# Religion and the
# Marketplace in the
# United States

# Religion and the Marketplace in the United States

Edited by

JAN STIEVERMANN, PHILIP GOFF

AND

DETLEF JUNKER

*Associate editors*

ANTHONY SANTORO

AND

DANIEL SILLIMAN

OXFORD
UNIVERSITY PRESS

# OXFORD
UNIVERSITY PRESS

Oxford University Press is a department of the University of
Oxford. It furthers the University's objective of excellence in research,
scholarship, and education by publishing worldwide.

Oxford   New York
Auckland   Cape Town   Dar es Salaam   Hong Kong   Karachi
Kuala Lumpur   Madrid   Melbourne   Mexico City   Nairobi
New Delhi   Shanghai   Taipei   Toronto

With offices in
Argentina   Austria   Brazil   Chile   Czech Republic   France   Greece
Guatemala   Hungary   Italy   Japan   Poland   Portugal   Singapore
South Korea   Switzerland   Thailand   Turkey   Ukraine   Vietnam

Published in the United States of America by
Oxford University Press
198 Madison Avenue, New York, NY 10016

Library of Congress Cataloging-in-Publication Data
Religion and the marketplace in the United States / edited by Jan Stievermann, Philip Goff, and
Detlef Junker; associate editors, Anthony Santoro and Daniel Silliman.
pages cm
Includes index.
ISBN 978–0–19–936179–3 (cloth : alk. paper)—ISBN 978–0–19–936180–9 (pbk. : alk. paper)
1. United States—Religion.   2. Business—Religious aspects.   I. Stievermann, Jan, editor.
BL2525.R46155 2015
201'.730973—dc23
2014031557

1 3 5 7 9 8 6 4 2
Printed in the United States of America
on acid-free paper

# Contents

PART THREE: *Religious Book Markets*

PART FOUR: *Religious Resistance and Adaptation to the Market*

PART FIVE: *Critical Reflection and Prospects*

# *Acknowledgments*

THE CONFERENCE FROM which this collection of essays grew was made possible by a generous grant from the Manfred Lautenschläger Foundation. We are very grateful to the foundation and to Dr. h.c. Manfred Lautenschläger personally for his enthusiastic support of this project.

For their invaluable help in preparing the conference we are indebted to our international board of advisers, especially to Christopher Bigsby and Hans Krabbendam. We also wish to thank the staff of the Heidelberg Center for American Studies for a good job in organizing the gathering. Special thanks are also due to Jennifer Adams-Massmann, who competently proofread the essays and helped to prepare the manuscript.

# *Contributors*

**Philip Goff** is the director of the Center for the Study of Religion and American Culture and a professor of religious studies and American studies at Indiana University Indianapolis. The author or editor of more than thirty volumes and nearly two hundred articles or papers on religion in North America, he has since 2000 been coeditor of *Religion and American Culture: A Journal of Interpretation.* His most recent edited volume, with Brian Steensland, is *The New Evangelical Social Engagement* (2013).

**Matthew S. Hedstrom** is an assistant professor of religious studies and American studies at the University of Virginia. He is the author of *The Rise of Liberal Religion: Book Culture and American Spirituality in the Twentieth Century* (2013). A former postdoctoral fellow at Princeton University, he is currently preparing a book on race and the search for religious authenticity in modernizing America.

**E. Brooks Holifield** is the Charles Howard Candler Professor of American Church History, emeritus, at the Candler School of Theology, Emory University. He is the author of numerous books on the history of American religion, on topics ranging from the history of the American clergy to the development of Puritan sacramental theology, including the landmark work *Theology in America: Christian Thought from the Age of the Puritans to the Civil War.* He is a fellow of the American Academy of Arts and Sciences.

**Detlef Junker** is the founding director of the Heidelberg Center for American Studies, a former director of the German Historical Institute in Washington, D.C. (1991–1994), and a former Curt Engelhorn Chair in American History at Heidelberg University. He has published and edited books on American history, transatlantic relations, German history, and theory of history in English and in German.

**Günter Leypoldt** is a professor of American literature at Heidelberg University, the author of *Cultural Authority in the Age of Whitman: A Transatlantic Perspective* (2009), and editor of *American Cultural Icons: The Production of Representative Lives* (2010). He is presently working on a study of literary and cultural charisma.

**Kathryn Lofton** is a professor of religious studies and American studies at Yale University. She is a historian of religion with a particular focus on the cultural and intellectual history of the United States. Her book, *Oprah: The Gospel of an Icon* (2011), uses the example of Oprah Winfrey's multimedia productions to analyze the nature of religion in contemporary America. Recent essays have explored the relationship between religious history and religious studies, the office cubicle as a religious artifact, the modernist–fundamentalist controversies, and the challenges attendant to the religious studies classroom. Lofton is currently researching several subjects, including the sexual and theological culture of early Protestant fundamentalism, the culture concept of the Goldman Sachs Group, and the religious contexts of Bob Dylan.

**Sarah M. Pike** is a professor of comparative religion and director of the Humanities Center at California State University, Chico. Pike is the author of *Earthly Bodies, Magical Selves: Contemporary Pagans and the Search for Community* (2001) and *New Age and Neopagan Religions in America* (2004) and has written extensively on contemporary Paganism, the New Age movement, the Burning Man festival, new religions in the media, environmentalism, and youth culture. She is currently writing a book about spirituality, youth culture, and radical environmental and animal rights activism.

**Katja Rakow** currently leads a research group on Pentecostal megachurches in a global context at the Karl Jaspers Centre for Advanced Transcultural Studies at Heidelberg University. She received her PhD in religious studies from Heidelberg University in 2010. Her research interests focus on the transcultural dynamics of religious history and the interrelation of religious discourses and practices with broader cultural patterns. Her fields of study are Tibetan Buddhism in the West and contemporary forms of Evangelicalism and Pentecostalism. Based on her research in the United States, she has coauthored *Religiöse Erlebniswelten in den USA* on the material culture of Lakewood Church in Houston, Texas.

**Anthony Santoro** teaches American religious, legal, and sport history at Heidelberg University (where he received his PhD) and the Heidelberg Center for American Studies. He is the author of several articles on religion and slave revolts, on the links between religion and capital punishment, and on professional football. He is also the author of *Exile and Embrace: Contemporary Religious Discourse on the Death Penalty* (2013).

**Daniel Silliman** teaches American religion and culture at Heidelberg University. His research interests include American evangelicals and Pentecostals, book history, atheism, and secularity. He is currently writing his doctoral dissertation at Heidelberg University on representations of belief in American evangelical fiction.

**Hilde Løvdal Stephens** holds a PhD in North American area studies from the University of Oslo (2012), with a dissertation on James Dobson and Focus on the Family. Her primary research interest is post-1945 American evangelicalism in national and transnational contexts. She has published articles in *American Studies in Scandinavia* and *Fides et Historia* and also writes for a wider audience, including teaching material for high school students.

**Jan Stievermann** is a professor of the history of Christianity in North America at Heidelberg University. He has written on a broad range of topics in the fields of American religious history and American literature, including articles for *Early American Literature*, *William and Mary Quarterly*, and *Church History*. His book *Der Sündenfall der Nachahmung: Zum Problem der Mittelbarkeit im Werk Ralph Waldo Emersons* (2007; *The Original Fall of Imitation: The Problem of Mediacy in the Works of R.W.E.*) is a comprehensive study of the coevolution of Emerson's religious and aesthetic thought. Together with Reiner Smolinski, he edited *Cotton Mather and "Biblia Americana"—America's First Bible Commentary* (2010). Most recently, he published with Oliver Scheiding *A Peculiar Mixture: German-Language Cultures and Identities in Eighteenth-Century North America* (2013). Currently, he is leading a team transcribing and editing volume 5 of Cotton Mather's hitherto unpublished *Biblia Americana*, the first comprehensive Bible commentary produced in British North America. For the Biblia project as a whole (10 vols.) he also serves as the executive editor.

**Mark Valeri** received his PhD from Princeton University and is the Reverend Priscilla Wood Neaves Distinguished Professor of Religion and Politics at the John C. Danforth Center on Religion and Politics at

Washington University in St. Louis. He previously was the Ernest Trice Thompson Professor of Church History at Union Theological Seminary in Virginia. His publications include *Law and Providence in Joseph Bellamy's New England* (1995) and *Heavenly Merchandize: How Religion Shaped Commerce in Puritan America* (2010).

**Grant Wacker** is the Gilbert T. Rowe Professor of Christian History at Duke Divinity School. He is the author of *Heaven Below: Early Pentecostals and American Culture* and a cultural biography of Billy Graham, *America's Pastor: Billy Graham and the Shaping of a Christian Nation.* Wacker taught at the University of North Carolina at Chapel Hill for fifteen years, served as an editor of *Church History: Studies in Christianity and Culture,* and is a past president of the Society for Pentecostal Studies and of the American Society of Church History.

# Religion and the Marketplace in the United States

# General Introduction

*Jan Stievermann, Daniel Silliman, and Philip Goff*

"IN OUR TIMES," R. Laurence Moore wrote in his landmark 1994 *Selling God: American Religion in the Marketplace of Culture*, "it is hard to imagine a religious organization whose operations are totally outside a market model."[1] The truth of that observation has not diminished in the intervening years. Things that once might have seemed overstated for effect are today quite literally the case. Moore wondered about a future where would-be prophets would have to "learn the ways of Disneyland in order to find their audience."[2] That was metaphorical then. It is an actual practice now. The fastest-growing evangelical church in the United States in 2012 was Triumph Church, a multisite megachurch in Detroit, Michigan, with more than 11,500 in regular attendance. Staff and volunteers at Triumph are trained by Disney Institute.[3] Twenty years ago, Moore speculated that religious leaders would struggle "to reach the many Americans who would feel perfectly comfortable at a prayer breakfast held under McDonald's generous golden arches."[4] He was invoking the fast food franchise to make a point. Since then, more than a few Christian outreach programs have been modeled on Ray Kroc's ideas. One can, for example, find drive-thru prayer ministries run by Seventh-day Adventists in California, Pentecostals in Florida and Michigan, Independent Christian Churches in Arizona and Texas, Methodists in Georgia and North Carolina, and even Lutherans in Massachusetts.[5]

These recent cases powerfully demonstrate that the embrace between American religion and the market has, if anything, become even stronger and more encompassing over the past twenty years. Religious adaptation of market techniques and technologies is everywhere and is, despite how things appear from a distance, just standard practice. The commodification of religion is likewise a fact of contemporary American culture. There is a danger, however, that these and other glaring examples of current commodifications of faith obscure not only the extraordinary complexity but also the long and diverse history of the relationship between religion and the marketplace in America. There is much more involved in the interaction of religion and marketplace than the straightforward declension narrative that is sometimes offered by journalists and critical adherents of the respective religious traditions.[6] Indeed, the story of religion and the marketplace in America is one of manifold, mutual, and often highly contradictory forms of interaction that extend far back before the time of drive-thru prayer, televangelism, or even the advent of consumer capitalism. Further, these glaring examples are themselves more subtle, contradictory, and multidimensional than they first appear.

In *God and Mammon*, Mark Noll noted that scholarship continues to struggle with the breadth and multiplicity of religion–market interactions. Even if the inquiry is restricted to just one religious group and to just one definite phase in economic history, as with Noll's edited volume subtitled *Protestants, Money, and the Market, 1790–1860*, it is very hard to do justice to the multidimensionality of these interactions. "The main reason that scholarship falls so short of the reality" it seeks to grasp, Noll dryly remarks, "is that the reality [is] extraordinarily complex."[7] Since Moore's *Selling God*, a veritable torrent of specialized scholarship has been expanding our understanding theoretically, thematically, and historically. And yet the subject, in many ways, still "dwarfs its historiography." For one thing, there are simply a lot of plots and characters in the larger story of American religion and the marketplace that have not yet been covered or need to be re-examined. Moreover, it continues to be a methodological challenge to rise to the extraordinary complexity of the subject and adopt what Noll calls an "integrated perspective that recognizes the fully connected relationship" of religion and marketplace,[8] with all of its negotiations, mediations, contingencies, and nuances.

The outgrowth of an international conference held at Heidelberg University in 2011, the essays in this collection take stock and make full use of the many significant studies published over the past two decades. They draw on the rich findings and various models put forth by scholars who have worked under the general rubric of American religion and the marketplace. At the same time, this volume aims to push the boundaries of the field in several ways. Our diverse international lineup of contributors makes space for the insights of Americanists from outside the United States on a topic laden with preconceived ideas and prejudices that very much demands a transatlantic perspective. It is also programmatically transgenerational, bringing together established and younger scholars, whose fresh research projects are going to define the future course of debate. The essays fill in historical lacunae, delve into neglected subjects, revisit familiar phenomena from different angles, and tentatively formulate new theoretical insights. They also take into account the substantial criticism that has been directed at some modes of studying religion and the marketplace and seek to further such critical discussion in pursuit of a more "integrated perspective." In order for the reader to better understand what this collection is trying to do (and not to do), and to appreciate more fully its innovative contribution, it seems helpful to review briefly the formation of the current scholarly discourse as well as some of the dominant narratives that have shaped the field in the past.

# *I*

Modern understandings of religion and the marketplace have grown from separate but parallel disciplinary studies in the 1980s and early 1990s. Some American historians working in religion, moving away from social history's emphasis on institutions and social forces, turned to "lived religion" categories of analysis, looking at faith within its larger cultural contexts.[9] Included in that matrix of culture was the development of the marketplace, replete with book sales, material possessions, and self-presentation, among others. Pathbreaking work by David Hall on Puritan reading ways and how they related to publishing turned historians' attention to the ways the mental worlds of Americans had shaped and been shaped by their surrounding material, economic, and political realities.[10] Jon Butler and Nathan Hatch, meanwhile, penned important and award-winning books about the diversity of early American religions and how groups competed for converts. Butler pointed to Baptists' "national spiritual markets," while Hatch showed how Methodists, especially, were entrepreneurs in a "divine economy."[11]

At the same time, social scientists were turning to a new way of interpreting religion in the United States, summarized by R. Stephen Warner in 1993 as simply "a new paradigm." A handful of scholars—Theodore

Caplow, Roger Finke, Andrew Greeley, Laurence Iannaccone, Mary Jo Neitz, and Rodney Stark—were shifting away from the traditional interpretation that religion would become either increasingly generalized so as to be empty or increasingly particularized so as to be relegated to the private sphere.[12] Instead, according to Warner, these sociologists and economists "learned from historians to view U.S. religion as institutionally distinct and distinctly competitive."[13] The analytic key to the new paradigm could be found in the disestablishment of churches at the American Revolution and the development of "an open market for religion."[14] Like the historians moving away from traditional social history, these scholars sought a new understanding that eschewed strictly institutional interpretations and allowed them to discuss religion in the United States as disestablished, culturally pluralistic, structurally adaptable, empowering, and voluntaristic. And, as was the case for the historians, a religious free market became for the social scientists a way to discuss such freedom. Stark and Bainbridge, for instance, offered a theory of the "religious economy."[15] This could be applied, then, to other nations in order to better comprehend the American situation. "Among Protestants, at least," wrote economist Laurence Iannaccone, "church attendance and religious belief both are greater in countries with numerous competing churches than in countries dominated by a single church."[16]

For a period, cultural historians and social scientists were on the same page. But while cultural historians Butler, Hatch, and then Moore had much in common with Bainbridge, Stark, and Iannaccone, the parallel paths soon became obscured. For various reasons, historians reacted negatively to the historical narrative offered by sociologists Finke and Stark in their 1992 *The Churching of America*. Reviews noted its overreliance on the economic model of the new paradigm, its dependence on outdated historiography, and its unawareness of the fine-grained histories that had already made a number of the arguments they were claiming were new.[17] Whether or not all of the criticisms were fair, a fault line was formed, and the apparent similarities between the work of historians interested in the marketplace of culture and the new paradigm of social scientists became less discussed. Indeed, to this day, historians tend to speak of Finke and Stark's book as metaphorically helpful but not historically significant. Social scientists, meanwhile, have dramatically advanced their part of the field using the new paradigm.[18] While cultural historians and new paradigm social scientists continue to have much in common, their work tends to exist along parallel paths with a median of trees between them.

Today, "religion and the marketplace" does not denote one theoretical approach or apparatus, any more than gender or ethnic studies do. It, rather, refers to a field of research, an interest in explaining various aspects of religious activities by looking at how they interact with different kinds of marketplaces. The conceptualizations of the marketplace used by scholars working within this general framework have been quite diverse, ranging from mostly metaphorical or analogous explanations of American religions in economic terms to quite literal examinations of business practices in the religious sphere. Equally varied are the phenomena and questions that these different concepts seek to address. For our purposes, one can distinguish three main categories of current religion and marketplace studies, although, of course, hardly any study only follows one approach. In practice there is, as always, much boundary-crossing, which blurs and complicates scholarly distinctions. Indeed, one thing that distinguishes many of the pieces assembled here is how they seamlessly move from one approach to the other or fruitfully combine them.

First, there are investigations of the literal, concrete intersections between market practices and religious beliefs and practices. Here, Moore's *Selling God* stands out as a widely influential work on religious forms of entrepreneurship and the use of marketing strategies for denominational growth. One important trend among studies of this type has been to push the focus of inquiry back into early American history. Thanks to a series of in-depth studies, we now have a much better sense of the coevolution of American religions and market practices from the early examples of the colonial commodification of religious products through the comprehensive economization of society during the nineteenth century and into the present era of postindustrial consumer capitalism.[19] Moreover, historians have examined various kinds of religious products in their respective historical and cultural contexts, such as the religious book market of the nineteenth century, contemporary rock music, and media culture.[20] Studies of the commodification of religious beliefs or practices, such as Leigh Eric Schmidt's *Consumer Rites*, and of ways these beliefs and practices are consumed,[21] such as Vincent J. Miller's *Consuming Religion* and Heather Hendershot's *Shaking the World for Jesus*, also fall in this category. One can still find instances where this sort of investigation provides the occasion for easy ironies or angry jeremiads, especially in more popular works.[22] More generally, though, there has been a notable effort to attend to the complexities of a phenomenon while avoiding assumptions about the loss of "religious depth" or other judgments based on one's own beliefs or political norms. Even the present iterations of the Prosperity Gospel have now been shown to stand in a much more ambiguous relation to the surrounding consumer culture than its crass and seemingly straightforward commercialism seems to suggest.[23]

Likewise abstaining from theological or moral evaluation, the majority of our essays, too, are interested (if not exclusively) in exactly these kinds of tangible exchanges. Daniel Silliman, for example, looks at how developments in American book markets were critical to the success of the evangelical apocalyptic fiction series *Left Behind*. Though the best-selling books are a religious phenomenon, he makes the case that it is important to understand them as market phenomena as well. Grant Wacker, further, shows how an intersection of practices is critical to understanding the ministry of Billy Graham. Over his sixty-year career, the celebrity preacher displayed uncanny business savvy. From careful control of media images to deft advertising techniques, from minutely managed organizational matters to his public associations with powerful figures from the worlds of business, politics, and sports, Graham's ministry cannot be understood separate from marketing and business practices. With both essays, the in-depth analysis of religion–market intersections offers new insight into subjects that have been widely studied. New complexities become apparent, specifically because of the attention paid to concrete examples of religion–market interaction. Several of our contributors are also pushing this type of study well beyond the confines of well-studied groups and traditions, too. Sarah Pike explores how the alternative economies of youth festivals such as Burning Man are critical to festival-goers' experiences of spirituality. In these temporary spaces, with a variety of religious and economic activities, there are ongoing negotiations between attendees' identities as spiritual selves and as secular consumers. Anthony Santoro opens up a similar dynamic of negotiation in his study of sports arenas. Santoro shows how stadiums are experienced as sacred through a variety of commercial practices in which consumers can participate. These studies are interested in the way that religious experiences are mediated by markets and the way that markets and market practices enable religious activities and experiences. They are, in a sense, micro studies. These studies examine the interactions and intermediations in great detail on, as it were, the ground, offering a very careful look at how this nexus works.

In the second category of current religion and the marketplace studies, scholars have looked at the relationship between religion and the marketplace in the United States by studying the interdependencies between the development of religious beliefs or rhetoric and the evolution of capitalist mentalities or economic theories and practices. Katherine Carté Engel's *Religion and Profit: Moravians in Early America* is an important example of this for the early period. This case study shows how for many colonial American communities, religious and economic conceptions defined and enabled one another in complex and changing ways that both encouraged economic experimentation and defined what true religion was. Exciting research has also been done on early twentieth-century American Fundamentalism, whose programmatic antimodernism, agrarian nostalgia, and cultural separatism have frequently been misunderstood as implying reservations toward new forms of industrialism and financial speculation. But in fact Fundamentalist businessmen such as Lyman Stewart can be found at the forefront of economic innovations, including wildcat investment capitalism, that stand in contrast to a traditional Protestant ethic of hard work but were nevertheless interpreted as authentic expressions of a conservative, Bible-centered theology.[24] For contemporary America, to cite one more example, Bethany Moreton, in a recent and widely praised book, investigates how the business practices and marketing language of Wal-Mart are deeply imbued with an evangelical theology that, in turn, has been very much shaped by late twentieth-century consumer capitalism.[25]

In our volume, several essays follow in this vein. Building on his book, Mark Valeri, for instance, examines how changing ideas of piety in Puritan New England informed the business practices of Boston merchants, shaping early American commerce. Valeri has examined these religious merchants' letters and finds that the two subjects are intertwined, in fact and theory. Looking at a more recent era, Hilde Løvdal Stephens demonstrates how belief in family values has functioned as both guarantor of capitalism and critique of capitalist society. Løvdal Stephens explains how, for a parachurch evangelical group such as Focus on the Family, beliefs about morality are related to beliefs about economics. Theories of capitalism are interdependent with ideas about the rightful regulation of sex. Matthew Hedstrom, similarly, sees a direct relationship between spiritual seeking and the emerging market for spiritual books in the mid-twentieth century. The ideals of eclecticism, open-ended pursuit, and self-improvement were religious ideas, all of which informed new publishing enterprises. Then, in the other direction, the ideas of the emerging book market had their own influence on the developing culture of spiritual quests. In each case, the picture that emerges from the very distinct studies is of complicated, interrelated ideas, which must be understood in their interconnections with each other.

The third broad category of research conducted currently under the heading "religion and the marketplace" is associated with the above-mentioned "new paradigm" of scholarship in the social sciences. It concerns relationships between religious groups, conceptualized as analogous to firms in capitalist economies. The locus classicus of this variety is Roger Finke and Rodney Stark's *The Churching of America*. They make the case that shifting religious landscapes should be examined via the dynamics of competition and supply and demand, in order to understand American religious vitality, diversity, and change. The mechanism of marketplace competition—especially, in their account, the impact of supply on demand—accounts for the growth and decline of various religious groups.[26] Besides the works cited above, it is worth mentioning here some examples of studies that have freely appropriated this model to explain the radical pluralization of America's religious landscape since the 1950s. Robert S. Ellwood and Wade Clark Roof, for instance, conceive of post-1960s religion in the United States as an increasingly diversified marketplace that continues to fine-tune its products to different target groups. By analyzing what has elsewhere been described as America's "quest culture" of "religious seekers" within the conceptual framework of "markets," these studies are able to make use of a variety of ideas, including supply and demand, consumers, and brands, and thus make religious practices legible by noting how they exhibit characteristics of market practices; these works align with other studies explicitly engaging with religious branding, such as Mara Einstein's *Brands of Faith*.[27]

The essays in this collection are certainly not averse to working with time-and-place-specific models of competitive religious marketplaces or to investigating supply-and-demand dynamics in particular enterprises. Katja Rakow, for example, is interested in how branding practices are at work in the life of a Texas megachurch. Daniel Silliman makes use of the supply-side idea, looking at how and where faith fiction is available, rather than why it is in demand. However, there is a notable caution not to overstretch these models into monocausal explanations for the rise and fall of denominations or types of spirituality, let alone for American religion as a whole. Indeed, one of the tendencies that this volume registers in current research within the broader framework of "religion and the marketplace" is that studies of the first and second type are going strong among cultural historians. At the same time, there seems to be increasing hesitation toward the third type of studies outside the social sciences. There is a shift from mostly quantitative toward more qualitative investigations with much more modest explanatory ambitions.

This tendency undoubtedly also has to do with an increasing awareness about the problems and flaws of several partly interlocking metanarratives about religion and economics, on which especially the third type of study, at least in its classical form, depended. As suggested above, our contributors all share this growing skepticism. They represent this turn to qualitative studies. Several of them critically engage with one or the other of the traditional metanarratives that were extremely influential in American religious studies. These metanarratives have been so influential in establishing "religion and the marketplace" as a subject, and are still so prominent in the background of much contemporary research, that they should be briefly reviewed here.

## II

There are two types of metanarratives of American religion and the marketplace in particular that should be briefly discussed. They have been so dominant as to sometimes, today, be accepted without reflection as something everyone knows. The studies in this volume all implicitly critique these metanarratives, but it is helpful to make those critiques explicit too. The first type of narrative about religion and economics might be called "the single-explanation approach." There are several varieties of this, each of which compartmentalizes religion and economics as more or less distinct spheres of human life that causally explain each other. The single-cause narratives have all been based on a contradistinction of religion as a quintessentially premodern element that will eventually be overwhelmed by a secular modernity driven by, among other factors, economic and technological innovation. Viewing religion and economics in an evolutionary struggle, this type of approach was thus inextricably tied into theories of secularization. The social power of religious institutions, the percentage of people who take religion seriously, and how seriously they take it are all assumed to decline with time, to use Steve Bruce's most recent and more moderate definition of what is sometimes called the standard theory of secularization.[28] In their classical nineteenth- and early twentieth-century formulations, theories of secularization even assumed an inevitable and total disappearance of religion. Two of the most influential single-explanation narratives, each with its own version of secularization theory, are those going back to Karl Marx, on the one hand, and Max Weber, on the other.

While the Marxist tradition seeks to use economics to explain religion, the Weberian tradition looks at religious beliefs to explain the rise of the modern market. Each in its own way is premised on the idea of a dialectics of influence and displacement between two ultimately irreconcilable forces. The emergence of the spirit of modern capitalism is explained in the Weberian tradition by a secularization of the traditional doctrines of Calvinism that are internal to it. For Weber, famously, the mystery of the beginnings of capitalism is how the necessary labor force is formed. Capitalism requires workers who are responsive to financial incentives that are completely separate from their needs. The secret of the market's ability to motivate workers to continue working after their needs are satisfied is, he writes, the secret of the doctrine of predestination, which teaches that one can never be satisfied as to the state of one's election.[29] The animating force of the market, which gives the market's mechanisms life, is to be found in how religion changes people. "The question of the motive forces in the expansion of modern capitalism is," he wrote, "above all, of the development of the spirit of capitalism."[30]

For the study of American religion, Weber's secularization theory has probably exerted a strong influence through Perry Miller's declension narrative of America's Puritan origins, as presented especially his *The New England Mind*. According to Miller, the increased economic activity of the once rigidly otherworldly and antimaterialist Puritans led to a secularization of New England society, as measured by a decline of communal religion and personal piety.[31] Although the evidence for such a declension has long been called into question, Katherine Carté Engel rightly asserts that especially early American studies continues to be "haunted by the theories of Max Weber and Perry Miller." As Engel writes: "Widespread historical perceptions of the interplay between the religious and the economic still reflect the assumption that the two were at loggerheads and engaged in an epic struggle marking the turn from a communal premodern to an individualistic and acquisitive modern."[32] Such myths can be quite powerful but are not accurate accounts of the very complicated relationships in actual existence.

The influence of the Marxian tradition on the study of American religion has been more oblique, but the logic of its single-cause explanation (the inverse of Weber's logic) still shows up especially in analyses of religious movements that were or are attractive to the poor and marginalized.

In the Marxian tradition, the question of the life force of religion is, in the final analysis, a question of economic realities. Religion is an illusion about real conditions, but, more importantly, that illusion is a product of the conditions. The inner logic of religion is the economic situation that made it necessary.[33] The tradition of Marxist historiography is stronger in Great Britain, where historians such as E. P. Thompson explained nineteenth-century Methodism as the misdirected energies of the working class, resulting from the class conflicts inevitable under capitalism. There are American versions accounting for religion as a species of false consciousness as well, especially with reference to new religious movements or groups attracting converts from among lower classes and racial minorities. Sean McCloud notes that the "deprivation thesis" dominated studies of "nativistic" and "revivalistic" movements in the 1950s, 1960s, and 1970s. In one study of almost three hundred small sects in American Christianity published in 1949 and republished in 1965, for example, all were deemed the product of poverty, regardless of the actual economic situations of adherents.[34]

The circular logic and oversimplifications of such theories have proved problematic for those who would study religious movements in any detail. They are inadequate when dealing with the intricacies and messiness of how religion and economics mesh in the "lived religion" of people then and now. While critics, academic and popular, might offer economic explanations for apparently peculiar religious practices, with further study, individual agency, actual practices, and the composition of religious groups have proved to be too complicated to be grasped by economic accounts alone. While theorists, as well as critical theologians, might define "the religious" and "the material" so as to be fundamentally opposed to each other, religious Americans then and now have usually been critical of certain kinds of economic practices while viewing others as being in harmony with or even important expressions of their faith. Recent studies of American religion and the marketplace, especially studies of the first and second types introduced above, are widely critical of both Weberian- and Marxist-style single-cause explanations. And so are, implicitly or explicitly, the essays in this volume. They share the sentiment of Noll when he writes, "Single-cause explanations—whether from the Bible, Max Weber, Karl Marx, E. P. Thompson, or any other authority—simply do not work as a satisfying explanation for religious–economic connections."[35] This volume, in line with much recent scholarship by historians and culturalists among religious studies scholars, holds such absolutist and transhistorical definitions to be questionable at best and proceeds on what might be called the "complexity assumption": it is assumed that religious beliefs and practices have always coexisted and interacted with diverse forms of economic ideologies and activities and that the two spheres can be neatly separated neither by the people in whose lives these spheres intersect nor by scholars on the observational or explanatory level. People might have alternatively or simultaneously seen religion and economics as partners and opponents, as threat and help, or as essential and irrelevant to each other, but they were never able to fully extricate one from the other.

Albeit in very different ways, even early Americans' religious endeavors were necessarily intertwined with economic activities, and many of them in fact understood their economic actions as religious. Consider, for example, Valeri's Boston Puritan merchants or the activities of that famous "peddler in divinity," George Whitfield, as portrayed by Harry S. Stout and Frank Lambert.[36] After the Revolution, instances of the simultaneous sacralization of economic activities and active marketing of faith are not hard to come by. They reveal the mutual transformations of American religion and capitalism in ways that defy any single-cause approach. John Turner, for instance, has reminded us of the diverse entrepreneurial projects of early Mormons during the era of the Jacksonian market revolution, ranging from treasure hunting to land speculation to wildcat banking, all in pursuit of an American Zion.[37] As B. M. Pietsch's recent study of California oilman and early Fundamentalist patron Lyman Stewart has shown, the potential for mutual transformation did not diminish where the forms of modern capitalism became totally unmoored from any notion of a Protestant work ethic, as with stock market speculations or, in Stewart's case, wildcat oil drilling. Stewart illustrates a form of business practice in which financial success through highly speculative risk-taking was not seen as "a natural reward for work, but a consequence of divine supernatural signs" and thus "re-enchanted the supposedly rational operations of modern capital. Stewart's economic ideals intermingled with his beliefs in dispensational premillennialism to create an economic and religious universe defined by the quest for hidden treasures and an overwhelming sense of urgency."[38]

In our collection, Matthew Hedstrom looks at how certain book publishing and reading practices in the mid–twentieth century aligned with a liberal conception of spiritual searching. The practice of one was, importantly, also the practice of the other. Those involved in the creation of

HarperSanFrancisco developed a business strategy of searching, nondog-
matic eclecticism. It is, in that sense, religious, in the tradition of William
James. The religious, at the same time, is commodified, with "William
James" becoming a product. By paying careful attention to the details and
emphasizing historical research, Hedstrom is able to arrive at some fascinating mutual mediations, showing the market of religion and religion
of the market. There is a dialectic there, but no world-historical claims.
The narrowness of the study is to its benefit. To abstract from that case
to a single-cause explanation would be to lose the most interesting parts.
Another example of this strategy is seen in Katja Rakow's essay on how
Joel Osteen is a "pastorpreneur." It would be easy enough to characterize
the prosperity preacher's talent for branding and subsequent success as
an example of secularization, of either the Marxist or the Weberian sort.
Rakow, however, is interested in a subtler and more careful point and
asks readers to look at the details of how religious practice and marketing
strategy seamlessly combine theoretically and as a matter of fact, for the
hierarchy of the church, those in regular attendance, and those who read
Osteen's books as part of their commercial-spiritual consumption habits.

   The complexity assumption emphasizes that economic and religious
forms have always been changing. Both *religion* and *economics* are very
capacious terms that historically encompass an enormous variety of ideas,
practices, and cultural and social formations. Indeed, people's business
practices and understandings of what constitutes the marketplace have
changed and varied at least as dramatically as their faith practices and
their understandings of what true religion is. One reason why traditional
formulations of the secularization theory predicted the disappearance of
religion in general is that they took as normative certain traditional forms
of religiosity whose often radical transformations in the context of modernization were then interpreted as disappearance. Having abandoned
such normative definitions, a slew of recent studies has demonstrated the
truth of Jon Butler's oft-quoted remark about "religion's surprising adaptability to modernity's conditions, certainly outside Europe, as well as the
adaptability of modernity to tolerate and absorb religiosity."[39]

   This is not the place to go into a full discussion of the ongoing debate
over how to theorize religion. Suffice it to say that we have followed the
lead of those scholars who, in the wake of the cultural turn, have argued
for de-essentializing religion and for understanding it as a social and discursive category that is as relational, contextual, and therefore fluid in
nature as other basic categories of human life and meaning-making, such

as gender, race, ethnicity, and national identity.[40] In other words, religion cannot be defined by permanent content or universal inherent features but, like other social and cultural categories, is very much contingent on its boundaries, which in every cultural and social formation are always contested and are "constantly being redefined in relation to new cultural circumstances and experiences"; part of this dynamic is that the meanings of religion necessarily depend on the equally contested and changing "discursive opposite": the secular. The chapters in this volume thus take "religion as a shifting historical category" whose protean nature eludes all teleologies and view "the intersections between religion and economic action in historically contingent ways."[41]

This is most obvious in those essays that look at phenomena that almost totally transcend churchly forms of a religion of dwelling (to use Robert Wuthnow's term) in a certain denominational or confessional tradition and belong to the wide and amorphous field of "seeker spirituality." Anthony Santoro, for one, shows how the experience of a sports stadium can be analogized to experiences of the sacred and, even more strongly, at points becomes essentially indistinguishable. The same thing can be seen in the work of Sarah Pike. She looks at how contemporary youth festivals create a space that is experienced as alternative to the market economy and is experienced as spiritual because of that separation. To enter into this space, attendees undertake pilgrimages and participate in various rituals, exorcising the market from themselves. At the same time, such festivals are also fully enmeshed in the market economy in practical terms and as a necessary condition for the kinds of consumption of spiritual experiences the attendees are seeking. The interrelation of religion and market, in these festivals, is delicate and fraught. It is something Pike can only explicate very carefully, by thinking about the relationship as dynamic and multidimensional and by liberating herself from traditional, preconceived notions of faith and worship. It is important to note that the essays dealing with these innovative forms of spirituality certainly look at how these forms of commodification have transformed traditional religious contents, but they do not assume that commercialization has inevitably diminished the intensity of religious experience or the investment of piety for those who partake in them. In fact, what they find is that, in these cases at least, the intensity and, as it were, otherworldliness are thoroughly related to the commercialization, though sometimes in contradictory ways.

Just as this collection eschews traditional grand theories of secularization, it also does not underwrite the kind of contrary wisdom in which religion–marketplace interactions have been interpreted as the American antidote to secularization. This brings us to the second metanarrative. Some of the most noted works inquiring into the relationship of religion and markets have been motivated by the idea that it explains "the American difference," why America seems so religious in comparison with other Western countries. There is an assumption, in these studies, that the secularization thesis is importantly right.[42] And America appears to be the exception. That exception has been explained as resulting from religious groups' ability to innovate, adapt, and, critically, compete. As R. Laurence Moore puts it, religion is not dying out in America, because in America it "operates in the marketplace of culture under the purest rules of *laissez-faire.*"[43] Along the same lines, Finke and Stark make the case that the mechanism of marketplace competition accounts for the growth and decline of various religious groups. Indeed, in Finke and Stark's account, free-market competition is *the* reason "why America shifted from a nation in which most people took no part in organized religion to a nation in which nearly two thirds of American adults do."[44] While entrepreneurial culture and a dynamic religious pluralism thus fueled the "churching of America," religious participation in Europe dwindled because the inability of the state-sponsored "monopoly church . . . to mobilize massive commitment is inherent in the segmentation of any religious economy. A single faith cannot shape its appeal to suit precisely the need of one market segment without sacrificing its appeal to another." Also, as Finke and Stark assert, "monopoly firms tend to be lazy."[45] The authors thus conceive of the rising and falling fortunes of religious groups as analogous to commercial fortunes in capitalist economies, driven by the dynamics of supply and demand. They understand American religious vitality and diversity as resulting from the deregulation that was disestablishment. Similar arguments, to cite another example, have been made by Robert D. Putnam and David E. Campbell in their well-received study *American Grace*. That work uses the idea of a "religious marketplace" to explain the startlingly high rates at which contemporary Americans change religions, which is to say, "the American difference," the way America has not secularized. As Putnam and Campbell note, "America is increasingly a domain of choice, churn, and surprisingly low brand loyalty. That is the demand side of the religious marketplace. On the supply side, we would expect successful 'firms' (denominations and congregations) in such a fickle market to be especially entrepreneurial in 'marketing' their product."[46]

Although we acknowledge that religion is more vital in the United States than in most other Western nations and that disestablishment and competition have played an important role in this, as they very likely did, it seems problematic to us to construct a grand theory of American religious difference based on these observations. Robert Wuthnow, among others, has noted that the "religious marketplace" theory threatens not only to become a new iteration of other classic "master narratives," such as the Puritan origins narrative or the Frontier Thesis, which claim to explain everything about American culture.[47] As such the theory of American religious difference also reinforces notions of national exceptionalism. More specifically, it has been noted that an overemphasis on competition can obscure other significant facets of American religious experience, such as cooperative and ecumenical efforts. These criticisms have been directed especially at Finke and Stark, whose embrace of underlying anthropological assumptions about *homo economicus*, as well as their prioritization of the supply side of religious competition, have been questioned.[48]

Closely related are concerns that by turning "religion and the marketplace" into one of the most important conceptual frameworks within which American religiosity is explained, scholars have made themselves complicit with ideologies advocating the thorough economization of all areas of life. We take these concerns about economization seriously, and it is one of our goals to further the critical dialogue on how to study American religion and the marketplace without totalizing either in one way or the other. Put differently, we wish to avoid contributing to the construction of a new and overarching metanarrative that makes economics the one key that fits every lock. For this purpose, the case studies in this collection are sandwiched by two metacritical essays. E. Brooks Holifield reviews some of the essential ideas involved in religion-and-the-marketplace explanations of American difference, questioning the clarity of that difference and further arguing that the explanations of the difference that does exist are quite limited. "For each explanation that is true," he writes, "a multitude of qualifications is required. Differences of degree do make a difference, and no single variable can explain any difference between Europe and America, whether religious or political. One certainly cannot appeal to the market alone as an explanation." Holifield offers strong reasons not to take this explanation as a master key to unlock all the secrets of American religiosity. In so doing, he sets the tone for the entire volume, which studiously avoids any kinds of overgeneralizations, including such about national differences.

In our final piece, Kathryn Lofton engages with the problem of how scholars in the field run the risk of playing into the ideology of neoliberalism and its triumphant narrative of the inevitable and total victory of the free market. It is possible, she warns, for studies to structurally reproduce neoliberal assumptions about individuals, their social relationships, and the highest form of individual fulfillment. It seems to us that the crucial remedy, besides critical self-awareness, is once again close attention to details and insistence on nuances and complexities. If it is true, as we think it is, that people's faith could never be neatly disentangled from their economic ideas and practices, this does not mean that American religious history somehow affirms the truth of one specific model of the economy, such as the free-market economy, or specific business and consumer practices, such as the ones Lofton describes in her analysis of the "Religion of Oprah."

Again, the economic sphere is as diverse and full of oppositions and genuine alternatives as the religious sphere. The communitarian economies of Engel's eighteenth-century Moravians and Turner's early Mormons can serve as reminders of this, just as much as more recent communitarian groups. Just because free-market capitalism is dominant and tacitly equated with "the economy" by most Americans (both religious and nonreligious) today and just because most forms of spirituality seem to be at ease with consumerism, we must not overlook that America was also home to the "Christian Socialism" of Walter Rauschenbusch and the early Reinhold Niebuhr and the dropout communities of the "Jesus movement" or that the contemporary anticapitalist "Occupy Wall Street" movement is also a religious movement in many ways.[49] Even in the more glaring examples of commodified religion and religious adaptation to markets, after all, closer examinations reveal complicated multidimensionality.

Overall, this volume has thus been undertaken in the spirit of a critical advocacy of the marketplace framework, one that is aware of its potential dangers and pitfalls even while it asserts its demonstrable usefulness. Even those who have voiced serious skepticism about potential totalizing tendencies of the conceptual framework have acknowledged its heuristic potential, if employed with circumspection. Wuthnow, for example, notes that while we should not make the mistake of constructing yet another master narrative, attending to the many specific reciprocities between religious and economic spheres is undoubtedly helpful and necessary.[50]

Analogously, scholars who are critical of the nationalist narratives in their discipline have propagated new transnational paradigms for American studies that likewise cannot afford to ignore the powerful ways in which the nation-state and nationalism have shaped the realities of U.S. culture and society on every level. Just as studying the nation-state does not necessarily make one an advocate of nationalism, we believe that paying attention to the interactions, interpenetrations, and interrelations of markets and religions need not imply a complicity with either specific beliefs held by any of America's denominations, the belief in the nation's competition-driven religious vitality as an essential feature of American exceptionality, or the quasi-religious belief in the market as the universal determinant of human life.

## III

This collection begins and ends with essays by highly respected scholars advocating critical self-awareness and attention to the potential pitfalls in the study of religion and the marketplace in the United States. E. Brooks Holifield extensively examines and evaluates the academic explanations for American religious vitality. He takes on the task of weighing and measuring Finke and Stark's thesis of disestablishment-produced competition between religious groups, looking at the data, the interpretations of the data, and the critical questions of definitions and terminology. The matter, Holifield finds, is anything but clear, and market-based metaphors for how Methodists related to Congregationalists or the German Reformed related to the Quakers do not eliminate the real complexities and persistent ambiguities of American religious vitality. Holifield then further considers a range of other accounts for the American difference, theoretical and historical, and makes a strong argument for what has been called the "complexity assumption." Setting the tone for the essays to follow, Holifield notes that "only a narrative, filled with contingencies," can account for religion in America. "Innumerable kinds of market relations have influenced religion," Holifield writes, and yet, "for each explanation that is true, a multitude of qualifications is required."

Chapters 2, 3, and 4 are focused specifically on American evangelicals. They each look at different aspects of the relationship between evangelicals and the marketplace, taking up different questions and examining different areas within the history of a single movement. Taken as a whole, the section shows that when one looks past the easy irony of drive-thru prayer chapels and televangelists soliciting donations, there are deeper substrata of interconnections waiting to be explored. Further, they demonstrate the promise of sustained examinations of a single tradition. The choice to focus on evangelicals is neither incidental nor, it is important to note, necessary. The subtle complexity and multidimensional intermediations of religion and the marketplace could have been exemplified with studies of Mormons and markets, Buddhists and markets, Jews and markets, or any of the many other religious traditions that make up the vibrant pluralism of America. In fact, it is our hope that the examinations of evangelicals here will inspire many such studies.

The focus on evangelicals for three chapters is, nonetheless, important for several reasons. First, American evangelicals have historically been at the forefront of market adaptations, from George Whitfield's advertising campaigns onward. In many cases, though by no means all, other traditions' engagements with marketplace practices were modeled on evangelical practices. Second, evangelicals' engagements with the marketplace have often been the focus of the problematic religion-and-the-marketplace narratives that this volume seeks to engage critically and move beyond. For reasons that have everything to do with cultural prominence and positioning, the declension narratives of the cheapening of religion in America are not normally about the commercialization and commodification of Santeria or Sikhism. Likewise, the problematic triumphalist narrative of the American difference of market-produced adaptability and vitality is not one that traditionally focuses on Jehovah's Witnesses or American Muslims. Studies of all those groups and traditions as they interact with markets, as well as of the many others in America past and present, are important and valuable. Our contention, though, is that the complexity of religion–market relationships is not just a matter of representing the range and variety of religious traditions. By looking in depth at the one tradition that has been at the center of reductive accounts, these three essays work to demonstrate the importance of a delicate touch in the examination of religion and the marketplace.

Mark Valeri opens this trio of chapters with a study of evangelical merchants in eighteenth-century Boston. He looks at how one cohort of religious businessmen combined commercial energy and evangelical sensibilities. This group of merchants was involved in two distinct developments: Commercial changes were connecting disparate local markets into Britain's capitalist empire; and a new kind of ministry, the revivalism

of itinerant ministers preaching heart conversion, was connecting disparate evangelicals into a transdenominational movement. Showing how
the two are connected, Valeri revisits Weber's Protestant ethic thesis and
makes a compelling case that American evangelicals had an outsized
effect on the beginnings of America's capitalist economy.

Shifting from the eighteenth century to the twentieth, Grant Wacker
demonstrates the ways in which Billy Graham, "America's pastor," adapted
to the market. Graham was a master marketer, and his ministry would not
have been possible apart from that. Examining the celebrity evangelist's
many modes of self-presentation over his sixty-year career, Wacker shows
how everything from his use of his rural roots and American vernacular
to his wardrobe to his public friendships with athletes and businessmen
can be understood through the relationship of religion and marketplace.

Hilde Løvdal Stephens then turns our attention to a contemporary
evangelical group's theoretical engagement with economic theory. She
looks at how the parachurch group Focus on the Family frames the traditional family and family values as the necessary guarantor of the freedom
of capitalism but also, importantly, as regulating capitalism. In its teachings, Focus on the Family has explained the importance of traditional
gender roles, the ethical regulation of sex, and even opposition to abortion
in terms of the interdependent relationship of capitalism and religious
morality. Its members are, Løvdal Stephens shows, critics of capitalism
and proponents, too. The widely disseminated and discussed doctrines of
family values are not often understood in terms of the marketplace, yet
they are integrally related in this case.

Chapters 5, 6, and 7 similarly share a single subject, in this case a specific market. Matthew Hedstrom, Günter Leypoldt, and Daniel Silliman
each turn our attention to the book market and look at the ways the economic ideas and practices of that market relate to and respond to religious
experiences. They show that this market is, in important ways, shaped
by and mediated by religious activities and, simultaneously, that some
religious practices, including but not limited to religious reading, are
dependent on the business of publishing and selling books in interesting and important ways. None of the authors suggest that the book market is somehow unique in this regard, only that, through looking at the
specifics of this market, critical insights can be made available. This is
not an exclusive claim. Other sorts of production and consumption can
be and have been studied to similar ends. Hedstrom starts this section
by examining the coevolution of middlebrow book-business practices and

liberal spirituality in the founding of HarperSanFrancisco, an imprint of HarperCollins. Hedstrom shows how the publisher's business strategy was built on liberal spiritual values, of the sort promoted by Ralph Waldo Emerson and William James. Those values, at the same time, were the values of a culture turning away from institutions and embracing a marketplace-based spirituality, the spirituality of middlebrow reading.

Moving from the middlebrow to the highbrow, Leypoldt offers a theoretical exploration of how the production of the cultural value of "serious" literature depends on economies of symbolic capital that run counter to the actual economics of bookselling. The singularization of a book or author is not unrelated to the market, Leypoldt explains, but neither is it related in a straightforward way. This essay looks at the singular Toni Morrison and at how her novels have been read in the context of Oprah's Book Club. Speaking directly to Kathryn Lofton's work, *Oprah: The Gospel of an Icon*, Leypoldt proposes that cultural value is a kind of consecration and that this sacrality happens within cultural economies.

Silliman concludes this section with an examination of the economic context for the *Left Behind* phenomenon. The apocalyptic fiction series's tremendous success at the turn of the twenty-first century has regularly been attributed to the anxieties of the audience. Silliman looks instead at the supply side of the market, exploring how the books' sudden popularity is connected to changes in how the works were produced and distributed. While not dismissing the importance of the question of why people chose to read *Left Behind*, he demonstrates that changes in the book market are critical to any understanding of the commercial and cultural juggernaut. Questions of how a book is produced and where it is available also have their place.

Taken together, these three essays show how book markets are tied up in religious experiences and practices. Whether it is mass-market fiction, spiritual self-improvement literature, or the heights of modernist experimentalism, the markets for these books are all relating to, responding to, and interacting with religion. These chapters demonstrate the value of sustained and detail-oriented examinations of specific economic sectors in the further study of the multidimensional nature of religion and the marketplace.

The next three essays—chapters 8, 9, and 10—study one specific type of interaction. They consider a variety of spiritual practices from different traditions and look at different sorts of economic activities but engage only one sort of religion–market relationship. If three chapters on evangelicals can be taken as examining religion *and* the marketplace, and three chapters on book markets can be taken as examining religion *in* the marketplace, these three chapters are devoted to religion *as* the marketplace. That is to say, Anthony Santoro, Katja Rakow, and Sarah Pike each turn our attention to contemporary cases of religious experience that are, in important ways, experiences of resistance or adaptation to the market.

Pike begins this trio of chapters with a consideration of youth festivals based on extensive interviews and her own participant observation. At Coachella music festival, Earthdance, Burning Man, and other such events, festival attendees at once resist the market economy and accommodate to it. There is a struggle for a sense of one's spiritual self, which Pike shows is a struggle with and against individuals' consumer identity, an attempt to escape the economic practices of consumption and also to adapt them. Both the rejection of the market and the uses of the market to achieve this rejection work together toward a discovery of a transcendent fulfillment. These people's spirituality, she shows, is not experienced as a separate sphere from economic transactions but, rather, as something antagonistically related to and also dependent on markets. Youth festivals, like Joel Osteen's branding, are spaces where markets, in some important ways, are religious. A sense of transcendent fullness is apprehended through consumer practices and through rituals exercised within a market framework. And yet, even this mode of the relationship between religion and market can, as Pike shows, be oppositional. In this mode of relationship, the economic and the spiritual are critically interlocked.

With Rakow's essay we move from the sacred space of youth festivals to the religiosity of a Texas megachurch's marketing. Rakow examines the branding practices of prosperity preacher Joel Osteen. Branding, Rakow explains, is a market practice of giving a product a supplemental aura, a sense of meaning that is additional to its physical form or practical purpose, thus allowing people to connect to the product more intensely. The product, that is to say, becomes spiritual. Osteen's message, inversely, is that spiritual practices produce tangible, physical results. Thus, when Osteen becomes a brand, the spiritual practice and the consumer experience, and the consumer practice and the spiritual experience, are merged.

Santoro ends the trio of essays by examining the importance of the interlocking relationship between the spiritual and the commercial in professional sports arenas. Looking at four National Football League stadiums in Cincinnati, Cleveland, Detroit, and Pittsburgh, Santoro shows that they were designed and constructed so that fans can, through their engagement with the stadiums, experience a sense of sacred space. Fans ascribe religious meanings to these spaces. When they buy tickets and attend games, participating in rituals and superstitions, they literally "buy into" the sacral narrative encoded into the physical space. Here, in the space of a football stadium, Santoro demonstrates how a sense of spiritual fullness and transcendence is produced through consumer participation in market practices.

Closing the collection, Kathryn Lofton considers the current neoliberal moment that is the present historical context for this volume. Building off her groundbreaking study of Oprah Winfrey and what she calls "spiritual capitalism," Lofton reflects on what it means for scholars that this is an age when the marketplace seems to blend seamlessly with the sale of spirituality. The task, Lofton says, is to carefully and thoughtfully extract the inextricable. At the same time, given the ubiquity of neoliberalism and the totalizing claims it makes for itself, and how it is so often presented and perceived not as one option but as the only one even imaginable, scholars must remain critical of their own potential complicity as they study these intersections of religion and market. It is necessary to study the valuations at work in this moment; it is nevertheless important not to tacitly and uncritically endorse those valuations. Echoing Holifield, Lofton ends the volume with a call for attention to detail and nuance, for modest methodology and cautious scholarship.

## *Notes*

1. R. Lawrence Moore, *Selling God: American Religion in the Marketplace of Culture* (New York: Oxford University Press, 1994), 274.

2. Ibid., 276.

3. Christy Scannell, "A Triumph in Detroit: #1 Fastest-Growing Church," *Outreach Magazine*, August 25, 2013, http://www.outreachmagazine.com/ideas/church-profiles/5463-a-triumph-in-detroit-1-fastest-growing-church.html.

4. Moore, *Selling God*, 276.

5. Kevin Simpson and Kellye Simpson, "Drive-Thru Prayers," *Pacific Union Church Support Services*, 2010, http://www.churchsupportservices.org/article/247/apply-it/drive-thru-prayers; Nigel Boys, "Has Convenience Gone Too Far? FL Church Has Drive Thru Prayer," *All Christian News*, July 25, 2013, http://allchristiannews.com/has-convenience-gone-too-far-fl-church-has-drive-thru-prayer/; Joe Lawlor, "Church Hosts Drive-Through Prayers," *USA Today*, July 28, 2008, http://usatoday30.usatoday.com/news/religion/2008-07-28-drive-thru-prayer_N.htm; Brian Webb, "Drive-Thru Prayer

Open for Business in North Phoenix," *ABC 15*, February 27, 2013, http://
www.abc15.com/dpp/news/region_phoenix_metro/north_phoenix/Drive-t
hru-prayer-open-for-business-in-North-Phoenix; Mark Collette, "Church
Keeps Worshipers in the Driver's Seat with Prayer on the Go," *Corpus Christi
Caller-Times*, February 9, 2013, http://www.courierpress.com/lifestyle/
prayer82320n-the-go; Brittany Smith, "Drive-Thru Prayer Service for Those
on the Go," *Christian Post*, December 28, 2011, http://www.christianpost.com/
news/drive-thru-prayer-service-for-those-on-the-go-65854/; Glenn Hannigan,
"Snellville UMC's Drive-Thru Prayer Ministry Is Vehicle for Reaching
the Unchurched," *North Georgia Advocate*, January 20, 2012, http://www.
ngumc.org/newsdetail/70431; Jimmy Tomlin, "Church Offers Drive-Through
Prayer," *Associated Press*, September 11, 2011, http://assets.matchbin.com/
sites/1140/assets/L01Z_091111e.pdf; Dan Adams, "Scituate Lutheran Church
Offers Drive-Through Prayers," *Boston Globe*, October 12, 2013, http://www.
bostonglobe.com/metro/2013/10/12/scituate-lutheran-church-offers-dr
ive-through-prayers/cf6SqQCupXa30XLNH4UgFM/story.html.

6. For a recent example of a liberal critique of the "evangelical-capitalist resonance machine," see William E. Connolly, *Capitalism and Christianity,
American Style* (Durham, N.C.: Duke University Press, 2008). Perhaps unex-
pectedly, some of the most aggressive recent attacks on religious adaptations to market logic have been evangelical Christians' self-critiques. See, for
example, Thomas Bergler, *The Juvenilization of American Christianity* (Grand
Rapids: Eerdmans, 2012); Brian F. Hulbutt, *Tasty Jesus: Liberating Christ from
the Power of Our Predilections* (Eugene: Wipf and Stock, 2013); Skye Jethani, *The
Divine Commodity: Discovering a Faith beyond Consumer Christianity* (Grand
Rapids: Zondervan, 2009); Brett McCracken, *Hipster Christianity: When
Church and Cool Collide* (Grand Rapids: Baker, 2010); Warren Cole Smith, *A
Lover's Quarrel with the Evangelical Church* (Franklin, Tenn.: Authentic, 2009);
Gordon T. Smith, *Called to Be Saints: An Invitation to Christian Maturity*
(Nottingham: IVP, 2013); and Tim Suttle, *Shrink: Faithful Ministry in a
Church-Growth Culture* (Grand Rapids: Zondervan, 2014).

7. Mark Noll, "Introduction," in *God and Mammon: Protestants, Money, and the
Markets, 1790–1860*, ed. Mark Noll (Oxford: Oxford University Press, 2002),
3–29, here 3.

8. Ibid., 7.

9. For more on this concept, see David D. Hall, ed., *Lived Religion in America: Toward
a History of Practice* (Princeton: Princeton University Press, 1997).

10. David Hall wrote a number of important articles in the 1980s along these
lines, culminating in his *Worlds of Wonder, Days of Judgment: Popular Religious
Beliefs in Early New England* (Cambridge: Harvard University Press, 1990).

11. Jon Butler, *Awash in a Sea of Faith: The Christianization of the American
People, 1550–1865* (Cambridge: Harvard University Press, 1990), 275; Nathan

O. Hatch, *The Democratization of American Christianity* (New Haven: Yale University Press, 1989), 101.

12. R. Stephen Warner, "Work in Progress toward a New Paradigm for the Sociological Study of Religion in the United States," *American Journal of Sociology* 98, no. 5 (March 1993): 1044–1093; Theodore Caplow, "Contrasting Trends in European and American Religion," *Sociological Analysis* 46 (Summer 1985): 101–108; Roger Finke, "Religious Deregulation: Origins and Consequences," *Journal of Church and State* 32 (Summer 1990): 609–626; Andrew Greeley, *Religious Change in America* (Cambridge: Harvard University Press, 1989); Laurence R. Iannaccone, "A Formal Model of Church and Sect," *American Journal of Sociology* 94 (1986), suppl.: S241–S268; Laurence Iannaccone, "Religious Practice: A Human Capital Approach," *Journal for the Scientific Study of Religion* 29 (September 1990): 297–314; Laurence Iannaccone, "The Consequences of Religious Market Structure," *Rationality and Society* 3 (April 1991): 156–177; Mary Jo Neitz, "Studying Religion in the Eighties," in *Symbolic Interaction and Cultural Studies*, ed. Howard Becker and Michael McCall (Chicago: University of Chicago Press, 1990), 90–118; Rodney Stark and Roger Finke, "American Religion in 1776: A Statistical Portrait," *Sociological Analysis* 49 (Spring 1988): 39–51.

13. Warner, "Work in Progress toward a New Paradigm," 1051.

14. Ibid., 1050.

15. Rodney Stark and William Sims Bainbridge, *The Future of Religion: Secularization, Revival, and Cult Formation* (Berkeley: University of California Press, 1985); Rodney Stark and William Sims Bainbridge, *A Theory of Religion* (New York: Peter Lang, 1987).

16. Iannaccone, "Consequences of Religious Market Structure," 157.

17. See, among others, Martin Marty, *Christian Century*, January 27, 1993; and Philip Goff, "Spiritual Enrichment and the Bull Market: Balancing the Books of American Religion," *Religious Studies Review* 22, no. 2 (Spring 1996): 106–112.

18. Two recent examples include two essays in Paul Oslington, ed., *The Oxford Handbook of Christianity and Economics* (New York: Oxford University Press, 2014): Robert Mochrie, "Economic Models of Churches," 421–437, and Charles M. North, "Regulation of Religious Markets," 472–511.

19. A recent survey study of this type is James Hudnut-Beumler, *In Pursuit of the Almighty's Dollar: A History of Money and American Protestantism* (Chapel Hill: University of North Carolina Press, 2007). On the colonial and early national periods, good examples include David G. Hackett, *The Rude Hand of Innovation: Religion and Social Order in Albany, New York, 1652–1836* (New York: Oxford University Press, 1991); Stephen Innes, *Creating the Commonwealth: The Economic Culture of Puritan New England* (New York: W. W. Norton, 1995); and Mark Valeri, *Heavenly Merchandise: How Religion Shaped Commerce in Puritan America* (Princeton: Princeton University

Press, 2010). On the nineteenth-century market revolution and its impact on antebellum religion, good examples include Stewart Davenport, *Friends of Unrighteous Mammon: Northern Christians and Market Capitalism, 1815–1860* (Chicago: University of Chicago Press, 2008); Lorman A. Ratner, Paula T. Kaufmann, and Dwight L. Teerter Jr., eds., *The Paradoxes of Prosperity: Wealth-Seeking versus Christian Values in Pre–Civil War America* (Champaign: University of Illinois Press, 2009); Mark S. Schantz, *Piety in Providence: Class Dimensions of Religious Experience in Antebellum Rhode Island* (Ithaca, N.Y.: Cornell University Press, 2000); Charles Grier Sellers, *The Market Revolution: Jacksonian America, 1815–1846* (New York: Oxford University Press, 1991); Kenneth Moore Startup, *The Root of All Evil: The Protestant Clergy and the Economic Mind of the Old South* (Athens: University of Georgia Press, 1997); William R. Sutton, *Journeymen for Jesus: Evangelical Artisans Confront Capitalism in Jacksonian Baltimore* (University Park: Pennsylvania State University Press, 1998); and Anthony F. C. Wallace, *Rockdale: The Growth of an American Village in the Early Industrial Revolution* (Lincoln: University of Nebraska Press, 2005). For the economics of televangelism, some good works include Moore, *Selling God*; Shayne Lee and Phillip Luke Sinitiere, *Holy Mavericks: Evangelical Innovators and the Spiritual Marketplace* (New York: New York University Press, 2009); and Jonathan Walton, *Watch This: The Ethics and Aesthetics of Black Televangelism* (New York: New York University Press, 2009).

20. On the mass media generally, including religious book markets, radio, television, pop music, and the Internet, some good works include Claire H. Badaracco, ed., *Quoting God: How Media Shape Ideas about Religion and Culture* (Waco: Baylor University Press, 2005); Candy Gunther Brown, *The Word and the World: Evangelical Writing, Publishing, and Reading in America, 1789–1880* (Chapel Hill: University of North Carolina Press, 2004); Lynn Schofield Clark, ed., *Religion, Media and the Marketplace* (New Brunswick, N.J.: Rutgers University Press, 2007); David Chidester, *Authentic Fakes: Religion and American Popular Culture* (Berkeley: University of California Press, 2005); Lori Anne Ferrell, *The Bible and the People* (New Haven: Yale University Press, 2008); Amy Johnson Frykholm, *Rapture Culture: Left Behind in Evangelical America* (Oxford: Oxford University Press, 2004); Michael J. Gilmour, *Gods and Guitars: Seeking the Sacred in Post-1960s Popular Music* (Waco: Baylor University Press, 2009); Tonja J. Hagen, *Redeeming the Dial: Radio, Religion and Popular Culture in America* (Chapel Hill: University of North Carolina Press, 2001); Matthew Hedstrom, *The Rise of Liberal Religion: Book Culture and American Spirituality in the Twentieth Century* (New York: Oxford University Press, 2012); Stewart M. Hoover and Lynn Schofield Clark, eds., *Practicing Religion in the Age of the Media: Explorations in Media, Religion, and Culture* (New York: Columbia University Press, 2002); Linda Kintz and Julian Lesage, eds., *Media, Culture, and the Religious Right* (Minneapolis: University of Minnesota Press, 1998);

John S. McClure, *Mashuo Religion: Pop Music and Theological Invention* (Waco: Baylor University Press, 2011); David Nord, *Faith in Reading: Religious Publishing and the Birth of Mass Media in America* (New York: Oxford University Press, 2004); Kathryn J. Oberdeck, *The Evangelist and the Impresario: Religion, Entertainment, and Cultural Politics in America, 1884–1914* (Baltimore: Johns Hopkins University Press, 1999); Daniel A. Stout and Judith M. Buddenbaum, eds., *Religion and Mass Media: Audiences and Adaptations* (London: Sage, 1996); Valerie Weaver-Zercher, *The Thrill of the Chaste: The Allure of Amish Romance Novels* (Baltimore: Johns Hopkins University Press, 2013); and Peter J. Wosh, *Spreading the Word: The Bible Business in Nineteenth Century America* (Ithaca, N.Y.: Cornell University Press, 1994).

21. For the scholarly debate on the commodification of Native American spirituality, see Philip Jenkins, *Dream Catchers: How Mainstream America Discovered Native Spirituality* (New York: Oxford University Press, 2004); and Christoph Ronwanién:te Jocks, "Spirituality for Sale," in *Religion and American Culture*, ed. David G. Hackett (New York: Routledge, 2003), 481–495. Other important works on the subject of religious consumption include Suzanne K. Kaufman, *Consuming Visions: Mass Culture and the Lourdes Shrine* (Ithaca, N.Y.: Cornell University Press, 2008); Kathryn Lofton, *Oprah: The Gospel of an Icon* (Berkeley: University of California Press, 2011); Christopher Owen Lynch, *Selling Catholicism: Bishop Sheen and the Power of Television* (Lexington: University Press of Kentucky, 1998); David Lyon, *Jesus in Disneyland: Religion in Postmodern Times* (Cambridge: Polity, 2000); Vincent J. Miller, *Consuming Religion: Christian Faith and Practice in a Consumer Culture* (New York: Continuum, 2004); Moore, *Selling God*; and Leigh Eric Schmidt, *Consumer Rites: The Buying and Selling of American Holidays* (Princeton: Princeton University Press, 1997).

22. Recent examples of popular condemnations of commercialized religion include Ross Douthat, *Bad Religion: How We Became a Nation of Heretics* (New York: Free Press, 2012); Becky Garrison, *Red and Blue God, Black and Blue Church: Eyewitness Accounts of How American Churches Are Hijacking Jesus, Bagging the Beatitudes, and Worshipping the Almighty Dollar* (San Francisco: Jossey-Bass, 2006); and Sarah Palin, *Good Tidings and Great Joy: Protecting the Heart of Christmas* (New York: Broadside, 2013).

23. See Kate Bowler, *Blessed: A History of the American Prosperity Gospel* (New York: Oxford University Press, 2013).

24. Douglas Carl Abrams, *Selling the Old-Time Religion: Fundamentalists and Mass Culture, 1920–1940* (Athens: University of Georgia Press, 2001); B. M. Pietsch, "Lyman Stewart and Early Fundamentalism," *Church History* 82, no. 3 (September 2013): 617–646. See also Sarah Hammond, " 'God Is My Partner': An Evangelical Business Man Confronts Depression and War," *Church History* 80 (2011): 498–519.

25. See also Connolly, *Capitalism and Christianity*; and Darren Dochuk, *From Bible Belt to Sunbelt: Plain-Folk Religion, Grassroots Politics, and the Rise of Evangelical Conservatism* (New York: W. W. Norton, 2012).

26. See also Larry Whitham, *Marketplace of the Gods: How Economics Explains Religion* (New York: Oxford University Press, 2010); and Lawrence A. Young, ed., *Rational Choice Theory and Religion: Summary and Assessment* (New York: Routledge, 1996).

27. See Robert Wuthnow, *After Heaven: Spirituality in America since the 1950s* (Berkeley: University of California Press, 1998).

28. Steve Bruce, *Secularization: In Defense of an Unfashionable Theory* (Oxford: Oxford University Press, 2011), 2.

29. Max Weber, *The Protestant Ethic and the Spirit of Capitalism* (London: Routledge, 2005), 24–25, 66.

30. Ibid., 31.

31. Perry Miller, *The New England Mind: From Colony to Province* (Cambridge: Harvard University Press, 1953). Miller's argument, based largely in intellectual history, was carried forward into social history by Bushman and others. See, for instance, Richard Bushman, *From Puritan to Yankee: Character and the Social Order in Connecticut, 1690–1765* (Cambridge: Harvard University Press, 1980).

32. Katherine Carté Engel, "Religion and the Economy: New Methods for an Old Problem," *Early American Studies: An Interdisciplinary Journal* 8 (Fall 2010): 482–514, 484.

33. Karl Marx, "Excerpt from *Towards the Critique of Hegel's Philosophy of Right*," in *Marx and Engels: Basic Writings on Politics and Philosophy*, ed. Lewis S. Feuer (New York: Doubleday, 1989), 263.

34. Sean McCloud, *Divine Hierarchies: Class in American Religion and Religious Studies* (Chapel Hill: University of North Carolina Press, 2007), 75–101.

35. Noll, "Introduction," 8.

36. Frank Lambert, *"Pedlar in Divinity": George Whitefield and the Transatlantic Revivals, 1737–1770*, new ed. (Princeton: Princeton University Press, 2002); Harry S. Stout, *The Divine Dramatist: George Whitefield and the Rise of Modern Evangelicalism* (Grand Rapids: Eerdmans, 1991).

37. John G. Turner, *Brigham Young: Pioneer Prophet* (Cambridge: Harvard University Press, 2012).

38. Pietsch, "Lyman Stewart and Early Fundamentalism," 619–620.

39. Jon Butler, "Theory and God in Gotham," "Theme Issue 45: Religion and History," *History and Theory* 45 (December 2006): 47–61, 53.

40. For a recent survey of the many theoretical attempts to define religion and the problems inherent in the diverse models, see Michael Bergunder, "Was ist Religion? Kulturwissenschaftliche Überlegungen zum Gegenstand der

Religionswissenschaft," *Zeitschrift für Religionswissenschaft* 19, nos. 1–2 (2011): 3–55.

41. Engel, "Religion and the Economy," 495.
42. See, for example, Pippa Norris and Ronald Inglehart, *Sacred and Secular: Religion and Politics Worldwide* (New York: Cambridge University Press, 2004), a comparative, longitudinal study of secularization worldwide. The authors tie it to social safety nets. Where they are strong, religion is weak; where they are weak, religion is strong. They also see America as a "deviant case."
43. Moore, *Selling God*, 7.
44. Roger Finke and Rodney Stark, *The Churching of America* (New Brunswick, N.J.: Rutgers University Press, 1992), 1.
45. Ibid., 11.
46. Robert D. Putnam and David E. Campbell, *American Grace* (New York: Simon & Schuster, 2010), 148.
47. Robert Wuthnow, "Religion," in *Understanding America: The Anatomy of an Exceptional Nation*, ed. Peter H. Schuck and James Q. Wilson (New York: PublicAffairs, 2008), 275–305, here 280–283.
48. See, for instance, Noll's critique: "The great difficulty for historians in putting the theory to use, however, is that it divorces explanation from the lived worlds of the historical participants. . . . Moreover, for Protestant connections to the economy, rational-choice theory offers little direct interpretation of the theological or religious meaning of either money or the accommodation of religious commitments to commercial practices" ("Introduction," 19).
49. For more on the Jesus People movement and communal living, see Larry Eskridge, *God's Forever Family: The Jesus People Movement in America* (Oxford: Oxford University Press, 2013). Rauschenbusch's and Niebuhr's views on economics are treated in Christopher H. Evans, *The Kingdom Is Always but Coming: A Life of Walter Rauschenbusch* (Waco: Baylor University Press, 2004); and Richard Wightman Fox, *Reinhold Niebuhr: A Biography* (New York: HarperCollins, 1987). For more on the religious elements of the Occupy movement, see Nathan Schneider, *Thank You, Anarchy: Notes from the Occupy Apocalypse* (Berkeley: University of California Press, 2013).
50. Wuthnow, "Religion," 281.

# PART ONE

*Reassessment*

# Why Are Americans So Religious? The Limitations of Market Explanations

*E. Brooks Holifield*

ALL OF US recognize the ambiguities of polls. They are reliable and unreliable at the same time, like a Lutheran righteous sinner. But we cite them anyway, and they do tell us something, despite ambiguities. Consider beliefs. In recent polls, 95 percent of Americans said that they believed in God, 66 percent in a personal God.[1] In Europe, 60 percent said that they believed in God, but only 31 percent in a personal God—a number that dropped to 15 percent in Sweden.[2] Seventy percent of Americans said that they believed in an otherworldly heaven; in Europe the figure was closer to 35 percent.[3] In Europe, 23 percent of the population said that they believed in hell, diversely defined; in America 70 percent said that they believed in hell, diversely defined, but only 6 percent of Americans foresaw even the remotest possibility that they would spend any time there.[4]

Or consider practices. At least 60 percent of Americans say that they belong to a church, synagogue, mosque, or temple. In Britain about 12 percent say that.[5] Forty percent of Americans say that they attend religious services in a typical week; in Europe 19 percent say that they attend more than once a month; in Britain, central France, and parts of Scandinavia the weekly number is about 5 percent.[6] Sixty percent of Americans say that religion is "very important" to them; in Western Europe, the corresponding figure is 21 percent.[7]

Such numbers cannot be taken at face value. They do not simply represent the world as it is but are self-representations. The difference between how Americans and citizens of other Western nations answer pollsters' questions is first of all about how they think of themselves and how they want to be thought of in the context in which the question is asked. It means something different to say that one is "very religious" in Picayune, Mississippi, than it does in Oslo. Someone might have many reasons to answer yes to such a question, and it might be misleading to interpret the "yes" as having one simple meaning.

But these numbers do reflect the way that Americans and Europeans think of themselves, and they reveal the gap between those self-identifications. Americans' statements about their religiousness certainly ring true to the European perspective on the difference between Europe and the United States. To Europeans, religion appears not only ubiquitous in America but also shockingly public. Journalist Robert Musik writes that to Europeans, American public life seems saturated with religion and that the Europeans find this simply baffling.[8] A colleague of the historian Hartmut Lehmann told of spending a year in Mannheim when he was a student. No one asked him about his religion. He then spent ten months at the University of Nebraska. People invited him to church, asked him "time and again" to which church he belonged, and loved to engage him in conversations about religion. Americans, he said, were remarkably "public" about their religious convictions.[9]

It was not always this way. Hugh McLeod is right when he argues that "the long sixties" marked a crisis in religion in both Europe and America.[10] But then the late 1970s catapulted American evangelicals and traditionalist Catholics to the covers of news magazines and the front pages of newspapers, while Western European societies seemed to become increasingly secular. Why?

Matters are always more complicated than they seem. Americans, for example, are not very knowledgeable about their religion. They remind one of the high school student cited by Richard Lederer who said that Martin Luther died a horrible death, being excommunicated by a bull. Despite the battles over the Ten Commandments in state buildings, only 35 percent of Americans could name half the commandments, and only 29 percent could remember that they say something about false gods.[11] About half of American Protestants could not identify Martin Luther, let alone remember the manner of his death.[12]

In the past fifteen years, moreover, a number of sociologists have found that while 40 percent claimed to attend religious services weekly, only about 20 percent actually did.[13] Further, the number of Americans who claim no religious affiliation apparently doubled between 1990 and 2009, rising from 8 percent to 16 percent of the population.[14] So maybe Americans are not quite as distinctive as they say they are, but they are distinctive in their eagerness to say it. This is puzzling, historically. In trying to explain it, we should remember one obvious point, namely, that differences of degree make a difference, and the differences of degree are matters of contingency, not necessity.

The most prominent contemporary attempts to explain why Americans seem so religious employ the idea of a religious marketplace. One can, of course, raise a variety of questions about religion and markets. Consider just fifteen of the different conclusions historians have reached in America in the past twenty years: They have argued that religion and the market had no relevant connection;[15] that religion legitimated markets and produced a disciplined workforce;[16] that religion checked the excesses of markets;[17] that colonial commercial success promoted both Christianity and millennial optimism;[18] that attitudes toward the market divided religious groups;[19] that churches inadvertently promoted the commercialization of religious holidays;[20] that gospels of wealth and prosperity flourished with unusual intensity in America;[21] that religious institutions "pioneered the organizational techniques that later appear in business corporations";[22] that denominations have used big business, its language, and its goal of efficiency as their model;[23] that churches and synagogues emulated secular markets to raise money;[24] that families adapted domestic religious rituals to consumer culture;[25] that affluence in the 1950s gave young people alternatives to church activities;[26] that religion stimulated Americans to create alternatives to the prevailing market economy;[27] that it provided a haven from a heartless market-driven world;[28] and that denominations provided markers of social and economic status.[29] Nonetheless, only a few theories of the religion–market relationship have a direct bearing on the question of why Americans seem, in some ways, more religious than Western Europeans. With these theories, historians have claimed to show that the cause of America's apparent religiousness is America's religious marketplace. They have made claims about necessity, rather than contingency. These theories need to be challenged.

The first and most prominent comes from the supply-side theorists who argue that the American separation of church and state created a

wide-open religious marketplace that outperformed the religious monop-
olies maintained by European state churches. Separation produced an
array of denominations—fifty-eight by 1850, more than 250 by now—that
competed for members. In the land of the free market, pastors, priests,
and rabbis sought, like the CEO of General Motors, to grow market share,
and the result was a religious America.[30] The numbers supporting this
argument are questionable, though. Estimates of attendance at religious
services before and after disestablishment and in the twentieth century
suggest that the separation of church and state had no dramatic effect on
religiosity. A case can be made that probably around 35 to 40 percent of
eighteenth-century colonial Americans regularly attended religious services, with some dips here and there, and that this did not change much
in 1850 or 1940.

The debate over membership, adherence, and attendance has carried conflicting definitions and assumptions. Patricia Bonomi and Peter
Eisenstadt defined "adherents" as "attenders" and their children; assumed
that each congregation had, on average, eighty families (400 to 480 persons); calculated the population in 1780 as 2,204,949; and concluded that
80 percent were "churched" in 1700 and 59 percent in 1780.[31] Rodney Stark
and Roger Finke, on the other hand, argued that 10 percent of the colonists
were "members" of churches. They assumed that each of the 3,228 congregations had, on average, seventy-five members and that the colonial population in 1776 stood between 2,421,000 and 2,524,000. In *The Churching
of America* they define "adherents" as members (rather than attenders) and
their children, and they calculate the colonial adherence rate as 17 percent
of the population.[32] According to Jon Butler, adherence could be defined as
"regular or steady attachment to institutional Christianity," but he tended
to interpret it as communicant membership, and he saw it as varying from
place to place, ranging from 8 to 40 percent, with a pattern of religious indifference, while James Hutson cites evidence that the population in 1770 was
only 2,100,000 and that the churches had on average five hundred to eight
hundred adherents (defined as attenders and their children). He concludes
that the adherence rate in New England and Virginia in 1750–1760 was
71 percent, a conclusion close to that of Bonomi and Eisenstadt. Hutson's
definition includes adherents who might have attended irregularly, but if
half made it to worship on a given Sunday, perhaps 35 percent of the population regularly attended.[33] Everyone recognizes that some colonies passed
laws requiring attendance, but everyone also agrees that the laws did not
fully attain their aim.

The figure of 35 percent attendance—a rough estimate, to be sure—assumes that each family had on average five to six persons; that some were too young to attend and someone had to stay home with them; that weather, old age, and illness kept others away; that distance and poor transportation sometimes made attendance difficult; that clerical short-ages, especially on the margins of settlement, reduced attendance; and that some adherents in the eighteenth century, as in the twenty-first, sim-ply felt no compelling reason to attend regularly. One-quarter of British immigrants arriving in the American colonies in the eighteenth century were convicts, and in Maryland they composed a quarter of the population during the thirty years before 1776—not a group likely to attend church in large numbers. A report from the rectors of eighty Anglican congre-gations in 1724 indicates that attenders outnumbered communicants by more than four to one but also that, from one parish to another, 10 to 70 percent of the parishioners might be absent on any given Sunday.[34] In Boston, Cotton Mather preached to as many as 1,600 people, and once in 1723 he described an attendance of one thousand as "thinner . . . than ordinary," but the average colonial meetinghouse in New England had far fewer seats than the one in which Mather preached. Brookline, Massachusetts, had 360 inhabitants in 1714, but the meetinghouse would hold only sixty-five of them.[35] In England, by comparison, a commission in the diocese of Lincoln in 1799 reported that about 33 percent of the pop-ulation attended churches and 16 percent of the adult population received communion.[36]

The federal U.S. Census in 1850 found 38,061 congregations, one for every 611 Americans. Using extrapolations from census data, Stark and Finke have argued that the members of these congregations made up about 21 percent of the population.[37] In Protestant churches, how-ever, attendance exceeded membership. When British traveler Andrew Reed toured the United States in 1835, he observed the difference. Six congregations in Lexington, Kentucky, had 3,200 attenders and nine hundred communicant members. In Danville, he found that 22 percent of the town's inhabitants were communicants but 57 percent attended; Morristown had 29 percent communicants and 71 percent attenders. In the largest Congregational church in Northampton, Connecticut, he counted 1,400 worshipers, while three hundred more attended in the sec-ond church. His reports make it plausible that the 21 percent membership rate proposed by Stark and Finke entailed a higher rate of attendance. If the average congregation in 1850 still ministered to eighty families—a plausible assumption given the highly rural character of the nation—then the rate of adherence, as defined by Bonomi and Eisenstadt, would have been 72 percent. If half of those adherents attended on a given Sunday, the attendance rate might have been around 36 percent nationwide. This figure is lower than Reed's count for selected larger towns but compatible with the conclusions of Stark and Finke and plausible in view of the large number of rural churches in less populated areas. It is also commensurate with other more focused and precise studies. Butler found that in New York City between 1855 and 1875, the number of worshipers ranged from a high of 35 percent (1855) to a low of 22 percent (1865), while in New York State the range went from 28 percent (1865) to 32 percent (1855), percentages higher than the membership rate but roughly consistent with the colonial pattern in 1780.[38]

By 1890, the number of congregations rose to 165,297, one for every 381 Americans. Membership in these congregations also rose. Stark and Finke figure that the membership rate by 1890 stood at 30 percent and that the inclusion of the children of the members would raise the rate to 45 percent. The meaning of membership, however, had also shifted as the large Protestant denominations relaxed their standards. By 1887, Josiah Strong surveyed thirty city congregations and found that only 56 percent of the members—not of the general population—attended worship.[39] Butler studied the surveys made by the Federation of Churches in New York City between 1896 and 1903. Two of them show that about half the Protestants, 80 percent of the Catholics, and 10 percent of the Jews in two New York districts reported attending regularly. Half the Baptists claimed to be "attending services with some regularity." Butler adds that a "less systematic survey" of Manhattan attendance in 1902 "showed about 38 percent of . . . [the] members attended . . . regularly," with Methodists claiming 50 percent and Jews, 10 percent.[40]

Numbers are easier to come by in the twentieth century. They show a decline in attendance in rural areas in the 1920s. Warren Hugh Wilson studied 713 small community churches and found that 16 percent of the Protestant rural population in the region he studied belonged to a church and that only 70 percent of that number was active.[41] Edmund de S. Brunner discovered in a study in 1921 of seventy counties in the rural South that the churches enrolled about 28 percent of the population, despite having held 211 "revivals" in the previous year. Only 20 percent of the churches had full-time resident ministers.[42] Brunner also looked at sixty-nine villages, largely in the Midwest, and found that 37 percent of the population was enrolled in a church, as opposed to 47 percent in the national census. But only 60 percent of the Protestant members in this largely Protestant region were "active."[43] The rural church reformers who carried out the surveys neglected one important group, the so-called emotional sects. Holiness and Pentecostal churches flourished in the rural areas during the 1920s, but to the reformers they seemed transient and inconsequential.[44] In fact, their inclusion would have resulted in higher numbers for both adherents and attenders. More recent analyses have claimed that in 1920, 43 percent of the population were still church members, and at the end of the 1930s 41 percent of the population claimed to attend regularly, but the other figures from the 1920s make the self-reporting about attendance suspect.[45]

Between 1935 and 1985, between 40 and 49 percent of the American population claimed to have attended churches or synagogues within the previous seven days. That figure remained relatively stable through the twentieth and early twenty-first centuries. The discovery that actual attendance was smaller in the late twentieth century, however, casts some doubt on the earlier twentieth-century figures.

Attendance seems to have declined since 1780, though it is difficult to know when the decline began. In any case, it seems highly unlikely that the separation of church and state produced a dramatic rise in attendance at services of worship.[46] Scholars who claim that membership rose during the nineteenth century are probably correct, but the meaning of membership changed in ways that make temporal comparisons relating to members at least as ambiguous as arguments about attenders. After 1865, it simply became easier to join one of the large Protestant denominations, and people joined who would never have submitted to the discipline imposed by many colonial congregations.

It is true that the probable attendance rates for the Americans exceeded those for Europeans during much of the nineteenth and twentieth centuries. In 1869, about 5 percent of the population in Berlin attended church on Sunday; in the early twentieth century 15 percent attended Mass in Paris; during the same period London had an average attendance of 22 percent; in Liverpool the number was 31 percent, closer to the American pattern. As in America, the lowest rates of religious practice in the early twentieth century could be found in some rural areas. In Hanover, the average church attendance in the inner city in 1870 was 5 percent, and in the suburban churches the number was still smaller.

Church customs—baptisms, marriages, and funerals—remained popular, but more active forms of participation often languished.

The difference, however, can hardly be attributed entirely to church–
state relations. The French separated church and state in 1905, a separation sharper than the American, and religious participation has not risen
in France. It has, in the long run, fallen.[47]

The supply-side argument may also overstate the dominance of
American colonial establishments. The Anglicans of South Carolina
gained a restrictive establishment in 1706, but they still had to compete
with at least nine other denominations, and one observer claimed in 1776
that dissenting Calvinist churches had more members than the established Anglicans.[48]

In fact, the theory may overstate the power of some church establishments in Europe and Britain. According to the British religious
census of 1851, the Church of England and the Church of Scotland had
to compete with at least fifteen other denominations, and about half of
Britain's churchgoers worshiped at Nonconformist chapels.[49] The options
increased after World War I, but religion in England still declined.[50] In
twenty-first-century Germany, the two large confessions, Evangelical and
Catholic, still have privileged relationships to the state, but Germany has
sixty Christian groups, most of them small, and thirty-three non-Christian
religious groups, also small, in addition to several varieties of Muslims.
How many options do you need to create a marketplace that significantly
increases religious participation?[51]

Additionally, the argument may overstate the negative effect of establishment on religious participation. In Virginia in 1724, for example, about
40 percent attended under monopolistic conditions, a number higher
than the ratio in New York State between 1855 and 1865.[52] In Europe, some
countries with virtually monopolistic churches—Ireland, Poland, and
Italy, for example—have had, in the recent past, rates of religious practice
as high as America's. To say that this reflects ethnic allegiance or political
identification might be true, but religion has frequently served multiple
purposes in the United States as well.[53]

Finally, religion flourished in nineteenth-century America not simply because the separation of church and state created a religious market but also because European immigrants, many of whom were already
religious, flooded into the country. In other words, nations with state
churches helped to make America more religious.

It is not that the separation of church and state, pluralism, and competition made no difference. It is, rather, that they made a difference in combination with a host of other things. Church–state separation gave laypeople greater authority over local religious institutions; prevented state certification of the clergy and therefore facilitated the democratization and numbers of religious leaders; and because of the ambiguity of the First Amendment to the American Constitution, generated controversial Supreme Court decisions, especially after 1962, that continue to mobilize religious activists and keep religion in the news. Thus, while the religious marketplace theory is deficient as an overall explanation, it is not entirely wrong. The religious market of the supply-siders is part of a larger picture.

A second market argument is that religion flourishes where people experience "social vulnerability, insecurity, and risk." The highest levels of religious practice are in the poorest countries of the world. Why, then, so much religion in affluent America? The answer: because its form of capitalism produces inequalities that generate vulnerability. The European welfare states, on the other hand, relieve anxiety and therefore dampen religious spirits.[54] But some of the most vulnerable in America—African American men in the inner city, for example—have low religious commitments, and some of Europe's most economically insecure regions—eastern Germany, for example—are not as religious as more affluent areas. In the nineteenth century, the poorest classes in Europe—the most vulnerable—were often the least inclined to attend churches and synagogues. Some were privately devout; many were decidedly not.[55]

The issue encompasses not only the poorest of the poor but also the working class. Christianity thrived in the United States, so goes one argument, partly because the churches were able to reach the working class, while the European churches were not. Some historians of labor in nineteenth-century America have discovered church growth in working-class neighborhoods, religious dimensions of working-class protest, alliances between the Catholic Church and working-class immigrants, and working-class attraction to Methodists and Baptists, by 1850 the two largest Protestant denominations.[56] And who can forget the early Pentecostals? Historians of labor in nineteenth-century Europe, on the other hand, have emphasized working-class alienation. They have pointed out that socialism functioned as a quasi-religion that drew workers from traditional religion, they have recalled church opposition to workers' strikes, and they have noted the low number of churches in working-class urban neighborhoods.[57] Hugh McLeod concluded that between 1870 and

1914 in Berlin only 10 percent of the working class attended churches; in London, about 12 percent; and in New York, where religion was often a marker of ethnicity, about 38 percent.[58] The differences, however, are not universal. Other historians have argued that in other parts of Europe and England, the working class remained as faithful and as active as the middle and upper classes.[59] Yet it does seem that the spread of working-class denominations in America, from Methodists and Baptists to early Pentecostals, as well as the working-class character of nineteenth-century Catholicism, made a difference. That may have resulted in a degree of difference between America and Europe.

A third market theory is relevant to the question of European and American difference: namely, that American religious groups created a "marketplace of culture" in which they learned how to reach the public by advertising; entertaining; exploiting the mass media; publishing mass-market books and magazines; promoting religion as a means to wealth and health; sponsoring leisure activities; and employing everything from magic lantern shows to radio, television, and Hollywood films to "sell God" in a consumer culture.[60] By the late nineteenth century, for example, American churches became social centers that performed an almost limitless number of nonreligious functions: Sunday school concerts, church socials, women's meetings, girls' guilds, boys' brigades, athletic clubs, scout troops, and military drill groups. One church reported in 1897 that "uniforms, guns, and equipment are as essential as the Bible and the Hymnal in the advance of our work."[61] By 1890, one observer spoke of a "complete revolution" in the social life of American congregations. Its symbol was the church parlor. In some denominations, he said, the parlor had become "almost as necessary as a pulpit."[62] When the Brooklyn pastor Henry Ward Beecher gave the Beecher lectures at Yale Divinity School in the 1870s, he told the students that he had one important piece of advice—to multiply picnics. There ought to be, he said, "such little gatherings as shall mingle the people together and make them like one another."[63]

In smaller American towns, the churches are still often the primary site for socializing. The late British historian Tony Judt traveled through America not long ago. Here is what he noticed in west Texas:

> Driving northwest from Dallas toward remotest Decatur . . . each settlement would be represented by a gas station or two, a dowdy (often shuttered) motel, the occasional convenience store, and little

clusters of trailer housing. But there was nothing to suggest community. Except the church. To a European eye, as often as not, it was little more than a warehouse topped by a giant cross. But the building stood out among the strip malls and ribbon housing. Religion is not just the only game in town—it is often the sole link to anything recognizably social. . . . If I lived in such a place, I too would join the Elect.[64]

It is quite likely that the social function of churches—and the connection of religion with mass entertainment—made, and makes, an important difference.

Yet churches in England in the nineteenth century were also places for recreation and social welfare. They had their Church Lads Brigades, Girls' Guides, and rifle drill groups along with picnics and church socials. Scottish Reformed congregations gravitated by the 1880s toward commercial advertising, church bazaars, music, literary readings, picnics, football, swimming, baseball, bowling, boxing, gymnastics, and cycling.[65] Germany and France soon emulated the British. One might think also of Oberammergau; the commercialization of Lourdes; Catholic fiestas; or the pop and rock music, parades, and drum groups at the German *Kirchentag*. Religious Europeans have also not been averse to their own forms of generating entertainment.

Nonetheless, there does seem to be a difference between Europe and America. It is hard to imagine that some American religious television shows could attract as wide a viewership in Europe as they do in America. It is hard to think that "Weightlifters for Christ" could become a popular touring group in European conservative churches, Christian exercise classes could attract so many participants, and Christian diet books could draw so many readers. Again, the difference is a matter of degree, but degrees make a difference.[66]

Some have argued, however, that revivalism created the foundation for the evangelicalism that today helps make America seem so religious. William Warren Sweet claimed more than half a century ago that the churches that used "revivalist methods" made America a religious nation.[67] More recently Charles Cohen has argued that revivalism became the "fundamental recruiting mechanism for nineteenth-century American Protestantism," helping to create "a new type of Christianity" that proved to be "admirably suited" as an "innovative instrument of Christianization" for the American setting.[68] Jay Dolan has shown that Catholics could be as revivalist as Protestants. On the other hand, William McLoughlin, who wrote the history of American revivalism, concluded that it made little difference. He believed that revivalist practices "hurt Protestantism more than helped it," and he argued that the rate of church membership growth was probably not "greatly influenced by revivalism."[69] Antebellum revivalism might have had an indirect effect. Donald Mathews long ago contended that revivals in the early nineteenth century formed an organizing movement that created religious congregations and therefore increased participation.[70] No straight line, however, extends from the revivals to the rate of membership growth in an expanding population.

Revivalism has never been isolated from market mechanisms. We have learned to think of the revivalist George Whitefield as an eighteenth-century "pedlar in divinity" whose immersion in a "thoroughly commercialized society" led him to conceive of a revival spanning the Atlantic, to employ innovative advertising, to take up the publishing trade, and to serialize his published sermons and sell them in large numbers.[71] We have also learned to recognize the market characteristics of Dwight L. Moody's innovative advertising and light shows and Billy Sunday's vaudevillian entertainment as well as his claim that it cost him only about $2.00 for each soul saved. A half-century later, Billy Graham perfected methods of mass mailings and televised rallies that influenced the advertising of American corporations (and political parties).[72]

Revivals, however, also swept through Wales and awakened Scotland. Children's revivals moved worshipers in Silesia. There were movements of Pietists in Germany, Switzerland, and the Netherlands. Moravians traversed the continent. Methodists and Baptists perfected revivalist techniques in Britain. Charles Finney and Dwight L. Moody enchanted the British, and Billy Graham held "crusades" in at least fifty-four British and Western European cities. Europeans had revivals, too.[73]

Yet there was a degree of difference. European revivals occurred in a context in which most Europeans identified themselves with established churches, and the religious institutions of European society, often stronger than American institutions, sometimes acted as a counterweight. In the early nineteenth century American revivalists reached multitudes of people who were moving from one place to another, people who had severed some of their relationships with their past, and therefore helped create new institutions and patterns of language. If one eliminated from today's poll numbers the nearly 30 percent of Americans who claim to have been "born again," America would look to the pollsters more like

Europe. Where did they get that language? From the New Testament, of course, but not the New Testament as read by the Council of Trent or Luther and Calvin. They read the New Testament through the lenses of Puritanism, Pietism, Methodism, and other forms of revivalism. The revivals therefore left an imprint on America, and they have some explanatory force, but they did not flow inevitably from the separation of church and state. They were a contingent, not necessary, series of events, and the context in which they occurred altered their influence.

Still other historians have argued that Christianity flourished because the American Revolution led to a democratizing of Christianity, with churches that required no educated clergy—indeed, preferred an uneducated clergy—and encouraged an earthy, witty, colloquial pastoral and preaching style.[74] This populist style has endured in America—even now only half the congregations in America have seminary-educated clergy—and the theologically unschooled sometimes serve megachurches.[75] Moreover, this populist style, in opening the pulpit to the theologically untrained, also opened it to people once excluded, including nineteenth-century African American preachers, slave and then free, who could reach slaves and freed people in ways that white preachers could not. The populist impulse helped make the black church the strongest African American institution in a segregated society. Remove the members of black churches from the polls, and America would look a little more like Western Europe.

The market had quite a lot to do with the rise of religious populism. The populist style fit a particular economic and educational niche—rarely the poorest of the poor, except in the case of some of the slave preachers, but, rather, yeomen farmers and aspiring craftsmen, predominantly middling and artisan classes. They were the same social constituency who later sent Pentecostal frenzy whirling through the United States and then the southern hemisphere.[76]

Nevertheless, a populist style of ministry did not ensure growth— antebellum Quakers were populists, and they declined proportionally in numbers in the nineteenth century. Mennonites had no trained clergy, and they remained a small, select group. There were populist preachers in England, Scotland, and Wales from the seventeenth century to the twenty-first, Hussite and Anabaptist preachers in central Europe, and prophetic visionaries in Lutheran Germany.[77] So populism alone cannot explain American religiosity, but the populist impulse has, to a degree, maybe to a significant degree, distinguished American from European religion and led to greater degrees of participation.

Still other historians have argued that American religion flourished because it adapted itself to American nationalism. Certain New England documents especially, such as Cotton Mather's *Magnalia Christi Americana* and John Winthrop's sermon on the Arabella, helped create an enduring mythology of America's special relationship with God:[78] "We are entered into a covenant [with God] for this work. . . . For we shall be as a city upon a hill, the eyes of all people are upon us."[79] The theme—even the very words—still resonates in American politics.

Americans have always been fascinated by a millennial theology with nationalist overtones. In the seventeenth century they saw New England as a New Israel. In the eighteenth, they sometimes confused republicanism and Protestantism, equated Britain and France with the Antichrist, and used millennialism to justify imperialism, which also, one might add, was never divorced from markets.[80] Forever after, some American churches saw it as part of their task to promote the aims of the nation, and from time to time they sold liberty bonds, recruited soldiers, blessed wars, and hung flags in their sanctuaries. Maybe American religion got confused with American nationalism, and that is why Americans seem to be so religious. A civil religion still flourishes in America, manifest in the language of politicians, references to the flag as sacred, prayers and chaplains in Congress, religious motifs on coinage, and the Pledge of Allegiance recited by American schoolchildren.

Religious nationalism, however, does not make America singular. The English also saw themselves as an "Elect Nation," the Spanish claimed a holy mission, and France viewed itself as a chosen nation destined to carry on the tradition of Israel.[81] In 1916, almost every place of worship in Britain displayed the Union Jack, often hanging above the communion table, and many Germans saw World War I as the last, best defense of Christian civilization.[82] Yet a civil religion does seem to elicit a greater degree of allegiance in America now than it does in most of Western Europe. It seems safe to bet that the proportionate number of national flags located in churches is significantly smaller in Western Europe. American nationalism and civil religion have made a difference—perhaps only to a degree, but these things matter.

Still other historians have implied that theology played a part, especially a form of theology that convinced Americans that the absence of religion meant the absence of morality. Many American Christians, even to this day, hold to a theology that identifies Christianity with honest and ethical behavior. That is probably the reason so many Americans say that they would not vote for a politician who does not profess religious belief— and the reason so many politicians speak of their piety in public.[83] A lot of European churches taught the same thing between the eighteenth and mid–nineteenth centuries, and a lot of Europeans also still identify Christianity with honest and ethical behavior, even though European politicians are less inclined to speak publicly about their religion.[84] A theology equating religion with morality made a difference in America, and it still colors American political life. Popular theology declares that Americans should not elect atheists; Europeans are not quite as worried about that. To a degree, the persistence and prevalence of this popular theology did make a difference.

Yet other historians have argued that America is more religious because America was an immigrant country and the church and synagogue, and later the temple and mosque, were among the few institutions that immigrants could bring from their home countries. For immigrants, the church was the center not only for worship but also for community life, group identity, recreation, matchmaking, and social advancement. Irish and German pastors and priests helped new immigrants find jobs, form insurance societies, create burial associations, and survive in ethnic enclaves. In 135 studies of immigration to America, 116 found religion to be an important agency of communal identity and support, material aid, and linguistic preservation, as well as worship with like-minded friends. Several recent studies have suggested that immigration tends to intensify religious commitments, at least in the first and second generations.[85]

Immigration did not always intensify religion, though. Orthodox Jewish immigrants often fell away in the late nineteenth and early twentieth centuries.[86] German exiles after the failed revolution of 1848 did not find that America made them more religious. In any case, religion in Western Europe has also drawn strength from immigration. Europe has seen successive waves of internal and external immigration, often voluntary, sometimes involuntary, ranging from movements into the old Austro-Hungarian Empire to the successive waves of Poles, Italians, Spaniards, Portuguese, and Turks who arrived in Germany and the Caribbean immigration to Great Britain. These immigrations sometimes intensified religious practice.[87]

Yet the sheer number of immigrants to America has brought successive waves of religious intensification. One need not agree with Timothy

Smith that immigration is a "theologizing" experience, or with Will Herberg that immigrants became American by being Protestant, Catholic, or Jewish, to see that immigration has left a deep imprint on religious participation in America. Without the most recent immigration from Latin America, the Catholic Church in America today would be quite different,[88] and America would look slightly more like Western Europe.

Finally, some historians have argued that American religion flourished because women made it flourish. From 1660 forward, women constituted—and still constitute—the majority of American churchgoers, and they have maintained the institutions, even when they were excluded from the pulpit.[89] In Catholic churches now, with no women priests, 80 percent of the local ministers are women. They cannot celebrate the Mass, but they lead the parishes.[90] Ann Braude has a point when she argues that American religious history is women's history. But that does not distinguish the United States from much of Western Europe. In nineteenth-century Europe, women were 60 percent of the membership; in early twentieth-century Germany they constituted 60 to 70 percent of the communicants. In later twentieth-century Britain, they were 65 to 75 percent of most congregations.[91] Callum Brown might not have been entirely right when he claimed that the departure of women from the churches led to religious collapse in Britain in the 1960s,[92] but his claim does accent the point that American women, to a greater degree than in Britain, sustained religious institutions.

One final explanation of American religious difference needs to be mentioned. In 1949, Arthur Schlesinger Sr. published a chapter on American culture that he entitled "Biography of a Nation of Joiners." In the nineteenth century Alexis de Tocqueville had noticed that "Americans of all ages, all stations of life, and all types of disposition are forming associations . . . of a thousand different types."[93] According to Robert Putnam, the number of nonprofit organizations listed in the *Encyclopedia of Associations* "more than doubled from 10,229 to 22,901 between 1968 and 1997."[94] Most of them are relatively small—and Putnam wrote his much-discussed book *Bowling Alone* in order to warn that the associative principle was appearing to wane. But the apparent tendency of Americans to join voluntary organizations of all kinds has, in all likelihood, raised the levels of religious participation. Europeans join voluntary organizations, too, but, to make a guess—and end with a sheer guess—they do not tend to join to quite the same degree, and that tendency makes a difference.

If Americans are more religious, in some ways, than Western Europeans, the reasons are many, and only a narrative, filled with contingencies, can provide a plausible explanation. The separation of church and state and the competitive religious marketplace form a piece of the answer, though only in connection with other events and movements. Innumerable kinds of market relations have influenced religion, but only alongside other kinds of social relations.[95] For each explanation that is true, a multitude of qualifications is required. Differences of degree do make a difference, and no single variable can explain any difference between Europe and America, whether religious or political. One certainly cannot appeal to the market alone as an explanation, though the market, too, has made a difference—a degree of difference.

## *Notes*

1. Gallup, "Religion in America 50 Years: 1935–1985," Report No. 236 (New York: Gallup, May 1985), 50. See also the 2011 Gallup poll, http://www.gallup.com/poll/147887/americans-continue-believe-god.aspx.

2. Yves Lambert, "New Christianity, Indifference, and Diffused Spirituality," in *The Decline of Christendom in Western Europe 1750–2000*, ed. Hugh McLeod and Werner Ustorf (Cambridge: Cambridge University Press, 2003), 71; Eva B. Hamburg, "Christendom in Decline: The Swedish Case," in McLeod and Ustorf, *Decline of Christendom*, 47; Olaf Müller and Detlef Pollack, "Churchliness, Religiosity and Spirituality: Western and Eastern European Societies in Times of Diversity," in *What the World Believes: Analyses and Commentary on the Religion Monitor 2008*, ed. Martin Rieger (Gütersloh, Germany: Verlag Bertelsmann Stiftung, 2009), 401.

3. Gallup, "Religion in America," 53; Lambert, "New Christianity," 71–72.

4. Albert L. Winseman, "Eternal Destinations: Americans Believe in Heaven, Hell," Gallup, May 25, 2004, http://www.gallup.com/poll/11770/eternal-destinations-americans-believe-heaven-hell.aspx; Lambert, "New Christianity," 71.

5. C. Kirk Hadaway, Penny Long Marler, and Mark Chaves, "What the Polls Don't Show: A Closer Look at U.S. Church Attendance," *American Sociological Review* 58 (December 1998): 741–742. Between 1967 and 1990, the Episcopal Church should have grown by 13 percent if we take at face value the percentage of Americans who claimed to be Episcopalians on social surveys; instead, Episcopal membership fell by 28 percent (742). For Britain, see Callum Brown, *The Death of Christian Britain: Understanding Secularization 1800–2000* (London: Routledge, 2008), 4.

6. Hadaway, Marler, and Chaves, "What the Polls Don't Show," 743; Christine Heyrman, *Southern Cross: The Beginnings of the Bible Belt* (New York: Alfred A. Knopf, 1997), 13; Brown, *Death of Christian Britain*, 4; McLeod and Ustorf, *Decline of Christendom*, 3. In America, 69 percent of the population say that they pray frequently; in Germany, the number is 26 percent (Hans Joas, "The Religious Situation in the United States," in Rieger, *What the World Believes*, 319).

7. Elaine Sciolino, Helena Fouquet, and Renwick McLean, "Europeans Fast Falling Away from Church," *New York Times*, April 25, 2009, A9.

8. Robert Musik, "That Old-Time Religion," *Atlantic Times*, July 2008, 17. In the 1960s, American scholars and theologians looked at America as secular, and they sometimes linked the secularity to the market. See Peter Berger, *The Sacred Canopy: Elements of a Sociological Theory of Religion* (New York: Doubleday, 1967). In his *The Secular City: Secularization and Urbanization in Theological Perspective* (New York: Macmillan, 1965), Harvey Cox saw the roots of secularity in the economic concentration that produced the city; Martin Marty in *The Modern Schism: Three Paths to the Secular* (New York: Harper and Row, 1969) compared America's "controlled secularity," which preserved religious symbols but secularized their content, with Europe's "utter secularity," antagonistic to religion, and Britain's "mere secularity," which was simply indifferent. He noted that the "business community" of the late nineteenth century had used religious symbols to validate commerce as "the locus of truth and value" (107). The idea of American secularity endured into following decades, often with a political subtext. In 1984, Richard John Neuhaus complained in *The Naked Public Square: Religion and Democracy in America* (Grand Rapids: Wm. B. Eerdmans, 1984) that American politics had become secularized (27); while twenty years later Mary Ann Glendon wrote in "The Naked Public Square Now" (*First Things* 15, no. 11 [November 2004]) about "state sponsored secularism" (13). In *The Secular Revolution: Powers, Interests, and Conflict in the Secularization of American Public Life* (Berkeley: University of California Press, 2003), Christian Smith seeks to uncover the agencies and interests whose strategies had produced a "secular revolution" in the United States (29). Smith finds business interests among the agencies that produced the secular turn.

9. Hartmut Lehmann, "Secular Europe versus Christian America? Re-examination of the Secularization Thesis," in *Transatlantische Religionsgeschichte 18. bis 20. Jahrhundert*, ed. Hartmut Lehmann (Göttingen: Wallstein Verlag, 2006), 147.

10. Hugh McLeod, *The Religious Crisis of the 1960s* (Oxford: Oxford University Press, 2007), 215–239.

11. Richard Lederer, *Anguished English* (Charleston, S.C.: Wyrick, 1987), 10; Kelton Research, "Ten Commandments Study," September 2007, http://www.opentheword.org, 1. See Lambert, "New Christianity," 70; George Gallup Jr., *The Role of the Bible in American Society* (Princeton: Princeton Religion Research

Center, 1990), 17; Stephen Prothero, *Religious Literacy: What Every American Needs to Know—and Doesn't* (San Francisco: HarperRow San Francisco, 2007), 21–38; "U.S. Religious Knowledge Survey," September 28, 2010, http://www.pewforum.org/2010/09/28/u-s-religious-knowledge-survey/.

12. "U.S. Religious Knowledge Survey." For British religious knowledge, see Vexan Crabtree, "Religion in the United Kingdom: Diversity, Trends and Decline," 2012, http://www.humanreligions.info/uk.html. For German religious knowledge, see Bernhard Grom, S.J., "Europa und die religiöse Ignoranz," 2003, http://www.stimmen-der-zeit.de/zeitschrift/archiv/beitrag_details?k_beitrag=1650249&k_produkt=1833386.

13. C. Kirk Hadaway and Penny Long Marler, "Did You Really Go to Church This Week? Behind the Poll Data," *Christian Century* 115, no. 14 (May 6, 1998): 472–475; Hadaway, Marler, and Chaves, "What the Polls Don't Show," 741–752; see also Penny Long Marler and C. Kirk Hadaway, "Testing the Attendance Gap in a Conservative Church," *Sociology of Religion* 60, no. 2 (Summer 1999): 176–185.

14. Jon Meacham, "The End of Christian America," *Newsweek*, April 13, 2009, 34–38; W. Bradford Wilcox, *When Marriage Disappears*, University of Virginia, National Marriage Project, 2010, http://stateofourunions.org/2010/SOOU2010.php; Robert Wuthnow, *The Restructuring of American Religion: Society and Faith since World War II* (Princeton: Princeton University Press, 1988), 167–172. In Italy also, 15 percent say that they never attend church. See Müller and Pollack, "Churchliness, Religiosity and Spirituality," 402.

15. See Michael Zuckerman, "Holy Wars, Civil Wars: Religion and Economics in Nineteenth-Century America," *Prospects: An Annual of American Cultural Studies* 16 (1991): 205–240. Zuckerman argued for multiple interrelations between religion and the marketplace.

16. Stephen Innes, *Creating the Commonwealth: The Economic Culture of Puritan New England* (New York: Norton, 1968), 101; Anthony F. C. Wallace, *Rockdale: The Growth of an American Village in the Early Industrial Revolution* (New York: Alfred A. Knopf, 1978), 350–397; Bethany Moreton, *To Serve God and Wal-Mart: The Making of Christian Free Enterprise* (Cambridge: Harvard University Press, 2009), 66, 101.

17. Mark Valeri, *Heavenly Merchandize: How Religion Shaped Commerce in Puritan America* (Princeton: Princeton University Press, 2010), 76; Jesper Rosenmeier, "John Cotton on Usury," *William and Mary Quarterly* 47, no. 4 (October 1990): 548–564; Mark Valeri, "Economic Thought of Jonathan Edwards," *Church History* 60, no. 1 (March 1991): 37–54; Kenneth Moore Startup, *The Root of All Evil: The Protestant Clergy and the Economic Mind of the Old South* (Athens: University of Georgia Press, 1997), 21–34; Lorman A. Ratner, Paula T. Kaufman, and Dwight L. Teeter Jr., *Paradoxes of Prosperity: Wealth-Seeking versus Christian Values in Pre–Civil War America* (Urbana: University of Illinois Press, 2009), 85–110.

18. Mark A. Peterson, *The Price of Redemption: The Spiritual Economy of Puritan New England* (Stanford, Calif.: Stanford University Press, 1997), 163–174.

19. Stewart Davenport, *Friends of the Unrighteous Mammon: Northern Christians and Market Capitalism, 1815–1860* (Chicago: University of Chicago Press, 2008), 56, 189; Rosalind Remer, "Old Lights and New Money: A Note on Religion, Economics, and the Social Order in 1740 Boston," *William and Mary Quarterly* 47, no. 4 (October 1990): 566–567.

20. Leigh Eric Schmidt, *Consumer Rites: The Buying and Selling of American Holidays* (Princeton: Princeton University Press, 1995), 106–243.

21. Catherine L. Albanese, *A Republic of Mind and Spirit: A Cultural History of American Metaphysical Religion* (New Haven: Yale University Press, 2007), 320–321, 439–442, 468; Donald Meyer, *The Positive Thinkers: A Study of the American Quest for Health, Wealth, and Personal Power from Mary Baker Eddy to Norman Vincent Peale* (New York: Doubleday, 1965; rev. ed., 1988), 281–299; Hannah Rosin, "Did Christianity Cause the Crash?" *Atlantic*, December 2009, 39–48; William C. Martin, "The God-Hucksters of Radio," in *Side-Saddle on the Golden Calf: Social Structure and Popular Culture in America*, by George H. Lewis (Pacific Palisades, Calif.: Goodyear, 1982), 49–55.

22. Peter Dobkin Hall, "Religion and the Organizational Revolution in the United States," in *Sacred Companies: Organizational Aspects of Religion and Religious Aspects of Organizations*, ed. N. J. Demerath III et al. (New York: Oxford University Press, 1998), 79–96; Douglas Carl Abrams, *Selling the Old-Time Religion: American Fundamentalists and Mass Culture, 1920–1940* (Athens: University of Georgia Press, 2001), 11.

23. Ben Primer, *Protestants and American Business Methods* (Ann Arbor: UMI Research Press, 1979), 118.

24. James Hudnut Beumler, *In Pursuit of the Almighty's Dollar: A History of Money and American Protestantism* (Chapel Hill: University of North Carolina Press, 2007), esp. 187–230.

25. Elizabeth H. Pleck, *Celebrating the Family: Ethnicity, Consumer Culture, and Family Rituals* (Cambridge: Harvard University Press, 2000), 1–20, 73–94.

26. McLeod, *Religious Crisis*, 104–105.

27. Katherine Carté Engel, *Religion and Profit: Moravians in Early America* (Philadelphia: University of Pennsylvania Press, 2009), 253.

28. Robert Booth Fowler, *Religion and Culture in the United States* (Grand Rapids: Wm. B. Eerdmans, 1989), 15–31.

29. Peter Berger, Grace Davie, and Effie Fokas, *Religious America, Secular Europe? A Theme and Variations* (Aldershot: Ashgate Publishing, 2008), 208.

30. For the supply-side theory, see Roger Finke and Rodney Stark, *The Churching of America* (New Brunswick, N.J.: Rutgers University Press, 1992), 1–21; Lawrence A. Young, ed., *Rational Choice Theory and Religion: Summary and Assessment* (New York: Routledge, 1997); Steven Pfaff, "The Religious Divide: Why

Religion Seems to Be Thriving in the United States and Waning in Europe,"
in *Growing Apart? America and Europe in the Twenty-first Century*, ed. Jeffrey
Kopstein and Sven Steinmo (Cambridge: Cambridge University Press, 2008),
24–52; Robert S. Ellwood, *The Fifties Spiritual Marketplace: American Religion
in a Decade of Conflict* (New Brunswick, N.J.: Rutgers University Press, 1997),
6. For opposition to the theory, see Roy Wallis and Steve Bruce, *Choice and
Religion: A Critique of Rational Choice Theory* (Oxford: Oxford University
Press, 1999), 57–60, 123–127, 141–152; Michael P. Carroll, "Upstart Theories
and Early American Religiosity: A Reassessment," *Religion* 34 (2004):129–
143; E. Brooks Holifield, "Toward a History of American Congregations,"
in *American Congregations*, vol. 1, ed. James W. Lewis and James. P. Wind
(Chicago: University of Chicago Press, 1994), 23–53.

31. Patricia Bonomi and Peter Eisenstadt, "Church Adherence in the
Eighteenth-Century British American Colonies," *William and Mary Quarterly*
39 (1982): 245–286.

32. Rodney Stark and Roger Finke, "American Religion in 1776," *Sociological
Analysis* 49, no. 1 (1988): 39–51; Finke and Stark, *Churching of America*, 26.

33. Jon Butler, *Awash in a Sea of Faith: Christianizing the American People*
(Cambridge: Harvard University Press, 1990), 4; James Hutson, "The
Christian Nation Question," in *Forgotten Features of the Founding: The Recovery
of Religious Themes in the Early Republic* (Lanham, Md.: Lexington Books,
2000), 111–132.

34. Roger A. Ekirch, *Bound for America: The Transportation of British Convicts
to the Colonies, 1718–1775* (Oxford: Oxford University Press, 1987),
4–5, 210; Kenneth Morgan, "The Organization of the Convict Trade to
Maryland: Stephenson, Randolph, and Cheston, 1768–1775," *William and
Mary Quarterly* 42, no. 2 (April 1985): 202; Bonomi and Eisenstadt, "Church
Adherence," 277–286.

35. Cotton Mather, *Paterna: The Autobiography of Cotton Mather*, ed. Ronald
A. Bosco (Delmar, N.Y.: Scholars Facsimiles and Reprints, 1976), 72; E. Brooks
Holifield, *God's Ambassadors: A History of the Christian Clergy in America*
(Grand Rapids: Wm. B. Eerdmans, 2007), 58 n. 55, 79 n. 28; William H. Lyon,
*The First Parish in Brookline* (Brookline: Riverdale, 1898), 8. The calculation of
seating capacity comes from a measurement based on the square footage of
sixteen churches outside Boston.

36. Nigel Ashton, *Christianity and Revolutionary Europe c. 1750–1830*
(Cambridge: Cambridge University Press, 2002), 259.

37. Roger Finke and Rodney Stark, "Turning Pews into People: Estimating 19th
Century Church Membership," *Journal for the Scientific Study of Religion* 25
(1986): 180–192.

38. Andrew Reed, *A Narrative of a Visit to the American Churches*, 2 vols.
(New York: Harper, 1835), vol. 1: 49, 99–176, 253; vol. 2: 106, 283.

39. Finke and Stark, "Turning Pews into People," 187; Josiah Strong, "Latent Power in the Churches," in *Parish Problems*, by Washington Gladden (New York: Century, 1887), 346.

40. Jon Butler, "Protestant Success in the New American City, 1870–1920," in *New Directions in American Religious History*, ed. Harry S. Stout and D. G. Hart (New York: Oxford University Press, 1997), 307.

41. Warren Hugh Wilson, *The Farmer's Church* (New York: Century Co., 1925), 40.

42. Edmund de Schweinitz Brunner, *Church Life in the Rural South* (New York: George Doran, 1923), 35, 59.

43. Ibid., 127.

44. James H. Madison, "Reformers and the Rural Church, 1900–1950," *Journal of American History* 75, no. 3 (December 1986): 663.

45. N. J. Demerath III, "Trends and Anti-trends in Religious Change," in *Indicators of Social Change: Concepts and Measurements*, ed. Eleanor Bernert Sheldon and Wilbur E. Moore (New York: Russell Sage Foundation, 1968), 353, 367.

46. Gallup, "Religion in America," 42.

47. Robert Gildea, *Children of the Revolution: The French, 1799–1914* (Cambridge: Harvard University Press, 2008), 441; Hugh McLeod, ed., *European Religion in the Age of the Great Cities 1830–1930* (London: Routledge, 1995), 14–17; Hans Otte, "More Churches—More Churchgoers," in McLeod, *European Religion*, 110–111. See also McLeod, *Religious Crisis*, 20.

48. Charles H. Lippy, "Chastized by Scorpions: Christianity and Culture in Colonial South Carolina, 1669–1740," *Church History* 79, no. 2 (June 2010): 261.

49. Graham S. Ward, ed., *The 1851 Religious Census of Northamptonshire* (Northampton, England: Northampton Record Society, 2007), 41; John A. Vickers, *The Religious Census of Sussex, 1851* (Lewes: Sussex Record Society, 1989), xxii. In England, Anglicans tended to have higher attendance in the south, and Nonconformists, elsewhere.

50. Callum Brown, *Religion and Society in Twentieth-Century Britain* (Harlow, England: Pearson, Longman, 2006), 118–120.

51. René Remond, *Religion and Society in Modern Europe*, trans. Antonia Nevill (Oxford: Blackwell, 1999), 36; Volkhard Krech, "Religionsgemeinschaften in Deutschland—Eine Religionssoziologische Bestandsaufnahme," in *Religiöser Pluralismus im vereinten Europa: Freikirchen und Sekten*, ed. Hartmut Lehmann (Göttingen: Wallstein Verlag, 2005), 116–144.

52. Lippy, "Chastized by Scorpions," 261; Newton B. Jenes, "Writings of the Reverend William Tennent," *South Carolina Historical Magazine* 61 (1960): 196–209; Bonomi and Eisenstadt, "Church Adherence," esp. the tables on 256–257, 277–286.

53. Lehmann, "Secular Europe versus Christian America?" 148.

54. Pippa Norris and Ronald Inglehart, *Sacred and Secular: Religion and Politics Worldwide* (Cambridge: Cambridge University Press, 2011), 106–108.

55. Hugh McLeod, *Secularisation in Western Europe, 1848–1914* (London: Macmillan Press, 2000), 86–92.

56. The tensions appear in Paul Johnson, *A Shopkeeper's Millennium: Society and Revivals in Rochester, New York, 1815–1837* (New York: Hill and Wang, 1978), 136–140; Sean Willentz, *Chants Democratic: New York City and the Rise of the American Working Class, 1785–1850* (New York: Oxford University Press, 1984), 77–78; Bruce Laurie, *Artisans into Workers: Labor in Nineteenth-Century America* (New York: Hill and Wang, 1989), 74–99, 133. For the religious dimensions of laboring-class life and protest, see Jama Lazerow, *Religion and the Working Class in Antebellum America* (Washington, D.C.: Smithsonian Institution Press, 1995), 9, 158; William R. Sutton, *Journeymen for Jesus: Evangelical Artisans Confront Capitalism in Jacksonian Baltimore* (University Park: Pennsylvania State University Press, 1998), 15, 44; Mark S. Schantz, *Piety in Providence: Class Dimensions of Religion Experience in Antebellum Rhode Island* (Ithaca, N.Y.: Cornell University Press, 2000); Herbert Gutman, "Protestantism and the American Labor Movement: The Christian Spirit in the Gilded Age," *American Historical Review* 72, no. 1 (October 1966): 74–101; Ronald Schultz, "God and Working Men: Popular Religion and the Formation of Philadelphia's Working Class, 1790–1830," in *Religion in a Revolutionary Age*, ed. Ronald Hoffman and Peter J. Albert (Charlottesville: University Press of Virginia, 1994), 125–155; Charles R. Morris, *American Catholics: The Saints and Sinners Who Built America's Most Powerful Church* (New York: Random House, 1997), 173.

57. Hugh McLeod, *Religion and Society in England, 1850–1914* (New York: St. Martin's Press, 1996), 64–65; Hugh McLeod, *Religion and the People of Western Europe, 1789–1989* (New York: Oxford University Press, 1997), 22–27; Brown, *Religion and Society*, 154; Jonathan Sperber, *Popular Catholicism in Nineteenth-Century Germany* (Princeton: Princeton University Press, 1984), 280–281; William G. Enright, "Urbanization and the Evangelical Pulpit in Nineteenth-Century Scotland," *Church History* 47, no. 4 (December 1978): 400–406.

58. Hugh McLeod, *Piety and Poverty: Working Class Religion in Berlin, London, and New York, 1870–1914* (New York: Holmes and Meier, 1996), 10, 32, 55.

59. Brown, *Death of Christian Britain*, 149–156; Thomas Walter Laquer, *Religion and Respectability: Sunday Schools and English Working Class Culture, 1780–1850* (New Haven: Yale University Press, 1976), 147–186; L. E. Ellsworth, *Charles Lowder and the Ritualist Movement* (London: Darnton, Longman, and Todd, 1982), 26–32.

60. Laurence R. Moore, *Selling God: American Religion in the Marketplace of Culture* (New York: Oxford University Press, 1994), 26, 59, 91, 106, 143; David Morgan, *Protestants and Pictures: Religion, Visual Culture, and the Age of American Mass Production* (New York: Oxford University Press, 1999), 179–196, 306;

Schmidt, *Consumer Rites*, 106–243; Kathryn Oberdeck, *The Evangelist and the Impresario: Religion, Entertainment, and Cultural Politics in America, 1884–1914*, New Studies in American Intellectual and Cultural History (Baltimore: Johns Hopkins University Press, 1999), 24, 297; Tona J. Hangen, *Redeeming the Dial: Radio, Religion, and Popular Culture in America* (Chapel Hill: University of North Carolina Press, 2002), 21–36; Julie Byrne, *O God of Players: The Story of the Immaculata Mighty Macs* (New York: Columbia University Press, 2003), 3–14; Christopher Owen Lynch, *Selling Catholicism: Bishop Sheen and the Power of Television* (Lexington: The University Press of Kentucky, 1998), 32–58; Gerald E. Forshey, *American Religious and Biblical Spectaculars* (Westport, Conn.: Praeger, 1992), 1–12; Heather Hendershot, *Shaking the World for Jesus: Media and Conservative Evangelical Culture* (Chicago: University of Chicago Press, 2004), 10, 35.

61. See Ithna T. T. Frary, ed., *Village Green to City Center* (Cleveland, Ohio: Euclid Avenue Church, 1943), 141, for the quotation; see also Jeffrey M. Burns, "Building the Best," in *American Catholic Parish*, vol. 2, ed. Jay Dolan (New York: Paulist Press, 1987), 41; Joseph J. Casino, "From Sanctuary to Involvement," in *American Catholic Parish*, vol. 1, ed Jay Dolan (New York: Paulist Press, 1987), 28.

62. G. B. Willcox, *The Pastor amidst His Flock* (New York: American Tract Society, 1890), 107–110.

63. Henry Ward Beecher, *Yale Lectures in Preaching* (New York: Howard and Hulbert, 1892), quotation on 159; see also 155.

64. Tony Judt, "Voyage Home," *New York Review of Books* 57, no. 9 (May 27, 2010): 29.

65. Brown, *Death of Christian Britain*, 44–45; Charles D. Cashdollar, *A Spiritual Home: Life in British and American Reformed Congregations, 1830–1915* (University Park: University of Pennsylvania Press, 2000), 159–163, 215–220; McLeod, *Secularisation in Western Europe*, 271–273.

66. Suzanne K. Kaufman, *Consuming Visions: Mass Culture and the Lourdes Shrine* (Ithaca, N.Y.: Cornell University Press, 2005), 18, 60; Marie R. Griffith, *Born Again Bodies: Flesh and Spirit in American Christianity* (Berkeley: University of California Press, 2004), 160–238.

67. William Warren Sweet, *Religion in the Development of American Culture 1765–1840* (New York: Charles Scribner's Sons, 1952), 146, 313.

68. Charles Cohen, "The Colonization of British North America as an Episode in the History of Christianity," *Church History* 72, no. 3 (September 2003): 567–568.

69. William McLoughlin, *Modern Revivalism: Charles Grandison Finney to Billy Graham* (New York: Ronald Press, 1959), 529; Jay Dolan, *Catholic Revivalism: The American Experience 1830–1900* (Notre Dame, Ind.: University of Notre Dame Press, 1978).

70. Donald G. Mathews, "The Second Great Awakening as an Organizing Process," *American Quarterly* 21, no. 1 (Spring 1969): 25–43.

71. Frank Lambert, "'Pedlar in Divinity': George Whitefield and the Great Awakening, 1737–1745," *Journal of American History* 77, no. 3 (December 1990): 812–837.

72. McLoughlin, *Modern Revivalism*, 529; Abrams, *Selling the Old-Time Religion*, 2–3, 27–35, 59–60; Marshall Frady, *Billy Graham: A Parable of American Righteousness* (Boston: Little, Brown, 1979), 279; Dolan, *Catholic Revivalism*, 3–13.

73. W. R. Ward, *The Protestant Evangelical Awakening* (Cambridge: Cambridge University Press, 1992), 54–92, 160–200, 269–355; "Billy Graham Crusade Statistics," http://www.billygraham.org/assets/media/pdfs/festivals/BGCrusadeChronology.pdf.

74. Nathan O. Hatch, *The Democratization of American Christianity* (New Haven: Yale University Press, 1989), 1–16.

75. Holifield, *God's Ambassadors*, 331; Mark Chaves, *Congregations in America* (Cambridge: Harvard University Press, 2004), 235.

76. David S. Lovejoy, *Religious Enthusiasm in the New World: Heresy to Revolution* (Cambridge: Harvard University Press, 1985), 41; John H. Wigger, *Taking Heaven by Storm: Methodism and the Rise of Popular Christianity in America* (New York: Oxford University Press, 1998), 49; Christopher H. Owen, *The Sacred Flame of Love: Methodism and Society in Nineteenth Century Georgia* (Athens: University of Georgia Press, 1988), 43–46. Dee E. Andrews, *The Methodists and Revolutionary America, 1760–1800* (Princeton: Princeton University Press, 2000), 9, 156–166, emphasizes that populist denominations sometimes included members from the wealthier classes. For Pentecostals, see Grant Wacker, *Heaven Below: Early Pentecostals and American Culture* (Cambridge: Harvard University Press, 2001), 197–216.

77. Dale A. Johnson, "The Methodist Quest for an Educated Ministry," *Church History* 51, no. 3 (September 1982): 304–320; Thomas Fudge, "Hussite Popular Religion," in *Popular Religion in Germany and Central Europe, 1400–1800*, ed. Bob Scribner and Trevor Johnson (New York: St. Martin's Press, 1996), 39; Jürgen Beyer, "A Lübeck Prophet in Local and Lutheran Context," in Scribner and Johnson, *Popular Religion*, 182; Patrick Collinson, *The Religion of Protestants: The Church in English Society, 1559–1625* (Oxford: Clarendon Press, 1982), 93–105.

78. E. Brooks Holifield, "The Abridging of Cotton Mather," in *Cotton Mather and "Biblia Americana"—America's First Bible Commentary*, ed. Reiner Smolinski and Jan Stievermann (Tübingen, Germany: Mohr Siebeck, 2010), 83–112; Oliver Scheiding, "The World as Parish: Cotton Mather, August Hermann Francke, and Transatlantic Religious Networks," in Scribner and Johnson, *Popular Religion*, 131–166.

79. John Winthrop, "A Modell of Christian Charity, 1630," in Edwin S. Gaustad and Mark A. Noll, *A Documentary History of Religion in America to 1877* (Grand Rapids: Wm. B. Eerdmans, 2003), 69.

80. Nathan O. Hatch, *The Sacred Cause of Liberty* (New Haven: Yale University Press, 1977), 89; Mark Noll, *America's God: From Jonathan Edwards to Abraham Lincoln* (New York: Oxford University Press, 2005); Harry S. Stout, *Upon the Altar of the Nation: The Moral History of the Civil War* (New York: Penguin Books, 2006), 46–51, 77; Ernest Lee Tuveson, *Redeemer Nation: The Idea of America's Millennial Role* (Chicago: University of Chicago Press, 1968), 52–79; James H. Moorhead, "The American Israel: Protestant Tribalism and Universal Mission," in *Many Are Chosen: Divine Election and Western Nationalism*, ed. William R. Hutchison and Hartmut Lehmann (Minneapolis: Fortress Press, 1994), 145–166.

81. Remond, *Religion and Society in Modern Europe*, 110; Frederick B. Artz, *Reaction and Revolution, 1814–1832* (New York: Harper, 1934), 117–118; A. F. Walls, "Great Britain: Carrying the White Man's Burden—Some Views of National Vocation in the Imperial Era," in Hutchison and Lehmann, *Many Are Chosen*, 29–50; Thomas Kselman, "France: Religion and French Identity—The Origins of the *Union Sacreé*," in Hutchison and Lehmann, *Many Are Chosen*, 57–80; Hartmut Lehmann, "Germany: 'God Our Old Ally'—The Chosen People Theme in Twentieth-Century German Nationalism," in Hutchison and Lehmann, *Many Are Chosen*, 85–109; Stephen Mitchell, "Sweden: Chosenness, Nationalism, and the Young Church Movement, 1880–1920," in Hutchison and Lehmann, *Many Are Chosen*, 231–250.

82. Brown, *Religion and Society*, 89; Martin Greschat, *Christentumsgeschichte II: Von der Reformation bis zur Gegenwart*, 2 vols. (Stuttgart: Verlag W. Kohlhammer, 1997), 209–213.

83. E. Brooks Holifield, *The Gentlemen Theologians: American Theology in Southern Culture 1795–1860* (Durham, N.C.: Duke University Press, 1978), 127–154; E. Brooks Holifield, *Theology in America: Christian Thought from the Age of the Puritans to the Civil War* (New Haven: Yale University Press, 2003), 172; Walter H. Conser Jr., *Church and Confession: Conservative Theologians in Germany, England, and America, 1815–1866* (Macon: Mercer University Press, 1984), 323.

84. Ashton, *Christianity and Revolutionary Europe*, 98.

85. R. Stephen Warner, "Immigration and Religious Communities in the United States," in *Gatherings in Diaspora: Religious Communities and the New Immigration*, ed. R. Stephen Warner and Judith Wittner (Philadelphia: Temple University Press, 1998), 15–18, 20–23; Richard Wormser, *American Islam: Growing Up Muslim in America* (New York: Walker and Co., 1994); Kambiz GhaneaBassiri, *Competing Visions of Islam in the United States* (Westport, Conn.: Greenwood, 1997), 44–48; Randall M. Miller and Thomas D. Marzik, eds., *Immigrants and Religion in Urban America* (Philadelphia: Temple University Press, 1977), xv, 17, 33, 77.

86. Jonathan Sarna, *American Judaism: A History* (New Haven: Yale University Press, 2004), 161, 224, 278; McLeod, *Piety and Poverty*, 107.

87. Brown, *Religion and Society*, 292.

88. Barry Kosmin and Seymour P. Lachman, *One Nation under God: Religion in Contemporary American Society* (New York: Harmony Books, 1993), 125–126, 132–143, 147–151.

89. Ann Braude, "Women's History Is American Religious History," in *Retelling U.S. Religious History*, ed. Thomas A. Tweed (Berkeley: University of Southern California Press, 1997), 87–107.

90. Dean R. Hoge and Jacqueline E. Wenger, *Evolving Visions of the Priesthood: Changes from Vatican II to the Turn of the Century* (Collegeville, Minn.: Liturgical Press, 2003), 129–131; Mark Chaves, *Ordaining Women: Culture and Conflict in Religious Organizations* (Cambridge: Harvard University Press, 1997), 21–25.

91. Chaves, *Ordaining Women*, 240–258; McLeod, *Religion and the People*, 28; Lucian Hölscher, *Geschichte der protestantischen Frömmigkeit in Deutschland* (Munich: Verlag C. H. Beck, 2005), 301.

92. Brown, *Death of Christian Britain*, 192, 195.

93. Alexis de Tocqueville, *Democracy in America*, ed. J. P. Mayer, trans. George Lawrence (Garden City, N.Y.: Doubleday, 1969), 513; Arthur M. Schlesinger, *Paths to the Present* (New York: Macmillan, 1949), 24–50.

94. Robert D. Putnam, *Bowling Alone: The Collapse and Revival of American Community* (New York: Simon and Schuster, 2000), 49.

95. Berger, Davie, and Fokas, *Religious America, Secular Europe?* 39–41.

# PART TWO

## *Evangelicals and Markets*

## 2

## *Weber and Eighteenth-Century Religious Developments in America*

### Mark Valeri

BOSTON MERCHANTS SAMUEL Philips Savage, Isaac Smith, David Jeffries, Ebenezer Storer, Peter Cally, and Simon Frost formed an impressive cohort during the early 1740s. As the rising generation of New England's commercial class, all in their twenties, they filled those years with frenetic activity. They traded in commodities, speculated in securities, rented properties throughout the town, invested in ventures such as manufacturers and private banks, and filed numerous lawsuits over unpaid debts and other contractual disputes. They traveled far and often—the eighteenth-century versions of today's frequent fliers. They made lengthy trips north through New Hampshire and Maine and south through Connecticut, New York, and Delaware. When not on such long journeys, they visited dozens of towns in western Massachusetts, buying and selling at every stop. When not on the road, they corresponded with each other and with agents throughout the Atlantic seaboard and in England. They helped shape New England's economy into an integrated market system, bound by the exchange of letters, money, and goods.[1]

They were busy in other ways as well. Each of these merchants jumped full force into the currents of evangelical Protestantism. When in Boston, they shuttled back and forth between two churches that were promoting revival: the Brattle Street Church and Old South Church. They gave each other the latest news of spiritual awakenings: how they had heard George Whitefield, Jonathan Edwards, or Gilbert Tennent or had witnessed a spiritual revival during their travels. They sampled evangelical, so-called New Light preaching in nearly every town they visited. They pondered their spiritual affections, fretted over the disposition of their souls, carefully tracked their agonizing movement toward conversion, and delighted when they came out the other side reborn. They urged hesitant colleagues to press on in spiritual matters. They were among those converts who shaped the revivals into an evangelical force called the Great Awakening.

The combination of commercial energy and evangelical sensibility in the lives of these merchants reflects larger historical developments in provincial New England. During the 1740s, the often disconnected and localized markets of a semiurban, semiagricultural economy coalesced into a domestic market order linked into Britain's commercial empire. At the same time, religious leaders promoted a new style of ministry focused on itinerant preaching, spirit-filled revivals, and emotionally fraught conversions: what has since become known as the beginning of evangelical Protestantism. Commerce and evangelicalism expanded in tandem. How should we understand this convergence? What exactly did revivalist Protestantism have to do with the activities of these Boston merchants, whose careers can stand in for the growth of early Anglo-American capitalism?

Studies of religion and capitalism give quite different answers, which, for simplicity's sake, can be gathered into two groups. Max Weber's "Protestant Ethic" thesis continues to shape the interpretations of historians who survey the broad scope of culture and capitalism in America, including such luminaries as David Landes, Benjamin Friedman, and Walter Russell Mead.[2] Following Weber, these scholars, as well as many early American economic historians,[3] limn the Protestant ethic as a source of self-disciplined rationality that led to capitalist industriousness. This reading of Weber minimizes the economic import of evangelical religiosity. Emotionalism and conversion-centered piety appear to have been fractious and irrational sideshows to a main event centered on bourgeois respectability and industrial prowess. The explicitly evangelical worldview of these Boston merchants was irrelevant to their economic spirit in such terms.

Yet from another perspective the revivals shaped the very origins of an Anglo-American religious tradition that has been identified with many of the most salient features of American capitalism, from popular communication techniques to consumer culture. To be sure, a previous generation of social historians emphasized the participation of the economically dispossessed in the revivals, contending that the Great Awakening marked a protest against a powerful mercantile class. This paradigm, however, hardly explains the sensibilities of these eighteenth-century Boston evangelical merchants. Richard Bushman long ago argued that evangelical theology displaced Puritan communalism and its resistance to commercial ambition: the born-again convert sallied forth into the market with a conscience freed from older economic inhibitions. Harry Stout suggested that New Light preaching fostered an improvisatory, oral culture set against authority and economic stasis. Turning the coin upside down, Frank Lambert and others have argued that New Lights deployed a vibrant print culture based on entrepreneurial modes of communication: epistolary networks, advertising, and rapid, time-sensitive publication. Even scholars of the putatively anticapitalist Moravians have gotten in on the act. Katherine Carté Engel recently has shown how the seemingly communitarian experiment in Moravian Bethlehem, Pennsylvania, came to depend on sagacious and cosmopolitan market strategies. These and other historical studies have led the American sociologist Roger Finke to identify eighteenth-century evangelicals among the creators of a "supply-side" religious economy. By Finke's account, evangelicals advertised their religious message as a commodity, the very abundance of which stimulated consumer demand, that is, popularity.[4]

To suggest some ways beyond this interpretive impasse between a Weberian dismissal of evangelicals from the story of capitalism and the assertion of an evangelical–market nexus, we should first review Weber's argument. By his account, medieval Christianity taught that individuals could calculate their progress toward salvation according to clearly defined moral laws. They therefore worked only enough to satisfy their immediate economic needs and devoted the rest of their energies to securing heavenly reward. Catholic teaching, in Weber's view, offered no cultural prompts to understand worldly labor as a divine calling. It therefore provided no motives to combat a natural instinct toward complacency—merely getting by with daily sustenance. It minimized economic planning, discouraged productive work, and led to feudal restrictions on economic energies.[5]

In contrast, Calvinists taught that divine sovereignty eclipsed ordinary (or ecclesiastically sanctioned) measures of religious merit. The Calvinist doctrine of predestination prevented individuals from assuming that they could know whether they had fulfilled the requirements for salvation. Such a lack of knowledge fostered anxiety. In response, Calvinists did not lapse into inactivity; rather, they worked all the harder to evidence their election to salvation by demonstrating that their lives, in fact, glorified God. They developed an incessant urge to prove themselves by what Weber called worldly asceticism, chiefly by way of the virtues of frugality, industriousness, and rationality. Calvinism thereby promoted voluntary—that is, free—labor because it produced individuals driven by internal motives. Religious conviction, rather than coercive external powers such as civil law or state intervention, drove production because it inculcated discipline. The conscience of the God-fearing individual overcame natural instincts toward economic complacency.[6]

Weber proceeded famously from that thesis to identify Puritan writers such as Richard Baxter as the ideal promoters of this free, rational, and self-disciplined labor. Yet, before discussing Baxter, Weber made an infrequently noted analysis of Protestants who by his reading displayed less productive mentalities than did their Calvinist counterparts. According to his typology, they included Pietists, Methodists, and Baptist sects. Along with their New England counterparts, they shaped what we have since come to know as eighteenth-century evangelicalism. Weber did not have at his disposal a clear definition of *evangelical* and did not use the term. Yet he clearly had in mind the religious movements that constituted the English and European versions of revivalism in particular. He referred to "the general awakening which followed Methodism everywhere," including New England. This was his rather imprecise formulation for the Great Awakening.[7]

Weber's analysis of these groups is complex but may be condensed into a straightforward assertion: they contributed little, if anything, to worldly asceticism and therefore to free labor. Indeed, they largely represented a countercapitalist mentality. According to the Protestant ethic, the various movements known under the term *Pietism*, especially Zinzendorf's Moravians, replaced the doctrine of election with an emotional assurance of salvation. While Catholics maintained an insistence that rejection of the world qualified one for salvation, and Calvinists fostered a kind of unknowing that bred worldly discipline, Pietists claimed to know by their affections that they were saved. They thereby reduced motives to worldly striving: they weakened "the inhibitions which protected the rational personality of the Calvinist from his passions."[8] Methodists went even further in this direction. Their closely regulated exercises in piety and precise accounts of progress toward conversion—the "method" itself, as Weber put it—assured believers of their spiritual status. The "emotional act of conversion" was measurable and so in the end "guarantees the *certitudo salutis* and substitutes a serene confidence for the sullen worry of the Calvinist."[9] Weber was so struck with the emotionalism of the Methodists that he hinted at psychosis: "only a neurologist" could fathom the "pathological character of Methodism." Whenever members of these groups promoted certitude about salvation they contradicted the Calvinist doctrine of predestination and therefore worldly asceticism. Whenever they emphasized emotional experience they undercut the Calvinist stress on rationality. This was hardly the bureaucratic mindset, or anxiety-driven calculation, of the Protestant ethic.[10]

To be sure, Weber recognized that many Baptists, as well as some Pietists and Methodists, produced a Calvinist-like moral anxiety despite their emotional and conversionist theologies. Baptists began with separatist and otherworldly tendencies, defining themselves by strict standards of moral purity. Yet this hypermoralism became rational in the urban milieus of England and the Netherlands. Even a Baptist merchant needed to keep his accounts diligently. "The strict morality of the Baptists," Weber allowed, "had turned in practice into the path prepared by the Calvinistic ethic" despite its foundations.[11] So, too, with Pietist writers such as Francke or the Pietists in Amsterdam. They tamed their emotionalism with dispassionate self-control. Methodists also calmed down. When Wesley developed his emphasis on Christian perfection and sanctification, he reintroduced the element of religious anxiety despite the assurance of salvation, making for a non-predestinarian way to worldly asceticism. To the extent that these evangelical groups became rationalized, however, they merely replicated what Calvinists had long taught. To the extent that they promoted worldly asceticism, and therefore free labor, they merely affirmed the Puritan personality. They added nothing to the story of religion and capitalism.[12]

Weber's concern to explain the development of free labor led him to emphasize Calvinist ideas that compelled individuals to production in a rational manner, that is, beyond the horizon of immediate needs and coercive obligations. Recent historians of capitalism, however, have stressed the labor and productive sectors of the economy less than Weber did. They have emphasized instead the distributive and consumer sectors: long-distance networks that linked producers and consumers into markets that spanned Europe and the American colonies. From a twenty-first-century perspective, capitalism has to do not merely with free labor but also with a highly monetized exchange in a global market.[13] To the extent that we emphasize this market-oriented exchange—the rules

and practices by which commodities and credit are priced and conveyed—
early evangelicals such as merchants Savage, Smith, and Jeffries appear to
have been crucial contributors to the development of capitalism and not
strange sideshows.

This reading requires an appreciation for the market as a social order
held together by cultural and economic conventions that crossed local and
national boundaries. Take, for example, the New England of the evangelical merchants. Its economy became integrated into a full-fledged market
order during the third, fourth, and fifth decades of the eighteenth century.
That is, in the domestic economy or trade within the region, prices for all
sorts of goods "converged": the cost of commodities rose or fell to the
same level across New England. Uniform prices indicated the spread of a
so-called rational economic order: speedy communication, highly mobile
merchants and customers, the publication of going rates for goods, widespread advertising, and, most importantly, a pattern of pricing for commodities and credit according to the laws of supply and demand rather
than local custom. The markets in which evangelical merchants participated, in classical economic parlance, tended toward equilibrium.[14]

In addition, merchants successfully integrated their trade into Britain's
transatlantic empire of goods. They achieved ready and reliable communication with London partners through a vast correspondence. They
employed factors and lawyers on both sides of the Atlantic. They followed
currency values and exchange rates in London, conforming to English
monetary standards. Trade with London increased markedly during the
1740s, filling Boston's shops with fashionable consumer items and send-
ing New World products eastward. The fantastically large numbers of
debt cases, which took up as much as 80 percent of county-court dockets,
spread formal legal protocols—modes of argument that applied equally in
London, Barbados, Boston, and western towns.[15]

The daily business activities of merchants such as Smith, Savage,
and Jeffries fit neatly into this economic narrative. The son of a middling
merchant father, Isaac Smith began his business with travels up and
down the New England seaboard, buying codfish and marketing his pur-
chases through Boston exporters. During the early 1740s he developed an
extensive correspondence with London merchants and invested in larger
ventures: timber products such as turpentine and whale oil sent to the
southern colonies, the Caribbean, and England in exchange for expensive
fabrics, silver utensils, and furniture. He continually tracked the going
rates for goods in and out of London, quickly adjusting his prices to match

those of other merchants. He prospered mightily as a result. In 1740 his receipts totaled £555. By 1745 they had risen to £19,600. Overdue notes and delayed payments frequently involved him in legal disputes, even as they evidenced the expansiveness of his business networks. He joined other high-powered merchants in several banking ventures and proposals to start a new manufactory in Boston.[16]

Smith focused his business on commodities. Meanwhile, his colleagues Samuel Philips Savage and David Jeffries formed a partnership in 1740, opening a shop in Boston, and worked the financial sector a bit more assiduously than Smith. They also participated in a massive volume of correspondence during the early 1740s. Their letter books trace a vast web of interconnected merchants and factors from Boston through the Carolinas and across the Atlantic to Lisbon and London. They also traded in expensive consumer items such as indigo, rum, crystal, and coffee, but after a few years they turned to real estate, financial securities, and monetary instruments. They underwrote insurance on shipping, purchased several properties in central Boston, invested in wharves and warehouses, funded dozens of shipping ventures, and eventually opened their own insurance office. They made huge profits from various credit schemes involving a dizzying complex of gold, bills of exchange, and bonds. The careers of Smith and other evangelical traders demonstrate what we mean quite specifically by the coalescence of a market order in colonial America.[17]

The integration of the market during the eighteenth century—the networks, price convergences, trade in credit, emerging consumer economy, and legal standards—depended not only on the rationalization of trade techniques but also on widely accepted cultural conventions. It rested on common scientific, moral, and political discourses that allowed transatlantic traders to communicate not only goods and monetary values but also notions of fashion and creditworthiness, which is to say "social respectability." We can identify one of these discourses with a strain of economic thought sometimes called mercantilism: the political economy of British commentators such as William Petty, Charles Davenant, and Nicholas Barbon and their popularizers.

While these early economic writers argued about various strategies to ameliorate England's economic woes—by enhancing economic production, trade, and overall wealth—they all advocated for market pricing, floating interest rates on credit, and political support for free trade. They did so by articulating a cycle of interconnecting claims about commerce and national interest. They claimed that England's freedoms, which promoted the virtue on which the commonwealth rested, depended on security against other, especially Catholic, nations. Empire secured those freedoms. International trade and colonization enlarged empire by extending English rule and funding the kingdom's navy and armies. Freedom of commerce and astute participation in the European and Atlantic markets enhanced trade. Free and expanding trade, in turn, depended on political liberties, the exercise of which, to return to the beginning of the cycle, promoted public virtue. The ideology of empire—England's Atlantic empire—thus circled through assertions that connected new commercial imperatives and the interests of the state. Proponents of this ideology assembled a social discourse that justified ambitious overseas commerce as a political and moral good.[18]

Weber dismissed mercantilism as an authoritarian regime uncongenial to bourgeois capitalism, but Joyce Appleby and Istvan Hont, among others, have shown how these political economists set the stage for later thinkers—most famously, Adam Smith—who criticized the promotion of heavy-handed political intervention into commerce. Petty, Davenant, and their colleagues pointed to the integrative power of a social theory premised on economic laws and natural social instincts. Mercantilists explained how individuals could operate according to rational rules and economies of self-interest and still pursue the common good. By describing free trade as an instrument of the state and a means to defend liberty, they linked moral virtue, patriotism, and market dynamics.[19]

The regnant Anglo-American moral philosophy of the 1730s and 1740s provided further theoretical justification for the conviction that individual dispositions or economic drives coalesced into forms of social solidarity. The most widely cited proponent of this moral philosophy—quoted by American *philosophes* such as Benjamin Franklin and evangelical preachers such as Boston's Benjamin Colman—was the third Earl of Shaftesbury. Shaftesbury taught that polite performance cultivated civility, enforced webs of social dependencies, and brought individuals pursuing their natural instincts, that is, commercial instincts, into a sociable union. He emphasized innate affections for, or internal dispositions to, social virtues such as benevolence. Fusing Newton's cosmology with Stoic natural philosophy, he argued that the social order tended by design toward balance and harmony. Individuals fit into this order by securing their happiness and public success as they followed innate tendencies to sympathy. Public communities reinforced this instinct for virtue by honoring sociability.[20]

Shaftesbury—admired especially by Addison; excerpted in *The Tatler, The Spectator,* and *The Guardian*; and narrated by popular writers such as Daniel Defoe—headed a long line of writers, including Lord Kames, Francis Hutcheson, and Adam Smith, who identified the bonds of social cohesion in the interior affections of individuals. They stressed the cultivation of benevolence and sympathy: moral affections that, informed by reason, formed bonds between individuals of different social stations. Smith made explicit the economic implications of their moral philosophy. Natural instincts bound economic actors together into a well-functioning and prosperous order without the interventions of traditional authorities such as the church or state.

Evangelicals sometimes opposed the theological implications of the new moral philosophy, but they consistently adopted its communication strategies and moral idioms. New Light clerical leaders taught their lay followers to understand the communication of religious sympathies across great distances as the means of social solidarity. Serialized accounts of awakenings, gathered and printed by Thomas Prince Jr., advertised a web of revivals centered in Boston, gave news of religious outpourings in Britain and Germany, reprinted sermons from famous preachers, and anticipated the formation of a worldwide union of evangelical sympathizers. Revivalists used innovative advertising tactics to announce their exploits. They also deployed the language of novelty, politeness, and emotional satisfaction to recommend their spiritual activities: a striking analog to cosmopolitan strategies to market new consumer goods. Wealthy merchants such as Smith and Savage funded a surge of publishing on behalf of revival, as well as missionary activity on the western frontier. They communicated their evangelical sentiments through channels of revival activity, correspondence, and commercial transaction. They followed itinerant evangelists while on business ventures and urged colleagues to attend preaching events. Their frequent letters and private reflections traced a map of evangelical networks marked by the same names (William Cooper and Benjamin Colman at Boston's Brattle Street Church, Jonathan Edwards, the itinerants Gilbert Tennent and George Whitefield) and the same events (sermons, revivals, and spiritual effusions). They found a cultural style and moral vocabulary that made for social integration despite geographical dislocation.[21]

Evangelical preachers also taught their devotees to shape themselves to cosmopolitan standards of sensibility and sociability. New Light leaders were all nurtured in the discourse of the leading moral philosophy with its attendant vocabularies: politeness, reasonableness, and benevolence. Jonathan Edwards drew deeply from Tillotson, Shaftesbury, and Hutcheson. He recommended their works to others, commending their moral teaching even as he denounced their latitudinarian theology. He insisted, most clearly in his *Charity and Its Fruits* and his *Religious Affections*, that the evangelical message be presented as persuasive in the public domain: that it should not only comport with but also supersede religious rationalism in the promotion of commonly held virtues such as benevolence.[22]

In effect, evangelicals and rationalists, even skeptics, presumed the same basis for social order: individuals united into a commonwealth by virtuous affections and reasoned discourse. This is why Benjamin Franklin and George Whitefield worked together so well and why Weber was not off-base when he suggested a similarity in social ethics between Franklin and Wesley. This also explains the mentalities of New England's evangelical merchants. Smith, Savage, and Jeffries rarely wrote at length about economic theories. Yet they did embrace the cultural constructs of the market. They occasionally traded witty poetry and satirical prose, shared periodicals that praised Isaac Newton, recommended the pursuit of natural moral virtue along with spiritual rebirth, and quoted moralists from the transatlantic republic of letters, whom Savage called "polite, worthy, and well Esteemed Gentlemen."[23] Virtuous social sentiment shaped aggressive profit-seeking, calculated exchange in credit, and hard-nosed litigiousness into civility.[24]

Taken together, the mandates of political economy, arguments of moral philosophers such as Shaftesbury, and evangelical adaptations of cultural fashion helped form the beginnings of a powerful social discourse: what we, following Jürgen Habermas, would identify with the liberal or bourgeois "public sphere." Habermas described the public sphere as a domain, created largely through the activities of eighteenth-century *philosophes* and political opposition writers, in which critical analysis or reason mediates between civil society (the private lives of citizens) and the absolutist state.[25] Early American historians interested in the rise of democratic discourse, especially literary scholars such as Michael Warner, embraced Habermas's analysis during the 1990s, but few commentators have drawn on Habermas to analyze the relationship between religion and the market during the eighteenth century.[26]

Although Habermas paid precious little attention to religion in his *Structural Transformation of the Public Sphere*,[27] his account suggests the importance of early evangelicals to the public sphere during this crucial period in the development of market capitalism. Much of his analysis rests on a discussion of how the private sentiments of those who did not embody established authority became public criteria for deliberating social policy. First, private spaces such as houses, inns, and salons became public when the bourgeoisie rubbed shoulders with nobility in conversations guided not by aristocratic privilege but by shared notions of reasonableness and civility. Second, writers created new literary forms, such as the epistolary novel, that narrated private affection (the internal voice of the heroine) and rendered it a subject for public observation. Third, commentators made private criticism, including analyses of politics and art, public through an unprecedented use of the press. As a result of such innovations, the ideas and interests of individual citizens coalesced into a social discourse without deference to court or crown. Habermas called this "public opinion."[28]

Habermas described the content of public opinion in political terms such as constitutional freedoms and consent, but we can use his notion to ponder the new conceptions of social authority reflected in the evangelical movement. His account of public opinion leads us to consider evangelicalism as liberal in the sense of validating the opinions and sentiments of private individuals whose religious experiences fell outside the bounds of customary ecclesiastical authority. Evangelical merchants noted how the religious controversies of the 1740s took place in previously private or unofficial enclaves—roadside stops, taverns, parlors—that served as settings for public debate. Removed from customary ecclesiastical domains, merchants who wrote about their encounters in these spaces gave less deference to received authority such as denominational loyalties and dogmatic convention than they did to standards of true piety. They considered itinerant revivalists to be models of godliness. They marveled at how New Lights preached in barns, on the street, and out of windows. They absorbed a form of religious critique, including rejections of the sacramental regimes or dogmatic traditions, that paralleled art criticism and opposition politics. The circulation of their observations through letters and even published accounts shaped new religious sentiments into a religious opinion apart from established institutions.

This religious mentality legitimated new economic ideals. In the public sphere, where public opinion trumped customary restraints on exchange, individuals constituted themselves into societies through shared affections common to all citizens. They divested themselves of inherited, class-based, or aristocratic forms of social authority. Detached from group loyalties, local customs, and traditional authorities, individuals could still travel about, literally or figuratively, and participate in a commonweal. They deposited, as it were, their economic strategies and social ideas into the public realm (especially through print) to be debated and approved to the extent that those deeds and ideas accorded with universal moral sentiments. In the public sphere, merchants were deemed to be sociable by virtue of their inner sentiments, even if they belonged to no guild, followed no custom, and remained fixed in no local community.

Thus, evangelical religion had everything to do with the emergence of a market premised on the coalescence of discrete exchanges into a system and the maintenance of civic society through common moral sentiment. It promoted and enhanced—indeed, lent transcendent meaning to—the ideal of individuals who formed solidarities through interior affections shared across great distances, displayed their virtues through polite gestures, and did so without deference to local and customary communities. They criticized many of New England's religious traditions, including filial pieties that emphasized the family and parish as the chief arenas for spiritual devotion. They stressed instead preaching and revival, two of the most mobile and emotionally affective forms of devotion. Evangelicals developed a religious discourse that confirmed the utility of reasonableness, inner moral dispositions, the mobility of ideas, and publicly oriented persuasion. Such evangelical expressions sanctified the public sphere and, with it, new modes of exchange in the emergent market.

In this, the evangelical version of what Habermas called the bourgeois public sphere, religion and commerce came together as twin expressions of the universal standards of sensibility and sociability. So the revivals themselves—all of the mobility of preaching, the focus on interior moral states, and the confidence in a dispersed yet united society—gave religious sanction to the confidence that free trade and piety, market behaviors and social solidarity, were compatible.

This, it seems to me, is what Weber missed in his discussion of eighteenth-century Pietists, Methodists, and Baptists. Contemporary commentators who restrict their understanding of Protestantism to Weber's version of worldly asceticism fail to account for the salience of early evangelicals. In so doing they minimize the religious and moral origins of capitalism when it developed into a transatlantic market in goods, credit, and intellectual commodities. The modern market, along with evangelicalism, matured in the public sphere. We need, to put it bluntly, Habermas to bring the story of religion and capitalism into the eighteenth century. When evangelicals transposed Christian practice into a mobile, preaching-centered religiosity that brought individuals into a community through their common affections, they carried an earlier ethos of free labor into the realm of global market exchange.

The story of religion and the market cannot be captured by fixed notions of either "the market" or "evangelicalism," as though all market systems were the same or all versions of evangelicalism, much less religion, interacted with the economy in similar ways. For the creators of Protestant evangelicalism, the market of their day arose as an economic means of social solidarity that challenged authoritarian, elitist, monopolistic, and economically restrictive policies. Merchants such as Savage and Smith embraced the ideal of like-minded individuals forming commercial and religious bonds through shared affections rather than through coercive traditions. What we have since come to know as early capitalism, like evangelical religion, bespoke solidarity along with equality and freedom. Nothing in their experience hinted at what we might see as later effects of market culture: secularization, individualism, or materialism.

Looking at it in this way, we should perhaps gain a deeper appreciation for the moral imagination that bound evangelicalism to the economy as it took shape in its eighteenth-century context. Many of the essays in this volume, including those by Hilde Løvedal Stephens, Grant Wacker, Daniel Silliman, and Katja Rakow, focus on the market strategies or other commercial impulses of evangelicals after the eighteenth century. The persistent engagement of evangelicals with commerce—the porous boundaries between evangelical piety and regnant cultural style—should not surprise us. The revival movement took shape in a public sphere that defined the free exchange of goods and ideas to be the moral mandates of public opinion.

## *Notes*

1. For the evidence from these merchants throughout this chapter, see Mark Valeri, *Heavenly Merchandize: How Religion Shaped Commerce in Puritan America* (Princeton: Princeton University Press, 2010), 234–249.
2. David S. Landes, *The Wealth and Poverty of Nations: Why Some Are So Rich and Some So Poor* (New York: W.W. Norton, 1998); Benjamin M. Friedman, *The*

*Moral Consequences of Economic Growth* (New York: Knopf, 2005); and Walter Russell Mead, *God and Gold: Britain, America, and the Making of the Modern World* (New York: Atlantic Books, 2007).

3. See, for example, Margaret Ellen Newell, *From Dependency to Independence: Economic Revolution in Colonial New England* (Ithaca, N.Y.: Cornell University Press, 1998).

4. For the appeal of the revivals to lower social classes, see Gary Nash, *The Urban Crucible: Social Change, Political Consciousness, and the Origins of the American Revolution* (Cambridge, Mass.: Harvard University Press, 1979), 198–232. For the Great Awakening and market sensibilities, see Richard L. Bushman, *From Puritan to Yankee: Character and the Social Order in Connecticut, 1690–1765* (1967; New York: W.W. Norton, 1970); Harry S. Stout, *The Divine Dramatist: George Whitefield and the Rise of Modern Evangelicalism* (Grand Rapids: Eerdmans, 1991); Frank Lambert, *Inventing the "Great Awakening"* (Princeton: Princeton University Press, 1999); Susan O'Brien, "Eighteenth-Century Publishing Networks in the First Years of Transatlantic Evangelicalism," in *Evangelicalism: Comparative Studies of Popular Protestantism in North America, the British Isles, and Beyond, 1700–1990,* ed. Mark A. Noll, David W. Bebbington, and George A. Rawlyk (New York: Oxford University Press, 1994), 38–57; and Katherine Carté Engel, *Religion and Profit: Moravians in Early America* (Philadelphia: University of Pennsylvania Press, 2009). For a helpful survey of the literature, see Mark A. Noll, "Protestant Reasoning about Money and the Economy, 1790–1860: A Preliminary Probe," in *God and Mammon: Protestants, Money, and the Market, 1790–1860,* ed. Mark A. Noll (New York: Oxford University Press, 2001), 265–294. Roger Finke's views may be sampled in his essay "The Illusion of Shifting Demand: Supply-Side Interpretations of American Religious History," in *Retelling U.S. Religious History,* ed. Thomas A. Tweed (Berkeley: University of California Press, 1997), 108–124.

5. Max Weber, *The Protestant Ethic and the Spirit of Capitalism,* trans. Talcott Parsons, foreword by R. H. Tawney (1958; Mineola, N.Y.: Dover, 2003), esp. 79–87. Weber's essay was first published in 1904–1905.

6. Ibid., passim.

7. Ibid., 142.

8. Ibid., 131.

9. Ibid., 140–141.

10. Ibid., 252 n. 165.

11. Ibid., 149.

12. Ibid., 132–133, 141–143.

13. See, for example, Charles E. Lindblom, *The Market System: What It Is, How It Works, and What to Make of It* (New Haven: Yale University Press, 2001); Niall Ferguson, *The Cash Nexus: Money and Power in the Modern World,*

1700–2000 (New York: Basic Books, 2001); Joyce Appleby, *The Relentless Revolution: A History of Capitalism* (New York: W.W. Norton, 2010).

14. Winifred Barr Rothenberg, *From Market-Places to a Market Economy: The Transformation of Rural Massachusetts, 1750–1850* (Chicago: University of Chicago Press, 1992); Bruce H. Mann, *Neighbors and Strangers: Law and Community in Early Connecticut* (Chapel Hill: University of North Carolina Press, 1987). On trade during the 1740s, see John J. McCusker and Russell R. Menard, *The Economy of British America, 1607–1789* (Chapel Hill: University of North Carolina Press, 1985), 35–50, 62–63, 91–111.

15. See Newell, *From Dependency to Independence*.

16. Valeri, *Heavenly Merchandize*, 237–238.

17. Ibid., 236–237.

18. Istvan Hont, *Jealousy of Trade: International Competition and the Nation-State in Historical Perspective* (Cambridge, Mass.: Belknap Press, 2005).

19. Joyce Oldham Appleby, *Economic Thought and Ideology in Seventeenth-Century England* (Princeton: Princeton University Press, 1978).

20. Nicholas Philipson, *Adam Smith: An Enlightened Life* (New Haven: Yale University Press, 2010), 24–55; Emma Rothshild, *Economic Sentiments: Adam Smith, Condorcet, and the Enlightenment* (Cambridge, Mass.: Harvard University Press, 2001), 218–252; Valeri, *Heavenly Merchandize*, 200–219.

21. Valeri, *Heavenly Merchandize*, 234–249.

22. Jonathan Edwards, *Charity and Its Fruits*, in *The Works of Jonathan Edwards*, vol. 8, *Ethical Writings*, ed. Paul Ramsey (New Haven: Yale University Press, 1989), esp. 129–271; Jonathan Edwards, *A Treatise Concerning Religious Affections* (Boston, 1746), in *The Works of Jonathan Edwards*, vol. 2, *Religious Affections*, ed. John E. Smith (New Haven: Yale University Press, 1959), esp. 383–461.

23. See Samuel Philips Savage to Simon Frost, April 8, 1744, Savage correspondence, Massachusetts Historical Society, Boston.

24. The evidence is found throughout the personal papers of the Boston merchants, for example, in the Savage correspondence quoted above. For Weber, see *Protestant Ethic*, 48–57, 175–176.

25. Jürgen Habermas, *The Structural Transformation of the Public Sphere: An Inquiry into a Category of Bourgeois Society* (1962), trans. Thomas Burger with Frederick Lawrence (1989; Cambridge: MIT Press, 1991).

26. Michael Warner, *The Letters of the Republic: Publication and the Public Sphere in Eighteenth-Century America* (Cambridge: Harvard University Press, 1990). The historiography of Habermas and early America is covered admirably by two essays from John L. Brooke: "Reason and Passion in the Public Sphere: Habermas and the Cultural Historians," *Journal of Interdisciplinary History* 29 (1998–1999): 43–67; and "Consent, Civil Society, and the Public Sphere in the Age of Revolution and the Early Republic," in *Beyond the Founders: New Approaches to the Political History of the Early American*

*Republic*, ed. Jeffrey L. Pasley, Andrew W. Robertson, and David Waldstreicher (Chapel Hill: University of North Carolina Press, 2004), 207–250. The use here of Habermas to analyze evangelical religion is prompted by Warner's unpublished lectures on the evangelical public sphere, available as an audio recording: Michael Warner, "The Evangelical Public Sphere," 2009 A. S. W. Rosenbach Lectures, March 23–26, 2009, University of Pennsylvania, Philadelphia.

27. Jürgen Habermas himself did not originally consider religion to have an important role in the development of the public sphere. In his *Theory of Communicative Action*, trans. Thomas McCarthy (Boston: Beacon Press, 1985), he argued that the public sphere needs to be based on reason and should be strictly secular, excluding religion. In his more recent thought, however, he has revised this position. In his dialogue with then-cardinal Joseph Ratzinger, published as *The Dialectics of Secularization* (San Francisco: Ignatius, 2006), Habermas praises Christianity for its contributions to the public sphere, especially in promoting reason. In *Between Naturalism and Religion: Philosophical Essays* (Malden: Polity, 2008), Habermas attends to postmetaphysical philosophy's reflexive appropriation of the "cognitive content" of religion, such as Walter Benjamin's use of the idea of messianic hope and Karl Marx's modification of the concept of the Kingdom of God, and sees religion as an important resource for modern societies, though religious ideas still need to be "translated" into secular terms before they can be publicly available.

28. Habermas, *Structural Transformation of the Public Sphere*, esp. 2, 25–56.

## 3

# Billy Graham, Christian Manliness, and the Shaping of the Evangelical Subculture

*Grant Wacker*

THIS CHAPTER ASKS a simple but important question: How did American evangelicals use the market system in general, and *cultural* capital in particular, to shape a distinctive subculture?[1] First, we need to consider evangelicals' nearly universal conviction that the world was their parish.[2] The desire for continual expansion proved intrinsic to the organism—part of its very DNA. Jesus's words, "Go into all the world and preach the gospel," served as its perennial marching orders. Uncounted examples come to mind, ranging from George Whitefield in the early eighteenth century to Joyce Meyer in the late twentieth century. "Speed the Light," the name of one of the most prominent of the movement's missionary agencies, reveals worlds within worlds about the tradition's expansionist impulse. Still more revealing is the agency's self-description: "The concept is simple: we give so others can speed the light of the gospel to a world in darkness."[3] When it came to evangelism, partisans experienced no setbacks, only challenges.

To be sure, several groups that bore important theological continuities with mainstream evangelicals do not readily fit the evangelical label, at least partly because they took an indirect approach to expansion or abjured it entirely. Some, like the Christian Reformed Church, an immigrant Dutch body, sought to grow mainly by holding onto the loyalty of their children and grandchildren. Others, such as the Covenant Church, embraced a soft-sell approach that effectively modeled St. Francis's advice: "Preach the gospel always. Use words if necessary." Still others, such as the Salvation Army, put their resources into costly endeavors such as homeless ministries that did not pay off in quantifiable ways.[4] And a trace, such as the disillusioned China missionary Pearl Buck, wrestled with the morality of any form of expansion if it meant disrupting another person's beliefs or another culture's integrity.[5]

Yet these comparatively minor streams in the great evangelical river formed the exceptions that proved the rule. For the vast majority, to be an evangelical was, virtually by definition, to seek more revenue, bigger churches, larger programs, greater influence, and enhanced effectiveness. To stand still was to marinate, a status little different from dying.

The question before us then is this: How did evangelicals achieve their aim of continual growth? Differently put, how did they actually do what they did?

Several answers come to mind, but one of the most compelling ones is that evangelicals understood not only how the market worked but also how to make it work for them. More precisely, they discerned religious needs and desires in the wider culture and then appropriated resources in the wider culture to meet them. Most conspicuously, they drew on a classically Enlightenment view of human ability, which depicted individual choice as a rational act of will unencumbered by ideology, tradition, or community. I shall discuss Billy Graham more later, but here it is worth noting that his magazine and network radio and television programs all bore the same telling title: *Decision*. Evangelicals' toolkits also included a realist or common-sense epistemology. This outlook affirmed that humans naturally possessed the ability to see the external world pretty much as it really was, free from the distorting effects of culture. (So goes the quip that "Interpretation" ranked as the shortest entry in any *Dictionary of Evangelical Theology*). And finally, they profited from a social location that enjoyed optimal tension with the mainline culture: just enough resistance to tighten the muscles but not enough truly to harm them.

However explained, evangelicals mastered the mechanics of the market as effectively as any group on the American religious landscape. The story of their success has been ably told elsewhere. One anecdote speaks for scores. At one point, Methodist churches, typically evangelical, outnumbered post offices.[6] In public, believers were quick to give all of the credit for their growth to the Holy Spirit and none to themselves. In private, however, they knew better. They knew that every church library secretly shelved the *Gospel of Adam Smith* next to the *Gospel of Luke.*

# *I*

The celebrity evangelist Billy Graham (born 1918) offers a useful case study for how evangelicals used cultural capital to achieve their aims. Graham offers more than just a case study, however. More than anyone else, he defined and channeled the swell of evangelical fervor that marked the long second half of the twentieth century. Graham did not create that swell; it was surging before he entered the scene. But he did fuel its energy and expand its scope. So how did he do it?[7]

The short answer is that he followed the same approach that most evangelicals followed. Like them, he discerned religious needs and desires in the wider culture and then drew on resources in the wider culture to meet them. The difference is that he did it with dramatically greater skill, for six decades, and with remarkably few missteps.

Multiple tactics blended to form a flexible yet coherent strategy. First came the preacher's organization, the Billy Graham Evangelistic Association, commonly known as the BGEA. Decade after decade this well-oiled machine staffed itself with efficient and fiercely loyal associates and assistants. Before the crusade meetings began, the BGEA oversaw saturation advertising with leaflets, billboards, bumper stickers, and radio and television spots. It orchestrated a meticulously organized system of neighborhood prayer meetings and door-to-door visits. During the meetings, participants heard nostalgic music, massive choirs, low-key fundraising appeals, folksy humor, and simple but powerfully effective sermons. They also heard an invitation to commit their lives to Christ. "Inquirers," as Graham called them, enacted their commitments through a clearly prescribed ritual of standing up and walking to the front, followed by another clearly prescribed ritual of talking with trained counselors and local clergy about their decisions. After the meetings, Graham maintained an imposing public presence through myriad publications, feature-length movies, radio and television programs, connections with business tycoons, public friendships with influential political figures, and a lasting eagerness to showcase his rural and Southern roots. Graham's reputation for marital fidelity, financial integrity, institutional probity, an unpretentious lifestyle, and personal humility undergirded everything else.

One of the more important but less appreciated aspects of Graham's relation to American society lay in the manifold modes of his self-presentation. In the balance of this chapter I wish to focus on his ability to model one of those modes. I will call it Christian manliness. With this phrase, I mean something like masculinity disciplined by an ethic of self-restraint.[8] Whether Christian manliness grew from biblical values, as insiders might have said, or from middle-class protocols, as outsiders might have said, or from both, as I would say, is a question that we probably cannot answer and which does not matter very much if we could. The point is that the combination of masculinity and self-restraint evoked an image closer to George C. Marshall than to George S. Patton, or perhaps closer to Charlton Heston than to Marlon Brando.[9] As far as I know, Graham himself never used the phrase "Christian manliness" or invoked the Muscular Christianity movement of the late nineteenth and early twentieth centuries.[10] Nonetheless, through an elusive combination of instinct and design he somehow discerned the power of that image. He took care to present himself in its terms, and Heartland America loved it.

## Looks

In Graham's career Christian manliness (hereafter, manliness) took multiple forms. Appearance constituted the most conspicuous one. Scottish genes and Nordic looks gave him a head start. When the preacher peered in a mirror, he saw the American male ideal: sculpted profile, blue eyes, square jaw, and flaxen hair. A retrospective written by the noted *Newsweek* columnist Ken Woodward started with the obvious: "His face was Hollywood handsome."[11] And if the face was Hollywood handsome, the physique was Hollywood trim: six feet two inches tall, 180 pounds, broad shoulders, and narrow waist. Graham took care to keep it that way too, with a regimen of jogging, weightlifting, mountain climbing, and, of course, golf.[12] Even when he was on the road, which was the majority of the time,[13] he maintained a schedule of rigorous daily exercise. One associate said that he was "hard as a rock." Especially before crusades, Graham claimed, he trained like a prizefighter.[14]

For the better part of sixty years, virtually every newspaper article about Graham—and there were thousands—commented on his appearance. The London *Evening News* called him "Charles Atlas with a Halo."[15] Popular magazines—especially women's publications—knew a good picture when they saw one. Some juxtaposed photos of him on one side of the page with shots of glamorous women on the other.[16] Fitness and nutrition magazines joined the parade. Even professional historians—a group not prone to notice realities as mundane as appearance—acknowledged the obvious. One found him "Olympian in size and handsomeness,"[17] while another said that he was to the media born, with his "laminated, heroic, commanding, Viking-like" visage.[18]

As Graham matured, he seemed to grow even better looking. The older preacher conveyed the image of the seasoned yet still virile male. A skillful dentist guaranteed the trademark million-dollar smile.[19] One journalist said that at age seventy-three "he looks like the aging athlete."[20] A *Time* magazine cover showed the familiar wavy mane, streaked with silver, and the familiar chiseled face, now deeply lined, all complemented by a sporty black blazer and white turtleneck. The simple caption read, "A Christian in Winter: Billy Graham at 75."[21]

The BGEA understood the power of rugged good looks in a media age. Appearance does not make a man better, one aide allowed, but it does reduce "the limitations a man faces if he is to present himself well."[22] When the historian Marshall Frady asked another aide what would have happened if the evangelist had been pudgy and scrappy of hair, the aide smiled, "Well, but he wasn't, was he? The Lord worked it out so that he wouldn't be."[23] Graham never said anything like that about himself, but clearly he appreciated the cultural power of a manly presence. He described his associate George Beverly Shea as a "handsome bass baritone" and his friend Prince Philip as "every inch a man's man."[24] When a *Harper's Magazine* profile depicted Graham's smile as "pleasant and manly," one suspects that the preacher took the compliment to heart.[25] After all, his rising visibility paralleled the rising visibility of Warner Sallman's paintings (which sold in the millions) of a tanned, angular, hirsute Jesus.[26]

As the decades passed, Graham also served as a role model for aging well, both physically and spiritually. He not only lived long but also lived long in the public eye. For nearly six decades he remained squarely on center stage and, not rarely, on the evening news. To be sure, Graham saw his share of aches, pains, and trips to the Mayo Clinic.[27] And age inevitably took its toll. In 1992 he admitted that he suffered from Parkinson's disease. The condition was serious, his wife remarked: "His Parkinson's disease is no joke. Overnight he has become an old man."[28] But the public never seemed to notice. What they noticed, rather, was resilience. One journalist observed that the "fire and energy" of Graham's youth had been replaced by a "gentleness brought on by the poignant reality that time is slipping."[29] The evangelist's public pronouncements focused on the deep-ened perspective born of years. "If you reach my age," he told a group of seminarians when he was seventy-nine, "you will wonder where the time has gone."[30]

And so he soldiered on, crusade after crusade, into his mid-eighties. In 2005, in his final meeting, he had to be helped to a platform to speak to nearly a quarter-million souls for the three nights of his outdoor cru-sade in New York's Flushing Meadows Corona Park.[31] The following year *Senior Living* magazine featured a snow-white yet smiling and absolutely square-jawed Graham on its cover.[32] As he approached age ninety-four, one admirer wrote that his ability to "accept illness and aging with peace" offered solace to others.[33] In his penultimate book, symptomati-cally named *Nearing Home: Life, Faith, and Finishing Well*, published in 2011, the nonagenarian Graham acknowledges that he suffered infirmi-ties. "Old age is not for sissies," he sighs.[34] But quietly disappearing into the twilight was never in the cards; such would undermine the image of Graham as the embodiment of manliness.

## Dress

Manly looks found their complement in manly threads. From the out-set, Graham seemed instinctively to know that he could never make a second first impression. A friend from his adolescent days remembered that he stood out with his navy jacket, white slacks, and white shoes.[35] Graham's attire changed with the setting. In 1940, he moved from the rural South to the suburban North. His destination was Wheaton College, located in Wheaton, Illinois, a decidedly uptown community twenty miles west of Chicago. The college enjoyed a reputation as the Harvard of the fundamentalist world, and that reputation applied to the social class of its students and faculty as well.[36] One historian aptly described the school as a "staid campus of pince-nez sanctitude."[37] Initially, Graham felt out of place, discomfited by his "Lil Abner" wardrobe and by his identifiably Southern accent.[38] Nonetheless, he adapted quickly, as photographs of him as a smartly dressed upperclassman attest.[39]

Out of college and onto the itinerant evangelist circuit, the aspiring preacher responded to the sartorial cues for a man in his line of work. In the late 1940s, as a traveling speaker for the parachurch organization Youth for Christ, he sported hand-painted ties—when he was not wearing a flashing (yes, flashing) bow tie, that is—and garish suits.[40] One writer called him "Gabriel in Gabardine."[41] Graham's breakout crusade in Los Angeles in 1949 showcased an evangelist changing with the setting. Photographs reveal a handkerchief billowing from a double-breasted suit coat pocket and shirts so stylish one writer billed him as a walking "Arrow collar man."[42] He looked the role. This protean ability to adapt without changing helped Graham seem to fit naturally into any situation, abetting the ease with which he came to epitomize manliness and helping him generate cultural capital in a variety of situations, to the benefit of his ministry.

For the most part, that is. In a classic case of misreading the cues, Graham and three associates showed up at a 1950 White House meeting with President Harry S. Truman decked out in cream-colored suits, hand-painted ties, rust-colored socks, and white buck shoes. Nearly fifty years later, Graham still cringed, remembering that Truman probably viewed them as if they were a "traveling vaudeville team."[43] As things turned out, underdressing proved the least of Graham's mistakes that day. He naively repeated the details of his conversation with the president to the press—and the president was furious. Yet the scene symbolizes Graham's awareness of the importance of self-presentation. He said that he had seen pictures of Truman in white buck shoes and felt that he should do likewise.

As the setting changed, so did the wardrobe. By the time of Graham's first major international crusade in London in 1954, his customary dress had evolved into smart business attire. Eventually the press spoke of his impeccably tailored "trademark" dark suits, starched white shirts, and ever-present accessory handkerchief.[44] In 1970, Graham scored a spot on a list of "Best Dressed Men."[45] He was well dressed but not *too* well dressed. No one thought of him as a fop or a dandy, which would have derailed him in the heartland. When photographers caught him at home, loafers, blue jeans, polo pullovers, and turtleneck sweaters prevailed. At work or play, the manly preacher was a haberdasher's dream.[46]

## Athletics

Manliness ideals also threaded through Graham's autobiographical reflections. When he told his family's story, he emphasized that both of his grandfathers had fought in the Civil War and that both had taken a bullet in battle.[47] His paternal grandfather, ironically named Crook Graham, emerges in Billy's accounts as something of a hell-raiser.[48] Though Billy gave no hint that he approved of Crook's behavior, he also gave no hint that he found it anything to hide. When Graham told his own story, he revealed the stereotypical preoccupations of an adolescent male in the South. Fast cars, pretty girls, and strutting behavior ranked high on the list. His father's Plymouth evidently saw its share of racing over country roads. Though Graham stressed that his romantic relationships remained chaste, he also portrayed himself as something of a swain with a zeal for smooching.[49] And Graham knew something about the real world, too: a farmhand named Pedro introduced him to tales of his "erotic experiences with women, probably embellished for my wide-eyed benefit." Pedro eventually got himself fired for trying to teach the young man how to chew tobacco.[50] A sanctimonious prude Graham never pretended to be.

In those autobiographical accounts, physical aggressiveness proved conspicuous. The teenage Graham had his share of fistfights, including bloody ones. After one altercation, he remembered, "I thought maybe I'd killed him."[51] When he was a student at Florida Bible Institute in Tampa he preached in jails, in trailer parks, and on street corners. It was a hard dollar. One saloonkeeper, irked by Graham's trawling for souls outside his establishment, marched outside and shoved him to the ground.[52] Undaunted, the aspiring evangelist continued to preach anywhere he could find an audience. Once, he recalled, "a gang of rowdies threw me down on the sidewalk . . . and ground my face in the gutter filth. I got my clothes all messed up, but I felt I was suffering for Christ's sake, and I jumped right back up and pronounced the Judgment of God on them."[53] Sometimes young folks made trouble for "the boy preacher'" during a sermon. Once, when he threatened to throw them out, a heckler stood, shook his fist, and stomped away. "I can do other things besides preach," Graham warned his audience: "If that fellow ever does that again, I'm going to give him the whipping of his life."[54] The accuracy of Graham's memories of those early adventures is less important than his willingness to write and talk about them years later. It would be cynical to suppose that he did it in order to win followers but obtuse to think that he remained unaware of the appeal of the image.

And then there was Graham's enduring love of baseball.[55] As a child he had shaken the hand of the great Babe Ruth; as an old man he still relished that moment and boasted about it.[56] He played first base on his high school team and one summer played a "few games" for a semipro team in Charlotte, N.C.[57] At one time, he might have aspired to go professional.[58]

True or not, the key point is that throughout his life, Graham often talked about his affection for the sport, and so did most biographers who wrote about him. In 2012, the front lobby of the Billy Graham Library in Charlotte still showcased a large photograph of the preacher in a determined left-handed batting crouch at home plate. Graham and America shared a field of dreams.

As a young evangelist, Graham not only esteemed sports but also linked athleticism with Christianity itself. To be sure, he remembered that in his salad days, he—like many Southern males—had resisted religion as "more or less sissy stuff. . . . It was all right for old men and girls, but not for real 'he-men' with red blood in their veins."[59] Preaching was no better.[60] Yet the example of a star football player—"a great athlete and a real man's man"—proclaiming the gospel eventually persuaded him otherwise.[61] Graham's very first crusade on his own (in 1947 in Charlotte, N.C.) featured Gil Dodds, the reigning American miler, racing six laps around the audience in a pseudo-competition against a local runner.[62] The idea struck fire. For the rest of the century, Graham's meetings highlighted testimonies from notable athletes. Graham also relished posing for photo ops with celebrity competitors such as Arnold Palmer and Muhammad Ali, grafting some of their cultural capital onto his own while mingling the different male ideals that he and they represented.[63]

The American public savored Graham's association with sports enough to pay for it. Popular media displayed photographs of him boating, jogging, treadmilling, and, especially, playing golf.[64] Since golf snapshots often showed him putting with influential people, including presidents of the United States, they carried additional implications about how sports offered Graham access to the highest echelons of power (not to mention the press's access to the mighty at play).[65] Graham's personal relationship with Lyndon Johnson captured special notice. The surface narrative focused on the enduring friendship between these two Southerners of exceptional power and charisma. But just beneath the surface ran another narrative that focused on the locker room camaraderie that partly defined that friendship. Golf, of course, marked much of it, but so did skinny-dipping in the White House pool and racing around the Pedernales backcountry in the president's convertible Lincoln.[66]

Though Graham never boxed, the press found that sport a useful metaphor for illustrating his bouts with the devil. The New York *Journal American* ran a telling cartoon on May 16, 1957, the day after his now-famous Madison Square Garden crusade opened in New York City.

It showed a muscular evangelist standing in the middle of a boxing ring with his gloved fists thrown high in triumph, while, bruised and battered, the devil skulked in the corner.[67] When Graham moved the meeting for one sweltering night in July from the Garden to Yankee Stadium, the press took care to note that the attendance of one hundred thousand made it the largest gathering on that site since Joe Louis had knocked out Max Baer for the heavyweight championship of the world.[68]

The image of a man of Herculean stamina also played a role in Graham's public presentation. Graham's great breakout crusade in Los Angeles in 1949 might well be called his great marathon crusade. In the eight weeks stretching from late September to late November, he held seventy-two meetings, preached sixty-five full sermons, and gave hundreds of additional talks to small groups and on the radio.[69] Yet that trial paled before the Madison Square Garden meeting, which ran from May 15 to September 1, 1957. Those months saw Graham preach exactly one hundred times in person to more than two million people.[70] He also spoke on live network telecasts almost every Saturday evening and made numerous individual appearances along the way. The celebrity pulpiteer had spent the preceding spring training like an athlete, jogging the rugged hills and country roads behind his home in North Carolina. Yet what stood out in his memory four decades later was the exhaustion—the utter, bone-crushing exhaustion—of the ordeal. "New York also took a toll on me physically," he remembered: "I left drained; I had lost twenty or more pounds. I have said in later years that something went out of me physically in the New York Crusade that I never fully recovered."[71]

Whether he recovered or not, one associate wrote that on average he continued to preach every other night year-round.[72] The autobiography yields an image of a man relentlessly on the go, flying from city to city around the world. As early as 1945 Graham logged 135,000 miles and received United Airlines' title as its top civilian passenger.[73] Though he took regular breathers—downtime at home and on Florida beaches— those moments of repose largely escaped the press's attention. What they saw and what they reported was a man always in a hurry.

The glamour of youthfulness counted, too. When Graham first hit the itinerant circuit in the dusty towns of central Florida in the late 1930s, the advance publicity recurrently underscored his youth, turning inexperience into a virtue. Said one poster: "HEAR BILLY GRAHAM / 21 Year Old Evangelist of Tampa, Florida / A Young Man With a Burning Message."[74] The image made good copy. A decade later a *Grand Rapids*

*Press* ad promised a winning combination of aptitude, appeal, preeminence, and athleticism: "Here's a Talent Line-up to Delight You!" Under Graham's photo, the caption read: "America's foremost youth leader and speaker. *A young athlete with a 20th Century Gospel Message.*"[75] Graham's first crusade in his hometown saw posters coupling youth with vitality. One featured Graham slightly crouched, with clenched fist thrust forward. Underneath ran the by-now familiar caption: "BILLY GRAHAM / America's Dynamic Young Leader and Evangelist."[76] Visual intimations of Graham as a man in the prime of life continued until he was well into his sixties.

Several factors played a role here. Part of it, of course, was that Graham fit the idealization, if not idolization, of post–World War II youth culture.[77] It was no accident that Billy Sunday and Aimee Semple McPherson had walked into the national religious limelight in the prime of their own youths in the 1890s and 1920s. Graham, too, portended a fresh start. Both Sunday and McPherson were gone by the time Graham's star began to rise in the late 1940s, so the field was his. To be sure, he was not the only contender, for a cluster of evangelists of comparable age jostled for center stage. But Graham somehow managed to combine athleticism, stamina, youthfulness, good looks, and Southern charm in a uniquely effective way.

Images of fresh vitality ran deep in the story of Graham's career. His ministry grew from a base in Youth for Christ, an organization that featured lively music, evangelistic fervor, and patriotic uplift in its stunningly successful Saturday night "rallies" across the United States and postwar Europe. Graham entered the movement just after it was organized in 1946 and soon became its first full-time paid evangelist.[78] He did not stay long. By 1947 or 1948—the data from those pre-celebrity years are too scant to say for sure— he launched out on his own. Photographic evidence from the earliest crusades intimates that he appealed to middle-aged to older audiences,[79] but by the 1970s, when Graham was in his fifties, he seemed especially to attract younger crowds. In 1970, he estimated that 60 to 70 percent of his audiences were less than twenty-five years old.[80] Though that figure seems high, sociological and journalistic evidence leaves little doubt that the preacher increasingly appealed to people well below the age of the typical churchgoer.[81]

## Moral Backbone

Though Graham's inclination to link sports with Christianity never disappeared, as the years passed he talked more about another form of manliness. We might call it moral backbone, a willingness to stand tall for the principles he believed in, often regardless of the consequences. This orientation manifested itself both in his personal deportment and in his punditry about national and world affairs.

The relation between personal deportment and moral backbone is more complex than it initially seems. On the one hand, Graham won wide recognition for his affable, easygoing style. Indeed, left-leaning critics targeted him for being too affable when he consorted with presidents who, they believed, needed a verbal slap rather than a pastoral word.[82] And his desire to get along with everyone led him to cultivate friendly relations with people of diverse if not mutually incompatible political and theological views. On the other hand—and this is the key point—he readily engaged real or perceived opponents in public debate, including audiences as diverse as Students for a Democratic Society at Columbia University and theology professors at Harvard Divinity School.[83] It is almost needless to say that academic elites held credentials that Graham, who never went to seminary, could only dream about. Yet in those situations he stood tall in his own way. Like a skilled barrister, he deflected barbs with a quick wit and a light touch. Always easy in his own skin, he never pretended to possess scholarly expertness. Yet time after time he deftly shifted the discussion onto moral or spiritual grounds where he felt comfortable. Besides uncounted public events of that sort, Graham took the initiative to meet or try to meet formidable foes in private to talk things over. Significantly, one of his most vocal critics, Reinhold Niebuhr,[84] refused, but others, especially journalists, accepted.[85] The main import is not the content of those exchanges or who scored more points but, rather, Graham's willingness to step into the ring in the first place.

Punditry about national and global affairs offered another forum for exhibiting moral backbone. In the early years of his ministry Graham consistently discerned rigor abroad and lassitude at home. He criticized Truman's handling of the Korean War because Truman dithered. Fight or get out, Graham counseled.[86] At the same time, communists' atheism had poisoned their souls but hardened their fists. That explained why visitors to the Soviet Union saw no drunkenness or pornography. In contrast, Americans' ceaseless pursuit of pleasure and amusement had left them soft and adrift.[87] Graham's anti-communism matched the most truculent warhorses in the State Department. One Chicago newspaper dubbed him "Communism's Public Enemy Number One"—a view echoed even in Soviet papers.[88] The preacher never endorsed Senator

Joseph McCarthy's hunt for traitors, but he did admire McCarthy's fear-lessness. He denounced "the pinks, the lavenders, and the reds who have sought refuge beneath the wings of the American eagle."[89] Graham sus-pected that internationalists in general and United Nations devotees in particular mistook compromise for peace.[90]

Yet the preacher changed as the world changed. In the later years of his ministry he grew less concerned about the peril posed by the Red Menace and more concerned about the peril posed by Soviet and American nuclear arsenals. To be sure, older forms of manliness persisted. Making clear that he was no pacifist, Graham insisted that nations retained both a right to defend themselves and an obligation to protect the weak. Nonetheless, as the years passed, the possible annihilation of the human race loomed increasingly large in his consciousness. Elbowing aside criticism from the religious and political Right, he issued increasingly sharp and frequent warnings about the gravity of the threat.[91]

This context frames one of the most publicized—and demonized—events of Graham's career. His plans to participate in a transparently ideo-logical "peace" conference in Moscow in 1982 aroused resistance from his family, his organization, and the U.S. State Department. He went anyway. From a public relations perspective the trip proved a mixed success. Hoping to facilitate harmonious relations between the Big Powers, as well as an invitation to return to preach the gospel, he seemed to polish the Soviet apple a bit too much. Graham's statements about the apparent freedom of religion in that country provoked stinging responses from the political Left as well as the political Right. The secular conservative columnist George Will called him "America's most embarrassing export."[92] Though Graham soon allowed that he had not spoken as carefully as he should have, he never backed down. However one assesses the wisdom of the trip and of some of his comments before and after it, there can be no question that he revealed steely determination in the face of unforgiving opposition.[93]

## Preaching

Graham's preaching style represented manliness of still another kind. First, of course, was the voice, a timbered baritone that *Time* journalists Nancy Gibbs and Michael Duffy describe as an instrument of "vast range and power."[94] His sound reminded many of his exact contemporary, the celebrated television anchor Walter Cronkite. Graham cultivated his gift. He not only trained his voice like an opera singer but also, for four hours before speaking, protected it by sequestering himself in the quiet of his hotel room.[95] In Graham's preaching, words became flesh, less delivered than fired. In high school, he said, he had chosen Bob Jones College because Jones had spoken at the school and he found the patriarch's commanding style impressive.[96] Later, at Florida Bible Institute, Graham paid attention to the assertive platform tactics of his evangelist elders, the paladins of an earlier generation. He also paid attention to celebrated national broadcasters such as Walter Winchell, Drew Pearson, Gabriel Heatter, and H. G. Kaltenborn. Verbal athletes, they had mastered the art of delivering words as fast as the tongue could speak and the ear could discern them.[97] And so it was that in the 1940s and 1950s Graham's audiences heard a verbal machine gun. One stenographer clocked him at 240 words a minute.[98] (Exactly how he did this with a distinctive Southern accent is not easy to explain.[99]) Timing counted. Staccato bursts and short pauses combined to form Graham's signature cadence. Volume counted, too. His sister Jean remembered that as a young evangelist, starting out in the late 1930s, he preached "so loud."[100] In 1949 *Time* magazine would call him "trumpet lunged," and *Newsweek* soon dubbed him the "Bible-shouting evangelist."[101]

Graham's authoritative voice lent itself to hard-hitting rhetoric and gestures. Believing that the average person possessed a working vocabulary of six hundred words, he favored one-syllable words, brisk verbs, and short sentences.[102] Military and athletic metaphors spiked the prose. "We used every modern means to catch the ear of the unconverted and then we punched them straight between the eyes with the gospel," he remembered.[103] Young people, especially, wanted a challenge. So when Graham preached to student audiences, he said that he gave them "the message of the gospel straight from the shoulder with no punches pulled."[104] The proof-text method of exegesis, which gathered—some said wrenched—short passages from different parts of the Bible, functioned as verbal ammunition.

The physical style of Graham's preaching changed as he did. In the beginning he paced relentlessly, by one account more than a mile in a single sermon.[105] Associate evangelist Cliff Barrows remembered that in the days before lapel microphones, his job was to sit behind the parson and continually unwind and rewind the cord.[106] With hair flying, arms swinging, and fists clenched, the young evangelist sprang up and down like a prizefighter, ducking, dodging, and delivering blows.[107] One observer dubbed him "the preaching windmill."[108] The middle-aged

Graham proved more stationary, but he still struck audiences as a man not to be toyed with. The scene seemed almost military. With his left hand thrusting a Bible high aloft and his right hand chopping like a meat cleaver, his baritone voice recurrently boomed, "The *Bible* says. . . ."[109] The older Graham's preaching style gradually slowed to the measured pace of a fireside chat. Gone were the explosive energy of the early decades and the clipped words of the middle decades. "At 75," said a reporter covering Graham's 1994 Cleveland crusade, the evangelist "no longer delivers with the rapid fire preaching frenzy that once prompted a writer to dub him 'God's machine gun.'" "These days," the reporter continued, "Graham doesn't need thunder to . . . preach convincingly. . . . [T]he power of his message comes from a surety that is absolutely serene."[110] Still, the no-nonsense bearing of a man who had seen many things and met many people allowed no eye to wander. Though Graham's preaching never rivaled the bombast of Billy Sunday or the theatricality of Aimee Semple McPherson, few mistook him for a black-robed cleric at Holy Trinity Lutheran, either.

## *II*

These considerations bring us back to the broader evangelical tradition and its relation to the market. When we measure adherents by the yardstick of their own ideals, which is the only fair way to do it, we find that their roundhouse embrace of market strategies, including their ready use of cultural capital, involved both losses and gains.

The loss side contained at least three kinds of problematic behavior. First, evangelicals' strategies sometimes baptized parts of the culture that even by their own norms they should not have baptized. Their showcasing of Christian beauty pageant winners, though an extreme case, serves as Exhibit A.[111] Second, their approach sometimes created the illusion that their own interests necessarily equaled the Lord's. Any activity that enlarged their institutional fortunes, financial and otherwise, often seemed, virtually by definition, to enlarge the Lord's as well. And finally, evangelicals' methods frequently privileged growth over nurture and breadth over depth. Though Graham himself never tired of saying that Christian commitment marked only the beginning of a lifetime of faith and service, many others got stuck on the counting part: tabulations of souls saved, bodies healed, and budgets met. They too easily forgot that some things should have been weighed rather than counted.

But if the market system involved losses for evangelicals, it also involved gains. Two stand out. The first and more obvious one pertained to the cultural meanings of growth. Persuaded that stabilization served as a euphemism for stagnation, and stagnation for deterioration, and deterioration for death, evangelicals proved extraordinarily *good* at doing what they determined to do. Observers do not have to embrace believers' theology, let alone their expansionist goals, to admire their entrepreneurial skills. There is no reason to think that evangelicals were smarter than other Christians. But their success suggests that they were, on the whole, more pragmatic, more willing to do whatever it took to achieve their goals. And that pragmatism stemmed from an underlying conviction that big questions were at stake—questions of sin, salvation, death, and eternal destiny. The second gain is less obvious but ultimately more important. The sum of it is that evangelicals' dependence on cultural capital typically rested on trust, and not on exploitation as the media often suggested. Trust was the invisible oil that lubricated the gears of their market relationships. In the words of one benefactor to the BGEA, contributions to Graham paid reliable dividends on the investment.[112] For millions of earnest believers, the movement itself paid reliable dividends on the investment. Grace was not less amazing for being dependable.

## *Postscript*

On April 23, 2012, the mail brought the newest issue of the *AARP Bulletin*, a monthly voice of the American Association of Retired Persons, nearly thirty-seven million strong. The front cover features, in bold red letters, these words: "Preacher Man: Living Life with Billy Graham." The referenced item turns out to be little more than a wisp of an article: a four hundred-word appreciation from a South Carolina member thanking Graham for serving as "the beacon"—the "moral compass"—for her and her family's life for more than fifty years. The important point here is not the substantive content of the piece, nice though it is, but, rather, that one of the most widely circulated periodicals in the world would showcase the legacy of a man approaching the century mark.[113] If evangelicals knew how to use the market, it is just as clear that the market knew how to use evangelicals' favorite son.

# *Notes*

I wish to thank my colleague David Morgan and my former student Anne Blue Wills for encouraging me to think about the role of gendered self-presentation in Graham's career. Though Anne and I pursued our research independently, we often reach similar conclusions. See especially Anne Blue Wills, "Billy Graham: Man of God, 1949–1954" (paper presented at the annual meeting of the American Society of Church History, San Diego, 2010).

1. Scholars' fascination with American evangelicalism seems to know no end. For a concise history of the tradition, see Douglas A. Sweeney, *The American Evangelical Story: A History of the Movement* (Grand Rapids: Baker Academic, 2005). For an astute summary of the state of the scholarship on the subject, see Darren Dochuk, "Evangelicalism," in *The Blackwell Companion to Religion in America*, ed. Philip Goff (Malden: Wiley-Blackwell, 2010), 550–558. In the same volume, see also the state-of-the-field essays by Paul Harvey ("Baptists"), Sylvester Johnson ("The Black Church"), Jonathan R. Baer ("Holiness and Pentecostalism"), D. G. Hart ("Reformed Tradition"), Christopher H. Evans ("Wesleyan Tradition"), and Wilbert Shenk ("Missions").

2. Of course this sentence represents an adaptation of John Wesley's most famous and perhaps most prescient words: "I look upon all the world as my parish. . . . I judge it meet, right, and my bounden duty to declare unto all that are willing to hear the glad tidings of salvation" (*Letters I*, in *Works* [Nashville: Abingdon, 1980], vol. 25: 616).

3. "About," *Speed the Light*, accessed April 15, 2012, http://stl.ag.org/about/. Speed the Light was founded in 1944 by the Assemblies of God's National Youth Ministries department. By 2012, it had raised more than $250 million for its worldwide work.

4. It is hard to document things that did not happen, but it is possible at least to gain a hint of broad patterns. See, for example, the survey articles on the evangelical tradition in America in the new and authoritative *Encyclopedia of Religion in America*. They focus on white and black Baptists, Presbyterians, Methodists, Pentecostals, and Independents; none mentions the Christian Reformed Church, the Covenant Church, or the Salvation Army. This focus suggests that the authors somehow sensed that those groups did not readily fall within the mainstream evangelical tradition. See Joseph S. Moore and Robert M. Calhoon's "Evangelicals: Nineteenth Century" and Randall Balmer's "Evangelicals: Twentieth Century" and "Evangelicals: Current Trends and Movements," all in *Encyclopedia of Religion in America*, ed. Charles H. Lippy and Peter W. Williams (Washington, D.C.: CQ Press, Sage, 2010), vol. 2: 796–804, 804–810, and 791–796, respectively.

5. Grant Wacker, "Pearl S. Buck and the Waning of the Missionary Impulse," *Church History: Studies in Christianity and Culture* 72 (December 2003): 852–874.

6. Peter W. Williams, *America's Religions: From Their Origins to the Twenty-first Century*, 3rd ed. (Urbana: University of Illinois Press, 2008 [1990]), 367.

7. Grant Wacker, "Billy Graham's America," *Church History: Studies in Christianity and Culture* 78 (September 2009): 489–511. The literature by and about Graham is vast. I have discussed some of the main texts in the first endnote of this chapter. See also the citations for the chapters in Andrew Finstuen, Anne Blue Wills, and Grant Wacker, eds., *American Pilgrim: The Worlds of Billy Graham* (forthcoming), and "Note on the Sources," in Grant Wacker, *America's Pastor: Billy Graham and the Shaping of a Nation* (Cambridge, MA: Harvard University Press, forthcoming, 2014).

8. Though historians tend to use the terms *manliness* and *masculinity* (like the adjectives *manly* and *masculine*) interchangeably, I have chosen consistently to employ *manliness* rather than *masculinity*. The etymological history here is complex. It suffices to say that *manliness*, which saw more use in the nineteenth century, connoted "sexual self-restraint, a powerful will, [and] a strong character," while *masculinity*, which saw more use in the twentieth century, connoted "physical force, aggressiveness, and male sexuality." Also, *manliness* connotes more cultural specificity—in this case, Victorian ideals of independence, strength, bravery, honor, and high-mindedness—while *masculinity* connotes more cultural generality—in this case, the "raw male power" characteristic of all men, regardless of time and place. See Gail Bederman, *Manliness and Civilization: A Cultural History of Gender and Race in the United States, 1880–1917* (Chicago: University of Chicago Press, 1995), 17–19 (quotations 18, 19); and Clifford Putney, *Manhood and Sports in Protestant America, 1880–1920* (Cambridge: Harvard University Press, 2001), 5.

9. In the past fifty years scholars have paid increasing attention to the images and functions of manliness/masculinity in American life. Much of this literature is ably summarized in Seth Dowland, "War, Sports, and the Construction of Masculinity in American Christianity," *Religion Compass* 5, no. 7 (2011): 355–364; and in Kathryn Lofton, "The Man Stays in the Picture: Recent Works in Religion and Masculinity," *Religious Studies Review* 30 (January 2004): 23–28. Lofton argues that images of masculinity in the works she surveys (1) are about gender, not sex; (2) historically change over time; (3) prove to be constructed in specific times and places; and (4) serve political purposes. Though I see no evidence that Graham was self-consciously aware of any of these characteristics of images of masculinity, all of them mark his career.

10. See Putney, *Manhood and Sports*, 206–207; and Tony Ladd and James A. Mathiesen, *Muscular Christianity: Evangelical Protestants and the Development of American Sport* (Grand Rapids: Baker Books, 1999), chaps. 4–7.

11. Kenneth L. Woodward, "Billy Graham Retrospective," prepared for use with his obituary, *Daily Beast*, manuscript in my possession.

12. Billy Graham, interview by David Frost, *Doubts and Certainties*, BBC, 1964.

13. Anne Graham Lotz, foreword to Billy Graham, *Living in God's Love: The New York Crusade* (New York: G. P. Putnam's Sons, 2005), 15.

14. Reported in Roger Bruns, *Billy Graham: A Biography* (Westport, Conn.: Greenwood Press, 2004), 3–4.

15. Quoted in William Martin, *A Prophet with Honor: The Billy Graham Story* (New York: William Morrow, 1991), 175.

16. Wills, "Billy Graham," 10.

17. Leonard I. Sweet, "The Epic of Billy Graham," *Theology Today*, April 1980, 85.

18. Marshall Frady, *ABC News*, Luce Press Clippings Television News Transcripts, December 20, 1979, 2; in original: "viking like."

19. John Corry, "God, Country, and Billy Graham," *Harper's Magazine*, February 1969, 37.

20. Rich, "The Autumn of Billy Graham," *Charlotte Observer*, August 23, 1992, ED.

21. *Time*, November 15, 1993, front cover.

22. Strober, *Graham*, 59–60.

23. Unnamed aide, quoted in Marshall Frady, *Billy Graham: A Parable of American Righteousness* (Boston: Little, Brown, and Company, 1979), 222.

24. Billy Graham, *Just as I Am: The Autobiography of Billy Graham* (San Francisco: HarperCollins, 1977), 85—hereafter cited as *JAIA*; and Billy Graham, "Billy Graham's Own Story: 'God Is My Witness,'" *McCall's*, June 1964, 64.

25. Corry, "God, Country, and Billy Graham," 39.

26. David Morgan, "The Face That's Everywhere," *Christian History and Biography* 91 (Summer 2006): 11.

27. *JAIA*, 424–425, 495, 601–602, 663, 741.

28. Ruth Graham, excerpted in Bill Adler, compiler, *Ask Billy Graham* (Nashville: Thomas Nelson, 2007), 228. Ruth added: "But there's a silver lining. Along with it, there's sweetness and gentleness."

29. Ken Garfield, *Charlotte Observer*, March 17, 1993, 1A.

30. Billy Graham, excerpted in Adler, *Ask Billy Graham*, 205.

31. "Publishers' Preface," in Graham, *Living in God's Love*, 13. The publishers reported an estimated total attendance of 242,000.

32. *Senior Living Resource Magazine*, Summer 2006, front cover.

33. Marsha Tennant, "What I Really Know about Billy Graham," *AARP Bulletin*, April 2012, 38.

34. Billy Graham, *Nearing Home: Life, Faith, and Finishing Well* (Nashville: Thomas Nelson, 2011), Kindle edition location 61.

35. Pauline Presson, quoted in Frady, *Billy Graham*, 76; see also 72.

36. Martin, *Prophet with Honor*, 69.

37. Frady, *Billy Graham*, 134.

38. *JAIA*, 60, 64; and Graham, "Billy Graham's Own Story," 204. The context leaves little doubt that Graham considered his Southern accent a social liability at Wheaton.

39. Photographs posted in the Billy Graham Museum, Wheaton (viewed August 2010).

40. Billy Graham, press conference, Philadelphia, June 7, 1972, Billy Graham Center Archives (BGCA), CN 24; *JAIA*, xxi; see also Frady, *Billy Graham*, 191.

41. "Billy Graham: Young Thunderer of the Revival," *Newsweek*, February 1, 1954, 44.

42. Quoted in James Morris, *The Preachers* (New York: St. Martin's Press, 1973), 384.

43. *JAIA*, xix. Graham said that *Time* reported that the suits were pistachio green, but he remembered them as cream-colored. A black-and-white photograph of the scene suggests that he was right—which may say something about the press's propensity to make a good story even better. The photo also shows that the four men were similarly though not identically attired. *JAIA*, xix and photo insert, 104ff.

44. Ken Garfield, *Charlotte Observer*, September 23, 1991, 1-A; Frady, *Billy Graham*, 5; uncounted press photographs, many of them collected in Russ Busby, compiler, *Billy Graham: God's Ambassador* (Alexandria, Va.: Time/Life Books, 1990).

45. *Charlotte Observer*, March 4, 1970, cited in Martin, *Prophet with Honor*, 383.

46. Martin, *Prophet with Honor*, 230.

47. *JAIA*, 3–4, 203; David Aikman, *Billy Graham: His Life and Influence* (Nashville: Thomas Nelson, 2007), 21.

48. *JAIA*, 3; Graham, "Billy Graham's Own Story," 124.

49. *JAIA*, 16; Billy Graham, in Curtis Mitchell, "I Was Born Again," *American Weekly*, January 16, 1955, 6; see also Grady Wilson, *Billy Graham as a Teenager* (Wheaton: Miracle Books, 1957), 9, 18–19.

50. Graham, "Billy Graham's Own Story," 196; and *JAIA*, 17.

51. Graham, "Billy Graham's Own Story," 122, 196 (quotation on 196); Billy Graham, in Mitchell, "I Was Born Again," 6; and Wilson, *Billy Graham as a Teenager*, 13, 23. On page 13, Wilson suggests that Graham did not initiate fights but then adds: "He could handle himself and didn't mind watching others [fight]."

52. John Pollock, *The Billy Graham Story* (Grand Rapids: Zondervan, 2003 [1985]), 25–26.

53. Billy Graham, quoted in Frady, *Billy Graham*, 128. These two incidents may have been the same, though the details differ enough to suggest different events.

54. Graham, "Billy Graham's Own Story," 202.

55. Ibid.; *JAIA*, 17–18; Wilson, *Billy Graham as a Teenager*, 7.

56. Billy Graham, Sacramento KCRA, Luce Press Clippings Television News Transcripts, September 9, 1983.

57. Ibid.; Martin, *Prophet with Honor*, 61.

58. *JAIA*, 18; Graham, *Nearing Home*, Kindle edition location 99. Many years earlier—closer to the fact—Graham acknowledged that he had never been good enough to play professionally ("Billy Graham's Own Story," 125, 196).

59. Billy Graham, "I Was 16 . . . and Loved Baseball," *Crusader: A National Evangelical News Monthly for the Philippines*, March 1963, 14.

60. Billy Graham, "Design for Decision," *Youth in Action*, November 1960, 5; Wilson, *Billy Graham as a Teenager*, 15, 24.

61. Billy Graham, in Mitchell, "I Was Born Again," 6. The athlete was Fred Brown.

62. Ladd and Mathiesen, *Muscular Christianity*, 96.

63. See, for example, the large photos of Graham with Muhammad Ali (twice) and Arnold Palmer hanging in the Billy Graham Library and Museum in Charlotte (viewed July 20, 2009).

64. See, for example, photographs of Graham in Charles Hirschberg, "The Eternal Crusader," *Life*, November 1994, 107 (boating); Strober, *Graham*, 72ff.; David Frost, *Billy Graham Talks with David Frost* (Philadelphia: A. J. Holman Company, 1971), 47 (jogging), 67; Curtis Mitchell, "Billy Graham's Physical-Fitness Program Can Help You," *Popular Science Monthly*, May 1965, 61 (treadmilling); "Resting Up to Save Souls," *Life*, December 26, 1955, 100; Harold H. Martin, "A Vivid Portrait of the Famous Revivalist Billy Graham," *Saturday Evening Post*, April 13, 1963, 20; and Jim Huffman, "Fame Hasn't Spoiled Billy Graham," *Minneapolis Tribune Picture Sunday Magazine*, December 12, 1965, 10 (golfing).

65. *JAIA*, photograph inserts, 424ff. and 680ff.; Billy Graham, "In His Own Words: Some Blunt Billy Graham Remarks on His Career, His Family, His Safety—and His Friend, Richard Nixon," *People Weekly*, December 22, 1975, 26; Nancy Gibbs and Michael Duffy, *The Preacher and Presidents: Billy Graham and the White House* (New York: Center Street, 2007), 206ff.

66. Martin, *Prophet with Honor*, 299; Harry Smith, "Billy Graham: A Personal Crusade," an episode of *Biography*, A&E, 1996; Billy Graham, interview by Monroe Billington, Billy Graham Oral History Interview, October 12, 1983, LBJ Presidential Library; *JAIA*, 408–409.

67. Andrew Finstuen, *Original Sin and Everyday Protestants: The Theology of Reinhold Niebuhr, Billy Graham, and Paul Tillich in an Age of Anxiety* (Chapel Hill: University of North Carolina Press, 2009), 135.

68. Bruns, *Billy Graham*, 78.

69. *JAIA*, 158.

70. Curtis Mitchell, *God in the Garden: The Story of the Billy Graham New York Crusade* (Garden City, N.Y.: Doubleday and Company, 1957), 9. Busby puts the attendance at 2.3 million (*Billy Graham*, 87).

71. *JAIA*, 323.

72. Busby, *Billy Graham*, 58.

73. Martin, *Prophet with Honor*, 92.

74. Photograph of poster displayed in the Billy Graham Center Museum, Wheaton College, Wheaton (viewed August 15, 2010).

75. Tommy Tomlinson, "First Crusade as Headliner: '47 in Michigan," *Charlotte Observer*, September 22, 1996.

76. Photograph of poster in the Levine Museum of the South, Charlotte (viewed April 15, 2010).

77. Grace Palladino, *Teenagers: An American History* (New York: Basic Books, 1996), 3–58.

78. Martin, *Prophet with Honor*, 90–94.

79. Busby, *Billy Graham*, 51.

80. Billy Graham, press conference, Baton Rouge, October 19, 1970, 4, BGCA, CN 24.

81. Ronald C. Wimberly, "Conversion in a Billy Graham Crusade: Spontaneous Event or Ritual Performance?" *Sociological Quarterly* 16, no. 2 (Spring 1975): 165; Larry Eskridge, " 'One Way': Billy Graham, the Jesus Generation, and the Idea of an Evangelical Youth Culture," *Church History: Studies in Christianity and Culture* 67 (1998): 83–106.

82. One could write a fat article, if not a fat book, on Graham's critics. For a sampler, see Pollock, *Billy Graham Story*, 88–90; and Wacker, "Billy Graham's America," 494.

83. Billy Graham, news conference, Portland, Ore., May 15, 1968, 11, BGCA, CN 24; *JAIA*, 422; Audiotapes T81 and T82, February 18–19, 1964, BGCA, CN 26.

84. *JAIA*, 301; George Champion, interview by Lois Ferm, June 29, 1979, BGCA, CN 141, Box 23, Folder 14.

85. Martin, *Prophet with Honor*, 182.

86. Billy Graham, *I Saw Your Sons at War: The Korean Diary of Billy Graham* (Minneapolis: Billy Graham Evangelistic Association, 1953), 63; William G. McLoughlin Jr., *Billy Graham: Revivalist in a Secular Age* (New York: Ronald Press Company, 1960), 114–115.

87. Billy Graham, "What Is God Like?" sermon on *The Hour of Decision*, revised 4c, January 1, 1951.

88. *Chicago Daily News* headline, 1953, quoted in Martin, *Prophet with Honor*, 167.

89. Billy Graham, "America's Decision," sermon #28 on *The Hour of Decision*, August 1, 1953.

90. Billy Graham, "Labor, Christ, and the Cross," sermon, September 1953, 6.

91. For one among scores of examples, see *JAIA*, 505.

92. George Will, "Let Us Pray for a Little Skepticism," *Washington Post*, May 13, 1982, A31. Will's actual words were, "Handcuffs are not America's most embarrassing export," but the context makes clear that Will meant that Graham filled that role.

93. *JAIA*, chap. 28; Aikman, *Billy Graham*, 157–170.

94. Gibbs and Duffy, *Preacher and Presidents*, 18.

95. Cathy Lynn Grossman, "The Gospel of Billy Graham: Inclusion," *USA Today*, May 16, 2005, accessed April 22, 2012, http://www.usatoday.com/news/religion/2005-05-15-graham-cover_x.htm.

96. *JAIA*, 34.

97. *JAIA*, 180.

98. Martin, *Prophet with Honor*, 96.

99. I owe this point to my friend John Akers.

100. Jean Graham Ford, e-mail to me, April 17, 2012.

101. "Trumpet-lunged" in *Time*, November 14, 1949, quoted in *JAIA*, 150; "Bible-shouting" in "In Passing: Holy Hood," *Newsweek*, March 5, 1951, 46.

102. Pollock, *Billy Graham Story*, 141.

103. Billy Graham, *Revival in Our Time* (Wheaton: Special Edition for Youth for Christ International, 1950), 3, quoted in McLoughlin, *Billy Graham*, 38.

104. Billy Graham, news conference, Columbus, Ohio, January 28, 1963.

105. Pollock, *Billy Graham Story*, 48.

106. Martin, *Prophet with Honor*, 114.

107. For a striking—and often reprinted—visual of the scene, see the full-page photograph in Busby, *Billy Graham*, 43.

108. Quoted without original source in Pollock, *Billy Graham Story*, 27.

109. This pattern is evident in virtually any of the videos of Graham's preaching in the middle years. For one conspicuous example, see the clip shown to visitors to the Billy Graham Library and Museum as they exit the display. The exact time and place are, significantly, not specified, presumably to convey an impression of the timeless and universal applicability of his message (viewed July 6, 2009).

110. David Hawley, "Billy Graham: 'God's Machine Gun,'" *Hamilton Spectator*, October 15, 1994, 1.

111. Mandy McMichael, "From the Altar to the Runway: Religion and Beauty Pageants in the American South" (PhD diss., Duke University, 2013).

112. Benefactor named and paraphrased by Torrey Johnson, in Torrey Johnson, interview by Lois Ferm, Billy Graham Oral History Program, #281, February 8, 1977, 28–29, BGCA, CN 141.

113. In March 2011 the circulation of the *AARP Bulletin* was 23,574,328, slightly eclipsed by its sister publication, *AARP Magazine*, at 23,721,626, making them the largest-circulation nonreligious publications in the world. The circulations of two publications posted by the Watchtower Bible and Tract Society (Jehovah's Witnesses) were nearly twenty million greater. See http://en.wikipedia.org/wiki/List_of_magazines_by_circulation (accessed April 25, 2012).

# 4

# Money Matters and Family Matters

## JAMES DOBSON AND FOCUS ON THE FAMILY ON THE TRADITIONAL FAMILY AND CAPITALIST AMERICA

*Hilde Løvdal Stephens*

"IF YOU WANT to be successful in life, do three things: graduate from high school, work full-time, and get married before you have children." So said Tom Minnery of Focus on the Family's public policy arm CitizenLink in a July 2012 video commentary entitled "Not Your Business." In this episode of *CitizenLink Report*, Minnery and colleague Stuart Shepard compared the economic policies of President Barack Obama and Republican presidential candidate Mitt Romney. Minnery's remark was a direct response to statements made by President Obama in Roanoke, Virginia, on how to succeed in America. Obama told the audience that "if you were successful, somebody along the line gave you some help," and insisted on the importance of teachers and infrastructure to help people move forward and achieve their goals in life. Minnery and Shepard saw Obama's claim as a dog whistle to union workers and those in favor of "big government" solutions to problems best left to individuals and families. This economic policy, they suggested, fails to acknowledge private enterprise as the backbone of American economy. They saw Obama's economic policy as ignoring the importance of individualism and family values in creating a sound economy, and they particularly objected to the president's apparent disregard for Americans who work hard and believe in the traditional family.[1]

This linking of economic issues and family values has long been a key theme of James C. Dobson and his organization Focus on the Family

(FotF; est. 1977).[2] Dobson began his career as a family expert with the publication in 1970 of *Dare to Discipline*, which he wrote as a response to the social and cultural changes of the 1960s. Like many evangelicals, Dobson and FotF take it for granted that God has ordained that America have a capitalist economic system. To them, the 1960s represent the great turning point in American history. For them, President Lyndon Johnson's Great Society epitomizes the federal government running amok and disregarding constitutional restraints on its authority via the establishment of a vast federal welfare system. That decade also saw the sexual revolution and a new wave of feminism, both of which ultimately expanded the range of options for what Americans can choose to do with their bodies. Whatever horror these events hold for those in the organization, Focus on the Family has been and is more than just a symbolic revolt against the 1960s enacting a longing for an imagined past. In the 1980s, Dobson became a leading evangelical representative for the emerging New Christian Right. Dobson and FotF staunchly defended President Ronald Reagan's financial policy of limited government and free-market capitalism and lauded his call for traditional "family values," the belief that social order is built upon the nuclear family. Anxious over the Left's call for more inclusive family policies and a move from the economic model of the 1950s, conservative evangelicals like Dobson would celebrate the 1950s vision of the family as the backbone of American economy and society. In Reagan's Americanism, call for "family values," and free-market message, Dobson and like-minded evangelicals found a set of values that could potentially turn the nation back to an imagined past where limited government and the traditional family together secured America's greatness.

Dobson owes his success, at least in part, to free-market capitalism. The massive expansion of FotF's work and outreach in the 1980s and 1990s came thanks to a booming evangelical consumer culture that went through a period of rapid growth in the decades following World War II.[3] Evangelical America enjoyed economic growth and established a massive institutional network of publishers and bookstores that thrived in a suburban, consumer-driven culture and gave Dobson a market on which to build his ministry. FotF participates in and contributes to the Christian consumer culture. Its periodicals are filled with advertisements for the latest videos/DVDs, books, and other "family-friendly" products. FotF is part of what Colleen McDannell calls "Material Christianity," a culture defined by *stuff*. Consumer evangelicalism—books, films, music, and knickknacks of various kinds—are central to everyday religious identity formation for many American believers. Simply put, *buying evangelical* is *being evangelical*.[4]

And yet, Dobson and FotF complicate the usual narrative of the evangelical embrace of the free market and consumer-driven capitalism. Over the years, evangelical America has struggled with how to serve God and not Mammon in an increasingly consumerist culture.[5] Dobson and FotF illustrate how contemporary evangelicals have turned to the "traditional family" to get the balance right. Seemingly paradoxically, the organization has endorsed Reagonomics while protesting the social and economic realities that have resulted from the economic structures that it celebrates. Traditional family values, FotF believes, are the basis for a free, capitalist America. At the same time, FotF uses these same family values as a lens through which to criticize consumerist America. FotF portrays traditional family values as the meaningful alternative to the heartless and stressful labor market and economic system marked by competition and the drive for success.[6] For FotF, the traditional family is a powerful and flexible symbol that serves as a guarantor of capitalism and a focal point for a critique of capitalist society.

During the tumultuous 1960s, Dobson watched the America he knew fall apart from the campus of the University of Southern California, where he completed his PhD in child development and later worked as an assistant professor. What he identified as prevalent sexual promiscuity and disrespect for authorities tested his vision of a good and stable America. Alarmed by what he saw happening around him, Dobson found support for his views in the theories of the late British anthropologist Joseph Daniel Unwin (1895–1936), whose 1935 address to the Medical Section of the British Psychological Society, "Sexual Regulations and Cultural Behavior," was republished in 1969 and distributed among Southern California's social conservatives.[7] It is easy to see why Unwin's theories caught on among Californians concerned about the sexual revolution and the future of capitalist America. In short, where Max Weber located the origin of capitalism in Calvinist theology, Unwin gave social conservatives a set of arguments that rooted Western capitalist economic systems in sexual behavior. Unwin tried to prove that sex had to do with much more than just sex; for Unwin, sex involved all aspects of a society and was part of what made such civilizations as the Aztec, Roman, and British empires successful. At heart, Unwin's project was about empirically testing the Freudian theory that regulated sexuality provided the energy needed to

build a society. Unwin examined the connection between sexual regulation and social and cultural patterns and concluded that contained sexuality made great civilizations possible. The address described three types
of cultures, from the most primitive and disorganized through those that
were somewhat organized up to highly organized and specialized societies. Each of these cultures, Unwin argued, was defined by sexual behavior. Where there was no regulation of sexuality, the culture could not
evolve. Where there was some regulation, the culture developed some sort
of organization. Only where sexuality was strictly regulated, he argued,
could highly developed and sophisticated cultures emerge. Sexual abstinence before marriage and restricted monogamy, Unwin explained, gave
a culture a surplus of energy to invest in institution-building and political
expansion. But, he warned, "the cultural process is not a one-way street.
A fall in the cultural scale is as possible as a rise."[8]

Dobson took Unwin's theory to heart. Beginning with *Dare to
Discipline*, Dobson has time and again referred to Unwin to prove that the
sexual revolution of the 1960s was not just about sex but, rather, marked
the start of a real revolution with the potential to bring America down. In
*Dare to Discipline*, Dobson turned to Unwin to explain why it was absolutely necessary to instill "responsible sexual attitudes" in American children in order for America to thrive in the future.[9] Further, in his 1975
book, *What Wives Wish Their Husbands Knew about Women*, Dobson
wrote: "Each culture has reflected a similar life cycle, beginning with a
strict code of sexual conduct and ending with the demand for complete
'freedom' to express individual passion. Unwin reports that *every* society
which extended sexual permissiveness to its people was soon to perish.
There have been no exceptions." Noting Unwin's claim that sex outside
marriage has literally brought down empires, Dobson argued that "man-
kind has known intuitively for at least fifty centuries that indiscriminate
sexual activity represented both an individual and a corporate threat to
survival."[10] In other words, a great civilization is not guaranteed to stay
great if people's sexual behaviors change. Unless Americans return to traditional family values, Dobson contended, the United States as he knows
it is in utter danger. A complete cultural collapse is possible, Dobson
warned; total social chaos is just a sexual revolution away.

We can see where the 1960s sexual revolution may have been terri-
fying for a generation of evangelicals marked by the Cold War critique
of "godless communism." After all, sexuality and gender roles were very
much at stake in the ideological battle between capitalist, theistic America

and the communist, atheistic Soviet Union. Proper gender roles and sexual behaviors played vital roles in early Cold War propaganda as keys to
upholding a free America against communist tyranny. Going against the
norm was perceived as a danger to the nation. Homosexuality was viewed
as particularly threatening. A deep-seated fear that homosexual men were
not able to withstand the lure of communism and were potentially able
to tear America down from within led to witch-hunts for homosexuals
within the federal government.[11] The emerging evangelical movement in
the 1950s chimed in. Cold warrior Billy Graham, for instance, connected
fighting against communism with fighting against sexual immorality
and even suggested that sexual promiscuity could harm America faster
than the communists could.[12] In the 1960s, Billy James Hargis and his
Christian Crusade protested against comprehensive sex education, which
Hargis perceived as another part of the plot for a communist takeover of
America.[13] In the 1970s, evangelicals would find ways to blend their fear
of communism with the call for "family values." The seasoned Catholic
anti-communist crusader Phyllis Schlafly would invigorate thousands
of evangelical women across the country to fight for the safety of their
families and the stability of the nation with her insistence that feminism
would tear America down. Traditional motherhood, she insisted, was a
cornerstone in the social order.[14] With groups like Focus on the Family, the
anti-communist heritage continued into the culture wars that emerged
out of the 1970s, shifting from a focus on communism to the broader
term *secular humanism* but retaining much of the rhetoric of uncontrolled
sex as a threat to America.[15]

Given the close link that Dobson and FotF saw between controlled sex
and a stable society, it is not surprising that they warned people about the
importance of having sex only in the right context. But they did more than
issue warnings: making sure people have good sex in the right context
became an urgent issue for Dobson and FotF. When Dobson and fellow
social conservatives grew alarmed by the decoupling of sexuality and marriage in the sexual revolution of the 1960s, they created their own version
of the sexual revolution. Dobson and other authors were part of a growing
industry of Christian advice literature dealing with marital sex. Christian
sex literature in many ways replicated what readers would find in secular
sex manuals, including counsel on various ways to enjoy their sex lives
more. Where evangelical sex manuals differed from secular versions was
in the evangelical belief that sex and desire reveal something profound
about the essence of male and female and their roles in society. Based on

an essentialist understanding of what it means to be a man or a woman, evangelicals insisted that God instilled certain qualities in the male and female bodies that make men and women fit for different roles in family and society. As Amy DeRogatis writes, these manuals express the belief that "God created men and women with natural sex desires, and those desires are related to male and female characteristics and how men and women should behave toward each other in the household, church, and society."[16] A woman's role as a domestic and nurturing wife and mother is coupled with her proper female sexuality, just as a man's role as protector and provider for the family is intertwined with his proper male sexuality. Through books such as *What Wives Wish Their Husbands Knew about Women*, Dobson has argued that men and women who live their sexuality and their God-given roles in family and society properly provide the best basis for a healthy nation and a stable economy.

Dobson took cues from George Gilder, who wrote one of Dobson's favorite works on marriage and society, 1973's *Sexual Suicide* (updated and revised into *Men and Marriage* in 1986). Gilder had a sociobiological approach to gender roles and linked sexuality and capitalism more directly than Unwin did in the latter's more general theory about sex and civilization. Written in the context of second-wave feminism, Gilder's work strongly criticized calls for gender equality and instead praised clearly defined gender roles as the source of women's power to influence society. The basis of his theory was that men's short-term and aggressive sexuality needs to be curbed and civilized into productive work. He wrote: "The crucial process of civilization is the subordination of male sexual impulses and psychology to long-term horizons of female biology." Put simply, "women domesticate and civilize male nature." According to Gilder, this gives women power over men and a key role in society. But if women refuse to play this role, they have the capacity to turn men into brutes instead of upright citizens. A woman, he contended, "can destroy civilized male identity by merely giving up [her] role."[17] Without a woman to impress and prove their masculinity to, Gilder believed, men would have no imperative to work for future goals, thus undercutting the basis of the American market economy. What women do with their bodies, then, is of particular interest to society. He wrote: "Women control not the economy of the marketplace but the economy of eros: the life force in our society and our lives. What happens in the inner realm of women finally shapes what happens on our social surfaces, determining the level of happiness, energy, creativity, and solidarity in the nation."[18] Sexuality, then, becomes the driving force of society, with women functioning as guardians of order and a healthy economy—as long as they control their erotic powers and curb men's sexuality.

Whereas Gilder left God out of the equation in *Sexual Suicide*, Dobson saw Gilder's explanation as a testimony of God's wisdom. In *Straight Talk to Men and Their Wives*, Dobson wrote:

> Suddenly, we see the beauty of the divine plan. When a man falls in love with a woman, dedicating himself to care for her and protect her, he suddenly becomes the mainstay of social order. Instead of using his energies to pursue his own lusts and desires, he sweats to build a home and save for the future and seek the best job available. His selfish impulses are inhibited. His sexual passions are channeled. He discovers a sense of pride—yes, masculine pride—because he is needed by his wife and children. Everyone benefits from that relationship.[19]

This balance between man and woman not only makes the national economic system work but also guarantees a healthy family economy. In *Bringing Up Boys*, Dobson borrowed imagery from a married couple he counseled who compared their relationship to a car. They described the husband as the family's pedal—the piece that moves the family forward and opens up the family's possibility to invest and expand its financial means—while a woman may best be described as the family's brake—the piece that makes sure that the man does not take risks that are potentially too costly. Together, husband and wife provide a balanced perspective on home economics, which in the end influence the nation's economy.[20] In other words, the gendered nature of both national and family economies is so delicate and balanced that forces that disrupt the balance between man and woman may bring down the entire economic system.

This understanding of sex and society underlies Focus on the Family's opposition to the federal welfare system. Over the years, FotF has attacked welfare as a route to economic destruction and cultural decline. The Great Society, the organization has insisted, was not so great but, rather, a dangerous threat to society. FotF views the growing welfare system in tandem with changing sexual morality. The welfare check, the logic goes, undermines women's need for men, which in turn turns men away from work and makes the economy crumble. Poverty is caused by men's lack of commitment to a family. Only if men and women marry will men have the impetus to work hard.

The concern over welfare is framed in racial terms. Echoing the racial discussion of welfare in the 1980s, FotF has largely portrayed welfare recipients as black and lower class. The black inner-city family functions as a worst-case scenario of what can happen to American society unless the welfare system is ended.[21] Based on this framework, FotF has teamed up with a host of conservative groups to turn government support to families from welfare to so-called marriage promotion since the 1990s.[22] Where the 1965 Moynihan Report described the black family as entangled in pathology, however, FotF has stressed that there is nothing wrong with the black family and community themselves. Rather, the organization frames the inner-city black family as a victim of a welfare system that has run amok, producing generations of matriarchal single-parent black families and black men without a sense of purpose. Moreover, inner-city black communities are simply *ahead* of other groups on the path toward the full disintegration of the family and the American economy.[23] The message is clear: the welfare system's unraveling of the black family could spread to other groups and tear apart the American family once and for all, with the downfall of America as the ultimate result.

The same premise underlies the fear of homosexuality as a potential threat to the entire civilization. Same-sex relationships lack the fundamental tension that underlies a healthy economy, FotF has argued. Hence, homosexuality in particular is a threat to the economy because of the belief that two men living for immediate gratification and uncivilized by women are not likely to be able to invest in the future and have long-term goals.[24] More important, however, is the fact that Dobson insisted, and continues to insist, that same-sex marriage undermines heterosexual marriage. In *Marriage under Fire*, Dobson argues that "we've already seen evidence from the Scandinavian countries that de facto homosexual marriage destroys the real McCoy. These two entities cannot coexist because they represent opposite ends of the universe." The economic and social implications of allowing couples of the same sex to marry may spell the end of the economy and Western civilization as we know it. After all, Dobson notes, this is what happened to all the great cities and empires of the past. Echoing Unwin's theory of sex and civilization throughout history, Dobson tells his readers that Sodom and Gomorrah, ancient Greece, and the Roman Empire were all brought down due to their liberal attitudes toward homosexuality.[25]

Women entering the workplace is yet another phenomenon that may shake the foundations of civilization. If masculine pride stems from working hard to provide for the family, then women bringing home the bacon may also challenge men's sense of commitment to the family. But whereas inner-city black families on welfare and same-sex couples are easy to target as threats against the gendered order undergirding a healthy economy, working mothers are more difficult for FotF to deal with. The organization itself has hired many working mothers; indeed, by the early 1990s, traditional homemakers made up only a minority of its audience.[26] Faced with the economic realities of the age, FotF has had a different take on working mothers than on homosexuality and the welfare system. Instead of warning against possible promiscuity and social collapse, FotF turned to a critique of consumerism and materialism. Women entering the workplace are often framed as a symptom of the conspicuous consumption that FotF deplores in modern America. The advice the organization has offered to couples in order to help them shift from two incomes to one reveals an assumption that a woman's paycheck can go to unnecessary *stuff*: the wife's income is often referred to as the *second* income, as money that may be squandered on extras and frequent vacations and not spent on food, housing, and savings.[27] This critique of consumerism is evident in how FotF believes that children are the losers in this culture. As a *Focus on the Family* magazine writer lamented in an article entitled "New Course for a New Decade," "Many of those who are having children—and could live on one income—are perfectly willing to risk their child to a child-care center in order to protect their career." Women who prioritize careers over mothering, the writer worried, may risk their children's happiness over access to more stuff, and he rhetorically asked, "Is it mere coincidence that the increased need for child care has paralleled society's increased consumerism?"[28]

Dobson and FotF champion a Christian faith in stark contrast to a consumer-driven culture. Dobson has portrayed his family as an ordinary family that has struggled financially and himself as someone who knows that sometimes one has to set aside one's desire for stuff in order to live a godly and family-friendly life. He often recounts the financial stress that he and his wife went through as young parents who had to make the tough decision to have Shirley Dobson quit her job and rely on one income when they discovered that their daughter was unhappy in her day-care center. Their financial stress had concrete consequences: they had to sell their second car in order to make it financially and put food on the table. As Dobson put it, "We sold (and ate) a Volkswagen."[29] Dobson's presentation of himself, then, contrasts starkly with televangelists such as Pat Robertson, Jim Bakker, and Kenneth Hagin, who have pushed what Lauren F. Winner describes as "Christian spirituality spiced with a diffuse cultural Reaganomics," flaunting their fortune and encouraging people not to settle for a Chevy but to pray for a Cadillac instead.[30]

While rejecting the prosperity gospel, Dobson has never stopped reminding his audience to trust in God to look after their needs. In his 1980 *Straight Talk to Men and Their Wives*, Dobson pointed to his own father as a great Christian role model. Dobson recounted growing up in a family that had to make a living on the meager and less-than-steady income his father made as an itinerant evangelist for the Church of the Nazarene. Having parents who had to turn to God for help paying their bills, Dobson explained, taught him to trust in God. He alluded to the prosperity gospel movement, writing, "God never made us rich, as some ministers promise today. But He never let us go hungry."[31] To Dobson, trusting in God is not to pray to God for a Cadillac but, rather, to have faith in a God who provides for his children and who shows his grace through people who share their money with those in need. At times, Dobson has even made statements that sound remarkably similar to the comments of progressive evangelicals such as Jim Wallis, Tony Campolo, and, more recently, Shane Claiborne. Dobson wrote:

> It is interesting to me that Jesus had more to say in the Bible about money than any other subject, which emphasizes the importance of this topic for my family and yours. He made it clear that there is a direct relationship between great riches and spiritual poverty, as we are witnessing in America today. Accordingly, it is my belief that excessive materialism in parents has the power to inflict enormous spiritual damage on our sons and daughters. If they see that we care more about things than people . . . the result is often cynicism and disbelief.[32]

Dobson has repeatedly warned his readers that materialism may take their focus away from what really matters in life and cautioned against finding solace in stuff over finding solace in faith and family. "If you hunger and thirst after great wealth—beware! Satan's objective is half accomplished already: this materialistic passion is paramount in American society," he wrote in *Straight Talk to Men and Their Wives*. To illustrate the godless materialistic worldview, Dobson told this story:

> Someone recently handed me a brochure published by Security Bank in California, which was designed to appeal to a gadget-minded culture. It asked the question, "What do you want to make you happy?" The remaining pages of the pamphlet listed the great sources of joy—a boat, a car, a stove, a television set, and refrigerator. I wonder if the executives at Security Bank actually believe that happiness can be purchased in the form of an appliance or a vehicle? If so, they should review the words of Jesus, who said, "Take heed, and beware of covetousness: for a man's life consisteth not in the abundance of the things which he possesseth." (Luke 12:15).[33]

Collecting stuff here on earth, then, is the opposite of God's plan for one's life and of a spiritually fulfilling existence.

Giving in to materialism may also threaten your children's future. Echoing Dobson's concern over the negative influence of welfare, he and FotF have routinely stressed the importance of teaching children how to manage money and how to work hard to get what they need and want. "Don't saturate the child with excessive materialism," Dobson preached in *Dare to Discipline*. Instead, he argued, children should learn the value of delayed gratification. They should learn the rewards of honest work and experience the joy of working toward a goal. A parent who simply gives his or her child all the toys and the clothes the child desires robs a son or daughter of the satisfaction of accomplishing something or earning something after having longed for it.[34] This, Dobson contended, undermines the very character needed to maintain a comfortable lifestyle in the future and neglects the work ethic needed to keep the economy going. He thus often warned against wealthy and aging parents leaving too large an inheritance to their adult children. Parents may have worked hard in order to make sure that their children have a better life than they had themselves, Dobson wrote, but by giving their children large sums of money they may simply rob them of the chance to "work hard, live frugally, save, build, and produce by the sweat of your brow."[35]

Dobson and FotF have often lamented that American families have become enmeshed in a consumer-driven economy where stuff is given higher priority than faith and family. In the midst of a thriving 1980s American economy and at the height of Reagan-era yuppie culture, a

*Focus on the Family* magazine article encouraged people to "Mak[e] Your Family Number One in '87." People had become more alarmed by a failing economy than by a failing marriage, the writer lamented. At a time when the economy was thriving, FotF juxtaposed the economy with the struggling family: "If half our major businesses failed," the writer argued, "we'd be in a panic. But when half of all first marriages end in divorce, too many of us accept it as some sort of scheduled stopover on the flight to fulfillment."[36] Instead, FotF encouraged people to pay attention to how they treat their families and neighbors. In the same issue of *Focus on the Family* magazine, a short article illustrated how shallow materialism and faithful family values collide and produce contradictory attitudes regarding the people in one's life. Pitting the shallow but successful corporate alpha male against the profound but moderately successful everyday dad, FotF argued that a good man is not "the Ideal Man" that "Madison Avenue, Hollywood and the National Football League have given us." Instead, FotF sided with the "Average Joe." The Average Joe is not a man who could live the fast-paced life of being a "living Ken to every blue-eyed, Barbie-doll woman," who has achieved great success in corporate America, wears stylish clothes, and has a fit and muscular body, good hair, and a beautiful girlfriend with whom he hits the nightclub scene. Instead, the Average Joe puts on his "polyester pants and a starched white shirt" and takes his kids to McDonald's between a Little League game and a church meeting. The author suggested that the empty and fast-paced lifestyle of corporate America—where profit, performance, and consumption outweigh loyalty and commitment—ultimately affects the way people relate to each other. The Ideal Man, the author recounted, eventually left his wife and children for his Barbie-like girlfriend and his Porsche. By contrast, the Average Joe, the real hero, spent his evenings with his wife, helped his friends when they were in need, gave generously to charity, and tucked his kids into bed at night after their daily evening prayer.[37]

Although men are to provide for their families, the ideal man is not a careerist but, rather, a caregiver who resists the pressure to work long hours. Dobson was cast as a role model for men who feel pressured into a stressful career at the expense of their families. He has repeatedly told the story of how he established FotF after having toured the United States, giving his family life seminars and telling parents how to raise their children and husbands how to love their wives while failing to walk the talk in his own life. Eventually, he concluded that being a family expert on the road undermined his role as a family man at home.[38] Dobson is not alone.

Over the years, *Focus on the Family* magazine has presented numerous sentimental stories of men who find themselves trapped in the modern labor market and pressured by the demand for fathers to provide for their families. In a piece titled "I'd Rather Be a Father," a writer flatly stated that "for many men, being a breadwinner isn't enough." This father yearned for time off from work and the chance to spend his evenings with his family. A career-oriented and materialist culture, he noted, does not encourage fathers to prioritize their children, even though they may desperately long for a closer relationship with them. According to this father, society simply does not encourage men to be caring fathers. "Who will congratulate the man who refuses to bring home a full briefcase every night or move every two years or to commute himself to death?" he asked, before aligning himself with fellow frustrated fathers: "Like an underground of resistance recognizing a password, some people close at hand will eagerly whisper their complicity in this common yearning."[39]

Dobson and his organization have often warned against a culture where consuming stuff not only has shaped the lives of American families but has also spilled over into how Americans relate to their own families. On occasion, modern consumer culture functions as a metaphor for how poorly Americans invest in family. As one *Focus on the Family* magazine writer put it: "In a sense, society's continual devaluation of the family is analogous to the way making toys has changed. Long ago, wooden toys were intricately handcrafted with time and care by their maker. As a result, they were functional, creative, and sturdy. Today, plastic toys are punched off assembly lines with little thought given to their quality. As a result, they rarely last more than a week."[40] FotF argued that, just as the short-term, consumer-driven economy cheapens toys, the hectic everyday lives of people in a modern-day society in which they are routinely told that they can "have it all"—a great job, all the new gadgets they want, and a family life—create a consumer-driven lifestyle that cheapens the relationships between husbands and wives, parents and children. By the 1980s, people had gotten used to quick fixes via modern, consumer-driven conveniences such as microwave ovens, drive-through restaurants, and computers and approached their family life in the same way. "We want our dreams to develop as if life were a speedy-print photo lab," a father and writer lamented. Attacking the concept of "quality time," he argued that true quality relies on quantity and presence. Whereas society had turned parents into "assembly-line parents," the readers were encouraged to turn parenting into a handicraft—a time-consuming and hands-on approach to family life that gives credit to the skills and processes involved in instilling values and beliefs in the next generation of Americans.[41]

FotF has suggested that materialism is a leading factor behind high divorce rates among evangelical as well as nonevangelical Americans. In "It's How It Ends that Matters," a guest writer laments in *Focus on the Family* magazine how today's weddings have become consumer-driven events instead of commitment-oriented ceremonies and suggests a correlation between costly weddings and short marriages. According to the writer, "Our culture has shifted from the spiritual and moral to the material and the immediate. We put more emphasis on how the marriage starts, but God is much more interested in how it ends!" In an earlier era, married couples had sparse weddings and managed money well, the writer argues. They knew what mattered and stayed married despite hardships. Today's newlyweds, on the other hand, start off with lavish parties but end up with unsatisfactory marriages. Whereas his parents and his grandparents paid a high price for their wedding vows, in that they knew that they were in it for life, the writer suggests, today's brides and grooms pay a high price for their wedding, in that they spend lots of money on *stuff* but fail to truly commit to their partner.[42]

The lavishness of modern weddings, however, is a minor issue compared with abortion. To FotF, abortion is the ultimate expression of a disrupted sexual order combined with materialism run amok. FotF presents abortion as the epitome of the consumerist attitude to human life and argues that aborted fetuses reveal that America sacrifices unproductive lives on the altars of convenience and careers.[43] Not only that, FotF has on occasion described what is often referred to as the abortion industry as an unscrupulous group of people ready to use aborted fetuses for their own gain. An article from 1988 entitled "Spare Parts from Babies—Are We Going Too Far?" reported that aborted fetuses may be the raw material in an inhumane industry that harvests tissue and spare parts from the fetuses to cure diseases.[44] Aborted fetuses become merely another resource to use and abuse.

A more common scenario, however, is to link abortion to slavery. According to FotF, Planned Parenthood devalues nonwhite Americans and carries on the legacy of slavery by handling black bodies as products from which they can make money. FotF has routinely insisted that Planned Parenthood intentionally sets up clinics in urban neighborhoods with a majority of black inhabitants in order to control or suppress the black population. This, supposedly, is a remnant of the eugenicist ideology that drove Planned Parenthood founder Margaret Sanger in the early 1900s. Not only that, FotF has posited that the family values movement carries on the legacy of the civil rights movement via its defense of the unborn black baby. The organization has teamed up with black antiabortion activists such as Kay Cole James and also promoted *Maafa 21*, a documentary that decries abortion as today's slavery and as part of a conspiracy to retain white control over the black population. For FotF, Planned Parenthood is nothing more than white supremacy packaged with liberal political correctness.[45]

Moreover, according to Dobson, Planned Parenthood is also the leading front for a greedy condom industry—a "safe sex cartel," as he put it—that preys on the bodies of innocent teenagers.[46] The backstory to Dobson's dislike of Planned Parenthood and related organizations stems from his service on the Panel on Teen Pregnancy Prevention under President Ronald Reagan, a panel from which Dobson and two other conservative panel members resigned in protest in 1988. In an interview with the *Chicago Sun-Times*, Dobson accused the rest of the panel of having "substituted their own ideology and course of action—that is, the wholesale distribution of condoms to teenagers supported by so-called value-free advice about sexuality"—instead of providing a plan for how to keep children from becoming sexually active in the first place.[47] Eventually, as Dobson explained in his 1992 *Children at Risk*, he came to understand what really drove the other panelists: money. "The motivation is not difficult to understand," he wrote: "Multiplied millions of dollars are generated each year in direct response to teenage sexual irresponsibility. Kids jumping into bed with each other are supporting entire industries of grateful adults." According to Dobson, "Physicians, nurses, medical suppliers, and bureaucrats" who support comprehensive sex education "owe their livelihood to the killing of unborn babies [and] would prefer that adolescents [not] abstain until marriage."[48] He continued: "Do you really believe they want to kill the goose that lays those golden eggs? . . . Imagine how many jobs would be lost if kids quit playing musical beds with one another!"[49]

The concern over comprehensive sex education is, of course, designed to help keep teenagers chaste. But sex education is also about preserving the American social and economic order. In *Children at Risk*, Dobson counseled against comprehensive sex education programs and, hearkening back to Unwin, asserted that "child and adolescent sexuality are . . . critical to the survival of the Judeo-Christian ethic, and indeed, to the continuance of Western civilization itself." Should America fail to teach her children to save sex for marriage, Dobson feared, the very basis of a healthy economy will disappear. Should children follow the advice of feminists and other secular humanists and reject the requirement of marriage before having sex, then "the culture [will be] deprived of the working, saving, sacrificing, caring, building, growing, reproducing units known as families."[50]

The link between abstinence and a stable society is particularly evident in the way FotF discussed its contribution to building a post-Marxist Central America. In the early 1990s, FotF was contacted by Central American governments that had replaced Marxist regimes and was asked to provide material on teaching sexual abstinence to children in public schools. FotF glowingly reported on this in connection with its twenty-fifth anniversary in 2002, highlighting how, after the moral emptiness left in the wake of Marxism, its sex education programs were providing these people with hope for the future. The future of Central America again looks bright, FotF reported, after decades of communist darkness thanks to chaste teens who, turning their hearts to Christ and saving themselves for marriage, may yet help build—or rebuild—nations gone astray.[51]

The battle continued on the home front. FotF and Dobson's new ministry Family Talk found a new and useful enemy in President Barack Obama. The president's support for comprehensive sex education and gay rights combined with an alleged connection to socialists only added more fuel in the culture wars that made Dobson and FotF heavy hitters in the Christian Right in the 1980s and 1990s. To them, the Cold War is not over but, rather, continues in a different form.[52] FotF has warned that the twin dangers of big government and comprehensive sex education still threaten to undermine America. In August 2013, CitizenLink published a guest commentary entitled "THE LIE 'America Is Just a Capitalistic Imperialistic Bully.' At a Public School Near You." Here, Julaine Appling draws direct lines from her childhood in Cold War America and the fear of missile attacks to the culture wars and the attacks on America in public schools. She writes, "What I didn't know for years later was that the philosophy and worldview of the Castros and Kruschevs of the world had taken firm hold in my homeland—and that those ideas, slowly worked into the fabric of our society, would one day destroy us without a missile ever being fired." Singling out big government and liberal attitudes in sex education, as well as evolution, she asserts that the safety of American children and the very future of America rely on parents taking control of the situation and teaching their children the values of capitalism and regulated sexuality.[53]

Dobson, with his new ministry Family Talk, and FotF, under the new president Jim Daly, continue to combine seemingly contradictory stances on the market. The traditional family, unimpeded by big government, is posited as the basis for a healthy economy, while, at the same time, it is threatened by the very consumer-driven economy that drives modern capitalism. They present themselves as the defenders of the innocent and vulnerable in a harsh and brutal economy. When they place the primary responsibility for securing American capitalism and protesting material-ism in the hands of ordinary husbands and wives, they echo the evan-gelical belief that changed hearts change society from below. The story of the relationship between the evangelical family values movement and Reaganomics and the free market is a complicated one indeed.

## *Notes*

1. "CitizenLink Report: Not Your Business," *CitizenLink*, accessed July 19, 2012, http://www.citizenlink.com/2012/07/17/citizenlink-report-not-your-business/.

2. After having gradually let a new generation take over leadership roles in his organization, Dobson left Focus on the Family for good in 2010. Jim Daly is now the new president and CEO of FotF. Dobson started a new radio ministry together with his son, Ryan James Dobson, called "Family Talk."

3. This was part of a broader trend. For instance, Lisa McGirr investigates the connection between fiscal and social conservatives in the New Right of Oregon County, while Bethany Moreton argues that the world's largest corporation, Wal-Mart, relied on family values to promote an economic ideology of the free market and explores how family values were used to sell more stuff and push an economic agenda. See Lisa McGirr, *Suburban Warriors: The Origins of the New American Right*, Politics and Society in Twentieth-Century America (Princeton: Princeton University Press, 2001); and Bethany Moreton, *To Serve God and Wal-Mart* (Cambridge: Harvard University Press, 2009).

4. Colleen McDannell, *Material Christianity: Religion and Popular Culture in America* (New Haven: Yale University Press, 1995). See also Heather Hendershot, *Shaking the World for Jesus: Media and Conservative Evangelical Culture* (Chicago: University of Chicago Press, 2004); Colleen McDannell, "Beyond Dr. Dobson: Women, Girls, and Focus on the Family," in *Women and Twentieth-Century Protestantism*, ed. Margareth Lamberts Bendroth and Virginia Lieson Brereton (Urbana: University of Illinois Press, 2002); Eileen Luhr, *Witnessing Suburbia: Conservatives and Christian Youth Culture* (Berkeley: University of California Press, 2009); and Dominic Janes, ed., *Shopping for Jesus: Faith in Marketing in the USA* (Washington, D.C.: New Academic Publishing, 2008). For Focus on the Family's relationship to the

evangelical publishing industry, see Dale Buss, *Family Man: The Biography of Dr. James Dobson* (Wheaton: Tyndale House Publishers, 2005), 41–43.

5. See, for example, Thomas Frank, *What's the Matter with Kansas? How Conservatives Won the Heart of America* (New York: Metropolitan Books, 2004); Gary Scott Smith, "Evangelicals Confront Corporate Capitalism: Advertising, Consumerism, Stewardship, and Spirituality, 1880–1930," in *More Money, More Ministry: Money and Evangelicals in North American History*, ed. Larry Eskridge and Mark Noll (Grand Rapids: W. M. Eerdmans Publishing Co., 2000); and Daniel K. Williams, "Evangelical Economics: Reexamining Christian Political Culture from a Market-Based Perspective," *Reviews in American History* 39 (2011), 175–184.

6. This turn to the family for comfort in a materialistic world is not limited to evangelical groups such as Focus on the Family. See, for example, Stephanie Coontz, *The Way We Never Were: American Families and the Nostalgia Trap* (New York: Basic Books, 1992), esp. 93–121.

7. Joseph Daniel Unwin, "Sexual Regulations and Cultural Behavior" (originally published by Oxford University Press, 1935; U.S. reprint, Trona, Calif.: Frank M. Darrow, 1969). Dobson also held a position at Paul Popenoe's American Institute of Family Relations in Los Angeles. It is likely that Popenoe was the one who introduced Dobson to Unwin. On page 2 of the foreword, publisher Frank M. Darrow recounts receiving a letter from Popenoe, who reportedly lamented that "the work of Unwin has been shamefully neglected by most sex educators."

8. Ibid., 15.

9. Dobson first refers to Unwin in James C. Dobson, *Dare to Discipline* (Wheaton: Tyndale House Publishers, 1970; 1976 reprint), 169.

10. James C. Dobson, *What Wives Wish Their Husbands Knew about Women* (Wheaton: Tyndale House Publishers, 1975; 1979 reprint), 97, 96.

11. See, for example, Elaine Tyler May, *Homeward Bound: American Families in the Cold War Era* (New York: Basic Books, 1988); David K. Johnson, *The Lavender Scare: The Cold War Persecution of Gays and Lesbians in the Federal Government* (Chicago: University of Chicago Press, 2004); and Daniel K. Williams, *God's Own Party* (New York: Oxford University Press, 2010).

12. For instance, in 1958, Graham told his audience in San Francisco that "salesmen of immoral literature do more to ruin the nation than communism" (Associated Press, "Billy Graham Cites Need for Less Lust, More Love," *Oscala Star-Banner*, May 15, 1958, 10). He would further explore his views on sexuality as a danger to civilization in his book *World Aflame* (New York: Doubleday, 1965), esp. 18–30.

13. For an overview of the battle over sex education, see Janice Irvine, *Talk about Sex: The Battles over Sex Education in the United States* (Berkeley: University of California Press, 2004), esp. 35–62.

14. See, e.g., David Farber, "Phyllis Schlafly: Domestic Conservatism and Social Order," in *The Rise and Fall of Modern American Conservatism. A Short History* (Princeton: Princeton University Press, 2010), 121.

15. May, *Homeward Bound*, 15.

16. Amy DeRogatis, "What Would Jesus Do? Sexuality and Salvation in Protestant Evangelical Sex Manuals, 1950s to the Present," *Church History: Studies in Christianity and Culture* 74, no. 1 (2005): 113.

17. George Gilder, *Sexual Suicide* (New York: Quadrangle, 1973), 23.

18. Ibid., 25.

19. James C. Dobson, *Straight Talk to Men and Their Wives* (Waco: Word Books Publisher, 1980), 157.

20. James C. Dobson, *Bringing Up Boys: Practical Advice and Encouragement for Those Shaping the Next Generation of Men* (Wheaton: Tyndale House Publishers, 2001), 28.

21. James C. Dobson and Gary Bauer, *Children at Risk: What You Need to Know to Protect Your Family* (Dallas: Word Publishing, 1990; 1994 reprint), 31, 106.

22. See Jean V. Hardisty, "Marriage as a Cure for Poverty? Social Science through a 'Family Values' Lens," in *Marriage Promotion Series, part II* (Somerville: Political Research Associates; and Oakland: Women of Color Resource Center, 2008); and Jean V. Hardisty, "Pushed to the Altar: The Right Wing Roots of Marriage Promotion," in *Marriage Promotion Series, part I* (Somerville: Political Research Associates; and Oakland: Women of Color Resource Center, 2008).

23. Jim Daly, "Black and White Problems," *Focus on the Family*, accessed January 31, 2011, http://www.focusonlinecommunities.com/blogs/Finding_Home/tags/bob.

24. Focus on the Family, "The Homosexual Agenda: What You Can Do," File: Focus on the Family, 1995–1998, Political Research Associates Archives, Somerville, 26; James C. Dobson, *Marriage under Fire: Why We Must Win This Battle* (Sisters, Ore.: Moltnomah Publishers, 2004), 53–56.

25. Dobson, *Marriage under Fire*, 47; see also 47–53.

26. Corwin Smidt, Lyman Kellstedt, John Green, and James Guth, "The Characteristics of Christian Political Activists: An Interest Group Analysis," in *Christian Political Activism at the Crossroads*, ed. William R. Stevenson Jr. (Lanham, Md.: University Press of America, 1994). Focus on the Family's audience has followed a general trend among evangelicals. A handful of ethnographic surveys suggest that evangelical women/mothers work outside the home at the same rate as nonevangelical mothers despite maintaining that a woman is called to be domestic. See Judith Stacey, *Brave New Families: Stories of Domestic Upheaval in Late Twentieth Century America* (New York: Basic Books, 1991); Christel J. Manning, *God Gave Us the Right: Conservative Catholic, Evangelical Protestant, and Orthodox Jewish Women Grapple with Feminism* (New Brunswick, N.J.: Rutgers University Press, 1999); and Brenda

E. Brasher, *Godly Women: Fundamentalism and Female Power* (New Brunswick, N.J.: Rutgers University Press, 1998).

27. See, for example, Larry Burkett, "Women Leaving the Workplace," *Focus on the Family*, March 1996, 11. However, this is not always the case. FotF has also recognized that sometimes a second income is necessary. In order for women to make an income without leaving the children during the day, FotF has regularly suggested working from home. See, for instance, Donna Partow, "Home-Based Business: Who Has Time for a Second Income?" *Focus on the Family*, June 1992, 5.

28. Bob Welch, "New Course for a New Decade," *Focus on the Family with Dr. James C. Dobson*, January 1990, 8.

29. Rolf Zettersten, *Dr. Dobson: Turning Hearts toward Home: The Life and Principles of America's Family Advocate* (Dallas: Word Publishing Group, 1989), 80.

30. Lauren F. Winner, "Reaganizing Religion: Changing Political and Cultural Norms among Evangelicals in Ronald Reagan's America," in *Living in the Eighties*, ed. Gil Troy and Vincent J. Cannato (Oxford: Oxford University Press, 2009), 191–192.

31. Dobson, *Straight Talk to Men and Their Wives*, 145. The basic message and the stories are repeated in updated versions of the book published as *Straight Talk to Men* (Carol Stream: Tyndale, 2003).

32. Dobson, *Straight Talk to Men and Their Wives*, 146.

33. Ibid., 144.

34. Dobson, *Dare to Discipline*, 43–44.

35. James C. Dobson, *Solid Answers: America's Foremost Family Counselor Responds to Tough Questions Facing Today's Families* (Wheaton: Tyndale House Publishers, 1997), 430.

36. Robert S. Welch, "Making Your Family Number One in '87," *Focus on the Family*, January 1987, 2–4.

37. Dean A. Ohlman, "The Ideal Man," *Focus on the Family*, January 1987, 5.

38. Zettersten, *Dr. Dobson*, 92–103; and Buss, *Family Man*, 57–59.

39. Eliot A. Daley, "I'd Rather Be a Father," *Focus on the Family*, June 1985, 7. Dobson and other fathers fit with what Bradford W. Wilcox describes as "soft patriarchs" in *Soft Patriarchs, New Men: How Christianity Shapes Fathers and Husbands*, ed. Alan Wolfe, Morality and Society Series (Chicago: University of Chicago Press, 2004).

40. Welch, "Making Your Family Number One in '87," 4.

41. Ibid.

42. William P. Farley, "It's How It Ends that Matters," *Focus on the Family*, February 2002, 14–15.

43. See also generally Susan Friend Harding, *The Book of Jerry Falwell: Fundamentalist Language and Politics* (Princeton: Princeton University Press, 2000); and Linda Kintz, *Between Jesus and the Market: Emotions that Matter in Right-Wing America* (Durham, N.C.: Duke University Press, 1997).

44. Dave Andrusko, "Spare Parts from Babies—Are We Going Too Far?" *Focus on the Family*, June 1988, 10–11.

45. Karla Dial, "Endangered Species," *CitizenLink*, accessed August 30, 2013, http://www.citizenlink.com/2010/06/01/citizenlink-endangered-species/.

46. James C. Dobson, "Dobson's Monthly Newsletter: Good News about the Family," October 1998, accessed February 2, 2010, http://www2.focusonthe-family.com/docstudy/newsletters/A000000320.cfm. FotF took down all of Dobson's newsletters when he left the organization.

47. "3 Quit Panel on Teen Pregnancy in Protest," *Chicago Sun-Times*, March 4, 1988, 6.

48. Dobson and Bauer, *Children at Risk*, 13.

49. Ibid., 14.

50. Ibid., 58.

51. Focus on the Family, *Focus on the Family: Celebrating Twenty-five Years of God's Faithfulness* (Colorado Springs: Focus on the Family, 2002), 262–265.

52. For claims about Obama's socialist bent, see, e.g., James Dobson, "Churchill and Obama Considered," *Family Talk Newsletter*, accessed August 30, 2013, http://drjamesdobson.org/about/commentaries/archives/2010-newsletters/Churchill_Obama_Considered. For examples of CitizenLink's recent attacks on Planned Parenthood, see, e.g., Carrie Gordon Earll, "Dig Deeper: A Case to Defund Planned Parenthood," *CitizenLink*, March 10, 2011, updated March 16, 2011, accessed August 30, 2013, http://www.citizenlink.com/2011/03/10/a-case-to-defund-planned-parenthood/?skip_splash=1. For CitizenLink's criticism of Obama's relationship to Planned Parenthood, see, e.g., Bethany Monk, "Obama Announces Planned Parenthood Support," *CitizenLink*, April 29, 2013, accessed August 30, 2013, http://www.citizenlink.com/2013/04/29/obama-announces-planned-parenthood-support/.

53. Julaine Appling, "Commentary: THE LIE 'America Is Just a Capitalistic Imperialistic Bully.' At a Public School Near You," *CitizenLink*, August 29, 2013, accessed August 30, 2013, http://www.citizenlink.com/2013/08/29/commentary-the-lie-america-is-just-a-capitalistic-imperialistic-bully-at-a-public-school-news-you/.

# PART THREE

*Religious Book Markets*

5

# The Commodification of
# William James

## THE BOOK BUSINESS AND THE RISE OF
## LIBERAL SPIRITUALITY IN THE
## TWENTIETH-CENTURY UNITED STATES

*Matthew S. Hedstrom*

"THERE IS THIS motif that you can't assume things are working, or that institutions are taking care of us," Clayton Carlson, the founding publisher and editor-in-chief of HarperSanFrancisco (HarperSF), told the *San Francisco Chronicle* in 1991. According to Carlson, this well-documented loss of faith in American institutions—loss of faith in government, schools, and churches dating from at least the 1960s and 1970s—formed the essential context for understanding religious publishing (his business) and American religion more generally in the late twentieth century.[1]

In short, Carlson thought that as faith in institutions waned, faith in the marketplace waxed. HarperSF's sales seemed to bear this out: in 1977, when Carlson led a group of thirteen staffers from Harper and Rowe's religion department in New York to their new office on the West Coast, the new press grossed $3 million; by 1991, HarperSF's revenues had grown nearly twelvefold to $35 million.[2] This small group of pioneers, charged with a mission to reinvent the religious publishing arm of one of America's historic firms, grew alongside its sales figures, reaching ninety by 1991. The modes of religious life rooted in churches, synagogues, parishes, and denominations may have suffered in the late twentieth century, but religious practices tied to American consumerism thrived, as Carlson saw firsthand. This observation about the critical differences between institutional religion and a free-floating, highly individualized form of religiosity enacted in consumption—a story well told by examining religious publishing—helps us make sense of some of the key, and often misunderstood, developments in twentieth-century U.S. religious history.[3]

For decades, the main story of American religion has been the apparent growth in numbers and power of conservative evangelicalism and the parallel demographic and political decline of liberal Protestantism. What in mid-century had been called the "mainline" or the Protestant "establishment"—not merely or even primarily because of sheer numbers but even more because of the political influence and cultural capital of its adherents and their institutions—was by the 1970s being eclipsed by the rising religious Right. Fueled by the backlash against feminism, civil rights, and legalized abortion, and by the growing importance of the Sunbelt in American economic and political life, conservative evangelicalism captured the nation's political and media attention, and the Republican Party, and held it for three decades.[4]

The story of evangelical success and mainline decline is one that may best be told through a traditional historical focus on ecclesiastical and political institutions. Simply put, the parallel universe of media groups and educational, parachurch, and political organizations that evangelicals built over the first half of the twentieth century, when they were in the cultural wilderness, proved more capable of responding to the myriad transformations of the 1960s, 1970s, and 1980s than did the ossified, "established" institutions of mainliners. Socially shunned by liberal elites and theologically committed to being "in but not of the world," evangelicals valued strong community boundaries and used their robust ecclesial infrastructure and new political operations such as the Moral Majority and the Christian Coalition to maintain clear identities and build political clout. In contrast, mainline churches and denominations, socially and culturally tied to power in mid-century, suffered from the same loss of authority as the government and secular universities did in the wake of Vietnam, Watergate, and the civil rights revolutions. As the mainline receded, evangelicals were ready and able to fill the vacuum.

This commonplace narrative of American religious history is true, and important, but incomplete. Its focus on the nexus of church and politics misses another critical dynamic, the dynamic of consumerism and culture—the dynamic that Carlson identified. Examining consumerism and culture foregrounds religious sensibilities and the mechanisms by which they are produced and propagated, rather than religious affiliations and their political consequences. To study consumerism and culture one must first bear in mind that culture and politics can never be fully disentangled, nor can church life and consumerism. Yet such a shift in focus does offer helpful new vantage points from which to view American religious life in the twentieth century. In addition, one must recognize that culture operates through institutions every bit as real as churches and political parties. In this sense, Carlson's opening observation was not quite accurate; Americans' loss of faith in institutions did not strike all institutions equally. Examining culture adequately, in fact, demands careful attention to its institutions, especially its market institutions, and the institutions of consumerism flourished even as those of church and denomination struggled in the late twentieth century. The story of religious publishing at Harper's, the subject of this essay, is the story of one such critically important cultural-religious institution.

In light of these observations, the central question of this essay becomes: how do our narratives of twentieth-century religious history change when we shift our focus from the institutions of churches and politics to the institutions of markets and culture? A deeper look at the religious publishing ventures of Harper's reveals surprising answers. Rather than the political ascendancy of conservative evangelicalism, this shift in focus helps us track the cultural ascendancy of liberal religion. Rather than the politicization of Billy Graham and Jerry Falwell, in other words, the story becomes the commodification of William James.

# *I*

Clayton Carlson brought Harper's religion department to San Francisco because he presciently saw the trends away from institutional religion and toward market-based innovation developing back in the 1960s and 1970s. Inspired in part by the "death of God" theology that had a brief vogue in the 1960s—a vogue captured in Harvard theologian Harvey Cox's surprise 1965 bestseller *The Secular City* and the notorious "Is God Dead?" cover story in the April 8, 1966, issue of *Time* magazine—Carlson began thinking about ways to reconceive religious publishing after the decline of mainline Protestantism. He found his formula in California. "You pick it, it's here," Carlson noted of California. "It's a traditionless culture." That freedom became a model: "People used to associate religious publishing with propaganda or an ideological party line. But we are not an advocacy publisher. . . . We try to choose the best and healthiest examples from each [worldview] and let the reader decide." Such an approach—an approach rooted in Emersonian spirituality and the logics of consumerism—perfectly matched the religious Wild West of San Francisco. According to the recollections of Carlson's associates from these years, his concerns about the enervation of traditional religion were alleviated by the vitality he witnessed in California. At the Esalen Institute in Big Sur, south of San Francisco, at the San Francisco Zen Center, and in the countless other examples of religious innovation and experimentation happening nearby, Carlson saw the future of religion, and religious publishing, in America.[5] "Stable cultures think California is so amorphous and frivolous," Carlson observed. But such openness, and even frivolity, suited the brave new world of postchurch religion: "In that sense, moving here has worked to our advantage."[6]

The success of Carlson's model for religious publishing may, at first blush, come as a surprise. After all, churches had traditionally been allies, even the best customers, of religious publishers. Yet Harper's, over many decades, had fashioned an ideology tailored to meet the religious demands of an increasingly diversified consumer culture. In the late twentieth century, as market-derived modes of thought and action increasingly replaced older collective norms embedded in government, communities, and churches, Harper's was ready. Carlson often jokingly referred to this ideology with the motto "We publish books to offend everyone," but framed the HarperSF outlook more positively in his interview with the *Chronicle*. "When a person asks primal questions and finds a book that promises some sort of insight, that's our reader," he observed. The move to San Francisco allowed the firm to explore as many avenues of insight as possible, from Christianity to Asian religions to psychological, feminist, and eco-spiritualities. Yet "the baseline, the common thing," Carlson concluded, summarizing the one idea that tied together the vast diversity of the company's publishing—and by implication American religion itself— "is the universal quest."[7]

The universal quest is a notion with powerful resonances and associations. Packed into this simple idea lie the dreams of religious utopians and imperialists, the hopes of the naive and the visionary. Many religions, of course, have proclaimed one universal God and one universal Truth—Judaism, Christianity, and Islam most notably. But the idea of the universal *quest* in the sense that Carlson proclaimed is a modern idea and far from universal. The now-widespread notion that all religions and all human beings are, at root, seekers after the divine, and that the many paths all point to the same destination, stems from a particular nineteenth-century cultural moment. Captured perhaps most evocatively in an American vernacular by Emerson's spirit of self-reliance and Whitman's image of the open road, the universal quest had become the central unifying idea among liberal religious Americans by the late nineteenth century.[8] William James, in his landmark *The Varieties of Religious Experience* (1902), gave this idea its most influential platform. James deployed the tools of modern science and philosophy to derive a purportedly universal taxonomy of the religious life. That modern scholars of religion have unmasked the narrowly liberal and Protestant—in other words, parochial and particular—presuppositions of Jamesian universalism should not distract from the powerful influence these ideas have had across the twentieth century and on into the twenty-first. In fact, the Protestant parochialism of James's science of religion accounted for much of its natural appeal to a largely Protestant American public, while its scientific universalism provided that public with the conceptual framework for its post-Protestant future.

The liberal religious sensibilities encapsulated in the notion of the universal quest now pervade American culture. Such liberal religious sensibilities appear in two related forms. The first is spiritual cosmopolitanism—a *religious* interest in *religious* others, from Jews doing yoga to Presbyterians reading the Dalai Lama and much more. The second is a ready incorporation of scientific modes of thought into religious outlooks, most especially through psychologically informed spirituality. Historian David Hollinger employs the terms *demographic diversification* and *cognitive demystification* to describe the processes by which nineteenth- and twentieth-century Americans became increasingly cosmopolitan and scientific as they accommodated their faith to a changing world. These processes certainly resulted in many individual and corporate instances of what might properly be called secularization, but also in the new forms of religious faith and practice captured by the term *post-Protestant*.[9] The emerging cosmopolitan and scientific religious orientations of the twentieth century, whether Protestant or post-Protestant, arose from the liberal accommodation to modernity and ambition to speak in a universal idiom.

Studies from the Pew Forum on Religion and Public Life and other venues demonstrate a modest rise in irreligion early in the twenty-first century but, even more tellingly, a widespread willingness to mix and match religious beliefs.[10] Sociologist Christian Smith, in his study of young adults published in 2009, finds that majorities agree with the propositions "many religions may be true," it is "okay to pick and choose religious beliefs without having to accept teachings of faith as a whole," and "it is okay to practice religions besides [one's] own."[11] According to Smith, these modern developments correspond to the very institutional decline Clayton Carlson identified. Echoing fellow sociologist Jay Demerath, Smith observes, "Liberal Protestantism's organizational decline has been accompanied by and is in part arguably the consequence of the fact that liberal Protestantism has won a decisive, larger cultural victory."[12] No place over the course of the twentieth century offers a better window into the mechanism by which this happened—the nexus of consumerism and culture through which this gospel of the universal quest spread—than Harper's religious publishing enterprise. Indeed, a deeper look into the history of Harper's reveals that Carlson's move to California in the 1970s, and his program to publish books "to offend everyone," stands at the apex of decades of efforts to craft a religious outlook suited for commercial success. In order to understand the spirituality of the baby boomers and their twenty-first-century children and grandchildren, we must go back to the 1920s, 1930s, and 1940s, when modern religious publishing began at Harper's.

## *II*

Mary Rose Himler, an executive with the Bobbs-Merrill publishing house, captured the challenges facing religious publishing in the mid-1920s. "Most religious books never reach the great bulk of the reading public," she declared, "because most religious books are bigoted and prejudiced, because a great many of them can be classified as textbooks for divinity students. Meanwhile, the American public knows exactly what it wants, whether it be automobiles, chewing gum or books and it buys that which gives it the most enjoyment, the better inspiration, the more interesting experience."[13] Religious publishing had long been dominated by the evangelistic and pastoral concerns of specific denominations and their publishing arms, yet the 1920s witnessed dramatic changes. The interwar years, according to historian Richard Wightman Fox, were "the critical decades in the consolidation of modern American consumer society," and in these years of consumerist ascendancy modern religious publishing was born as well. Aware of the psychic and spiritual dislocations wrought by the war, the theological rancor of the modernist–fundamentalist controversies, mass culture, increasing consumerism, and the profusion of new scientific and theological knowledge, publishing and religious leaders worked together to craft new structures for the promotion of religious reading. They devised religious book clubs, curated book lists for libraries, organized a religious book week and other reading campaigns, and, perhaps most critically, launched new publishing ventures designed to bring Jamesian liberalism to the mass market.[14]

In response, the sales of religious nonfiction skyrocketed in the late 1920s. What had been the sixth-best-selling genre in 1900 became the second best-selling by 1928, behind only adult fiction, ahead of biography, history, poetry, and even juvenile literature. Sales of new religious titles increased steadily enough by the mid-1920s that book industry insiders announced the advent of "a decided religious renaissance."[15] "Religion and religious books," noted *Publishers' Weekly* in 1927, had quickly become "a very live topic."[16] Publishers and booksellers looked at the modernization and professionalization of the publishing industry, in particular at the sophisticated marketing of the new general-trade religious literature, and recognized an important shift in the fundamentals of their business. According to one measure, the portion of total book sales accounted for by religious books increased 34 percent from 1925 to 1929 alone.[17]

Then came the Crash. In October 1929, when the bottom fell out of the stock market, and then in the coming months and years as the economic crisis metastasized into the Great Depression, the sense of jubilant optimism surrounding religion and religious books crashed as well. Commentators soon began to speak and write of a "religious depression" that corresponded with the economic depression, and the business of buying and selling books, including religious books, suffered greatly. Total book sales dropped from 219,276,000 in 1927 to 197,259,000 in 1937, but within this drop religious books suffered particularly severe losses: as a percentage of total books sold, religious books declined by 45 percent in the years from 1931 to 1935.[18] This sharp decline occurred not simply as a function of the generally dismal economic climate, since religious books suffered a significantly greater drop in sales than other kinds of books. Rather, the sales of mass-market religious books plummeted as part of the broader fate of liberal institutional Protestantism in these years.[19]

When sociologists Robert and Helen Lynd returned to Muncie, Indiana, in the mid-1930s to follow up on their pioneering *Middletown* study of the previous decade, they found that the congregations of the mainline churches seemed "older than formerly," perhaps because "sermon topics in 1935 are interchangeable with those of a decade ago."[20] In spite of a resurgent Social Gospel, institutional liberal Protestantism had failed to mount an adequate response to the national emergency. As one informant in the Lynds' study remarked, "The depression has brought a resurgence of earnest religious fundamentalism among the weaker working-class sects . . . but the uptown churches have seen little similar revival of interest."[21] The long-term, historic decline in the Protestant mainline—the decline that prompted Clayton Carlson to reinvent Harper's religion department in California—had its roots in the dark days of the 1930s, as did the consumerist pathway to HarperSF's post-Protestant success.

The crisis in the churches largely accounts for the drop in the overall sales of religious books, since the largest sectors of religious publishing consisted of texts for clergy and devotional literature for the laity. Yet the Depression cut deeper than economics, deeper even than institutional religion—and here, paradoxically, was hope for religious publishing. In its most intimate manifestations, in the hearts and minds of men and women, the crisis of the 1930s furthered the reach of the psychological and cosmopolitan spirituality of Jamesian liberalism. The Depression, remarked journalist and social historian Frederick Lewis Allen, "marked millions of people—inwardly—for the rest of their lives." Behind the raw numbers measuring joblessness and foreclosures "were failure and defeat and want visiting the energetic along with the feckless, the able along with the unable, the virtuous along with the irresponsible."[22] While many contemporary observers, such as the informants of Helen and Robert Lynd, saw the churches as offering little to those in spiritual as well as economic crisis, those hurting in the Depression years were not without recourse. The modern literature of soul care that was marketed so aggressively in the 1920s found a steady audience among the American middle class of the 1930s. Indeed, although the liberal Protestant establishment began its period of long decline in these years, liberal spirituality continued to rise. Formal liberal religious theology in prominent pulpits and seminary professorships gave way in many places to the emerging neo-orthodoxy, yet popular religious explorations at the margins of liberal Protestantism continued to flourish.

Beginning in the mid- and late 1920s, as the publishing industry professionalized and modern religious literature rose in prominence, a number of prominent New York general-trade presses restructured their religious publishing practices, frequently by establishing specialized religion departments, and emerged as key players in this new field. These houses, especially Harper & Brothers, Scribner's, and Macmillan, embraced the marketplace with renewed vigor in the late 1920s and 1930s and, despite their deep connections to institutional Protestantism, recast their businesses in more explicitly commercial terms. As the Depression undercut faith in the mainline churches, these modern religious publishing houses continued to provide a steady stream of books, many reflecting traditional Protestantism but many others emphasizing newer spiritual vocabularies. All told, the business of religious books from the Depression years forward greatly accelerated the already significant popular trend toward liberal religious sensibilities.[23]

The most significant of the new religion departments established in the late 1920s was at Harper & Brothers. When the publisher launched its religion department in late 1926, it turned first to Walter S. Lewis to guide its operations. Lewis had managed the Book Department of the Presbyterian Board of Publication for ten years and had been active in the American Booksellers Association. Harper & Brothers was one of the esteemed New York houses, dating back to 1817, and for much of the nineteenth century was perhaps the nation's leading publisher of books and magazines. For many decades, each succeeding Harper generation that ran the family firm consisted of remarkably devout Methodists and shrewd businessmen, and the firm flourished. This record of prosperity persisted into the 1890s, when a national economic downturn and uncharacteristic mismanagement required a bailout from J. P. Morgan and ultimately the imposition of outside control. Harper's subsequently struggled through the early years of the twentieth century, but by the mid-1920s a regime of strict financial discipline and the hiring of a new generation of young, professional-minded executives set the firm back on a promising course, finally clear of debt. The new direction featured a program of professionalization and specialization that resulted in a textbook department and a business book department, and with the renaissance in religious books in the 1920s the firm decided to enter that expanding field as well. Harper's turned to Lewis, who had a solid track record in the field, and eagerly launched its foray into religious books.

In a published statement summarizing why Harper's had entered the field of religious books, the firm noted, "the last ten years have witnessed a widely-recognized increase in the demand for this type of literature" and promised to "devote all possible energy, discrimination and enterprise in

promoting the publication and distribution of these books with the intention of making the new department an important part of their general
business."[24] The announcement noted the passionate interest in religious
matters due to the simmering modernist–fundamentalist controversies
and the significant emergence of radio preaching as factors that seemed
to drive readers to the bookstores in increasing numbers. Harper's lured
Lewis with the intention to produce "outstanding books of a religious, ethical, and theological character," but Lewis was unable to see that agenda
develop in any significant way. He died in February 1928, just over a year
after his appointment as the founding head of the department. In April,
Harper's hired the young Eugene Exman as his replacement.

Exman ran the religion department at the venerable New York publishing house Harper & Brothers from 1928, just over a year after the
department was established, until his retirement in 1965, a period during
which Harper's became a leading trade publisher—perhaps the leader—
in the field of religion. The key challenge Exman faced early in his tenure
was the crisis of the Depression. He saw the need to tap into the existing market provided by churches whenever possible, but ultimately his
vision was to disentangle religious books from theological books, so that
religious books might continue to sell even as the churches, and books
aimed at church workers, faltered. Though an active church member
himself, Exman recognized, as he put it, that "vast numbers of persons
find little satisfaction in the activities and rituals of ecclesiastical bodies,
yet are intelligently interested in religion."[25] The future of modern religious books, to Exman, lay with those, in his words, "who want above all
else to be intellectually honest, who, weary of their own conceit, search
for reality wherever it may be found."[26] As many churches struggled during the depths of the Depression, Exman forged the religious sensibility
that would guide Harper's to success amid the collapse of the mainline
decades later.

Exman's personal story closely tracks the larger story of liberal
Protestantism, and liberal religion more broadly, over the middle decades
of the twentieth century and provided him with a unique opportunity to
guide Harper's into its post-Protestant future. A bookish University of
Chicago Divinity School graduate and member of the famed Riverside
Church in New York his entire adult life, Exman became a seeker, a spiritual explorer and experimenter, in midlife. His tale shows how changes
that were happening in the larger intellectual and religious culture of the
period operated in conjunction with the transforming realities of the book

business to facilitate the dissemination and popularization of Jamesian religious liberalism in the twentieth century. His expansive spiritual interests and penchant for personal awakenings, so evident in his midlife transformation, had deep roots. At seventeen, Exman had what he later termed a "mystical experience."[27] Reflecting back on this and other spiritual awakenings in his life, Exman described "a heightening of reality; a higher sense of unity and a more profound sense of being, a sense of order and of beauty."[28] This early moment of transcendent clarity obviously impressed Exman greatly, as it became the touchstone against which he measured similar experiences nearly forty years later.

Exman's religious journey followed an ordinary enough path when, in 1922, at age twenty-two, he ventured to the Divinity School at the University of Chicago. "I remember saying," he wrote later in life, "after that adolescent experience, that I would never need to doubt God again," but "the unity of knowledge I had then was not intellectually retentive." The rigorous environment of the Divinity School at Chicago, the leading center of rationalized liberal theology in the country, brought Exman to a period of doubt.[29] "Living in a secular, cynical society, as I did as a graduate student in Chicago," he later recalled, "I swung completely away from this belief" in God and the unity of all things, beliefs that had seemed so certain only a few years earlier.[30]

Exman arrived at Harper's deeply formed by these early experiences. His personal story meshed with the larger story of liberal religion and print culture in the interwar period, allowing him to use his own experiences to craft a successful vision for the religion department at Harper's. Exman guided the department according to a simple mission statement, printed on the back of each catalog the department produced: "to publish books that represent important religious groupings, express well-articulated thought, combine intellectual competence and felicitous style, add to the wealth of religious literature irrespective of creedal origin, and aid the cause of religion without proselyting for any particular sect."[31] The motto certainly made good business sense, allowing Exman and Harper's to find and develop books that would sell "irrespective of creedal origin"—a more genteel version of Clayton Carlson's later aim "to offend everyone"—but the mission of Exman's department also reflected his personal commitment to "search for reality wherever it may be found." This combination of good business sense and an earnest "search for reality" drove his openness to the best-selling authors who made Harper's such a success in the bleak 1930s, when it published huge bestsellers from mainstream liberals such as Harry Emerson Fosdick as well as from eclectically metaphysical writers such as Emmet Fox and Glenn Clark.

Exman's desire to "aid the cause of religion without proselyting for any particular sect" resulted in an openness to spiritual innovation that served the department well in the mass marketplace. As it turns out, Eugene Exman was soon to become the living embodiment of that culture. In early January 1941, the forty-year-old Exman wrote to one of his authors about a forthcoming book: "I've been moved much by what you have written here; I've been [led] recently to enlarge my own spirituality so you were speaking not to an editor, perhaps, as much as to a fellow seeker."[32] From the early 1940s onward, Exman ventured far and wide in cultivation of this enlarged spirituality. Along with the British expat Gerald Heard—who taught a mix of liberal Protestantism, Vedanta-inspired meditation, and psychological science—and the writer Aldous Huxley, Exman helped establish Trabuco College, a meditation center in Southern California. Trabuco was short-lived—it did not survive the 1940s—but it was a truly remarkable site of California-style innovation while it lasted, a direct inspiration for the openness Carlson would later find at Esalen. The mystic and popular comparative religionist Huston Smith spent time at Trabuco, as did the Indian theosophist Krishanmurti, along with Huxley and Heard and a number of World War II conscientious objectors. Each of these figures published significant works with Exman at Harper's, but especially notable are Smith's *The Religions of Man* and Huxley's *The Perennial Philosophy*. These books were national bestsellers and introduced generations of Americans to the universal quest, the idea of the unity of all religions found in mystical experience. Exman summarized the meaning of Trabuco in tellingly Jamesian terms, explaining that there he found a "spiritual synthesis of the scientists, the psychologists, and the mystics."[33] This formulation captured Exman's ambitions both for himself and for his religion department at Harper's.

In the late 1950s, Exman embarked on his most exotic spiritual adventure, participation in a study of the spiritual significance of LSD. Aldous Huxley and others at the time were just beginning their inquiries into LSD, and Exman partook in these experiments, led by Huxley, Heard, and Bill Wilson, the founder of Alcoholics Anonymous, whom Exman had known since the 1930s, when he advised Wilson on the publication of the Big Book of Alcoholics Anonymous. Exman later told an international conference on parapsychology and pharmacology that his experience with LSD induced the strong sense that his "personality had to be crucified," a loss of ego he found painful and frightening yet which led, "at the height of the experience," to the insight that he "could not have salvation alone."[34] He concluded, however, that while it did provide "an empirical basis on which to go to people who are skeptical . . . we should not by any means think that this is something we can discuss openly," for "whether you have the mystical experience, non-induced by the drug, or the experience of spiritual reality induced by the drug, you are open to suspicion."[35] Rather than through LSD, then, Exman hoped for the transformation of American churches and religious life through mystical experience more broadly understood. "We have many orthodox people in theology," he wrote: "This is my field. I know something about the organized church, and some of my best friends are theologians. I know how awfully hard it is for them to break the shell of orthodoxy. They verbalize, they intellectualize, and this is the spiritual experience, paradoxically, that they are talking about."[36] Exman found the drug spiritually instructive but ultimately limiting and did not continue to pursue the divine through psychedelics; Smith reached a similar conclusion, and Huxley, too, urged caution, while the acid evangelists Timothy Leary and Richard Alpert merrily pressed on. But Exman never lost his faith in the centrality of mystical experience to the life of the spirit. In 1960 he wrote an essay, "Search for Meaning," in which he continued the same focus on depth psychology, mystical ways of knowing and experiencing the divine, and the search for God beyond any destination as the very essence of what it means to be human.[37] Seen against this backdrop, the decision of Clayton Carlson to move the Harper's religion department to San Francisco seems less like a revolution and more like an act of filial piety.[38]

Alongside these ever-expanding spiritual explorations, Exman carried on his highly successful work in the religion department at Harper's. He certainly brought a stellar group of writers into the Harper's fold.[39] In addition to Fosdick, Fox, Clark, Heard, Huxley, and Smith, the theologians H. Richard Niebuhr, Paul Tillich, Dietrich Bonhoeffer, Karl Barth, and Rudolf Bultmann were all Exman authors in the 1930s, 1940s, and 1950s, as were Catholic Worker founder Dorothy Day, African American mystic Howard Thurman, and Martin Luther King Jr. Exman's personal story, and the story of his religion department at Harper's, thus brought together the theological and ethical concerns of mainline Protestantism with an adventurous, boundary-crossing, psychologically informed spiritual cosmopolitanism.

Exman's vision for the religion department at Harper's—to divorce the "religious" from the "theological," and most certainly from the "ecclesiastical," and to move beyond the creedal concerns of denominational houses and, instead, promote a free-flowing "search for reality"—was made possible by the burgeoning consumer culture of post–World War I America. Certainly, religion and the market had a deep, shared history in the United States, but those in the book business had traditionally viewed their product as unique and even sacred, not a commodity to be hawked like soap.[40] But this genteel concern for the sacredness of book culture began to break down amid the consumerist triumphalism of the 1920s. The increased willingness to treat the book, including the religious book, as but one more commodity in a consumer culture provided the critical context for Exman's work at Harper's.

As radical as the changes in religious publishing were in the 1920s, however, the commodification of religious reading that occurred must not be seen as a sign of secularization. While consumerist sensibilities certainly eroded the communal norms essential to vital institutional religion, in the broader arena of culture, consumerism and religion made an easy accommodation. In a 1921 editorial entitled "The Habit of Reading," Rufus Jones, a Quaker, argued, in fact, that proper religious reading demanded participation in the consumer marketplace. "It is not enough to read capriciously and sporadically, to borrow a book occasionally and then have done with it," he argued: "I am pleading for the ownership of books and for *the cultivation of the habit of reading*." Proper religious reading, for Jones, meant reading in a very specific manner. "The true and effective way to read an illuminating book," he counseled, "is to read it, pencil in hand, to mark cardinal passages, to make notes, and to digest the message which the book contributes." Jones then added, to make sure his point was clear: "That means that the book ought, if possible, to be owned rather than borrowed." One must own religious books because when reading religiously, in his words, "one needs to go back again and again to a good book, to reread marked passages, and to become literally possessed of it."[41] A good book can possess us, according to Jones, only if we first possess it.

By the end of the decade religious publishers were fully on board. "Man to man," declared Charles Ferguson, former head of the Religious Books Department at Doubleday, Doran, in a speech to his fellow bookmen and -women in 1930, "there is reward on earth for some book-seller or group of booksellers who will take religious books seriously and make a normal, intelligent effort to handle them on a sound, commercial basis." "I believe," he added, "with all the fervor of a salesman that there is money in religious books, just as there is in stories of crime and sto-ries of sex."[42] Though aware of the lingering fear of some in the trade of treating their product as just another commodity—and aware, as well, of the parallel notion from many booksellers that popular religious texts were beneath the intellectual and aesthetic standards of serious book cul-ture—Ferguson would have none of it. "I often hear urged the irrelevant objection that religious books are full of piffle," he proclaimed: "What of it, when books on philosophy, self-improvement, the care and feeding of dogs, and contract bridge are open to the same criticism? . . . I don't know why it is that a bookseller will think he has to be an apostle to sell reli-gious books."[43] Ferguson, Exman, and other industry leaders who estab-lished the mores of the rapidly commercializing religious book business arrived at a quintessentially capitalist solution to these dilemmas, a solu-tion designed to appease both religious concerns and secular book deal-ers: sell "piffle" along with quality and let the market sort it out. This decision to trust the market set the course for much of twentieth-century religious culture.

The tale of Exman, Harper's, and the commercialization of religious publishing in the mid–twentieth century helps us see that the spiritual eclecticism so often associated with the 1960s and 1970s in fact has much deeper cultural roots. Even more significantly, the tale of Exman and Harper's helps us see *how* the avant-garde religious liberalism of William James and other turn-of-the-century elites came to characterize in popu-larized, simplified form the religious sensibilities of so many ordinary Americans less than a century later. In her study of therapeutic culture, sociologist Eva Illouz contends, "A critique of culture cannot be adequately waged before we understand the mechanism of culture: how meanings are produced, how they are woven into the social fabric . . . and why they come to organize our interpretation of the self and others."[44] In the book marketplace of the mid-twentieth century, we see just such a mechanism of culture in operation. The decision to sell religious books like chewing gum, to no longer fear the charge of "piffle" but, rather, to embrace the values and institutions of market culture, transformed not only the reli-gious book business but also the opportunities available to religious seek-ers in the marketplace of ideas. Very few twentieth-century Americans followed Eugene Exman's example directly and joined Vedanta centers or embarked on psychospiritual experiments with LSD. Most Americans, after all, were not friends with Gerald Heard or Aldous Huxley. But the religion department at Harper's did follow Exman's lead and head off to California, both metaphorically and literally, and much of popular American spirituality followed along.

In 2008, the *San Francisco Chronicle* followed up on its interview with Clayton Carlson from seventeen years earlier, turning once again to the publishing business to take the nation's spiritual temperature. (HarperSF had been rechristened HarperOne the year before.) In the midst of ongoing war and financial collapse, Mark Tauber, senior vice president and publisher of HarperOne, reported, "So many people are disillusioned."[45] By 2012, nearly 20 percent of Americans were religiously disaffiliated, a number that rises to one in three among those under age thirty.[46] Yet, as was true nearly two decades earlier, sales of religious books were booming early in the twenty-first century, outpacing all other segments of the industry. Tauber understood that his readers were "looking for hope and comfort" in the face of adversity but knew, as Carlson had, that fewer and fewer Americans were finding that hope in government or church. "We publish everything from the Dalai Lama to Billy Graham to the Bible to books on Buddhism from a gay perspective," Tauber declared, offering the formula for commercial success and spiritual succor that Exman had pioneered seventy years earlier: "Philosophically, we don't want to be pinned down. We publish something to offend everyone."

## *Notes*

1. Clayton Carlson, quoted in Patricia Holt, "Harper's Spiritual Quest," *San Francisco Chronicle*, June 2, 1991, Sunday Review, 1.
2. In 1991 the most significant assessment of this turn from community was Robert Bellah, Richard Madsen, William M. Sullivan, Ann Swidler, and Steven Tipton, *Habits of the Heart: Individualism and Commitment in American Life* (Berkeley: University of California Press, 1985). More recently, see Robert D. Putnam, *Bowling Along: The Collapse and Revival of American Community* (New York: Simon and Schuster, 2000).
3. Holt, "Harper's Spiritual Quest," 1.
4. See especially Robert Wuthnow, *The Restructuring of American Religion: Faith and Society since World War II* (Princeton: Princeton University Press,

1988); and Darren Dochuk, *From Bible Belt to Sunbelt: Plain-Folk Religion, Grassroots Politics, and the Rise of Evangelical Conservatism* (New York: W. W. Norton, 2011).

5. E-mail correspondence with current and former HarperSF and HarperOne staffers Mark Tauber, Greg Brandenburgh, and Thomas Grady, in author's possession.

6. Holt, "Harper's Spiritual Quest," 1.

7. Ibid.

8. See Leigh Eric Schmidt, "The Making of Modern Mysticism," *Journal of the American Academy of Religion* 71, no. 2 (June 2003): 273–302.

9. David A. Hollinger, "The Accommodation of Protestant Christianity with the Enlightenment: An Old Drama Still Being Enacted," *Daedalus* 141, no. 1 (Winter 2012): 76–88, republished in *After Cloven Tongues of Fire: Protestant Liberalism in Modern American History* (Princeton: Princeton University Press, 2013), 1–17.

10. The two most important such studies are from the Pew Forum on Religion and Public Life: "Many Americans Mix Multiple Faiths: Eastern, New Age Beliefs Widespread" (http://www.pewforum.org/2009/12/09/many-americans-mix-multiple-faiths) (Pew Research Center: Washington, DC, December 2009); and "'Nones' on the Rise: One-in-Five Adults Have No Religious Affiliation" (http://www.pewforum.org/2012/10/09/nones-on-the-rise) (Pew Research Center: Washington, DC, October 2012).

11. Christian Smith with Patricia Snell, *Souls in Transition: The Religious and Spiritual Lives of Emerging Adults* (New York: Oxford University Press, 2009), 135.

12. Ibid., 287. Smith's argument here draws on N. Jay Demerath III, "Cultural Victory and Organizational Defeat in the Paradoxical Decline of Liberal Protestantism," *Journal for the Scientific Study of Religion* 34, no. 4 (1995): 458–469. It is echoed quite influentially in David A. Hollinger, "After Cloven Tongues of Fire: Ecumenical Protestantism and the Modern American Encounter with Diversity," *Journal of American History* 98, no. 1 (2011): 21–48.

13. Mary Rose Himler, "Religious Books as Best Sellers," *Publishers' Weekly*, February 19, 1927, 691.

14. Richard Wightman Fox, "Epitaph for Middletown: Robert S. Lynd and the Analysis of Consumer Culture," in *The Culture of Consumption: Critical Essays in American History, 1880–1980*, ed. Richard Wrightman Fox and T. J. Jackson Lears (New York: Pantheon Books, 1983), 103. For religious publishing before the twentieth century, see Candy Gunther Brown, *The Word in the World: Evangelical Writing, Publishing, and Reading in America, 1789–1880* (Chapel Hill: University of North Carolina Press, 2004); David Paul Nord, *Faith in Reading: Religious Publishing and the Birth of the Mass Media in America* (Oxford: Oxford University Press, 2004);

Rennie B. Schoepflin, "The Mythic Mission Lands: Medical Missionary Literature, American Children, and Cultural Identity," in *Religion and the Culture of Print in Modern America*, ed. Charles L. Cohen and Paul S. Boyer (Madison: University of Wisconsin Press, 2008), 72–104; William Vance Trollinger Jr., "An Outpouring of 'Faithful' Words: Protestant Publishing in the United States," in *A History of the Book in America*, vol. 4: *Print in Motion, The Expansion of Publishing and Reading in the United States, 1880–1940*, ed. Carl F. Kaestle and Janice A. Radway (Chapel Hill: University of North Carolina Press, 2009), 359–375.

15. In 1928, there were 1,135 new adult fiction titles and 776 new religion titles published. Figures come from Dorothea Lawrance Mann, "Selling Religious Books," *Publishers' Weekly*, February 22, 1930, 973.

16. "The Religious Renaissance," *Publishers' Weekly*, February 19, 1927, 684.

17. Eugene Exman, "Reading, Writing, and Religion," *Harper's Magazine* 206 (May 1953): 85. Exman's figures show religious books, narrowly construed, accounting for 6.1 percent of total book sales in 1925 and 8.2 percent in 1929.

18. Ibid. Religious books accounted for 8.5 percent of all books sold in 1931 and only 4.7 percent of those sold in 1935.

19. For data on the "religious depression," see Wuthnow, *Restructuring of American Religion*, 25–26. The phrase itself comes from Robert T. Handy, "The American Religious Depression, 1925–1935," *Church History* 29 (March 1960): 3–16.

20. Robert S. Lynd and Helen Merrell Lynd, *Middletown in Transition: A Study in Cultural Conflicts* (New York: Harcourt, Brace, 1937), 297–298.

21. Ibid., 301.

22. Frederick Lewis Allen, *The Big Change: America Transforms Itself* (New York: Harper & Brothers, 1952), 248–249.

23. For an overview of Protestant religious publishing from 1880 to 1940 that briefly touches on these commercial developments, see Trollinger, "Outpouring of 'Faithful' Words."

24. "Why Harpers Have Entered the Field of Religious Books," *Publishers' Weekly*, February 19, 1927, 695.

25. This is notably parallel to nineteenth-century developments in evangelical publishing, as detailed by Brown, *Word in the World*.

26. Eugene Exman, "Modern Religious Books," *Publishers' Weekly*, February 20, 1932, 841–842.

27. Biographical sources for Exman include *The National Cyclopaedia of American Biography*, vol. 62 (New York: James T. White and Co., 1984), 119; the obituary in *Publishers' Weekly*, October 20, 1975, 38; and the obituary in the *New York Times*, October 12, 1975, 73.

28. Eugene Exman, "Individual and Group Experiences," in *Proceedings of Two Conferences on Parapsychology and Pharmacology* (New York: Parapsychology Foundation, 1961), 10.

29. On the intellectual climate at the University of Chicago Divinity School in these years, see Gary Dorrien, *The Making of American Liberal Theology: Idealism, Realism, and Modernity, 1900–1950* (Louisville: Westminster John Knox Press, 2003), 151–208.

30. Exman, "Individual and Group Experiences," 10.

31. Eugene Exman, *The House of Harper: One Hundred and Fifty Years of Publishing* (New York: Harper and Row, 1967), 287–288.

32. Eugene Exman to Thomas R. Kelly, January 4, 194[1], Box 12, Thomas R. Kelly Papers, Mss. Collection 1135, Quaker Collection, Haverford College Library, Haverford, Pa. Exman misdated this letter as 1940. Leigh Schmidt quotes this same excerpt from Exman's letter to Kelly in *Restless Souls: The Making of American Spirituality* (San Francisco: HarperSanFrancisco, 2005), 260. Schmidt develops in rich detail the interconnections among Kelly, Rufus Jones, Gerald Heard, Aldous Huxley, Douglas Steere, and Christopher Isherwood, a group of seekers with whom Exman felt great kinship and who were instrumental in his own spiritual explorations. See ibid., 227–268.

33. Exman, "Reading, Writing, and Religion," 86.

34. Exman, "Individual and Group Experiences," 11. On LSD and American spirituality in this period, see Jay Stevens, *After Heaven: LSD and the American Dream* (New York: Atlantic Monthly Press, 1987).

35. Exman, "Individual and Group Experiences," 13, 12.

36. Ibid., 11.

37. See Aldous Huxley, *The Doors of Perception* (New York: Harper and Brothers, 1954); and Huston Smith, *Cleansing the Doors of Perception: The Religious Significance of Entheogenic Plants and Chemicals* (New York: Tarcher, 2000).

38. Eugene Exman, "Search for Meaning," in *Search for Meaning*, by Eugene Exman, Thomas E. Powers, and Douglas V. Steere (Rye, N.Y.: Wainwright House, 1961), also published in *Hibbert Journal* 62, no. 239 (1962): 275–283.

39. See, for example, Eugene Exman, "Religious Book Publishing," in *What Happens in Book Publishing*, ed. Chandler B. Grannis (New York: Columbia University Press, 1957), 330–342. Exman also served as chairman of the Religious Publishers' Group, a consortium of the major national religious publishers affiliated with the National Association of Book Publishers.

40. See, for example, Laura J. Miller, *Reluctant Capitalists: Bookselling and the Culture of Consumption* (Chicago: University of Chicago Press, 2007). On selling religion like soap, see "The New Evangelist," *Time*, October 25, 1954, 56–64.

41. Rufus M. Jones, "The Habit of Reading," *Watchword* (Dayton), March 13, 1921.

42. Charles W. Ferguson, "Selling God in Babylon," *Publishers' Weekly*, February 22, 1930, 969.

43. Ibid., 970.

44. Eva Illouz, *Saving the Modern Soul: Therapy, Emotions, and the Culture of Self-Help* (Berkeley: University of California Press, 2008), 4–5.

45. Heidi Benson, "Publisher Glories in Readers' Soul-Searching," *San Francisco Chronicle*, April 11, 2008.

46. Pew Forum on Religion and Public Life, "'Nones' on the Rise."

# 6

## Literature and the Economy of the Sacred

### Günter Leypoldt

HOW CAN WE think about the relation between the marketplace and the sphere of cultural value? Critics of contemporary culture have been concerned that the global commercialization of our lives has led to an "erosion" or "contraction of the sacred" even as it has increased the market for "low-intensity" spiritualities and consumerist "lifestyle" religions.[1] There is much to suggest, however, that the expansion of the cultural marketplace has not eroded but broadened and diversified the formerly more overarching sacred space of traditional religion, producing "multiple sacred forms that exert complementary and conflicting fields of influence."[2] One of the most important of these fields of influence, as I will argue in the following, has emerged from institutions of literature and the arts. In this essay I will explore the sacred economy of literary institutions by looking at Toni Morrison's encounters with Oprah Winfrey.[3]

Pierre Bourdieu's history of the "literary field" suggests that with the modernization of culture, profane and sacred economies of literary production have mutually intensified one another in a complex process of reciprocal constitution. While the accelerating print markets since the 1700s have extended the domain of short-lived literary commodities, they have also created new spaces of consecration that are (paradoxically) both market-internal (subsidized by the rising commercial turnover) and market-sheltered (protected from pure economic reason). With the mid-nineteenth-century industrialization of the book, the cultural system tipped toward the "loser wins"[4] phenomenon in the arts that continues to shape our sense of cultural relevance today: the highest literary prestige falls to writers and artists who make little or no economic profit and do not receive public support (Wordsworth around 1800, say, T. S. Eliot in 1925, or Toni Morrison in the early 1970s). This implies that the commercialization of culture has not diminished; it has intensified the consecration of literature and disconnected literary sacrality from its traditional Scriptural basis. The canonicity of John Milton's *Paradise Lost* (1667) today owes little to its Christian theme and a great deal to its aesthetic affinities with the modernist sensibility that dominates the most relevant literary institutions.[5]

## *I  Singularization, Sacralization*

Literary market shelters encourage the formation of professionalizing expert cultures ("avant-gardes") that detach themselves from mainstream sensibilities. The production of literary avant-gardes thus resembles the process by which art museums, memorials, and sites of memory convert ordinary commodities into priceless collection pieces. Igor Kopytoff and Arjun Appadurai have theorized this conversion process as "singularization."[6] They suggest that singularity is thrust upon things that are removed from ordinary cycles of consumption and consequently partake of the quality of the sacred.[7] Likewise, avant-gardes in literature and the arts tend to draw their aura ("autonomous," "disinterested," "priceless") from their momentary distance to large-scale consumption.

How precisely do singular objects relate to the large-scale commercial market? Appadurai notes that many singularities defy sharp distinctions between markets and their outside.[8] But rather than invoking unstable borders between well-defined spheres—a "scrambling" of the "sacred–profane distinction"[9]—I suggest that we imagine cultural objects as possessing two bodies, in Kantorowicz's sense.[10] There is thus a "mortal" body of things that circulates through the profane world of commercial exchange (where it may be locked in rapid cycles of being desired, used, exhausted, and discarded) and a more enduring, iconic, mystical, transubstantiated body that invokes contact with a higher order. While the former inhabits the "lower" economies of quotidian consumption, where it gratifies short-term desire, the latter body provides us with long-term values beyond the ordinary.[11] These simultaneous materialities of things follow differing rhythms of growth and decline: the most mundane commodities (shower gels, toothpastes, entertainment media, BMWs) can acquire a second, socially magical existence when the poetics of branding connects them to an imagined space above the quotidian (think of the little transcendences that link the supermarket to the museum or the church).[12] At the higher end of the spectrum, the most consecrated objects (Picasso paintings, rare antiques, modernist poems, ancient relics, Shakespeare) develop parallel lives in a secondary process of commoditization that ranges from auctioneers trying to price the priceless to the merchandising of reproduced cultural icons in "heritage" markets and museum shops.

If literary critics have treated the twin materiality of artifacts with suspicion, this is due to a sense, ingrained in our scholarly habits, that the fundamental reality of a work precedes its institutional or commercial lives. The artwork's sacred or profane body is made a secondary matter for reception historians to be considered separately from a prior, more central aesthetic event. In this essay I will argue that it is unhelpful to distinguish between an artwork's power—its aesthetic-emotional and ethico-moral attraction—and the "social magic" or "charisma"[13] it acquires within markets and consecrating institutions.

## II  Morrison, Oprah, and the Positionality of the Sacred

*The Oprah Winfrey Show* was the highest-rated U.S. talk show almost from its inception in 1986 until its conclusion in May 2011. "Oprah's Book Club" became a regular feature in 1996, shortly after Winfrey had shifted her programming toward themes of moral and spiritual uplift ("Change Your Life TV"), distancing herself from the tabloid scandals that surrounded the daytime talk show genre in the mid-1990s.[14] Her own celebrity and her show's national media presence produced the legendary "Oprah effect,"[15] which converted her selections into immediate bestsellers and made her a tastemaker in the market of serious literature for middle-class audiences.[16] Toni Morrison visited Oprah's Book Club four times, forming an iconic relationship that began with the book club's second episode in October 1996 (featuring *Song of Solomon*).[17] Morrison was then already an internationally acclaimed novelist who represented the cutting edge of literary innovation. Her literary credentials aided Oprah's

efforts toward genre-gentrification, while the Oprah effect propelled even
her more experimental works onto the paperback bestseller lists.[18]

In what sense, however, has the Oprah phenomenon evidenced a
"reading revolution," as some critics have suggested?[19] The debate about
Oprah's effects on U.S. literary culture overlaps with a longer dispute
about whether or how the contemporary mediascape has lessened traditional high/low distinctions. No doubt, the recent shifts in taste and the
emergence of cultural "omnivores" and "niche cultures" have blurred the
more rigid lifestyle demarcations that Bourdieu famously drew from data
he collected in the 1960s and 1970s in France.[20] But audience mobility
has its limits: just because Morrison successfully entered the world of
Oprah, as a charismatic Nobel laureate, does not mean that the sphere
of the experimental novel has merged with the more commercial market
of network television. Rather, *institutionalized* avant-gardes (Wordsworth
in the 1830s, T. S. Eliot during the 1950s, and Morrison since the 1990s)
resemble rare museum pieces: their higher and lower social lives flourish
within different social atmospheres.[21]

## III   *Morrison's Two Bodies*

When Morrison praised Oprah's Book Club in 1996 for infusing her 1977
novel *Song of Solomon* with "new life that is larger than its original life,"[22]
she in fact conflated two bodies of her work that deserve to be kept apart.
The lower (i.e., more quotidian) body of a Morrison text, as object of entertainment, edification, or instruction, arguably thrives best among audiences whose reading habits allow them to "consume" her often opaque
prose with a certain ease. Experiencing a novel like *Song of Solomon*
as ordinary reading (a "page-turner," meaningful commentary on the
African American condition, or source of redemptive self-knowledge)
requires a degree of familiarity with recent literary tradition. Such
familiarity would seem most likely within the social sphere of Wendy
Griswold's "reading class," the "highly educated, affluent, metropolitan"
social elite that constitutes about 15 percent of the general population in
today's developed countries.[23] By contrast, within the atmospheres of less
restrictive cultural markets (the popular terrain of Michael Crichton, say,
or Dan Brown), Morrison's consumption value shrinks behind her symbolic power. The question that immediately presents itself, of course, is
why readers of more popular fiction should care about Nobel-enhanced

symbolic power: What if Toni Morrison's novels leave me cold while eminently noncanonical works (Janice Radway's romances, say)[24] strike me with a powerful sense of affective intensity or redemptive self-knowledge? But given our tendency to distinguish our desires into higher and lower forms,[25] it seems perfectly possible to prefer reading genre fiction for its immediate uses and still have a sense that Morrison's writing embodies higher, more long-term values that require special training and a more professionalized readerly attitude. Since the higher location of the Nobel Prize—the aura of the elite networks and institutions attached to it—is part of a public structure of feeling, we do not need to have access to the profane value of Toni Morrison's work (as source of pleasure or practical uses) in order to feel the cultural authority she represents.[26] It is, rather, that her cultural authority makes it desirable to gain more immediate access to her work: being touched by the profane body of a Morrison novel brings us more closely in touch with the Western canon and the authority it represents. Truly enjoying the consecrated (rather than just recognizing its superiority) can be perceived as a form of cultural upward mobility.

The Princeton episode of Oprah's Book Club devoted to Morrison's experimental novel *Paradise* (1997) provides an instructive example.[27] When Oprah and her studio guests tried to make *Paradise* a source of "therapeutic"[28] meaning, the novel's resistance did not diminish its manifest attraction. We might even say that its descent to daytime television heightened the artifact's mystique, perhaps in a way similar to how conventional languages can become socially magic from the perspective of those unfamiliar with the relevant codes—medieval books among the illiterate, the Latin Mass for non-Latin speakers, or consecrated museum pieces for the uninitiated.[29] In the mood of critical realism we might rejoin that the perceived sacrality in this case is a mirage: the ignorance of codes leads to a mystification of a perfectly ordinary artifact, whose pseudo-sacred aura will disappear in the bright light of adequate skills (i.e., literacy in the Middle Ages, knowledge of basic Latin for Catholics, acquaintance with experimental prose for Oprah's guests). But imagined realities can be real in the performative sense.[30] The sacred body of a book is a mirage only if we reduce literary experience to a relatively simple process of communication, thus limiting literature's function to the transfer of encoded messages. To a degree, such a view of the literary underlies Oprah's concept of reading as transformative "connection" with a work's themes and characters. The difficulty of accessing *Paradise* indeed motivated Oprah to move the session to a Princeton classroom ("We needed help," she said, since some readers "couldn't make it to *Paradise*").

Toni Morrison, by contrast, considers literary reading to be less about access to meaning (emotive or cognitive) than a fascinating and unsettling encounter with alterity. Her position recalls a long-standing "negative theology" in the history of literature and art criticism that holds cognitive uncertainty to be constitutive of, rather than detrimental to, aesthetic experience. To cite an example of this tradition in the more recent philosophy of art, Alexander Nehamas suggests that beauty is "the enemy of certainty" because "we find things beautiful" when we sense that we "have not exhausted them" and "still desire" to "possess" and "know" them better.[31] In this view, Oprah's desire to "get" *Paradise* (to possess and inhabit the novel, with Morrison's guidance, as a therapeutic object) can be considered an appropriate response to textual otherness, the "pull" of uncertainty or negativity produced by Morrison's opaque prose.[32] And Morrison's comments at the Princeton session would seem to confirm this viewpoint: she pointed out that rather than writing a novel that could be reduced to an idea or thesis ("a book in which there was a formula and a perfect conclusion and that was the meaning and the only meaning"), she had wanted to create with *Paradise* an open literary space that, by withholding positive clues, would entice its readers toward more "powerful" ways of engagement. When her high-modernist technique baffled Oprah's guests ("Ms. Morrison, are we supposed to get it on the first read?"), she stressed the importance of audience participation ("I wanted the weight of interpretation on the reader") and suggested that forcing readers to face an unfamiliar world heightens their aesthetic experience and their ethico-moral astuteness. As Oprah put it in class: "Wise author that [Toni Morrison] is, she knows the rewards are twice as great when we readers get to unlock the secrets on our own." Whereas Oprah takes the readers' "light-bulb moments"[33] to depend on moments of *anagnorisis*, the recognition of positive knowledge ("secrets" to be "unlocked," as she put it), Morrison's negativity-based view of art suggests that the epiphanic power of literature unfolds precisely when the text *keeps* its secrets, resisting semantic or conceptual translation into positive knowledge.[34]

Morrison's aesthetics of uncertainty fails to tell the whole story, however, because it reduces the magnetic power of *Paradise* to a question of form: a Gumbrechtian presence "beyond hermeneutics" emerges from a textual resistance to closure, as if the relentless negativity of *the work* were enough to stimulate the reader's desire to penetrate and inhabit

Morrison's novel.[35] I wish to argue, rather, that in order to understand the novel's force of attraction (the power with which it draws the reader's hermeneutic energies) we need to look at how *Paradise* connects us with cultural authority.

## IV   *Oprah and the Question of Social Trust*

Lucien Karpik's recent study on the market of "unique" cultural products is helpful here because it relates the "economics of singularities" to the production of social trust.[36] Karpik demonstrates that uncertainty, rather than being a privilege of experimental art, pertains to a great many quotidian consumer choices: if we seek a good wine, an interesting new novel, the latest electronic gadget, a high-quality jazz recording, or even relatively mundane professional assistance (an excellent lawyer or psychoanalyst, say), we intuitively reach for what seems an open market of goods and services. But we will in fact rely on a variety of "judgment devices" (*dispositifs*) to help us "dissipate the opacity of the market."[37] Karpik points out that the "judgment-markets"[38] of cultural products differ significantly from the simpler "price-markets" that deal with more or less familiar merchandise (for example, basic foods we know well enough to evaluate on the basis of supply and demand). Judgment-markets are less transparent than price-markets because cultural values inevitably pose a degree of qualitative uncertainty that complicates economistic equations. One can reasonably compare two brands of breakfast cereal, but the Beatles and the Stones or Toni Morrison and Barbara Kingsolver are incommensurable. Our decision to choose one singularity over another will thus depend on complex regimes of evaluation that involve larger networks of cultural expertise and authority. In order to make the right decision—find the definitive recording of Beethoven's Ninth, the highest achievement in the experimental novel, or an excellent presidential candidate—we fall back on "coordination regimes" to which we need to extend a certain degree of trust.

As Oprah's encounter with Morrison shows, the issue of trust is key to the singularization of literary works. Experimental artifacts do not attain singularity simply because their perceptional difficulties impede their commoditization. The outside of the commodity sphere contains all manner of qualitatively uncertain things that are nonetheless experienced as trivia or trash. Perhaps the most intuitive reaction to artworks that truly elude our horizon of expectation is therefore to wonder whether familiarizing ourselves with the perplexing object is worth the trouble. The magic of the Oprah label lies in its power to convince her readership that the effort of engaging with a selected novel is justified (i.e., by the rewards of transformative connection). In her 1996 announcement of Morrison's *Song of Solomon* as a book club selection, for example, Oprah urged her audiences to have faith in her choice even if the novel's literariness might entail moments of readerly toil ("I encourage you to stay with Ms. Morrison, stay with the author. Put your trust in her because she knows what she's doing").[39] The relevance of trust became even more apparent when, in the Princeton episode, one of Oprah's studio guests signaled that while she had approached *Paradise* with sincere belief in its therapeutic potential ("I really wanted to read the book and love it and learn some life lessons from it"), her actual reading experience shook her faith in Oprah's authority ("[*Paradise*] was so confusing I questioned the value of a book that is that hard to understand, and I quit reading it"). When Oprah rejoined by justifying Morrison's use of literary unfamiliarity ("You have to open yourself up; it's like a life experience"), her guest accepted the lesson and promised to retackle the novel. Regardless of whether or not Oprah's advice was taken, the exchange illuminates how we distinguish between valuable and specious uncertainties. The question of whether such a novel as *Paradise* seems worth exploring hinges on our trust in its "connection" to the sort of higher cultural sphere that Edward Shils has called society's "charismatic" center.[40]

## V   *Charisma, Fullness*

Charismatic centers are culturally mediated "imagined spaces" that affect us with the aesthetic-emotional intensities and ethico-moral certainties typical of the phenomenology of the sacred. We experience these spaces in terms of a power or attraction we often describe in the vague semantics of the numinous or the sublime: the "presence" of a celebrity icon, the "aura" of a consecrated artwork or canonical literary text, the "radiance" of a priceless collection piece or a memorial object, the "magic" of sacralized social or political rituals, or the "charm" of rarefied lifestyles or manners. The function and perceptual feel of charismatic centers can be elucidated with Charles Taylor's notion of "fullness." Taylor relates the experience of fullness to any "place of power" that people perceive as a "deeply moving" and "inspiring" and "motivating intensity,"[41] one that embodies "some activity, or condition" where "life is fuller, richer, deeper, more worthwhile, more admirable, more what it should be." Taylor's metaphor of "spatial orientation" refers to people's sense of how they are " 'placed' or 'situated' in relation" to fullness and whether they are "in 'contact' with it."[42] The idea of a "sense" of fullness implies a tacit, practical kind of knowledge (a "feel for the game") that affects us more directly than rationalized propositions or conscious creeds. As Michael Warner puts it, fullness is therefore "not in itself a belief" but "the sense of something larger or more deeply meaningful about which we may have beliefs."[43]

## VI   *Charisma and Social Space*

How does our experience of charismatic fullness relate to the rituals and apparatuses of consecration that divide social practices along the lines of a sacred/profane distinction? Whether or not Oprah embodies for us "something larger than ourselves" does not depend on her use of religious narratives (her characteristic rituals of confessional and redemptive reading)[44] but, rather, on her institutional power as a media icon. This power seems eminently relational; it varies across social space. As we can gauge from comments by reviewers and academic critics, more bookish audiences tend to perceive Oprah's Book Club as an important mediator of literary works whose credentials as literary singularities, however, are established elsewhere (above "our heads," as Winfrey said at Princeton). In one sense, the site-specificity of Oprah's magic has to do with the differences in readerly training that characterize the divide between professional and lay audiences.[45] But this does not make institutional charisma a mechanical function of cognitive knowledge or skills. Since any labor-intensive practice in the arts can be dismissed as empty professionalism, the value of reading skills does not hinge on the amount of labor invested in it but, rather, on the degree to which specific kinds of labor embody cultural authority.

Take, for example, the book-length response to the Oprah phenomenon by the published poet Kathleen Rooney. Similar to the disgruntled studio guest at the Princeton session, Rooney admits to having failed to read through Morrison's *Paradise* because she doubted the value of a novel that struck her as "unnecessarily cryptic and impenetrable in style and composition."[46] Rooney can dismiss a Nobel Prize–winning writer as a formalist because she feels at home in the academic institutions that play a more significant role than televised book clubs in shaping Morrison's cultural prestige. In contrast to Oprah's audiences, Rooney mentions her inability to cope with *Paradise* with pride rather than shame,[47] and she flaunts the symbolic weight of her academic credentials by distinguishing between high-literary works that merit multiple rereading ("James Joyce's *Ulysses*, for instance, or even *The Sound and the Fury* by Morrison's antecedent William Faulkner") and those that, like Morrison's *Paradise*, are "needlessly muddled" and "deliberately and unnecessarily obfuscating."[48] Since this finest of distinctions—between gratuitous and justified literary difficulty—is ultimately unverifiable (as defenders of Morrison's novel would surely protest), whether or not we find Rooney's rejection of Morrison convincing depends on our faith in the judgment devices on which her verdict is based. This faith in turn depends on our trust in the consecrating institutions to which these judgment devices are linked. As Oprah's self-conscious gesture toward Morrison attests, the institution that produced *Paradise* ("Princeton") trumps her book club.[49]

It is helpful here to consider the pecking order of consecrating institutions in historical context. As Giorgio Agamben reminds us, " 'To consecrate' (*sacrare*) was the term that indicated the removal of things from the sphere of common law."[50] In premodern societies this process obviously rested on the steep hierarchies of direct political power: a ninth-century warrior king in medieval Europe could authorize a saint's relic more or less single-handedly.[51] Secularist narratives tend to attribute the waning of the cult of relics to the excarnation of religion or simply the waning of belief. More productive explanations, I think, look at how the economies of the sacred changed with the dispersal of consecrating agencies across multiple, economically embedded institutions. To the degree that symbolic power ramifies, fewer central organs are able to define the gold standard of singularization—no single institution today can deconsecrate, say, Duchamp's ready-mades, the Louvre's *Mona Lisa*, or Toni Morrison's *Beloved*. Yet the ramification of authority does not mean that power is everywhere and nowhere. As Shils's spatial image of a charismatic "center" suggests, the broadening of the overarching canopy of religious sacrality into multiple sacred spaces has not simply leveled the field; it has created a new "gravitational pull," in Gordon Lynch's formulation, that is now "simultaneously exerted by different sacred forms."[52] Just as the flattening of social hierarchy has increased rather than diminished people's need for local distinction, today's consecrating institutions differ along various scales of influence, varying in the degree of trust they muster, the felt sense of charismatic attraction they generate, and thus the amount of cultural centrality they invoke.[53]

## VII   Oprah's Gift

Of course, the realities of cultural hierarchies jar with our democratic sense that the literary canon should be determined by representative publics rather than small professional elites. The natural temptation is therefore to dismiss charismatic consecration as an authoritarian fantasy that can be dispelled by a dose of enlightened reflection. This temptation is apparent in the media scandal over Jonathan Franzen's public remarks after Oprah announced *The Corrections* as a book club selection in September 2001. Franzen stumbled into a public relations debacle when in a string of promotional interviews during his book tour he voiced his ambivalence about his association with the Oprah label. The media fastened on his comments about literary taste—in a radio interview he had placed himself "solidly in the high-art literary tradition" and mentioned that Oprah's more sentimental ("schmaltzy") selections made him "cringe." When Winfrey promptly rescinded her invitation ("It has never been my intention to make anyone uncomfortable or conflicted"),[54] Franzen backpedaled with a series of apologetic retractions. He conceded that the high/low distinction was "meaningless"[55] and that he had "no one but myself to blame."[56]

But blame for what exactly, other than having badly managed his media appearance? The most vehement condemnations came from critics who took Franzen's discomfort itself as an offensive gesture: one does not cringe about popular culture unless one looks down upon the mainstream. It was assumed that Franzen's felt dislike presupposed a creed or ethics that justifies such dislike. In the manner of the New Atheist critique of religious belief as essentially consisting of false propositional statements about the world (fantasies rather than verifiable realities), Franzen was accused of a faith in the existence of "the middle-brow" that critics attributed to the "sacred conversations" of a reactionary "priesthood of English professors."[57] Understandably, Franzen declared himself an unbeliever: "I know," he said to the *Chicago Tribune* in November 2001, "the distinction between high audiences and low audiences is false."[58]

Franzen presumably meant to acknowledge the equal dignity of all tastes, and who would want to disagree? But how does such an abstract philosophical position affect the empirical realities of our embodied reaction to differing aesthetic atmospheres (the sense of upward or downward movement that gives us a bodily "unease" of being "out of place")?[59] Rooney's engagement with Oprah is a revealing case in point: highly critical of Franzen's insensitivity, she prefaces her account with a disclaimer that her academic expertise as a reader does not "negate the value" of the experience of any less educated member of Oprah's club, who "may deal with fiction in a *different* way than a member of the academy."[60] This democratic principle has not prevented Rooney from experiencing Oprah's more accessible picks as painfully simple, predictable, and overly schematic and sensational,[61] nor has her theoretical tolerance mitigated her aversion to what she perceives as Oprah's "studiously immature" and "sophomoric"[62] response to literature. Rooney and Franzen both "cringe" in the atmosphere of the middlebrow because their embodied sense of high and low (or singular/cheap, sacred/profane, pure/impure, etc.) goes deeper than their ideas (ethical, political) about this distinction.

The more vexing question, to be sure, is how our orientation toward fullness relates to our socioinstitutional position. Let me, for the sake of clarity, overstate the issue in the one-sided vocabulary of economic investment: it is hard to see how any author who competes mainly in the restricted literary market, where success is defined by prizes instead of large print runs, would be unambiguously pleased about crossing over into the large-scale atmospheres of the middlebrow book club and daytime TV.[63] This does not mean, as critics have suggested, that highly credentialed authors cannot at the same time be thrilled (as Franzen indeed was) when the Oprah effect turns them into national bestsellers. But unlike Toni Morrison—who arrived at Oprah's Book Club as a museum object whose radiance remains untouched by the profanity of secondary commoditization—Franzen faced a greater degree of tension between the two economies that polarize the field. His financial gains from Oprah's endorsement had to be weighed against a potential loss of prestige, even if the risk of such a loss had never in fact been that great, as Franzen presumably realized soon enough in the erupting scandal. His immediate apology for "rudeness" suggests that he sensed how far the public fixation on his comments devalued the symbolic currencies that normally make the Oprah effect a win-win situation for all participants in the exchange. We can view the book club segment as Oprah's financial investment (a Maussian "gift")[64] in a cultural economy of prestige: Hosting Nobel Prize winners in order to "get the whole country reading again"[65] is an expensive business, paid for with low ratings, but its symbolic returns have given *The Oprah Winfrey Show* a cultural clout beyond the reach of any other contemporary daytime talk show. Franzen's public discomfort was "rude" in that it reversed the symbolic significance of his scheduled appearance on the show—Oprah gains little from meeting an acclaimed author whose media image has come to symbolize her middlebrow inferiority.

Of course the vocabulary of investments and returns conceals as much as it reveals, and it risks raising the specter of bad faith or naiveté—Oprah *believes* that she is enchanted by the power of *Paradise*, while the discerning sociologist tells her that she is really after social distinction. But while it is disingenuous to deny Oprah's real gains in the exchange,[66] it is no less reductive to "expose" these as the "deeper" reality of her literary interests. Since the "social magic of institutions" can "constitute just about anything as an interest,"[67] Oprah's felt sense of fullness during the encounter with Morrison may be every bit as real as the prestige she draws from it.

## *Notes*

1. Bryan Turner, *Religion and Modern Society: Citizenship, Secularization and the State* (Cambridge: Cambridge University Press, 2011), 297.

2. Gordon Lynch, *The Sacred in the Modern World: A Cultural Sociological Approach* (Oxford: Oxford University Press, 2012), 135.

3. For an application of the following theory of sacralization to broader trends in literary history, see my "Singularity and the Literary Market," *New Literary History* 45, no. 1 (2014): 71–88.

4. Pierre Bourdieu, *The Field of Cultural Production: Essays on Art and Literature* (New York: Columbia University Press, 1993), 39.

5. By drawing attention to the larger socioinstitutional contexts of this development I wish to avoid the more polemic sense in which the term *sacralization* is often used, as shorthand for a pseudo-religious strategy of domination. Lawrence Levine's influential thesis of the "sacralization of culture," for example, attributes the late nineteenth-century emergence of elitist opera, Shakespearean theater, and art museums to intentional gatekeeping mechanisms by which the Gilded Age upper classes in the United States shored up traditional class hierarchies (*Highbrow/Lowbrow: The Emergence of Cultural Hierarchy in America* [Cambridge: Harvard University Press, 1990]). On a more productive use of *sacralization*, see Hans Joas, *The Sacredness of the Person: A New Genealogy of Human Rights* (Washington, D.C.: Georgetown University Press, 2013).

6. Igor Kopytoff, "The Cultural Biography of Things: Commoditization as Process," in *The Social Life of Things*, ed. Arjun Appadurai (Cambridge: Cambridge University Press, 1996), 64–94; Arjun Appadurai, "Introduction: Commodities and the Politics of Value," in Appadurai, *Social Life of Things*, 1–63.

7. The museum studies scholar Krzysztof Pomian has theorized collection pieces as *sémiophores*, things that become symbolic of the "invisible" as soon as they are withdrawn from the sphere of quotidian use (*Collectors and Curiosities: Paris and Venice, 1500–1800* [New York: Polity Press, 1990], 30, 32). Accordingly, artists and the collecting elites become "semiophore men [*des hommes sémiophores*]," who distinguish themselves by their proximity to the sacred, as opposed to mere "thing-men [*des hommes-choses*]" (32) who occupy the lower social regions of quotidian production. See also Stefan Lauber, *Von der Reliquie zum Ding: Heiliger Ort–Wunderkammer–Museum* (Berlin: Akademie, 2011).

8. Appadurai, "Introduction," 17.

9. Colleen McDannell, *Material Christianity: Religion and Popular Culture in America* (New Haven: Yale University Press, 1995), 4–8.

10. E. H. Kantorowitcz, *The King's Two Bodies: A Study of Medieval Political Theology* (Princeton: Princeton University Press, 1957). Jeffrey Alexander has applied the image of the king's two bodies to the political performances in American elections, suggesting that the victories of Reagan, Clinton, and Obama had to do with their ability "to enter into myth" by growing "a sacralizing and mythical second body," "an iconic surface that allows audiences an overpowering sense of connection with the transcendental realm of the nation's idealistic political life." Because "Obama [had] grown this second body" in the 2008 election he was "no longer just a human being—a skinny guy with big ears, a writer, an ordinary man, but a hero." By contrast, the "mythical public body" of less successful politicians (McCain in 2008, Carter in 1980, Nixon in 1960) remained so "weak and puny" that they were perceived as "politician rather than myth" (Jeffrey Alexander, "The Democratic Struggle for Power: The 2008 Presidential Campaign in the USA," *Journal of Power* 2, no. 1 [April 2009]: 65–88, here 75).

11. Charles Taylor has shown how in the process of "strong evaluation" "our desires are classified in such categories as higher or lower, virtuous and vicious, more and less fulfilling, more and less refined, profound and superficial, noble and base" ("What Is Human Agency?" in *Human Agency and Language: Philosophical Papers vol. 1* [Cambridge: Cambridge University Press, 1985], 15–44, here 16).

12. See, for example, Slavoj Žižek's take on "cultural capitalism," where the consumption of organic apples or products from Starbucks (with its "coffee ethic" and "'Ethos Water' program") implies connection to a higher realm of meaning ("we are not merely buying and consuming" but "simultaneously doing something meaningful," such as "showing our capacity for care and our global

awareness, participating in a collective project" (*First as Tragedy, Then as Farce* [London: Verso, 2009], 52–54).

13. Pierre Bourdieu, *Language and Symbolic Power*, ed. John B. Thompson (Cambridge: Polity, 1992), 117–126.

14. On Oprah's programming makeover, see Wendy Parkins, "Oprah Winfrey's Change Your Life TV and the Spiritual Everyday," *Continuum: Journal of Media and Cultural Studies* 15, no. 2 (2001): 145–157; and Kathryn Lofton, *Oprah: The Gospel of an Icon* (Berkeley: University of California Press, 2011), 3–4. On Oprah's distinction from tabloid culture, see Janice Peck, "Literacy, Seriousness, and the Oprah Winfrey Book Club," in *Tabloid Tales: Global Debates over Media Studies*, ed. Colin S. Sparks and John Tulloch (Oxford: Rowman and Littlefield, 2000), 229–250; and Laura Grindstaff, *The Money Shot: Trash, Class, and the Making of TV Talk Shows* (Chicago: University of Chicago Press, 2002), 25–27.

15. D. T. Max, "Oprah Effect," *New York Times Magazine*, December 26, 1999, sec. 6, p. 36.

16. On the problems of defining middle-class or middlebrow reading, see Tim Aubry, *Reading as Therapy: What Contemporary Fiction Does for Middle-Class Americans* (Iowa City: University of Iowa Press, 2011), 10–16.

17. Oprah subsequently selected Morrison's *Paradise* (1997) for January 1998, *The Bluest Eye* (1970) for April 2002, and *Sula* (1973) for April 2002, the last pick before the book club went into a period of remission, until it reappeared in June 2003 with a focus on classic authors.

18. The print run of *Song of Solomon*, for example, increased by about one million copies in the six months after Oprah's endorsement. See Daisy Maryles and Dick Donahue, "The Oprah Scorecard," *Publishers Weekly*, April 21, 1997, 18.

19. Cecilia Konchar Farr, *Reading Oprah: How Oprah's Book Club Changed the Way America Reads* (Albany: State University of New York Press, 2005), 2. See also Jim Collins, *Bring on the Books for Everybody: How Literary Culture Became Popular Culture* (Durham, N.C.: Duke University Press, 2012), 5–6.

20. See Alan Warde, David Wright, and Modesto Gayo-Cal, "Understanding Cultural Omnivorousness: or, The Myth of the Cultural Omnivore," *Cultural Sociology* 1, no. 2 (July 2007): 143–164. On "niche culture," see Chris Anderson, *The Long Tail: Why the Future of Business Is Selling Less of More* (New York: Hyperion, 2006).

21. Whereas emergent avant-gardes gain their prestige by recognition from a small professionalized cultural establishment (Bourdieu speaks of "charismatic consecration"), institutionalized avant-gardes become more widely known cultural icons to the degree that their canonicity entails a secondary commoditization (Wordsworth as a leather-bound Victorian commodity, T. S. Eliot lecturing in 1950s football stadiums, or Toni Morrison on *Oprah*).

22. *The Oprah Winfrey Show*, Harpo Production Inc., November 18, 1996. See Edith Frampton, "Toni Morrison, Body Politics, Oprah's Book Club,"

in *The Oprahfication of American Culture*, ed. T. T. Cotton and K. Springer (Jackson: University Press of Mississippi, 2011), 145–160, here 146.

23. Wendy Griswold, *Regionalism and the Reading Class* (Chicago: University of Chicago Press, 2007), 65.

24. Janice A. Radway, *Reading the Romance: Women, Patriarchy, and Popular Literature* (Chapel Hill: University of North Carolina Press, 1984).

25. Cf. Taylor, "What Is Human Agency?"

26. As anyone who went through reading lists of third-level literary education knows, the attraction of difficult canonical works is of a different kind than more directly accessible "pleasures" of reading. There is a variety of terms, within literary aesthetics, attempting to conceptualize this difference, from the ancient distinction between the beautiful and the sublime to Roland Barthes's eccentric opposition between the *plaisir* of reading realist fiction and the *jouissance* of losing oneself in Joyce's modernist *Ulysses*.

27. Unless otherwise indicated, all citations from Oprah's show refer to the thir-teenth book club episode (*The Oprah Winfrey Show*, Harpo Production Inc., March 6, 1998) devoted to Morrison's *Paradise*. In contrast to Oprah's usual practice, the episode took place in a classroom at Princeton University and featured Oprah, Toni Morrison, and twenty-two selected guests. See Michael Perry, "Resisting Paradise: Toni Morrison, Oprah Winfrey," in *The Oprah Affect: Critical Essays on Oprah's Book Club*, ed. Cecilia Konchar Farr and Jamie Harker (Albany: State University of New York Press, 2008), 119–140; Timothy Aubry, "Beware the Furrow of the Middlebrow: Searching for Paradise on The Oprah Winfrey Show," *Modern Fiction Studies* 52, no. 2 (Summer 2006): 350–373; Rona Kaufman, " 'That, My Dear, Is Called Reading': Oprah's Book Club and the Construction of a Readership," in *Reading Sites: Social Difference and Reader Response*, ed. Patrocinio P. Schweickart and Elizabeth A. Flynn (New York: Modern Language Association of America, 2004), 221–255.

28. On *The Oprah Winfrey Show*'s relation to therapeutic discourse, see Eva Illouz, *Oprah Winfrey and the Glamour of Misery: An Essay on Popular Culture* (New York: Columbia University Press, 2003). On the therapeutic in postwar literary culture, see Aubry, *Reading as Therapy*, 26–31.

29. On medieval books as holy objects, see Christopher De Hamel, "Books and Society," in *The Cambridge History of the Book in Britain, vol. II: 1100–1400*, ed. N. Morgan and R. Thomson (Cambridge: Cambridge University Press, 2008), 3–10. On the Latin Mass, see Amy Hungerford, "Don DeLillo's Latin Mass," *Contemporary Literature* 47, no. 3 (2006): 343–380.

30. See Jeffrey Alexander, "Iconic Consciousness: The Material Feeling of Meaning," *Society and Space* 26 (2008): 782–794, here 783.

31. Alexander Nehamas, "The Return of the Beautiful: Morality and the Value of Uncertainty," *Journal of Aesthetics and Art Criticism* 58, no. 4 (Autumn 2000): 393–404, here 402.

32. *Paradise* is a challenging novel by most accounts: key information about the protagonists and their setting is withheld or scattered across the narrative and often focalized through the perspectives of various badly informed and sketchily described characters. In the manner of modernist fiction (the Faulkner novel, for example), the story world has to be culled from a series of indistinct impressions that upon first reading fail to add up to a coherent and causally rich picture. See Aubry, "Beware the Furrow of the Middlebrow," 358.

33. On Oprah's concept of "light-bulb" or "aha moments," see Lofton, *Oprah*, 185.

34. This view recalls the negative theology of romantic art religion, which assumes that by eluding conceptual interpretation, aesthetic forms can become a higher, subtler language. Morrison is no romantic mystic, but her interest in musical form—her attempts at aural definitions of black identity, for example—is related to the shift toward aural images of singularity that first emerged around 1800, when the semantic indeterminacy of music (which eighteenth-century aesthetics had still considered a weakness of the medium) became a mark of its expressive power, as a "language *above* language" that carried a higher presence (God, Democracy, National Character, etc.) but in a subconceptual idiom that could only be intuited and felt. See Carl Dahlhaus, *The Idea of Absolute Music* (Chicago: University of Chicago Press, 1989).

35. Hans Ulrich Gumbrecht, *The Production of Presence: What Meaning Cannot Convey* (Stanford, Calif.: Stanford University Press, 2004). Because Gumbrecht situates the production of presence with formal beauty, his theory of art recalls Ezra Pound's formalist definition, where modernist artwork, by evading semantic closure, turns the text into "a radiant node or cluster" "from which, and through which, and into which, ideas are constantly rushing" (Ezra Pound, *Early Writings: Poems and Prose* [London: Penguin, 2005], 289).

36. Lucien Karpik, *Valuing the Unique: The Economics of Singularities* (Princeton: Princeton University Press, 2010).

37. Ibid., 44.

38. Ibid., 112.

39. *The Oprah Winfrey Show*, Harpo Production Inc., October 18, 1996. For more, see Kaufman, "That, My Dear, Is Called Reading," 230.

40. Shils suggested that modern societies revolve around symbolic "centers" that consist of deeply felt, irreducibly "charismatic" values. See Edward Shils, *The Constitution of Society* (Chicago: University of Chicago Press, 1982), sec. II. Whereas Max Weber limited "charisma" to extraordinary (*außeralltägliche*) forms of authority (as an irrational force only intermittently disrupting the normal course of modern organizational rationality), Shils envisaged an "attenuated, mediated, institutionalized charismatic propensity" at the level of "the routine function of society," a specifically cultural authority that "not only disrupts social order" but "also maintains or conserves it" (120, 257). Anticipating Robert Bellah's influential concept of "civil religion," Shils suggested that the

most revered and prestigious values of a society induce the sort of intuitive "deference" in its members that is reminiscent of more traditional experiences of the sacred. See Stephen Turner, "Charisma Reconsidered," *Journal of Classical Sociology* 3, no. 1 (2003): 5–26.

41. Charles Taylor, *A Secular Age* (Cambridge: Harvard University Press, 2007), 5.
42. Charles Taylor, *Sources of the Self: The Making of the Modern Identity* (Cambridge: Harvard University Press, 1989), 43. Taylor suggests a tripartite spatial constellation: there is a "sense of orientation" toward "fullness" that "also has its negative slope," where one experiences "above all a distance, an absence, an exile, a seemingly irremediable incapacity ever to reach this place; an absence of power." And often one's location is imaged as "a kind of stabilized middle condition," defined by the feeling that one has "found a way to escape the forms of negation, exile, emptiness, without having reached fullness" (Taylor, *Secular Age*, 6). This condition of the "normal" combines a "stable, even routine order of life," on the one hand, with some meaningful practices, on the other. The middle position works so long as "the routine, the order, the regular contact with meaning in our daily activities, somehow conjures, and keeps at bay the exile, or the ennui," while at the same time it assures "some sense of continuing contact with the place of fullness; and of slow movement towards it over the years" (ibid., 7).
43. Michael Warner, Jonathan VanAntwerpen, and Craig Calhoun, *Varieties of Secularism in a Secular Age* (Cambridge: Harvard University Press, 2010), 11. Taylor describes a "general structure of our moral/spiritual lives" (*Secular Age*, 7) that cuts across the religious/secular divide: since all cultures (secular or not) recognize some kind of spiritual or moral "hypergoods," it is important, according to Taylor, to understand the culture-specific production of fullness rather than just to assume that certain cultures lack such experiences (or lost them in the course of modern disenchantment).
44. See Lofton's comparison of Oprah's Book Club with the self-cultural reading rituals of such late nineteenth-century reform movements as the Chautauqua Institution (*Oprah*). See also Trysh Travis, "'It Will Change the World if Everybody Reads This Book': New Thought Religion in Oprah's Book Club," *American Quarterly* 59, no. 3 (September 2007): 1017–1041.
45. John Guillory, "How Scholars Read," *ADE Bulletin* 146 (Fall 2008): 8–17.
46. Kathleen Rooney, *Reading with Oprah: The Book Club that Changed America*, 2nd ed. (2005; Fayetteville: University of Arkansas Press, 2008), 82.
47. Ibid., 81.
48. Ibid., 82.
49. The main institution behind Rooney's book is E. M. Forster's *Aspects of the Novel* (1927), which will seem weightier in Oprah's world than in the practice space of professionalized criticism. And again, the issue of symbolic prestige might partly concern the question of appropriate intellectual labor (whether

the use of Forster will feel like "over-" or "undertheorization") but mainly concern critical consecration (whether Foster is deemed profanely "dated" or singularly "fresh").

50. Giorgio Agamben, *Profanations* (New York: Zone, 2007), 73–74.

51. As long as the market for relics remained relatively unregulated, the sacredness of a bone depended on its perceived authenticity, which in provincial settings hinged on the performative action of political or religious rulers ("I hereby remove this bone from profane space"). See Patrick Geary, "Sacred Commodities: The Circulation of Medieval Relics," in Appadurai, *Social Life of Things*, 169–194.

52. Lynch, *Sacred in the Modern World*, 135.

53. At the risk of simplification we might imagine cultural authority as a landscape with higher and lower regions: a plateau of academically credentialed gatekeepers (the Nobel Prize, the culture of the school) towers over a less prestigious but more profitable region of serious fiction (the National Book Award, the *New York Times Book Review*), which slopes downward (via more gentrified mediascapes from HBO to independent film) toward the more commercialized territories of genre fiction and mainstream television and film and, further down, to mass-mediated valleys of tabloid culture. This landscape has, of course, a tenuous empirical basis—it is real only insofar as it occurs in certain people's embodied sense of fullness. Our recognition of this landscape has a great deal to do with which sort of body is accepted as representative.

54. Susan Schindehette, "Novel Approach," *People Magazine*, November 12, 2001, 83–84, here 83.

55. David Kirkpatrick, "'Oprah' Gaffe by Franzen Draws Ire and Sales," *New York Times*, October 29, 2001, http://www.nytimes.com/2001/10/29/books/oprah-gaffe-by-franzen-draws-ire-and-sales.html.

56. Julia Keller, "Franzen vs. the Oprah Factor," *Chicago Tribune*, November 12, 2001, http://articles.chicagotribune.com/2001-11-12/features/0111120196_1_jonathan-franzen-authors-pulitzer-prize-winning-novel.

57. Collins, *Bring on the Books for Everybody*, 21.

58. Keller, "Franzen vs. the Oprah Factor."

59. Pierre Bourdieu, *Pascalian Meditations* (New York: Polity, 2000), 184–185.

60. Careful to dissociate herself from the harsher critics of Oprah's Book Club, Rooney stresses that she has learned how to tolerate difference: she says that in the "original draft" of her book she had still "announced with great fanfare" that she was "'qualified' to distinguish good literature from bad" ("owing to my extensive literary education"). Yet upon "further thought" she had realized how "reactionary" it would be to believe "that only a minority of trained professionals can interact critically with texts" (*Reading with Oprah*, 78–79).

61. Ibid., 85ff. Such as Alice Hoffman's *Here on Earth* (1997), Chris Bohjalian's *Midwives* (1997), Anita Shreve's *The Pilot's Wife* (1998), Maeve Binchy's *Tara Road* (1998), and Elizabeth Berg's *Open House* (2000).

62. Rooney, *Reading with Oprah*, 159.

63. See James English, *The Economy of Prestige: Prizes, Awards, and the Circulation of Cultural Value* (Cambridge: Harvard University Press, 2005).

64. See Annette Weiner, *Inalienable Possessions* (Berkeley: University of California Press, 1992); Maurice Godelier, *The Enigma of the Gift* (Chicago: University of Chicago Press, 1999); and Mark Osteen, *"Gift or Commodity?" The Question of the Gift: Essays across Disciplines* (London: Routledge, 2002), 229–247.

65. *The Oprah Winfrey Show*, Harpo Production Inc., September 17, 1996.

66. While Farr and Aubry are right that Oprah did not have immediate financial gains from books she promoted, her symbolic returns are considerable and (given the proverbial absence of free gifts) may well reconvert themselves into economic value. See Farr, *Reading Oprah*, 20; and Aubry, *Reading as Therapy*, 46.

67. Pierre Bourdieu and Loïc Wacquant, *An Invitation to Reflexive Sociology* (Chicago: University of Chicago Press), 117.

# 7

# *Publishers and Profit Motives*

## THE ECONOMIC HISTORY OF *LEFT BEHIND*

### *Daniel Silliman*

THE HISTORY OF the success of *Left Behind* is a history of a market transformation. The fiction series capitalized on a number of developments in the market for evangelical books and was the vehicle for a number of important breakthroughs as well. While the series's place in American culture has not been explained in these terms, either popularly or academically, an account of the market's transformation with and through *Left Behind* is critical to understanding the books' phenomenal popularity.

The apocalyptic fiction series coauthored by Tim LaHaye and Jerry B. Jenkins is not unique in this regard. Understanding the nature and dynamics of book markets is important to understanding where, when, and in what numbers books are consumed. This is as true of popular fiction today as it is of the historic publications of canonical works of Western literature. Words on the page, printed and bound, have "rearranged the cognitive universe and reoriented man within it," as book historian Robert Darnton writes of the masterwork of the Enlightenment, the *Encyclopédie*.[1]

Yet, to do that, those words first had to be printed, shipped, and sold.[2] The speculations of the great *philosophés* depended on the workaday speculations of publishers.[3] The imaginings of best-selling novels depend on the imaginations of agents, editors, publishers, distributers, and booksellers. Economic histories of books are important for this reason. The point is not to dismiss or downplay the theologies, ideologies, worldviews, and individual agencies at work. It is, rather, to put them in the context of the economic conditions through which they are communicated. When ideas are in books, the realities of book markets enable, limit, and shape the distributions of those ideas.

Whereas some attention has been given to the publishing histories of transformative, canonical works of the past, less attention has been paid to contemporary publishing phenomena. With popular faith fiction and popular fiction generally, commercial success is typically explained in terms of consumers' shifting needs and desires, without regard for the supply side of the market. The result can be a kind of facile Hegelianism. As Janice Radway writes in her landmark study of romance fiction readers, this is a tendency that has led to critical misconceptions:

> Because literary critics tend to move immediately from textual interpretation to sociological explanation, they conclude easily that changes in textual features or generic popularity must be the simple and direct result of ideological shifts in the surrounding culture. . . . [However,] it may be true that Harlequin Enterprises can sell 168 million romances not because women suddenly have a greater need for the romantic fantasy but because the corporation has learned to address and overcome certain recurring problems in the production and distribution of books for a mass audience.[4]

Commercial success is too often seen as evidence only of a shift in the zeitgeist, while how, concretely, that popularity was achieved is not examined. Without lapsing into economic determinism, it seems fair to say that how corporations change and how the market changes to produce fiction and get it to readers are critical to understanding the place of those commodities in contemporary culture. "Publishers and profit motives," Radway writes, "must be given their due."[5]

Evangelical fiction has been a significant feature of the American landscape in the late twentieth and early twenty-first centuries. Its ubiquity has attracted much interest, and important academic work has been done interpreting some of the many, many novels published since Janette Oke's *Love Comes Softly* was released by Bethany House in 1979.[6] Important work has also been done in ethnographic research of some communities of readers, examining the nuanced and sometimes subtle ways in which these texts are used.[7] The history of the market for this fiction, however, has largely escaped notice. Besides some cursory treatments of commercial developments, the history of the industry of specifically evangelical fiction, written with evangelical Christian commitments and produced by evangelical publishers, has not been told.[8]

This essay will examine one pivotal period of that history, the phenomenal commercial success of the much-discussed *Left Behind* series. These thirteen novels and three prequels, published between 1995 and 2007, have had a significant religious and cultural presence in America. They have been an important part of evangelicals' engagement with American culture for more than two decades and are deeply connected with the turn of the millennium, the rise of the religious Right, and the U.S. response to the terrorist attacks of 2001. For that reason, they have been widely studied and have forced more than one journalist to explore the theological thickets of premillennial dispensational eschatology. They have been discussed, dissected, dismissed, dissed, praised, and criticized. The narratives of rapture and tribulation and even the name, *Left Behind*, have become part of America's common vocabulary and part of the cultural imagination. This, however, was made possible through the transformation of markets that the books benefited from and facilitated. The history of how a corporation managed to overcome serious market limitations to produce and distribute the apocalyptic novel series to a mass audience is thus an important story. Examining the economic history behind *Left Behind* serves to deepen and broaden the explanation of those novels' place in contemporary culture. It can also serve to demonstrate the value of economic accounts of religious commodities and the need to study the transformations of markets that make significant aspects of religion and culture possible.

## *I   To Reach Two Audiences*

From the very beginning, the *Left Behind* project was commercially minded. Tim LaHaye has said that he had the idea for the opening scene of the first novel in the mid-1980s.[9] The idea that it could be the start of a novel, however, and that that novel could have an impact on American culture, came later. In the late 1980s, Pentecostal-minister-turned-novelist Frank Peretti demonstrated new possibilities of evangelical fiction. In a market crowded with Christian romances, his novel of spiritual warfare, imagining the supernatural forces battling behind the scenes of a small-town instantiation of the American "culture war," opened publishers to the thought of other varieties of fiction. *This Present Darkness* sold only 4,200 copies in the first six months, but many readers returned to Christian bookstores and bought more copies for their friends.[10] In the second six months, 10,000 more copies were sold. In the six-month period after that, another 20,000 copies were sold. The evangelical publisher Crossways then decided to promote the novel with a national publicity campaign and sold 60,000 more copies in the subsequent six-month period.[11] It was a significant number for evangelical retailers at that time and enough to convince LaHaye that "fiction is what most people seem to want to read."[12]

The quality of Peretti's writing and his obvious kinship with popular mainstream writers such as Stephen King and Michael Crichton also caused evangelical publishers to wonder about crossover potential.[13] The distribution network of Christian Booksellers Association stores was limiting, and authors and publishers were always interested in reaching a broader public through the American Booksellers Association. The problem was, as Peter Kladder Jr., the president of the evangelical publisher Zondervan, said in 1980, "a significant share of our potential market never enters a Christian bookstore."[14] Kenneth N. Taylor, who was influential in the founding of the Christian Booksellers Association in 1950 and founded his own evangelical publishing company in 1962, accepted estimates that 90 percent of evangelicals did not frequent Christian bookstores. "Then there are the three quarters of the American population who do not count themselves as evangelicals," Taylor said: "It is our obligation to try to reach them with books that will attract them to the Lord. That is why I am just as concerned about distribution as I am about publishing."[15] Peretti's success seemed to point toward the possibility of wider distribution.

Both financial and evangelistic reasons account for the desire to reach a broader public, and Peretti's hits in 1986 and 1989, *This Present Darkness* and *Piercing the Darkness*, "earned Christian fiction a tiny space on the shelves of the major bookstores," according to industry observers.[16] They showed that it was possible to sell evangelical fiction—and a lot of it. They showed, further, that one of the main limitations was distribution. Starting in the 1990s, one big, persistent question among evangelical book producers was how to repeat Peretti's triumph and expand upon it. LaHaye, from the start, thought that a novel dramatizing the rapture and its aftermath could do what other books had failed to do and reach beyond the core audience of evangelical readers.

Jerry B. Jenkins recalls that the potential of apocalyptic fiction was discussed in his first meeting with LaHaye. "I was impressed," he said, "that he wanted to reach two different audiences. He wanted to encourage the church, those who were already persuaded. And he wanted to persuade unbelievers."[17] This is not to say the coauthors of *Left Behind* envisioned the phenomenon it would become. They thought they "had something pretty good," according to Jenkins, but pictured sales figures similar to Peretti's. Jenkins, for his part, would have been thrilled to move 200,000 copies of *Left Behind*.[18]

The choice of Jenkins as coauthor to realize the fiction signaled market ambitions. Jenkins had demonstrated an ability to respond to the market and write for the market. He was not precious about his craft but saw it as a craft. At the time, he had written and cowritten 125 books for the Christian market, including nineteen adult mystery novels and eighteen evangelical biographies.[19] Though he slowed down in later years, at the time *Left Behind* was written, his output was forty to sixty pages per day.[20] If this made him a hack, a mass-market man, Jenkins did not have a problem with that. "I make no apologies for writing for the masses," he later said: "I am one of them."[21] Jenkins was not LaHaye's first choice, though. The first choice was reportedly Peretti.[22] Peretti declined, however, possibly for theological reasons, possibly for aesthetic reasons. When he did, Jenkins was recommended. Jenkins was known for his adaptability. He was ambitious and willing to work as part of a team, and he accepted the proposed arrangement. LaHaye would outline the story and set out the apocalyptic timeline, while Jenkins produced the actual words on the page.[23]

## II   *The Influence of Agents*

The two men were brought together, notably, by a book agent, S. Rickly "Rick" Christian. Christian was one of the first agents to work with evangelical authors, specializing in the evangelical book market. Before the 1990s, there were no agents in that field, no one mediating between publishers and authors, representing authors' interests and negotiating their contracts with Christian publishers. The industry had been slow to adopt practices that could seem to conflict with its ministry ethos. Business deals had been negotiated with handshakes and prayer and the common understanding that all involved were brothers and sisters in Christ.

American evangelicals were not necessarily opposed to economic competition and free-market practices, though. The slogan at the tenth annual Christian Booksellers Association was "He Profits Most Who Serves Best," the motto of Chicago businessman Arthur F. Sheldon and the Rotary International.[24] The evangelical book industry shared the sentiment. It was widely believed that business enabled ministry and that good business was good service. As the industry developed, it increasingly adhered to the standards and practices of the secular industry, including author representation. By the 1990s, this included the practice of agents representing authors. Popular pastor Charles Swindoll hired a lawyer to get the best possible deal for his work *Grace Awakening*, which was published in 1990, and others immediately followed.[25] The move was transformational. Some criticized the development as a sign of the industry's willingness to compromise the gospel message for profit, but others saw it as a way to get that message to those who would not hear it otherwise.[26] Both LaHaye and Jenkins were in the later camp. Both were also represented by Rick Christian.[27]

Christian, for his part, was a sometimes fierce critic of publishers and argued bad business practices were responsible for some of the persistent problems in the evangelical book market. "I saw books that went unread," he said, "not because they were poorly written but because nothing was spent to let people know they existed." If that made his relationship with the publishers contentious on occasion, he accepted that. On his desk sat a framed quote: "One of the signs of Napoleon's greatness is the fact that he once had a publisher shot."[28] Agents, as Christian understood it, could force publishers to do better business.[29] Rights and royalties were, of course, one aspect of agent–publisher negotiations, but another critical item was publishers' promises to reach the widest possible audience. Christian saw his role in the conception of *Left Behind* as making sure the project had a real commercial chance.

This was the market environment *Left Behind* came into. LaHaye was interested in "two audiences," and Christian connected him with Jenkins. Jenkins's prodigious pace meant that he could turn the first book out in under twelve working days, and it had the style and form of popular action-adventure movies, as Amy Hungerford has shown.[30] The book was shopped around, and though Christian initially had trouble placing the manuscript with a press, it was ultimately sold to Tyndale. In part, this was because Tyndale was a leader among evangelical presses in breaching the general book market.[31] The company's representatives convinced

Christian, Jenkins, and LaHaye that Tyndale would seize every commercial opportunity, distributing the work as widely as possible, possibly even reaching a nonevangelical, non–Christian Booksellers Association audience. The publisher bought the book with a $50,000 advance, which was split evenly between the coauthors, minus the agent's percentage.

Tyndale's president and CEO, Mark Taylor, faced some internal skepticism that there was a market for the novel, but he held firm. He said, "I believe we could sell half a million of these."[32] That guess was more than double what Jenkins hoped to sell but 62.5 million fewer than what they actually sold.

## III  *Efforts to Reach the General Market*

Tyndale House was not the first Christian publisher to make significant inroads into the general market. Between 1970 and 1990, Zondervan did as much as any publisher to put evangelical books into mainstream distribution channels, but the process was anything but smooth. Twenty years of effort saw some success but also demonstrated the many systemic difficulties of distributing evangelical books in what industry experts call the American Booksellers Association market. In the early 1970s, the Grand Rapids, Michigan, publisher partnered with Bantam Books for broad distribution of Hal Lindsay's nonfiction book on the "last days" and Christ's imminent return, *The Late Great Planet Earth*. Zondervan printed the first run of 10,000 and granted Bantam the rights to a mass-market paperback edition for distribution to the general market. The book was a wild success and ranked as the number-one best-selling nonfiction title of the decade. Bantam sold more than 7.2 million copies of *The Late Great Planet Earth* by 1980, and Zondervan sold nearly three million.[33]

*The Late Great Planet Earth* bridged the chasm between the two markets, evangelical and general, but it was a small bridge. A few evangelical works of nonfiction were distributed more broadly in the following years—Tyndale's *The Living Bible* in 1972 and 1973, Revell's *The Total Woman* in 1974, Zondervan's *Joni* in 1976—but no regular route from evangelical publication to mass-market distribution was established.[34]

In part this was because nonevangelical publishers and booksellers did not always know what to do with religious titles. Even a book with sales as significant as Hal Lindsey's could seem mysterious to a clerk in an airport bookstore, as Zondervan's cofounder Pat Zondervan found while waiting for a flight in Anchorage, Alaska, in the mid-1970s. The airport bookshop carried several copies of *The Late Great Planet Earth*. However, because of the word *planet* in the title, the book of eschatology had been shelved in the section for ecology.[35] Another persistent issue was that authors who wanted to reach beyond Christian bookstores and had the ability to attract the attention of the big New York publishers tended to skip the smaller evangelical houses altogether. Billy Graham, for example, consistently brought manuscripts to nonevangelical publishers when he thought the books would have general appeal. He turned to evangelical publishers only with smaller volumes he expected would sell only to Christian Booksellers Association shoppers.[36] Despite an initial breakthrough in the 1970s, evangelical publishers thus struggled throughout the 1980s to get their books into nonevangelical distribution channels, with only limited success.

Even major efforts faltered. Zondervan, leading the way, launched a campaign in 1980 promoting "a wedge of seven Zondervan books intended to open an ongoing channel into the general book market."[37] The books were specially selected for that project and included a fictionalization of the biblical story of Esther, an apocalyptic interpretation of economic and political developments in the Middle East, and a self-help book about interpersonal relationships. Promoted by a marketing expert recently hired away from Hewlett-Packard and the former president of a New York ad agency, the evangelical books were pushed on New York City bookstores, in hopes of proving Zondervan's stock's wide commercial potential. In that year's annual report, however, the publisher's president told shareholders that "the effort did not reap as great a success as hoped for."[38]

When the company was purchased by Harper & Row in 1988, becoming the evangelical imprint of one of the world's largest publishers, many expected that would change the market. Some, in fact, feared that change. Writing in the theologically and culturally conservative evangelical newsmagazine *World*, Gene Edward Veith warned that the corporate takeover could corrupt and compromise the standards of evangelical publications. "As ministries turn into big business," Veith wrote, "theological integrity can easily give way to marketing considerations. . . . [C]ut-throat competition, coupled with theological looseness, can lead to promotion of a new, watered-down, pop Christianity."[39] Yet, despite hopes for and concerns about big change, little actually happened. Access to the general market was still limited, with evangelical publishers still restricted to evangelical retail outlets. The arrangement with Harper offered Zondervan financial stability in exchange for access to the Christian Booksellers Association market.[40] The company did not, however, guarantee that it would promote Zondervan titles through its established distribution networks. Mostly, it did not. The company already had a religion division in San Francisco, which Matthew Hedstrom has written about. Harper's sales reps were largely unfamiliar with evangelical books and did not dedicate themselves to selling the products of the Grand Rapid's press.[41] Though they promoted Bibles and a few titles such as 1990's *Tom Landry*, the spiritual autobiography of the Dallas Cowboys' coach, few Zondervan books found their way onto general-market bookstore shelves, despite the new corporate owners.[42]

For someone such as LaHaye, whose goal was "to reach two different audiences," this was the cardinal concern. Tyndale was attractive to the men behind *Left Behind* because, in the mid-1990s, the Carol Stream, Illinois, publisher had found another route to the book-buying masses. Following the model set out by the mass-market paperback publishers that had been blocked from bookstores during the paperback explosion of the 1950s and 1960s, Tyndale bypassed the American Booksellers Association stores, finding alternative means of distribution and stocking its books in nonbook retail outlets.[43] At about the same time that LaHaye and Jenkins's book agent was looking for the best deal for *Left Behind*, Tyndale was making a distribution deal with Wal-Mart.

## IV   *Wal-Mart and Evangelical Fiction*

As Bethany Moreton has shown in *To Serve God and Wal-Mart*, the big-box retailer based in Bentonville, Arkansas, went to great lengths to adapt to the religious mores of consumers. The company trumpeted the values of middle-class American shoppers. For instance, Wal-Mart portrayed consumption as a service women could do for their families, positioning itself as a haven for traditional families harried by the economy and the apparently hostile culture of coastal elites. Savings and value were emphasized, and the value of the work of providing for one's family on a budget was recognized as Wal-Mart sought to identify with the worldview of its core consumers.[44] In the mid-1990s, one important way to communicate this connection between the corporation and its customers was by stocking religious and family-friendly books.

Wal-Mart's biggest competitor, Kmart, learned this lesson the hard way when B. Dalton Bookseller, a chain of mall bookstores owned by

Kmart, began to stock erotic books as well as pornographic magazines. The American Family Association, a nascent religious Right organization, called for evangelicals across the country to boycott Kmart. A week before Christmas 1990, evangelicals were informed that "K Mart is one of the largest retailers of pornography in America," and they were urged to call the company in protest. They were also urged to shop at "family-oriented stores" such as Wal-Mart.[45] The group was particularly scandalized by a line of novels produced by a New York publisher, Blue Moon Publishing, featuring sadism and masochism in narratives with underage female protagonists. Between 1990 and 1994, the boycott was promoted in 160,000 churches and on hundreds of evangelical radio stations. Boycott materials were distributed to an estimated twenty million people.[46] The extent to which the five-year campaign against Kmart was successful can be disputed—a Kmart spokeswoman said the boycott was notable "in some regions of the country"—but Wal-Mart responded to the agitation by establishing distribution deals with evangelical publishers.[47] Thomas Nelson, the Nashville-based publisher of the New King James Bible, built a display room in Bentonville to show Wal-Mart executives what a Christian book section would look like in their stores.[48] Soon, Thomas Nelson's sales were going through a limited number of Wal-Mart stores, and the retailer was considering stocking more evangelical books at more of its stores. The change was immediately noted. "There's never been such a tumultuous time in our industry," said Doug Ross, then the president of the Evangelical Christian Publishers Association.[49] When Tyndale started publishing the *Left Behind* series in 1995, it was with one eye on these changes, this newly expanded and expanding market.

Despite mass-market ambitions and its eventual commercial triumph, the first *Left Behind* novel was produced with caution. Tyndale hedged its bet with the first run, printing a modest 35,000 hardback copies. Even more cautiously, only 20,000 dust jackets were made, to save on costs if a third or more of the first printing just ended up going to the shredder.[50] The first volume was distributed through Christian Booksellers Association channels. The three subsequent volumes—*Tribulation Force* in 1996, *Nicolae* in 1997, and *Soul Harvest* in 1998—were also sold mainly at Christian retail outlets.[51] They were successful in those markets, becoming a hit among the "relatively small group of mostly evangelical readers" who were connected to each other in "reading networks of family, friends, and church members."[52] The series's success, up to that point, was notable for evangelical fiction but not a phenomenon by general-market standards. According to the *New York Times*, the first four books sold a combined three million copies by fall 1998, "about as many as the typical John Grisham novel."[53] That was still enough, though, to trigger recognition from *Publishers Weekly*, enough to get a story about the series published in the *New York Times*, and enough to pique the interest of Wal-Mart executives.

## V   Apollyon *Breaks Through*

The end-times series went from evangelical hit to publishing phenomenon in 1999, when Wal-Mart agreed to stock *Apollyon*, the fifth book in the series, in about three hundred stores.[54] Wal-Mart was expanding the experiment it had started with Thomas Nelson and agreed to distribute the works published by Tyndale. The *Left Behind* series was promising for Wal-Mart because it had an established brand and proven sales record. There was also a sense that the impending turn of the millennium would provoke interest in all things apocalyptic. The Y2K panic, which focused on fears that computers would fail when the date changed from 1999 to 2000, had become a small industry, generating widespread interest in apocalypticism. Though the *Left Behind* series made no mention of the end of the twentieth century or computer failure, and actually took a decidedly positive stance on technology, the product fit the retailer's sense of the zeitgeist.[55]

With a special prologue for readers new to the series, *Apollyon* was published in February 1999. It was the fifth book of the series but the first to be made available to a mass market. The impact was immediate. Sales jumped, and booksellers took notice. Other big-box retailers and warehouse wholesalers, such as Sam's Club, Costco, and even Kmart, stocked the book as well.[56] Significant numbers of books were moved through the relatively new online book retailer Amazon.com, and the book also found space on the shelves of a recently expanded chain of suburban bookstores, Barnes & Noble. That company had just refined its strategy of superstores and had more than eight hundred such stores in suburban areas across the country.[57] According to the president of the Evangelical Christian Publishers Association, Barnes & Noble's expansion across middle America had "created enormous amounts of shelf space that stores had to fill," and the company adopted a liberal attitude toward titles that would fill it.[58] Seeing a book moving quickly at nontraditional outlets, Barnes & Noble sought to stay competitive by stocking the same titles.

With sales then moving through multiple channels, and more channels than any previous evangelical novel had, *Apollyon* made a notable appearance on national bestseller lists. It became the first novel published by an evangelical press to appear on *Publishers Weekly*'s annual bestseller list. Within a year, it had sold 3.5 million copies, more than the previous four titles combined, making *Left Behind* "the most successful Christian fiction series in history."[59]

*Apollyon* was not the only evangelical fiction title to make that year-end list in 1999, though. Tyndale followed the book's success with another *Left Behind* sequel that same year. The general market was breached, and the strategy established. A mere six months after *Apollyon* was published, the sixth title in the series was released. *Assassins*, written in about eleven days at Jenkins's intense pace, was published in August 1999 and sold almost one million copies in the first week. It made the *New York Times* Best Seller List, an unheard-of feat for evangelical novels, taking the number-two spot. It stayed on the list for thirty-nine weeks.[60]

## VI   Success after the Turn of the Millennium

The success would seem to prove that LaHaye was right about the possibility of an evangelical apocalyptic novel appealing to the masses. It would seem to prove that evangelical publishers, which had been pursuing general-market distribution channels since the 1970s, were right to think that more people would read their books if only they had access to them. The triumph of *Left Behind* is directly related to the transformation of the evangelical book market. That, however, was not the consensus explanation of the books' commercial success. The books were seen instead as a symptom of a sudden outbreak of psychic insecurity, most likely having to do with the pending millennium. Religious historian Paul Boyer, for example, attributed the enormous popularity of *Left Behind* to "the public preoccupation with the year 2000."[61] Even LaHaye speculated that perhaps the series was a success because of a "one-time window of opportunity" created by the approaching millennium.[62] The ways in which systemic supply-side problems had been solved to distribute the books to the widest possible audience were not taken into account. To basically all observers, it seemed that consumers' apocalyptic anxiety was the driving force behind the series's commercial success.

But then nothing happened, and still sales continued. When the calendar changed without any computer crashes or serious interruption of the global economy, Tyndale was busy making bigger and bolder plans for the seventh book in the series, *The Indwelling*. Convinced that the books sold well because of the expanded market, the company sought to expand the market even more. *The Indwelling* was promoted with a nearly $1 million budget. This was a significantly more aggressive promotional campaign than evangelical novels had received up to that time. Tyndale funded special book displays for Wal-Mart and Barnes & Noble, and the authors were sent on a ten-city promotional tour. Ads were placed in *USA Today* and on ABC radio and Rush Limbaugh's popular conservative talk radio program. The publishers, like never before in the history of the evangelical publishing industry, were placarding a vast portion of the media landscape with news of a novel's release.[63] As Tyndale vice president Ron Beers said, "Before . . . it was like pulling teeth to get significant publicity for our books. Now the entire nation is a platform for us."[64]

In anticipation of the sales, production was ramped up. It is normal to think of and speak of books being produced in response to demand, but it is clear in the case of *The Indwelling* that the books were printed in anticipation of demand. Tyndale's staff was increased from 200 employees to nearly 350, the office was expanded by 25,000 square feet, and a new 60,000-square-foot warehouse was constructed specifically for the *Left Behind* books.[65] An additional 80,000 square feet of warehouse space was rented.[66] Four printing plants worked for forty days to print the first run of two million books. It took seventy-nine semitrucks to deliver *The Indwelling* from the presses to the stores on May 23, 2000, and those trucks went to Christian stores, American Booksellers Association stores, big-box retailers, and Amazon.com distribution centers. "This," said Daisy Maryles, executive editor of *Publishers Weekly*, "is a phenomenal number of books we're talking about." In fact, the first print run of the seventh book was more than fifty-seven times the first run of the first book in the series. Within two weeks, 1.9 million copies were sold. *The Indwelling* became Amazon.com's best-selling novel that month and debuted in the top spot of the *New York Times* bestseller list, an unheard-of accomplishment for evangelical fiction.[67]

Some noted at the time that the fiction's success undercut existing explanations for its popularity. "Until now," reporter Dinitia Smith wrote, "the five-year-old series seemed propelled by the national fixation on the year 2000, with its apocalyptic themes. But even though interest in the millennium has died down, *The Indwelling* is doing better than previous books in the series."[68] A reporter for Great Britain's *Guardian* made the same point. Where it had been "assumed that the success of the earlier novels in the series had been part of conservative America's mounting excitement over the approach of the millennium," Martin Kettle reported, "the anticlimax of the start of the new millennium has done nothing to dampen enthusiasm for the series."[69] The book remained on the *New York Times* bestseller list for thirty-five weeks.

## VII   *Continued Success, Continued Expansion*

The success of the series continued from there, though many observers found themselves unable to explain the market phenomenon. The eighth book of the series, *The Mark*, was supported by the same sort of ad blitz that Tyndale had used to promote *The Indwelling*. There was a first printing of 2.5 million hardbacks in November 2000, and *The Mark* appeared as the number-one best-selling novel on the *New York Times* list the next month. It remained a *New York Times* bestseller for thirty-two weeks.[70] The series was, at that point, judged to be the fastest-selling adult fiction of all time.[71] Tyndale hired a public relations expert just to focus on the *Left Behind* series. A new vice president of operations was hired to improve order processing and fix the workflow problems created by the tremendous sales volume. The success also created a new market for Tyndale's other titles and its backlist. Further, the company started accepting more books for publication and increased the total number of titles produced by about one-third. Stores that had never carried Christian books before—and even stores that were not known for carrying books—began to stock the *Left Behind* series, including regional grocery stores and beauty care outlets such as Avon.[72] By the end of the year 2000, Tyndale had spent $3.5 million on book promotions, and there was widespread recognition that the industry had changed.[73]

Tyndale's earnings more than tripled between 1997 and 2000.[74] The success was marked as a major transformation of the evangelical book-publishing industry. "The *Left Behind* series got everyone's attention," said Rolf Zettersten, the newly named vice president of a Christian division of Warner Books in 2000: "The moguls have discovered that there's this great big population out there that's willing to spend money on Christian products." Zettersten had worked for Focus on the Family in the 1980s, a prominent evangelical gatekeeping organization, and then for

Thomas Nelson in the 1990s. Consistently, he had heard evangelicals say that they were excluded from the media marketplace because of the prejudices of those in the top spots of the secular industry. By 2000, though, *Left Behind*'s commercial success was obviously warmly welcomed by booksellers, and mainstream publishers were interested in establishing their own lines of evangelical books, hiring people such as Zettersten to tell them how. Where previously evangelical products had been marginalized, even ignored, now these books were hailed as great business. For some in the evangelical publishing industry, this came as a revelation. "There may have been some prejudices" against evangelicals in major media corporations, Zettersten said, "but I can assure you that those prejudices do not overshadow media companies' desire to run profitable businesses."[75] Before *Left Behind* broke through to the general market, the word many industry insiders used to describe evangelical fiction publishing was *ghetto*. After 2000, it was not conceivable to imagine the market that way anymore. "Many of the old barriers," reported *Christianity Today*, "have been obliterated."[76] The commercial success could not be explained away as a culture-wide outbreak of anxiety, or a one-off fluke, but was recognized, if not by cultural historians and literary critics, as a transformation of the market.

In 2001, Tyndale planned to continue and build on its success. It scheduled the production of nearly three million copies of the ninth *Left Behind* title, *Desecration*, or roughly one for every one hundred Americans. Jerry Jenkins said that the sales could only be described as "astronomical," far beyond the 200,000 copies he had hoped to sell when the series was first conceived.[77] Tyndale's marketing director described the series as "out of our control."[78] The publisher set aside a promotional budget of $2 million for *Desecration*, more than the earnings from any of the books before Tyndale broke into the general market. The novel was released one month after the terrorist attacks of September 2001 and became the best-selling title of the series. *Desecration* even knocked John Grisham off the top of *Publishers Weekly*'s annual bestseller list, a place Grisham had held every year since 1994. The novel also attracted the attention even of mainstream media organs that had previously ignored *Left Behind*, such as *Time Magazine* and the *New York Review of Books*.

Sales were actually only slightly higher than for previous volumes, however. *The Mark* sold 2.5 million copies in the first few months, and *Desecration* sold 2.9 million copies between its October publication and the end of the year.[79] There was a spike in sales, as there were with many books in the aftermath of 9/11. One chain reported that Bible sales increased by 27 percent the week after the Twin Towers collapsed, and Quran sales increased by even more than that. A number of publishers rushed out new versions of books on Islam, terrorism, the politics of the Middle East, prophecy, and finding God in times of tragedy. Others expanded print orders of books that were already slated for publication. The change was not as dramatic as many imagined, though. Booksellers worried as much about having too many books related to recent events as about not having enough. The best-selling book on Amazon.com in the week of the historic terrorist attack was actually Oprah Winfrey's book club pick, *The Corrections*, by Jonathan Franzen.[80] The ninth installment of *Left Behind* sold, and sold well, but not in numbers unimaginable apart from world historical events.

## VIII   *9/11 and the Anxiety Thesis*

Despite this, the novel's success was widely attributed to consumers' anxieties caused by the attacks and the new global war on terror. Journalists and scholars alike explained the series's success in this way. *Time* profiled Jenkins and LaHaye in summer 2002 and breezily attributed the series's commercial triumph to "this volatile moment." "It's fair to speculate," the magazine reported, "that last year's installment would not have outsold John Grisham's *Skipping Christmas* to become the biggest novel of 2001 if the planes had not crashed."[81]

The series's share of the market, though, was well established before 2001, and sales continued apace for the tenth and eleventh titles of the series, published in 2002 and 2003, respectively. When the first prequel, *The Rising*, was released in spring 2005, it also took the top slot on the *New York Times* bestseller list. Jenkins made this point in 2003, in interviews promoting his solo book, *Soon*. "We had a spike in sales" after 9/11, he said: "But the series was already going crazy, and it's stayed at that pace since then."[82]

Attributing the series's sales to cultural anxieties seemed—and seems—intuitively right to many, though the evidence does not support that interpretation. It is true, as Jason Bivins has convincingly argued, that the novels are filled with "the erotics of fear" and seek to situate readers in interpretive frames where "fearful dreams and messianic optimism promise certitude but yield an erotics and a demonology that pull against, or at least defer, this promise."[83] Nevertheless, how readers read and how they position themselves in response to texts are quite complicated. Both quantitative and qualitative studies show that *Left Behind* readers and their motives and psychological needs cannot be easily characterized.

The Barna Group, a respected polling organization that specializes in studies of evangelicals, looked at the consumption of evangelical media in 2002. It found that Christian-produced books, television, and music reached far beyond the believing masses. In fact, there were twenty-seven million Americans who were not self-identified churchgoers, and another fifteen million who said that they were not associated with Christianity in any way, who had, nonetheless, consumed some form of Christian media in the previous month. About 70 percent of all Americans—more than twice the percentage of evangelicals in the country—told the Barna Group pollsters that they had read a Christian book besides the Bible in the previous months. One out of every seven atheists and agnostics, notably, read Christian books such as *Left Behind* in 2002.[84] It strains credulity to conceive of all those readers as reading out of expressions of more or less identical anxiety. Popularity, as Ien Ang has argued, is an extremely complex thing. "Totalizing accounts of 'the audience,' "[85] she writes, where an "audience is taken-for-grantedly defined as an unknown but knowable set of people, not more, not less,"[86] tend to occlude more than they explain.

Sometimes critics, while explaining the success of *Left Behind* with the anxiety thesis, indirectly demonstrate the true range of readerships attracted to the series. "I picked them up," notes Gordan Harber in an otherwise snarky review published in the *New York Sun*, "because I was intrigued by their particular combination of entertainment and eschatology."[87] Though he distinguishes himself from what he imagines to be the intended audience, Harber also speaks for many, many readers of the series.

When the books were sold everywhere where books are sold, reviewed widely, and discussed widely, the *Left Behind* books were read for a wide variety of reasons.[88] Many likely read the books out of curiosity, many from an ironic distance, and many to see what "those people" really believe. There were also those who read the book to please a friend or family member, as Amy Johnson Frykholm shows in her study of *Left Behind* readers, *Rapture Culture*. In fact, although Frykholm's ethnographic work focused on readers who were within an evangelical milieu, she found that a number of readers had very ambivalent relationships to the novels. Of course there were those who used the novel to give form to their anxieties about their lives, the world, and cultural changes, but Frykholm also spoke to readers who found the apocalyptic scenario dramatized in *Left Behind* to be a source of humor.[89] She found many readers within the evangelical communities read the popular fictions because of how that connected them to their communities and she found a number of practicing evangelicals used the theology of the books to raise questions about the evangelical doctrines they were taught in their churches.[90] Frykholm's readers also repeatedly emphasized the books' fictionality and the extent to which fiction reading is creative and a kind of play.[91]

The novels' commercial success is not unrelated to the sometimes traumatic historical changes of the late twentieth and early twenty-first centuries. The "anxiety thesis," however, which explains the phenomenon of this fiction as resulting from widespread psychic insecurities, dramatically oversimplifies the many diverse motives of the fiction's mass audience. It misses, further, that an important part of the success of the books was how they were designed to appeal to a mass audience, to readers who read for different reasons. As Jenkins said, the hope, from the very beginning, was "to reach two audiences." The success, the triumph of the series that made it such a ubiquitous presence throughout American culture, was that it reached so many different sorts of readers who read for so many different reasons. To account for how that happened, it is important to examine how the evangelical fiction market changed.

The story of the phenomenon of *Left Behind* is not a simple story of consumers who were suddenly anxious. Closer examination reveals that the history of the fiction's commercial success is the history of a market transformation. When the first novel was published, evangelical fiction was restricted to the Christian Booksellers Association's distribution channels, and sales were limited. After evangelical publishers struggled to overcome those limitations for many years, Tyndale found a way to reach a wider audience, getting its books to nonevangelical retailers. *Left Behind*, designed from the beginning for broad appeal, was the vehicle. By the year 2000, fully half of all of *Left Behind*'s sales were outside the traditional Christian market. The novels "made their way into Wal-Mart and other mass merchandisers, plus Barnes & Noble, Borders and Chapters— even airport bookstores, rare venues for evangelical Christian books."[92] The effects of this were evident industry-wide. According to *Christianity Today*, *Left Behind* was one of the fifty most influential evangelical books of the twentieth century because of how it transformed evangelical publishing. "The book," the magazine reported, "launched a marketing empire that launched a new set of rules for Christian fiction."[93] The number of faith fiction titles available from evangelical and nonevangelical publishers increased from about 500 in 1990 to more than 2,500 in 2004. By the middle of the first decade of the twenty-first century, publishers were printing more than four hundred new evangelical novels per year.[94] With genres multiplying and production increasing, sales grew, too. Evangelical publishing was estimated to be a $1 million-per-year business in the 1980s. By the 2000s, Wal-Mart alone was selling more than $1 million worth of evangelical publishers' products annually.[95] Things changed, and that change can be seen in an examination of the economic history of the *Left Behind* books. Publishers and profit motives must be given their due.

## *Notes*

1. Robert Darnton, *The Business of the Enlightenment: A Publishing History of the "Enyclopédie" 1775–1800* (Cambridge: Harvard University Press, 1979), 7.
2. Robert Darnton, "What Is the History of Books?" in *The Book History Reader*, ed. David Finkelstein and Alistair McCleery (Abingdon, England: Routledge, 2006), 9–26.
3. Darnton, *Business of the Enlightenment*, 3.
4. Janice Radway, *Reading the Romance: Women, Patriarchy, and Popular Literature* (Chapel Hill: University of North Carolina Press, 1991), 19–20.
5. Ibid., 45.
6. See, for example, Crawford Gribben, *Writing the Rapture: Prophecy Fiction in Evangelical America* (Oxford: Oxford University Press, 2009); Jason Bivins, *Religion of Fear: The Politics of Horror in Conservative Evangelicalism* (Oxford: Oxford University Press, 2008); Peter Gardella, "Spiritual Warfare in the Fiction of Frank Peretti," in *Religions of the United States in Practice, vol. 2*, ed. Colleen McDannell (Princeton: Princeton University Press, 2001) 328–345; Valerie Weaver-Zercher, *Thrill of the Chaste: The Allure of Amish Romance Novels* (Baltimore: Johns Hopkins University Press, 2013); Glenn W. Shuck, *Marks of the Beast: The "Left Behind" Novels and the Struggle for Evangelical Identity* (New York: New York University Press, 2005); Anita Gandolfo, *Faith and Fiction: Christian Literature in America Today* (Westport, Conn.: Praeger, 2007); Amy Hungerford, *Postmodern Belief: American Literature and Religion since 1960* (Princeton: Princeton University Press, 2010); Bruce David Forbes and Jeanne Halgren Kilde, eds., *Rapture, Revelation, and the End Times: Exploring the "Left Behind" Series* (New York: Palgrave Macmillan, 2004).
7. See, for example, Amy Johnson Frykholm, *Rapture Culture: "Left Behind" in Evangelical America* (Oxford: Oxford University Press, 2004); Lynn S. Neal, *Romancing God: Evangelical Women and Inspirational Fiction* (Chapel Hill: University of North Carolina Press, 2006); and Weaver-Zercher, *Thrill of the Chaste*.

8. Heather Hendershot's landmark book *Shaking the World for Jesus: Media and Conservative Evangelical Culture* (Chicago: University of Chicago Press, 2004) examines many market developments but does not look at novels. Collen McDannell's *Material Christianity: Religion and Popular Culture in America* (New Haven: Yale University Press, 1995) devotes an important chapter to Christian retail stores but does not focus on book sales. McDannell writes that "while books and music are prominently displayed in the stores, it is the gifts, clothing, jewelry, art, and novelties that catch the eye" (222). Neal gives a brief history of the market for evangelical romances in *Romancing God*, and Jonathan Cordero takes a sociological look at the role of gatekeepers in the evangelical publishing industry in "Producing Christian Fiction," *Journal of Religion and Popular Culture 6*, no. 1 (Spring 2004), http://utpjournals.metapress.com/content/a78o18347302664u/. One of the more extensive treatments of Christian fiction book markets is in Weaver-Zercher's 2013 study of Amish romances. Weaver-Zercher gives two chapters of *Thrill of the Chaste* to the market conditions of Amish romances, covering new and important ground.

9. "Dr. Tim LaHaye Bio," LeftBehind.com, n.d., http://www.leftbehind.com/03_authors_testimonials/bio_lahaye.asp; Gribben, *Writing the Rapture*, 136.

10. Bruce Bickel and Stan Jantz, *His Time, His Way: The CBA Story: 1950–1999* (Colorado Springs: CBA, 1999), 94.

11. *Where There Is a Vision: The Inspiring Story of God's Faithfulness through Fifty Years of Publishing the Good News* (Westchester, Ill.: Good News Publishers, 1988), 102.

12. Steve Rabey, "No Longer Left Behind," *Christianity Today*, April 22, 2002, http://www.christianitytoday.com/ct/2002/april22/1.26.html; Jerry B. Jenkins, *Writing for the Soul* (Cincinnati: Writer's Digest, 2006), 3.

13. Gene Edward Veith, "Whatever Happened to Christian Publishing?" *World*, July 12, 1997, http://www.worldmag.com/1997/07/whatever_happened_to_christian_publishing/page1.

14. James E. Ruark, *House of Zondervan* (Grand Rapids: Zondervan, 2006), 161.

15. Harold Myra, "Ken Taylor: God's Voice in the Vernacular," *Christianity Today*, October 5, 1979, 21–22.

16. William Lobdell, "Christian Fiction Finally Has a Prayer of Selling," *Los Angeles Times*, July 6, 2002, http://articles.latimes.com/2002/jul/06/local/me-fiction6.

17. Carl E. Olson, "LaHaying the Rapture on Thick," *Catholic Culture*, n.d., http://www.catholicculture.org/culture/library/view.cfm?recnum=4621.

18. Dick Staub, "Jerry Jenkins's Solo Apocalypse," *Christianity Today*, September 1, 2003, http://www.christianitytoday.com/ct/2003/septemberweb-only/9-15-23.0.html.

19. Jenkins, *Writing for the Soul*, 10; "Books," Jerry B. Jenkins, n.d., http://jerry-jenkins.com/books/.

20. "Jerry Jenkins on Writing the Left Behind Series," LeftBehind.com, November 20, 2003, http://www.leftbehind.com/03_authors_testimonials/viewAuthorInteractions.asp?pageid=876&channelID=79.

21. Jeff Gerke, "Please Welcome . . . Jerry B. Jenkins," *Where the Map Ends*, n.d., http://www.wherethemapends.com/Interviews/jerry_jenkins.htm.

22. Daniel Radosh, *Rapture Ready! Adventures in the Parallel Universe of Christian Pop Culture* (New York: Scribner, 2008), 94.

23. Jenkins, *Writing for the Soul*, 3.

24. Bickel and Jantz, *His Time, His Way*, 100; Paul P. Harris, *This Rotarian Age* (Chicago: Rotary International, 1935), 96–98.

25. Rabey, "No Longer Left Behind."

26. Veith, "Whatever Happened to Christian Publishing?"

27. Jenkins, *Writing for the Soul*, 1–2.

28. "FAQ," AliveCommunications.com, n.d., http://www.alivecommunications.com/question-and-answer/.

29. Rabey, "No Longer Left Behind."

30. Hungerford, *Postmodern Belief*, 123.

31. Rabey, "No Longer Left Behind."

32. Jenkins, *Writing for the Soul*, 6.

33. Ruark, *House of Zondervan*, 123–127.

34. Ibid., 125–126.

35. Ibid., 127–128.

36. Ibid., 71.

37. Ibid., 160.

38. Ibid., 160–161.

39. Veith, "Whatever Happened to Christian Publishing?"

40. Ruark, *House of Zondervan*, 168. Zondervan was purchased for $56.7 million, or $13.50 per share, after a financial scandal shook the company and led to a series of hostile takeover attempts. The sale to Harper & Row marked the end of what *Publishers Weekly* called Zondervan's "decade of travail." Part of the purchasing agreement allowed Zondervan to retain a mission statement declaring it a "company seeking to glorify God and serve Jesus Christ." It was also understood that Zondervan would remain separate and distinct from Harper's other religious imprint, with the former continuing to operate in Grand Rapids and the latter in San Francisco.

41. Ibid., 200.

42. Ibid., 169.

43. See Charles A. Madison, *Book Publishing in America* (New York: McGraw-Hill, 1966), 547–556; Kenneth C. Davis, *Two-Bit Culture: The Paperbacking of America* (Boston: Houghton Mifflin, 1984); and Laura J. Miller, *Reluctant Capitalists: Bookselling and the Culture of Consumption* (Chicago: University of Chicago Press, 2007), 38–39.

44. Bethany Moreton, *To Serve God and Wal-Mart: The Making of Christian Free Enterprise* (Cambridge: Harvard University Press, 2010).

45. "News of Interest to Christians: K Mart Adds Child Pornography to Book Line; Now Carries Adult Porn, Homosexual Porn and Child Porn," *Sword of the Lord*, December 21, 1990.

46. "AFA Boycott Helps Drop Kmart Profits, Force Closing of 110 Stores," *American Family Association Journal*, November/December 1994, 22.

47. Dan McGraw, "KMart Pays a Steep Price," *U.S. News and World Report*, November 13, 1995, 90.

48. A. J. Kiesling, "Religion Publishing's Black Hole," *Publishers Weekly*, March 22, 2004, http://www.publishersweekly.com/pw/print/20040322/34743-religion-publishing-s-black-hole.html.

49. "Christian Publishers, Retailers Unhappy with Spring Arbor," *Publishers Weekly*, November 16, 1998, http://www.publishersweekly.com/pw/print/19981116/19734-christian-publishers-retailers-unhappy-with-spring-arbor.html.

50. Jenkins, *Writing for the Soul*, 6.

51. Cindy Crosby, "Left Behind Fuels Growth at Tyndale House," *Publishers Weekly*, May 10, 2001, http://www.publishersweekly.com/pw/print/20010507/38487-left-behind-fuels-growth-at-tyndale-house.html.

52. Frykholm, *Rapture Culture*, 7, 40.

53. Laurie Goodstein, "Fast-Selling Thrillers Depict Prophetic Views of Final Days," *New York Times*, October 4, 1998, http://www.nytimes.com/1998/10/04/us/fast-selling-thrillers-depict-prophetic-view-of-final-days.html?pagewanted=all&src=pm.

54. Crosby, "Left Behind Fuels Growth at Tyndale House."

55. Ibid.; Frykholm, *Rapture Culture*, 124–127.

56. Crosby, "Left Behind Fuels Growth at Tyndale House."

57. "Barnes & Noble History," *Barnes & Noble Booksellers*, n.d., http://www.barnesandnobleinc.com/our_company/history/bn_history.html.

58. Rabey, "No Longer Left Behind."

59. Rabey, "Apocalyptic Sales Out of This World," *Christianity Today*, March 1, 1999, http://www.ctlibrary.com/ct/1999/march1/9t319a.html.

60. Hendershot, *Shaking the World for Jesus*, 178.

61. Goodstein, "Fast-Selling Thrillers Depict Prophetic Views of Final Days."

62. Rabey, "Apocalyptic Sales Out of This World."

63. Dinitia Smith, "Apocalyptic Potboiler Is Publisher's Dream," *New York Times*, June 8, 2000, http://www.nytimes.com/2000/06/08/books/apocalyptic-potboiler-is-publisher-s-dream.html?pagewanted=all&src=pm.

64. Crosby, "Left Behind Fuels Growth at Tyndale House."

65. Corrie Cutrer, "Publishing: Left Behind Series Puts Tyndale Ahead," *Christianity Today*, November 13, 2000, http://www.ctlibrary.com/ct/2000/november13/20.26.html.

66. Crosby, "Left Behind Fuels Growth at Tyndale House."

67. Smith, "Apocalyptic Potboiler Is Publisher's Dream."

68. Ibid.

69. Martin Kettle, "Apocalyptic Fundamentalists Set to Shove Harry Potter Aside," *Guardian*, June 9, 2000, http://www.theguardian.com/world/2000/jun/09/books.booksnews.

70. Crosby, "Left Behind Fuels Growth at Tyndale House."

71. Stephen McGarvey, "Nothing but a God Thing," *CrossWalk*, n.d., http://m.crosswalk.com/archive/nothing-but-a-god-thing-1108584.html.

72. Crosby, "Left Behind Fuels Growth at Tyndale House."

73. Cutrer, "Publishing."

74. Ibid.

75. Rabey, "No Longer Left Behind."

76. Ibid.

77. McGarvey, "Nothing but a God Thing."

78. Rabey, "No Longer Left Behind."

79. "'Left Behind' #9, 'Desecration,' Is Top Seller for 2001," *PR Newswire*, February 26, 2002, http://www.prnewswire.com/news-releases/left-behind-9-desecration-is-top-seller-for-2001-two-christian-books-lead-the-lists-76170457.html.

80. Teresa F. Lindeman, "Seeking Answers through Books," *Pittsburgh Post-Gazette*, October 7, 2001, http://old.post-gazette.com/businessnews/200 11007books1007bnp2.asp.

81. John Cloud and Rancho Mirage, "Meet the Prophet," *Time Magazine*, July 1, 2002, http://ti.me/75vURZ.

82. Staub, "Jerry Jenkins's Solo Apocalypse."

83. Bivins, *Religion of Fear*, 35, 211.

84. Barna Group, "Christian Mass Media Reach More Adults with Christian Message than Do Churches," *Barna Group*, July 2, 2002, http://www.barna.org/barna-update/article/5-barna-update/77-christian-mass-media-reach-more-adults-with-the-christian-message-than-do-churches.

85. Ien Ang, *Desperately Seeking the Audience* (London: Routledge, 1991), x.

86. Ibid., 2.

87. Gordan Harber, "The Ministry of Fear," *New York Sun*, August 23, 2004, http://www.nysun.com/arts/ministry-of-fear/681/.

88. One helpful way to conceptualize the possible, general orientations readers can take toward a text is suggested by theorist Stuart Hall in "Encoding/decoding," in *Culture, Media, Language*, eds. Stuart Hall, Dorothy Hobson, Andrew Lowe, and Paul Willis (New York: Routledge, 1996), 128–138. He suggests that readers can take a "dominant" position, accepting and identifying with the meaning and ideology of the text. Readers can also, however, take an "oppositional" position. They identify with a hermeneutic that they believe enables them to, in a sense, "see through" the text. There is also a third possible position, that

of "negotiated" reading. These readers, Hall says, generally accept the larger frame and much of the message but adapt it "to local conditions."

89. Frykholm, *Rapture Culture*, 108–109, 119.

90. Ibid., 39–66.

91. "Over and over again in interviews," Frykholm writes, "I ask the question, 'Are these books accurate? Is this the way the world is going to end?' Over and over again, I receive the same answer, 'Yes, but they are just somebody's interpretation. They are only fiction'" (ibid., 133). These readers' position on the truth and fictionality of *Left Behind* does not seem particularly unique to that series. As James Wood has written, readers "try on" the reality of fiction, in a game "of not-quite-belief" (*The Broken Estate: Essays on Literature and Belief* [New York: Picado, 2000], xxi).

92. David E. Horton, "Looking at Left Behind," *On Mission*, circa 2000, http://www.onmission.com/onmissionpb.aspx?pageid=8589964399.

93. "The Top 50 Books that Have Shaped Evangelicals," *Christianity Today*, October 6, 2006, http://www.christianitytoday.com/ct/2006/october/23.51.html?paging=off.

94. Claire Kirch, "The Main Debate," *Publishers Weekly*, March 28, 2005, http://www.publishersweekly.com/pw/print/20050328/20061-the-main-debate.html.

95. Moreton, *To Serve God and Wal-Mart*, 91.

## PART FOUR

*Religious Resistance and Adaptation to the Market*

# 8

## Selling Infinite Selves

### YOUTH CULTURE AND CONTEMPORARY FESTIVALS

*Sarah M. Pike*

RIDING AWAY FROM the Temple of Transition, a cathedral-like structure created at Burning Man in 2011 to memorialize dead loved ones, I rode out on my bicycle across a barren stretch of the Black Rock Desert. A set of white pillars soon loomed before me, and when I looked closely, I saw "Ten Tenets" posted on them, including "Do not covet world peace or any other conclusion. Life is alive with infinite possibilities and infinite worlds. . . . Go out and seek miracles on a day at Burning Man." Of the many slogans expressed at the annual Burning Man arts festival, this one is as good as any to sum up what many "Burners" believe to be their spiritual mission at the festival: to seek the miraculous and infinite possibilities made available to them by the festival. But the tenet also captures the sentiments of a growing number of Americans—many of them young—attending large-scale music and art festivals that take place outside religious institutions and yet serve as spiritually charged destinations of annual pilgrimage.[1] While the news media and other observers typically stress the secular nature of music and art festivals, their unbridled excesses, and their financial success, festival-goers locate gatherings such as Burning Man and Earthdance at the center of their spiritual lives.[2]

The proliferation and growth, especially among younger attendees, of gatherings such as Coachella (a music festival in Indio, California), Earthdance events occurring across the country, Faerieworlds (outside of Portland, Oregon), and Burning Man (in Nevada's Black Rock Desert) suggest that the diversity of festivals is a feature of the American religious landscape that is being reshaped by young adults exploring spirituality outside institutional religion.[3] Jeet Kei Leung, a festival organizer and musician, calls these events "transformational festivals" that "rejoin sacred ritual with secular festival."[4] According to participants, such events offer opportunities for pilgrimage, transformation, and spiritual experience without requiring commitment to specific creeds or doctrines. While most of these events were not originally intended to be spiritual destinations, for many of their participants they have become sacred spaces for exploring, in the words of the Ten Tenets, "infinite possibilities and infinite worlds."

The infinite worlds that festivals offer are made possible in part by their construction as places apart from daily life and especially in contrast to a consumer society.[5] Festivals are sacred destinations set apart in festival-goers' minds from what Burning Man participants call the "default world." However, because many festivals involve corporate sponsorship and expensive tickets, necessitate the purchase of goods, and make use of social media, festival-goers remain quintessential consumers. Even utopian festival spaces far removed from ordinary life are permeated by the marketplace. Blending big business with possibilities for spiritual transformation, festivals embody the contradictions that many Americans face when they try to create alternative religious models: the market creeps in. In order to make festivals into attractive spiritual destinations separate from consumer society, festival-goers must negotiate between their identities as spiritual selves and as secular consumers. Festivals, then, are important sites for exploring some of the contradictions and issues involved with young Americans' spiritual seeking in the context of market forces. At the same time, the landscape of American festivals offers clues to trends in young Americans' spiritual concerns at the beginning of the twenty-first century.

## *I   Youth Spirituality and Twenty-First-Century Festivals*

If you are a twenty-something Californian, between June and September you have the pick of dozens of festivals that combine music, art, green lifestyles, and spirituality.[6] Atheist or Christian, you can "buy" these spiritual vacations for several hundred dollars or more. Twenty-first-century festivals of music, art, and spirit exist on a spectrum from the most secular, such as Coachella, with its unabashed commercialism, to the most explicitly spiritual, such as Earthdance, which is promoted as "a festival of spiritual consciousness, environmental political activism and awareness." Although many festivals are located on the West Coast, others take place across the country; the largest, in fact, is Bonnaroo, held every summer on a seven hundred-acre farm in rural Tennessee. Most festivals take place in remote or rural locations, and most participants camp on or near festival sites, although a minority stays in nearby hotels. Although unaffiliated with any particular religious tradition, these festivals include motivational speakers, yoga and dance, workshops on healing arts, indigenous cultures, shamanism, rituals, shrines, altars, and smaller sacred spaces within festival grounds.

All of these resources provide a map for personal transformation. In a survey of Burning Man participants in 2000, 63 percent of respondents either agreed or strongly agreed that "Burning Man has changed my life."[7] In news coverage as well as promotional self-descriptions these festivals often reference each other, lending further credence to the sense many observers and participants have that they are very much part of a shared movement. Pagan blogger and festival-goer Jason Pitzl-Waters observes, "Faerieworlds, for example, is very much in the tradition of fantasy-oriented European festivals like Castlefest, merged with Pagan, Burner, and Tribal elements."[8] Local news coverage of Faerieworlds describes the festival as "a Bonnaroo staged in Middle Earth,"[9] and *Common Ground* magazine describes Earthdance as a "festival that combines the artistic liberation of Burning Man with the socially responsible conscience of the Oregon Country Fair."[10] Participants in different festivals clearly recognize each other as belonging to a trend of young Americans blurring the boundaries between leisure time and spiritual engagement.[11]

While each of these events has distinctive features, they all experienced steady growth during the first decade of the twenty-first century.[12] Although festivals attract all ages, participants are disproportionately young Americans between eighteen and thirty years old, and the increasing attendance at festivals over the past decade is largely due to an increase in young adult attendees.[13] Coachella had become so large (75,000 attendees in 2011) that in 2012 it split into two festivals. Earthdance, which started in California and was held in eighteen locations in 1997, had spread to more than five hundred locations in seventy-five countries by 2011. And Faerieworlds, just over ten years old in 2011, added a new fall harvest event that year in addition to its annual summer solstice gathering.[14] Burning

Man's attendance has increased every year since its founding in 1986, and it sold out for the first time ever in 2011 at 50,000 tickets.[15] The proliferation of festivals that cater to young Americans of diverse religious backgrounds and serve as spiritual destinations is an important but overlooked aspect of young adults' spiritual experience outside religious institutions.[16]

Many of the young Americans who attend festivals consider themselves to be "spiritual, but not religious," by which they mean institutionally unaffiliated.[17] They belong to the ranks of the "unchurched," described by religious studies scholar Robert Fuller in his 2001 book, *Spiritual, but Not Religious: Understanding Unchurched America*: Americans who disavow membership in churches, synagogues, or other traditional religious institutions.[18] While festivals also include participants who identify as Christian, Jewish, Pagan, and so on, for many young adults, festival settings encourage talk of "spirituality," rather than religious identities linked to particular traditions.[19] The context of these events varies from giant parties to holidays from work to places to see one's favorite band, dress up and dance for hours, and enjoy what participants describe as spiritual experiences within a spiritual community.

## II   A Short History of American Festivals as Spiritual Destinations

Spiritually charged gatherings attracting young adults have a long history in the United States. These events exemplify what Catherine Albanese has called the metaphysical tradition in American religious history. In *A Republic of Mind and Spirit*, Albanese's exhaustive study of metaphysical religion, she identifies a strand of American religiosity that she argues is just as central as evangelicalism or mainstream denominations in shaping American religious life. According to Albanese, metaphysical religion is characterized by the following: "a preoccupation with mind and its powers"; a "predisposition" toward ancient theories of "correspondence" between self and cosmos; beliefs that mind and universe are dynamic and full of energy; and a "yearning for salvation understood as solace, comfort, therapy, and healing."[20] While not all of these characteristics are present at all festivals, many of them shape festival-goers' experiences and expectations.

Contemporary music and art festivals with metaphysical themes belong to a tradition of collective occasions that, to borrow historian Jon

Butler's phrase, first flourished in the "spiritual hothouse" of the nineteenth century. Chautauquas, outdoor revivals, camp meetings, lyceum programs, and Spiritualist conventions were all intended to transform the minds and spirits of nineteenth-century men and women—and especially young men and women. I want to look briefly at these earlier American events in order to contextualize contemporary festivals in a tradition of American worship where outdoor collective gatherings have promised and provided transformative experiences and offered alternatives to other religious options.

Like contemporary festivals, these nineteenth-century events were consciously experienced apart from the rhythms of daily life. Camp meetings were "religious holidays," according to historian R. Laurence Moore: sites to travel to by leaving home and thus abandoning everyday domestic and work routines, even if only to journey to the outskirts of town, where tents were set up in farmers' fields. As Moore and others have argued, nineteenth-century gatherings blended sacred and secular activities.[21] Goods and services were available for purchase, so that, even though these spaces were set apart from daily life, they remained implicated in the marketplace. Nineteenth-century camp meetings and early twentieth-century Chautauquas represented not the disappearance of religion, as secularization proponents expected, but, rather, its commoditization. As Moore observes, "Religious influences established themselves in the forms of commercial culture that emerged in the nineteenth century, turning the United States into a flowering Eden of leisure industries by the middle of the twentieth."[22]

Moore suggests that, as religious experience was commoditized, Americans were "learning to purchase 'culture' as a means of self-improvement and relaxation."[23] In this way multiple meanings and desires converged on the beaches, farms, and wooded areas where many of these earlier gatherings were held. Like music and art festivals of the twenty-first century, earlier events served as vacation retreats, provided opportunities for conversion experiences, and exposed their participants to new ideas and lifestyles. Further, like their twenty-first-century counterparts, they were suspect in their effervescence.

"Critics complained," Moore writes, "but the setting of the revival, for the space of the few hours or days, often protected practices that were elsewhere forbidden."[24] Camp meetings, then, were often seen as subversive and suspect in their challenge to acceptable religious practices.[25] Historian Nathan O. Hatch observes that critics of camp meetings "perceived a manifest subversiveness in the form and structure of the camp meeting itself, which openly defied ecclesiastical standards of time, space, authority and liturgical form."[26] According to Hatch, outsiders were threatened by the "intense enthusiasm of congregated masses, the unbridled communal force and overwhelming power that swept over these occasions."[27] The sense of these events as excessive and boundaryless contributed to their attractiveness as spiritual destinations.

The Chautauqua movement flourished later in the nineteenth century, following in the footsteps of camp meetings and lyceums and, like them, successfully blending sacred and secular activities. The Chautauqua circuit began as an adult education movement focused around lectures and nondenominational Christian preaching. A Methodist minister and businessman organized the first Chautauqua in 1874 in western New York, and by 1900 there were two hundred pavilions in thirty-one states featuring opportunities for education as well as entertainment.[28] As with their camp meeting forebears, a carnival-like atmosphere prevailed at these gatherings. By 1924, tens of thousands of Americans had visited Chautauqua tents and enjoyed their diverse programming, which blended vacation time with study and entertainment.[29] On the program were teachers, preachers, explorers, travelers, scientists, politicians, singers, violinists, pianists, bell-ringers, glee clubs, bands, orchestras, concert companies, quartettes, quintets, sextets, elocutionists, jugglers, magicians, whistlers, and yodelers.[30] The great number of Chautauquas, as well as the absence of any central authority over them, meant that religious patterns varied greatly among them. Some were so religiously oriented that they closely resembled church retreats, while more secular Chautauquas with their animal acts and trapeze acrobats competed with vaudeville in theaters and circus tent shows. Chautauquas positioned themselves carefully vis-à-vis the marketplace, providing a wide variety of services for participants. In this way, Chautauquas are one of the best examples from the early twentieth century of sites offering an infinite world of experience and yet detached from any particular religious affiliation.

As sites of spiritual experience, contemporary festivals also have roots in American and British countercultural events of the late 1960s and early 1970s, such as the Summer of Love gatherings in San Francisco, the 1969 Woodstock festival in New York, and the Glastonbury Festival (founded in 1971) in England.[31] Nineteenth-century collective practices such as channeling and mental healing enjoyed a resurgence of popularity in gatherings like these and others in the 1960s. The promotion of a "Human Be-In" gathering in San Francisco's Golden Gate Park in 1967 promised a "Gathering of the Tribes" with language that sounds much like today's festival marketing. The identification with "tribe" and the turn to Asian and Native American cultures for spiritual wisdom developed during 1960s countercultural events. Tens of thousands of participants showed up in Golden Gate Park to hear Timothy Leary, Allen Ginsberg, and other famous 1960s figures speak, as well as to dance to the music of popular 1960s bands such as Jefferson Airplane.[32] Unlike many twenty-first-century festivals, 1960s festivals were often free or cost little; nevertheless, clothing, jewelry, and other consumer goods also had a part in these earlier festivals.

Contemporary American music and art festivals that also function as spiritual destinations have their counterparts in other countries as well as in the past. Some European festivals are also largely geared toward young adults, such as Fusion Festival in Germany (founded in 1997)[33] and the Polish Woodstock festival, Przystanek Woodstock, which attracted half a million attendees from all over the world in 2009.[34] What these events share may be captured, at least in part, by journalist Erik Davis's moniker "the cult of experience." Davis suggests that Burning Man is characterized by "the ultimate attention economy: what participants exchange are the willingness, and the opportunities, to submit to new experience."[35] In Burning Man founder Larry Harvey's words, "Beyond belief, beyond the dogmas, creeds, and metaphysical ideas of religion, there is immediate experience."[36] By the 1990s, raves—large-scale music and dance events that started to become popular in the 1980s—had blended with the "outdoor experience of the West Coast" and contributed to the development of festivals focused on art (Burning Man), music (Coachella), and dance (Earthdance).[37] Many festivals also incorporated aspects of contemporary Pagan festivals, such as being timed to coincide with solstices and equinoxes and including opening and closing circles.[38] As Pagan blogger Jason Pitzl-Waters observes on his blog, *The Wild Hunt*, "These festivals have adopted practices and rituals from modern Paganism, incorporating opening and closing circles, altars, invocations of sacred land, and pre-Christian (often Goddess) imagery."[39] This movement of festivals that integrate youth culture, contemporary Paganism, and the legacy of the 1960s counterculture suggests a trend in the global West that crosses national boundaries, creating sites of communal and spiritual meaning for large crowds of young adults from Poland to California.

## III   How Festivals Became Extraordinary Places

Geographer Rob Shields describes powerful sites like festivals as "an imaginary geography vis-à-vis the place-myths of other towns and regions which form the contrast which established these sites as liminal destinations."[40] Participants create and maintain festival boundaries through the place myths they share with each other. They work before, during, and after festivals at making an extraordinary experience set apart from their lives "back home."[41] When they describe festivals as special places apart from daily life, festival-goers identify festivals with their spiritual selves and the rest of their lives with secular society.[42] Nadia, who attended Coachella in 2011, pointed out in her review of the festival that "live music for me is like going to a place of worship. It's an environment where I feel completely free."[43] Carrie, a graduate student in her twenties, explained to me that Burning Man "is my religious holiday."[44] As holidays that stand in stark contrast to the quotidian, festivals exemplify David Chidester's description of American sacred spaces in which "sacred meaning and significance, holy awe and desire" turn a place into "a site for intensive interpretation."[45] These events are sites of intensive interpretation where meaning becomes concentrated at specific times, such as the summer solstice, and in particular spaces, such as the Black Rock Desert, where Burning Man takes place. Burning Man's and Coachella's locations in remote desert areas, like the hills of Kentucky where nineteenth-century camp meetings were held, are strange and wild to the city dwellers who make up the majority of their communities and provide a sensual and aesthetic contrast to the everyday world back home.

In order to heighten the contrast to life back home, festival-goers emphasize the preparation and journey to the festival space, dress in special clothing, and ritualize the passage through festival boundaries in order to mark these sites as separate from ordinary life. The festival experience begins days or even months in advance, as festival-goers plan and prepare for the event to come. They tell stories of extraordinary experiences and share photos and videos online and in person, creating expectations for the upcoming event. They make costumes, divide up cooking duties with camp mates, work on art projects, decide which bands and musicians they most want to see, buy items to bring, and, for Burning Man, even construct portable altars to memorialize dead loved ones at Burning Man's temple.[46] In this way, mundane things and daily life are already becoming consecrated, even outside the festival, as memories and expectations are evoked in these acts of preparation and facilitated through social networking on Facebook and other sites.[47]

Armed with expectations, festival-goers embark on a pilgrimage-like journey to sites that are usually far away from home, driving for hours and sometimes days to remote deserts, farms, and woods removed from urban life: "Coachella is a pilgrimage; a journey to a sleepy, out-of-the-way area in the scorching desert known mainly as a place to retire. They plan their trips months in advance, pack days before the festival and drive hours to get to it."[48] Accounts of even the most secular festivals, such as Coachella and Bonnaroo, are couched in the language of pilgrimage and sacred space. Angela, an undergraduate student, told me that she had found traveling to Coachella to be a sacred pilgrimage and the festival site to be the location of her spiritual community.[49] Blogger Andrew Smith describes going to Bonnaroo—"trekking down to Manchester, Tennessee for another music festival"—as a "limitless emotional and spiritual experience," which for him "touches the body and soul like embarking on a mission trip or a fishing trip or a combat mission—where music fandom stretches your physical limits."[50] In this way, many festival-goers liken their pilgrimage to festival sites to other kinds of special journeys that take them away from ordinary concerns.

Once they arrive, they are usually forced to wait in long lines at festival entrances, an ordeal that heightens their sense of arriving at a special destination. Burning Man's entrance gate, where participants often wait for hours, includes a "Greeter's Station" where costumed or nude greeters welcome arrivals to the festival with exclamations of "Welcome home!" Festival boundaries are also sharpened by a search of some sort (for illegal substances or stowaways). One Coachella participant described arrival in this way:

> How does one describe heaven? You really can't cause my idea of heaven is a place where each person has an individualized sense of total consciousness and joy. For me, heaven is getting out of the car and walking towards the gates, barely able to restrain the urge to sprint and scream and giggle because the excitement is totally overwhelming. Saint Peter isn't at the gates of my heaven. A townie with an electronic scanner and a slight dependency on crystal meth works the gate here. You present your ticket and are given passage to the other side. 5 stages of music, plus the Do-Lab, are the choirs of angels and they JAM. . . . It's got to be heaven.[51]

Once they enter festival grounds, being in "heaven" means participants know that they have entered a different realm of the senses. Festival spaces sound, smell, and look different: Music permeates the sites, while nature is visibly present, as are crowds of other people. Cars are not allowed in most areas, so participants must walk or bicycle around festival grounds. Work schedules are replaced by festival time. Festival-goers' bodies are also subject to sun, heat, rain, and other conditions that highlight their physical vulnerability. In accounts of the festival, bodily experiences that are both positive (feelings of love and pleasure) and negative (being hot in the intense midday desert sun or buffeted by torrential rains) are often mentioned to explain how the festival experience was special and different from ordinary life. In her review of Coachella, Geneva exclaims, "Who knew spending one weekend sweating my butt off in the desert, roaming grass fields in search of good bands and being a dirty, barefoot hippie would be the MOST AMAZING WEEKEND OF MY LIFE?! This is definitely one of the best memories I'll ever have of my youth."[52] Whether suffering or delighted, participants experience their bodies differently in festival space. Significantly, the festival self is not just an inner state of consciousness but is experienced though the body and movement as festival-goers explore dance, costume, face paint, masks, and nudity and buy new clothes and jewelry.

Events such as Burning Man and Faerieworlds that emphasize individual creativity and costuming as art forms offer particularly vivid aesthetic contrasts to life back home. For many festival-goers, their undressed or beautifully adorned festival bodies are the inverse of what they wear outside festival bounds.[53] Donning fairy wings or body paint helps to underscore festival-goers' identification with cultures of the past and with child selves of their own pasts, including the memories and inner histories that they bring with them to festival sites. Faerieworlds organizers describe dressing up in this way: "In a world where we are bombarded daily with so much information, young people want to believe there is more to the world than they see and that maybe they are magical. This is why faerie believers wear wings: they are symbols of flight, freedom and beauty and declarations of identity: I am more than what you see, I walk in two worlds."[54] The phrase "walking in two worlds" perfectly captures the festival experience of being an ordinary human being, on the one hand, and an extraordinary festival-goer wearing magical costumes or adorned with body paint, on the other. Erik Davis notes that "one of the first signs that you have stepped across the threshold into the festival is the difference in dress. . . . Style can channel your unique twist on the universe, but style can also be a way to affirm, and create, clan."[55] Festivals bring together the world of inner consciousness, which is made more accessible through adornment, with routines that are similar to those in ordinary life, such as eating and sleeping. What they buy and choose to wear marks participants as belonging to festival communities and suggests that they are ready and willing to walk in another world.

Bringing forward the child self of one's own past into the present through dress up and play is one important way to express the "infinite selves" made possible by festivals. The inner space of one's own past may be reshaped and reimagined in the festival space, especially through childlike play. A pedal-powered "Spinnin' Anemone Carousel" was featured at Burning Man in 2001, and Burning Man's 2008 event listing included "Tricycle Alley Open Track Time" hosted by a camp called "Tricycle Alley," which invited all interested participants to "come celebrate your inner child on our fleet of lightning fast tricycles."[56] While children themselves are present at most festivals, although generally not in large numbers, play areas equipped with giant seesaws, swings, roller rinks, and trampolines are designed especially for adults.[57] Thus, the sense of festivals as extraordinary worlds encourages participants to access their own experiences of childhood within a communal context of experimentation and play.

Another way in which festivals offer access to other worlds and stand in contrast to the rest of society is by linking participants to what they imagine to be a larger tribal community. Festivals sell neotribalism by linking festival communities to the pasts of the festival sites themselves and to indigenous cultures worldwide, although few indigenous people participate in these festivals. When they do attend, they are often accorded a special position. Burning Man has held workshops by Shoshone and Washoe Indians from western Nevada where the event takes place, and in 2011 Earthdance featured "Incan shamans" and a "Native American Elders Wisdom Council."[58] Some festivals are timed to occur during equinoxes and solstices in order to create connections to indigenous communities and the cultures of the European pre-Christian past that festival-goers believe lived more harmoniously with the cycles of the seasons. Faerieworlds organizers have made a point to play up this connection in their promotional materials: "We bring the tribes back together," claim Faerieworlds organizers, "at critical moments that have been celebrated through the ages."[59] As the Faerieworlds website puts it,

> At Harvest, we gather the Faerieworlds community in a communal feast to enjoy the best of our local, food, wine, beer and of course, our extraordinary arts and crafts, within an intimate festival village atmosphere around the Standing Stones. Together we will enjoy nature's bounty, shop our Mythic Marketplace, listen to amazing bands from around the country and across the world, and dance around a bonfire that celebrates the passing of the Summer Sun and welcomes the arrival of the Autumn Equinox. But most important, we will recognize and honor the friends and relationships that bind us to each other and create this wonderful inspiring, Faerieworlds community.[60]

In promotional materials for the festival, visions of a harmonious past and hopes for creating tribal communities across time and space are knit together in such a way as to attract participants.

But festivals do not simply recreate an imagined primordial past around "Standing Stones"; rather, they bring the past into a technologically advanced future by creating global communities on the Internet. Earthdance organizers explain how "what started as an event focused on electronic dance culture has grown to include all types of music genres, spiritual traditions and even indigenous tribes."[61] Festival neotribalism is not mainly about being deeply connected to a landscape as indigenous communities might be; it is about connecting with like-minded others across the planet. The highlight of Earthdance is when every Earthdance event around the world plays a specially created track called the "prayer for peace" at exactly the same time and all participants join the prayer at exactly the same moment, made possible by a synchronized clock that all Earthdance organizers consult: "Midnight in London, morning in Sydney and afternoon in California, it is a very powerful moment that unites every dance floor."[62] Bodies moving in space and time in northern California are mirrored by other bodies praying and dancing in the same way in Sydney, Australia, and other festival sites around the world. Marcelle, who participated in Earthdance's prayer in 2010, remembers feeling a sense of belonging to this global movement: "I really loved the mass meditation that took place all around the world. It was so powerful to know that I am part of such a huge powerful focus/meditation/vibration of mass consciousness. . . . It was the most beautiful feeling."[63] In this way festivals come to represent for their participants an ideal community that links humans to each other and to the nonhuman world. In festival space and time, festival-goers imagine that they can touch and see other worlds, other forms of consciousness, and other cultures of the past with which they resonate.

In order to imagine the festival as a place of self- and collective transformation, tribal community, and timeless power, festival-goers often criticize the outside world and mark festivals as sites of inversion, creating what philosopher Michel Foucault calls "heterotopias." Foucault suggests that there are marginal sites in every culture that "are something like counter-sites, a kind of effectively enacted utopia in which all the others are simultaneously represented, contested, and inverted."[64] One of the issues that festivals try to work out through inversion and contestation is festival-goers' relationship to the environment. For instance, in order to celebrate their perceived connection to indigenous cultures that lived more lightly on the land and to further mark their festival community as special and separate from the world outside, festival-goers make efforts to be "green" by creating sustainable festival practices. As alternatives to the world participants hope to leave behind, festivals claim to promote a sustainability-minded and earth-friendly atmosphere. Promotional materials and participants' accounts emphasize their efforts to live more sustainably, at least within the time and space of the festival.

Earthdance notes in "We Choose Green" that "the Earthdance festival strives to implement greening policies wherever possible. This includes on-site recycling and trash sorting, the use of eco-dinnerware by our vendors, bio diesel fuel for generators, ride share boards, soy based inks and recycled paper for flyers, etc."[65] Most festivals also promote and facilitate carpooling in order to reduce fuel consumption as people travel to them, such as "Carpoolchella" advertized on Coachella's website. Burning Man's motto "Leave No Trace" is facilitated by an elaborate recycling camp and rules that require participants to take everything out with them. Burning Man's camping area, Black Rock City, includes an "Alternative Energy Zone." Even a more explicitly commercial festival such as Coachella promotes its interactive recycling bin art walk, human-powered sound stage, and golf carts, powered by wind, solar, biodiesel, ethanol, and liquid petroleum gas.[66] The "Urban Land Scouts" at Bonnaroo are festival volunteers who help promote ecologically friendly practices. Bonnaroo's organizers urge participants to "stop by the Carbon Shredders booth this year to earn a patch from the Urban Land Scouts, ride a bike to power a lightbulb. . . . All joining together to help you learn ways to reduce your carbon footprint!" Bonnaroo offers participants workshops that will expand their "global consciousness," where they can "learn about issues from global warming to water protection to human rights issues. Learn how to reduce your carbon footprint with the Carbon Shredders. Learn the how-to's and benefits of eating locally, either from your own garden or from local farms, at the Victory Garden workshops."[67] Here are practices aimed at young Americans attending a music festival who will leave the festival behind but can take home skills and knowledge with them.

## IV   *Mass Consumption for a Soft Footprint*

For participants, festivals become utopian destinations that offer blueprints for a future in which corporations do not infringe on every area of their lives. Offering locally made goods and food and showcasing alternative energy sources are important ways that festivals work to create a sense of difference from the world outside. Burning Man seems to be at the extreme by promoting a gift economy and banning all buying and selling except for ice and coffee drinks in the organization's "Center Camp." Marketing professor Rob Kozinets describes Burning Man as "a place outside the gravitational pull of the market," and the festival works hard to live up to this ideal.[68] Gifting expresses both the nostalgia many festival-goers have toward other cultures that value gifting and the desire of many Burners to move toward a future in which community relationships are not shaped by market forces. While Burning Man only allows gifting, other festivals that include the buying and selling of goods envision a future filled with small businesses and fair-trade products: "Earthdance has become a global event unlike any other, with more than 350 locations contributing to, and building the energy of peace on our shared planet. It is this consciousness that we want to bring to your festival here in California and this consciousness we want reflected in our marketplace."[69] Festivals often explicitly state an intention to challenge capitalism and corporate-driven media by offering handmade local and sustainable goods and services. The Earthdance website highlights this intent: "We are in a transitional phase of the global marketplace business practices. A time when positive business practices will be encouraged, and business practices that profit without just return to the community will be let go. We require all importers to belong to a fair trade organization or its equivalent. We choose vendors who support living wages and safe and healthy conditions for workers in the developing world."[70]

Most participants at Earthdance and other festivals see themselves as ecologically minded and open to the sustainable practices made available at festivals.[71] In fact, these aspects are important components of their identities as spiritual seekers. And yet these ideals are often contradicted by festival-goers' practices, revealing the limits of temporary utopian communities and the ways consumerism permeates these supposedly alternative spaces. Festival organizers and participants grapple with the contradictions posed by the festivals' very existence as temporary destinations that are most easily reached by motor vehicles and usually involve traveling long distances. Faerieworlds bills itself as a "soft footprint event" that donates to the Circle of Life foundation and the Cascades Raptor Center, but festival-goers spend a lot of money and use a lot of fuel to get to a place where they can celebrate making a soft footprint.[72] Going to a special natural environment that seems wild and pure necessitates the consumption of fuel and leaves an impact on the natural environment.[73]

While festival communities and individual festival-goers work hard to shore up the boundaries that separate their temporary tribe from the outside world, they do not leave that world behind. They buy clothes and make altars to bring to festivals and buy music and other things at festivals to bring home. While criticism of capitalism and consumer society is widespread at many festivals, and most explicitly at Burning Man, such critiques coexist uncomfortably with festival-goers' actual consumer practices. Burners spend thousands of dollars on elaborate camp decorations, costumes, and art projects to take with them to their utopia. Because the event's organizers forbid buying and selling, most Burners buy an assortment of products to bring with them: LED wire, elaborate costumes, masks, and wood and other raw materials for building structures and art pieces, although some Burners do choose to make art and costumes out of secondhand and repurposed clothes and objects. While Burning Man often requested that participants cover over any corporate logos, as the festival has grown, parts of Burning Man's Black Rock City increasingly resemble a Ryder rental truck convention.

Not only do corporate products appear everywhere on the bodies and in the camps of festival-goers, but many festivals are sponsored by large corporations. In 2011, Earthdance, which champions sustainable goods, listed sponsors including Knudsen, Santa Cruz Organics, Frey Vineyards, and Lagunitas Brewing; Knudson and Santa Cruz are both owned by the giant U.S. manufacturer of preserves, J. M. Smucker Co.[74] Coachella's website celebrated its corporate partnerships and "a joint venture from Intel and the saucy New York–based media conglomerate Vice encouraging cross-genre artistic and technical collaboration" on some art installations and stages.[75] State Farm Insurance and Ford Motor Company, meanwhile, have sponsored some events at Bonnaroo.[76] Clearly, the outside world intrudes on festival space through the presence of large corporations at these sites, which want to promote a sense of a "simpler lifestyle," and through enjoying the advantages of a technologically advanced consumer society with a myriad of goods to enhance festival experience and adorn participants' bodies.

The spiritual commitments of festival-goers shape their economic practices because festivals *create* demands for goods and services. Festival-goers buy and bring to festivals what they imagine they need to fully realize the infinite possibilities of festival space. The festivals then expose them to a whole new realm of lifestyle items, such as handmade jewelry, fair-trade clothing, organically grown food, and other items marketed as sustainable and thus desirable. Although individual choice is pushed as the norm, the emphasis on green living, costumes, masks, jewelry, and body paint creates a kind of conformity and expectation, as the common distinction at Burning Man between "tourists" and "spectators" suggests.[77]

## V    Convergence Spirituality: Festivals as Gatherings of the Counterculture of the Internet

Festivals must straddle the distinction between alternative anticapitalist utopia and consumer culture. As they look to the past for meaning and wisdom, they simultaneously flaunt the use of new technologies as these experiences travel across the Internet through photo-sharing sites and Facebook. The apparent boundaries of temporary festival settings have expanded to include buying tickets months in advance, then packing and unpacking, and finally sharing photos, videos, and stories online. While these annual events are bounded in space and time, new media enable the sharing of images and experiences, which in turn influences ongoing identity-creation and cultural forms—websites and next year's festival—as well as exchanges of information, resources and consumer goods. Products available at festivals are often also available at any time online. These porous boundaries of the festival experience might be understood as a kind of twenty-first-century "convergence spirituality," to borrow media scholar Henry Jenkins's concept of contemporary convergence culture, which involves the "flow of content across multiple media platforms, the cooperation between multiple media industries, and the migrating behavior of media audiences."[78] For Jenkins, convergence culture is by nature participatory, since "convergence occurs within the brains of individual consumers and through their social interactions with others."[79] Earthdance's synchronized prayer linking festival communities across the globe, festival-goers' online reviews of festivals, YouTube videos of their favorite performers and art pieces, and handmade sustainable clothing marketed on the Internet all render obsolete any sense that the festival is bounded in time and space. The festival *is* set apart as an extraordinary and special space, and yet it is not contained, because of all the ways that old and new technologies converge in the minds and consumer practices of festival-goers. As one festival musician put it, "These are gatherings of the counterculture of the Internet, the Web 2.0 generation."[80] Contemporary festivals have become sites of self-definition among young Americans where modern media forms such as blogs and websites converge with ancient religious symbols, invented rituals, and material cultures to create new spiritual experiences and identities.

Yet festivals also highlight the problems that arise because of such convergences. Inside and outside festival space, festival-goers respond to the tension between their utopian ideals and the presence of consumerism and free-market capitalism through the use of irony. Some festivals poke fun at received wisdom—and especially at institutional religion. Performance artist Reverend Billy Talen and his "Stop Shopping Gospel Choir" make regular appearances before Burning Man crowds to preach anticonsumerism. The Reverend's "Church of Stop Shopping" supports resistance to global capitalism in favor of independent shops, community gardens, and local economies:

> Consumerism is normalized in the mind of the average person, sometimes we even refer to ourselves as consumers forgetting that we are also citizens, humans, men, women, animals. We forget that we share many resources, public spaces, libraries, information, history, sidewalks, streets, schools that we created laws and covenants and governments to protect us, to support us, to help us. . . . The subjugation of these resources and these laws to the forces of the market demands a response.[81]

If festivals offer infinite worlds and infinite possibilities, they also recognize limitations. At the same time that they both contest and replicate the world festival-goers say they have left behind, these destinations serve as spaces to play with and reconfigure elements of the world outside, as the gospel of "Stop Shopping" suggests. In this case, by distancing themselves from institutionalized churches and choirs, festival-goers strengthen their identities as participants in a new form of spirituality. At Burning Man, such a stance involves antireligious art and the use of irony and juxtaposition. The 1998 Burning Man guide to events describes "The Temple of Idle Worship" as a "spiritual powerpoint" of the event but warns that "it makes no difference in what way you recognize this power as all forms of rituals and observance are meaningless here."[82] When I visited the temple itself that year, a sign warned me that "you can light candles and prostrate yourself all you want, but your prayers won't be answered; the deity is napping." Festival-goers are not always given a clearly charted spiritual path to follow at festivals—this is the nature of infinite possibilities.

Contemporary festivals remain ambiguous sites of religious identity-making for young Americans who are trying to work out how to integrate practices of consumption and anticonsumption with spiritual seeking. Clearly, the boundaries of identity are porous for many attendees, so that multiple and sometimes contradictory commitments exist simultaneously. It is implicit that to enjoy, experiment with, and create new spiritualities, you have to buy expensive tickets, camping supplies, and special clothing or costumes and travel—consuming fuel—to remote locations where you can express your spiritual identity in spaces set aside for that purpose. Although many young people attending Burning Man or Earthdance bemoan the corporatization of spirituality and art, they are participating in a time-honored American pastime of perpetuating the market society at the same time that they want to upend it, even with attempts to substitute gifting and other economies in its place.

Festival bodies and festival tribes exist in two worlds: the ideal and the real. If festivals continue to grow and young Americans with spiritual yearnings continue to flock to them, this tension will prove challenging to the utopian expectations and creative meaning-making embodied by these sacred destinations.

## Notes

1. They capture what historian of American religions Catherine L. Albanese has described as the "renewed and far more encompassing metaphysical spirituality"

of the early twenty-first century (*A Republic of Mind and Spirit: A Cultural History of American Metaphysical Religion* [New Haven: Yale University Press, 2007], 511).

2. American studies scholar Jeremy Hockett describes media "distortions" of events such as Burning Man in "Participant Observation and the Study of Self: Burning Man as Ethnographic Experience," in *Afterburn: Reflections on Burning Man*, ed. Lee Gilmore and Mark Van Proyen (Albuquerque: University of New Mexico Press, 2005), 68–73.

3. Although these festivals are explicitly not associated with any religious traditions, the closest being Neopaganism or the New Age movements, they share many characteristics with large-scale Christian music festivals such as Cornerstone, which are also geared toward young people.

4. Jeet Kei Leung, "Transformational Festivals," TedXTalks, 2010, http://tedx-talks.ted.com/video/TEDxVancouver-Jeet-Kei-Leung-Tr.

5. See Sarah M. Pike, "Desert Goddesses and Apocalyptic Art: Making Sacred Space at the Burning Man Festival," in *God in the Details: American Religion in Popular Culture*, ed. Katherine McCarthy and Eric Mazur (New York: Routledge, 2010 [2001]), 154–173.

6. Kyer Wiltshire and Erik Davis, *Tribal Revival: West Coast Festival Culture* (San Francisco: Lovelution Press, 2009).

7. Allegra Fortunati, "Utopia, Social Sculpture, and Burning Man," in Gilmore and Van Proyen, *Afterburn*, 163.

8. Jason Pitzl-Waters, "Transformational Festival Culture," *The Wild Hunt*, October 2, 2011, http://www.patheos.com/blogs/wildhunt/2011/10/transformational-festival-culture.html; Sarah M. Pike, *Earthly Bodies, Magical Selves: Contemporary Pagans and the Search for Community* (Berkeley and Los Angeles: University of California Press, 2001). Large Christian gatherings such as the Cornerstone music festival also have many similarities to spiritual festivals that have no connection to Christianity. For an excellent account of Cornerstone, see Andrew Beaujon, *Body Piercing Saved My Life: Inside the Phenomenon of Christian Rock* (Boston: Da Capo Press, 2006).

9. "Faerieworlds Celebrates 10 Years," KVAL News, June 16, 2011, http://www.kval.com/communities/springfield/194981141.html.

10. "Earthdance: The Global Festival for Peace," http://earthdancelive.com/. Accessed September 30, 2011. Earthdance is an annual event that occurs around the Autumn Equinox (usually Sept. 20–21) both in real time and space in local communities and as a virtual, synchronized prayer linking dancers around the world.

11. Other events also have significant overlap with these festivals, especially Rainbow gatherings and Renaissance festivals such as the Northern California Renaissance Faire. See Michael Niman, *People of the Rainbow: A Nomadic Utopia* (Knoxville: University of Tennessee Press, 2011 [1997]).

12. Festivals try to be racially and ethnically inclusive but draw mainly middle-class Americans. Statistics from Burning Man censuses suggest that Burning Man's population is also largely white.

13. A Burning Man census shows an increase (proportionately) from 2006 to 2010 in the eighteen- to thirty-year-old age group. See "Afterburn Reports," Burning Man, http://afterburn.burningman.com/.

14. Begun six years ago by event producers Robert Gould and Emilio & Kelly Miller-Lopez, Faerieworlds is inspired by the art of Brian Froud. Froud, who created the fantasy classic *Faeries* with Tolkien artist Alan Lee, was also the conceptual designer for the landmark Jim Henson films *The Dark Crystal* and *Labyrinth*. "Faerieworlds 2011 Harvest," Faerieworlds, http://www.faerieworlds.com/harvest/press.html. Renaissance festivals such as the Northern California Renaissance Faire feature participants dressed in elaborate costumes that include "fairy costumes" as well as period dress. See Northern California Renaissance Faire, http://www.norcalrenfaire.com/.

15. Burning Man, http://www.burningman.com.

16. Christian Smith and Melissa Lundquist Denton, *Soul-Searching: The Religious and Spiritual Lives of American Teenagers* (Oxford: Oxford University Press, 2005); Lisa D. Pearce and Melissa Lundquist Denton, *A Faith of Their Own: Stability and Change in the Religiosity of American Adolescents* (Oxford: Oxford University Press, 2011); Conrad Cherry, Betty A. DeBerg, and Amanda Porterfield, *Religion on Campus* (Chapel Hill: University of North Carolina Press, 2001).

17. Lee Gilmore, *Theater in a Crowded Fire: Ritual and Spirituality at Burning Man* (Berkeley and Los Angeles: University of California Press, 2010), 45–57.

18. Robert C. Fuller, *Spiritual, but Not Religious: Understanding Unchurched America* (New York: Oxford University Press, 2001).

19. They fit many of the characteristics of the spiritual practitioners described in Courtney Bender's ethnography, *The New Metaphysicals: Spirituality and the American Religious Imagination* (Chicago: University of Chicago Press, 2010), 5–7.

20. Albanese, *Republic of Mind and Spirit*, 13–15.

21. R. Laurence Moore, *Selling God: American Religion in the Marketplace of Culture* (New York: Oxford University Press, 1995). According to Moore, by the 1840s lyceums had become more commercialized, with little distinction between the religious and the secular (57). Water cure advocates vied with traveling medicine men for customers, and mesmerists and phrenologists provided entertainment. Moore discusses Chautauqua Sunday school institutes at 151. See also Leigh Eric Schmidt, *Consumer Rites: The Buying and Selling of American Holidays* (Princeton: Princeton University Press, 1995).

22. Moore, *Selling God*, 5.

23. Ibid.

24. Ibid., 45–46.
25. Leigh Schmidt discusses the "peddling of festivity" at church festivals and hawkers waiting on the outskirts of camp meetings to sell "food, liquor, patent medicines, books, ballads, shoe polish, and daguerreotypes" (*Consumer Rites*, 21).
26. Nathan Hatch, *The Democratization of American Christianity* (New Haven: Yale University Press, 1989), 50.
27. Ibid., 52.
28. "Traveling Culture: Circuit Chautauqua in the Twentieth Century," Library of Congress, http://www.loc.gov/teachers/classroommaterials/connections/traveling-culture/history.html.
29. In its Jubilee Year of 1924, thirty million Americans visited Chautauqua tents (ibid.).
30. "Attend Chautauqua, You'll Enjoy It," http://www.campusschool.dsu.edu/myweb/history.htm.
31. One Bonnaroo participant explicitly invoked the legacy of the counterculture in describing his encounter with some Krishna Consciousness devotees at Bonnaroo in 2011 who were chanting "Hare Krishna": "This welcome flashback to the early 1970s calibrated our inner spaciousness in a way that we could spread across the weekend" (Andrew William Smith, "Bonnaroo's Decade of Dust and Dreams: Jacket's Sonic Beauty, the Sightings of Ben Sollee, and So Much More," *Interference*, June 19, 2011, http://www.u2interference.com/15086-bonnaroo%E2%80%99s-decade-of-dust-dreams-jacket%E2%80%99s-sonic-beauty-the-sightings-of-ben-sollee-so-much-more/).
32. Michael Bowen, "The 'Human Be-In' Poster," *San Francisco Bay Guardian*, August 24, 2007, http://www.sfbg.com/category/author/michael-bowen. On 1960s roots of contemporary festivals, see Sarah M. Pike, *New Age and Neopagan Religions in America* (New York: Columbia University Press, 2004), 67–88.
33. Charly Wilder, "A Summer Festival with a Communal Theme and No Ads," *New York Times*, June 23, 2009, http://intransit.blogs.nytimes.com/2009/06/23/a-summer-festival-with-a-communal-theme-and-no-ads/.
34. Woodstock Festival Poland, http://www.en.wosp.org.pl/woodstock_festival/about_woodstock_festival_poland; and "The Polish Woodstock," *Time*, http://content.time.com/time/photogallery/0,29307,1915346,00.html.
35. Erik Davis, "Beyond Belief: The Cults of Burning Man," in Gilmore and Van Proyen, *Afterburn*, 21.
36. Quoted in ibid.
37. Leung, "Transformational Festivals." For more on raves and other dance music gatherings, see Graham St. John, *Technomad: Global Raving Countercultures* (Sheffield: Equinox Press, 2009).
38. See Pike, *Earthly Bodies, Magical Selves*.

39. Pitzl-Waters, "Transformational Festival Culture."

40. Rob Shields, *Places on the Margin: Alternative Geographies of Modernity* (New York: Routledge, 1991), 112.

41. Anthropologist Victor Turner contrasts flexible, egalitarian liminal events to the stratified, normal world in *Dramas, Fields, and Metaphors: Symbolic Action in Human Society* (Ithaca, N.Y.: Cornell University Press, 1974), 200–201.

42. Pike, "Desert Goddesses and Apocalyptic Art."

43. Nadia G., Coachella review, Yelp, February 11, 2012, http://www.yelp.com/biz/coachella-indio-2?q=Nadia.

44. Conversation with the author, July 2011.

45. David Chidester, "Introduction," in *American Sacred Space*, ed. David Chidester and Edward T. Linenthal (Bloomington: Indiana University Press), 14.

46. Sarah M. Pike, "No Novenas for the Dead: Ritual Action and Communal Memory at the Temple of Tears," in Gilmore and Van Proyen, *Afterburn*, 195–213.

47. For some examples, see the thousands of messages on Burning Man's discussion board, http://eplaya.burningman.com/. See also Burning Man's Facebook page, http://www.facebook.com/BurningMan.

48. Jesus A. Vargas, "A Local's Journey from 'Coachella the City' to 'Coachella the Music Festival,'" *Coachella Unincorporated*, April 16, 2012, http://coachellaunincorporated.org/2012/04/16/a-local%E2%80%99s-journey-from-%E2%80%9Dcoachella-the-city%E2%80%9D-to-%E2%80%9Ccoachella-the-music-festival%E2%80%9D/.

49. Conversation with the author, March 2, 2007.

50. Smith, "Bonnaroo's Decade of Dust and Dreams."

51. Nate M., Coachella review, Yelp, February 15, 2011, http://www.yelp.com/biz/coachella-indio-2?hrid=LOi7LRPSsv__96cqyPVeaw. Accessed September 28, 2011.

52. Geneva, Coachella review, Yelp, http://www.yelp.com/biz/coachella-valley-music-and-arts-festival-indio-2. Accessed September 28, 2011.

53. Catherine Albanese argues that an important development in twenty-first-century metaphysical religion is that the mind acquires a body, so that emphasis increasingly lies on the "enlightened body-self" (*Republic of Mind and Spirit*, 514).

54. "Faeries Prepare to Descend on Eugene, Oregon," *Send2Press Newswire*, July 16, 2007, http://send2press.com/newswire/print/news_2007-07-0716-005.shtml.

55. Wiltshire and Davis, *Tribal Revival*, 50.

56. "What, Where, When," Burning Man program, 2006.

57. Wiltshire and Davis, *Tribal Revival*, 91–101. Faerieworlds promotes its family-friendly environment, while at Burning Man the presence of real children has sometimes been controversial. For example, see a discussion thread titled "Going to Burning Man" on the Berkeley Parents Network, http://parents.berkeley.edu/recommend/places/burningman.html.

58. Drift Dodgers, "New Discoveries at Earthdance 2011." http://lostinsound.org/earthdance-2011-videos-review/.

59. Faerieworlds, http://www.faerieworlds.com. Accessed September 30, 2011.

60. "What Is Faerieworlds Harvest?" Faerieworlds, http://www.faerieworlds.com/harvest/what.html.

61. Eric Wendt, "Earthdance 2011," *Synthesis*, September 21, 2011, http://synthesis.net/earthdance-2011/.

62. Ibid.

63. "Earthdancer Testimonials," Earthdance, http://earthdance.org/event/. Accessed December 15, 2011.

64. Michel Foucault, "Of Other Spaces," *Diacritics* 16 (1986): 23.

65. "We Choose Green," Earthdance, http://www.earthdancelive.com/festival-info/we-choose-green. Accessed December 15, 2011.

66. See http://www.coachella.com/festival-info/sustainability.

67. "Planet Roo: Activities and Attractions," http://108.59.242.87/activities/planet-roo.aspx. Accessed September 30, 2011.

68. Robert V. Kozinets and John F. Sherry Jr., "Welcome to the Black Rock Café," in Gilmore and Van Proyen, *Afterburn*, 88.

69. "Vendor Opportunities," Earthdance, http://earthdancelive.com/get-involved/vendor-opportunities. Accessed December 15, 2011.

70. Ibid.

71. Kozinets and Sherry, "Welcome to the Black Rock Café," 92–93.

72. "Faerieworlds Celebrates 10 Years."

73. Burning Man's motto of "Leave No Trace" is everywhere at the festival, but every year bags of trash litter the roads leading away from the festival site, resulting in rants and complaints in online forums.

74. "Sponsor's Page," Earthdance, http://www.earthdancelive.com/sponsors-page. Accessed December 1, 2011.

75. August Brown, "Stages Are Set for a Coachella Art Spectacular," *Los Angeles Times*, April 10, 2011, http://articles.latimes.com/2011/apr/10/entertainment/la-ca-coachella-stage-20110410.

76. See http://108.59.242.87/activities/there-tent-state-farm.aspx and http://corporate.ford.com/news-center/press-releases-detail/pr-2011-ford-fiesta-mixing-it-up-at-32726.

77. Stories abound about the pressure to participate and the discomfort of those who are not sure how. See, for example, "You Are Burning Man," Burning Man, http://www.burningman.com/participate/you_are_burning_man.html.

78. Henry Jenkins, *Convergence Culture: Where Old and New Media Collide* (New York: New York University Press, 2006), 2. Religious studies scholar Lee Gilmore makes this connection on a Burning Man blog in which she draws parallels between what she calls DIY spirituality and Jenkins's concept of convergence culture. Lee Gilmore, *The Burning Blog*, http://blog.burningman.com/author/lgilmore/.

79. Jenkins, *Convergence Culture*, 3.

80. Leung, "Transformational Festivals." But Burning Man's anticorporate positions and other festivals' efforts to expose their participants to sustainable practices also travel home with some participants. An important way that festival-goers cross boundaries between the festival as a place apart and the world outside and back home is through social service and charitable giving. Immediately following Hurricane Katrina, a group of Burning Man participants went to New Orleans to help and later formed "Burners without Borders," an organization of festival-goers that continues to engage in other kinds of social service activities. Other festivals donate large sums of their proceeds to local charities.

81. "About Us," Reverend Billy and the Church of Stop Shopping, http://www.revbilly.com/about-us.

82. Pike, "Desert Goddesses and Apocalyptic Art," 161.

## 9

# Religious Branding and the Quest to Meet Consumer Needs

### JOEL OSTEEN'S "MESSAGE OF HOPE"

*Katja Rakow*

ON NOVEMBER 28, 2010, the *Miami Herald* announced that televange-list Joel Osteen was coming to Miami's AmericanAirlines Arena and that "10,000 fans" were expected to attend the event. The article described Osteen as "pastor of the country's biggest church, prolific author, and one of the most recognizable faces of U.S. Christianity."[1] Osteen is senior pas-tor of Lakewood Church in Houston, Texas, based in the Compaq Center, former home of the NBA's Houston Rockets. Lakewood's 2005 move into the Compaq Center gave the church a substantially larger venue—the church now seats 16,000 and boasts 9,000 parking spaces. Lakewood is one of the biggest nondenominational megachurches in the United States; with four English-speaking services and two Spanish-speaking services per week, it draws up to 45,000 weekly worship attendants from various ethnic, racial, and socioeconomic backgrounds. Osteen's Sunday services at Lakewood are broadcast on religious, secular, and international televi-sion channels. His *Joel Osteen* program has the highest Nielsen ratings a religious show has ever had in American history, with an estimated seven million viewers per week.[2] In September 2011, he published his fourth self-help book, *Every Day a Friday: How to Be Happier 7 Days a Week*.[3] The book was heavily advertised via his TV program, his website, TV features, and interviews, as well as via social media networks such as Facebook. Within just a few weeks, *Every Day a Friday* made its way onto the *New York Times* bestseller list, just as Osteen's three previous books had.[4] Osteen's "A Night of Hope" events are held in huge, sold-out stadiums all over America and, like his services at Lakewood Church, combine contemporary Christian praise and worship music presented by the Lakewood music ministry team with encouraging messages from Osteen, his wife, Victoria, and other members of the Lakewood Church ministry.[5] This was the event that the *Miami Herald* expected to draw ten thousand to the AmericanAirlines Arena.

For all of his success, Osteen's message is often attacked and dismissed as "cotton candy Gospel" or "Christianity Lite" because of his emphasis on hope, empowerment, prosperity, and inspiration without mentioning "sin, suffering or redemption."[6] The dominant profile of Osteen carried by the mainstream media, however, is that of "the smiling preacher," an image upheld by Osteen's readers, viewers, and worship service attendees, who describe his message as overwhelmingly positive, encouraging, and uplifting.[7] This message has made him the "most popular preacher in the country"[8] and broadened his influence beyond North America.[9]

Joel Osteen may be the perfect embodiment of a "pastorpreneur" in today's consumer society. Consumerism, backed by an increasingly globalized mediascape and the growing influence of neoliberalism, has become the dominant sociocultural and economic order in the years following World War II.[10] In 2003, John Jackson coined the neologism *pastorpreneur* to designate a pastor of a modern church organization who is at the same time a savvy businessman.[11] The pastorpreneur employs entrepreneurial strategies and combines elements from consumer culture and popular culture in packaging and distributing his message and growing his church. Osteen is not unprecedented; rather, he is the latest in a long line of enterprising evangelical preachers offering their respective generations a relevant interpretation of Protestant Christianity.[12] Well-known historical examples such as George Whitefield in the eighteenth century, Charles Finney in the nineteenth century, and Norman Vincent Peale, Billy Graham, and Robert Schuller in the twentieth century have also been able to package and present religion in entertaining and edifying ways that appealed to their contemporaries while also provoking criticism from the dominant religious establishment.[13] Each pastorpreneur not only attracted the masses but also adopted the available cultural practices and technologies of his era to bring his message to ever-broader audiences. The earliest pastorpreneurs spread their messages through newspapers and pamphlets, while later generations used books, radio, and television broadcasts. Today's evangelists also employ the Internet and social media networks.[14] As Laurence Moore notes, there has been an ongoing "interpenetration of American religion and commercial popular culture"[15] for more than a century. Religious institutions and clergy have exerted, and continue to exert, their influence via inventive contributions to the cultural marketplace and thereby have turned religion itself into a market commodity. Without the benefits of formal legal establishment, churches and religious leaders had to offer their products and services not only in a competitive religious market but also in the cultural market of the leisure industry. As early as the nineteenth century, the nexus of commercial and popular culture stimulated innovative and entertaining religious products and services that were shaped by and catered to popular tastes and thereby secured the public importance and cultural centrality of Protestant Christianity.[16] According to Moore, advertising, publicity, and business methods have been seen as valuable approaches to expand the reach of the church since at least the early twentieth century, but given the successes and methods employed by earlier pastorpreneurs such as Whitefield and Finney, we may well say that they have been seen as valuable tools for significantly longer than that.[17]

Explanations of religious change in terms of a religious market metaphor often employ one of two approaches: (1) the supply-side approach, which stresses both the role of restrictions and deregulations in the religious marketplace and the innovative contributions of religious suppliers as perpetrators of religious change, or (2) the demand-side approach, which attributes religious transformations to modified consumer needs and perceptions as well as to broader developments in the cultural sphere that account for shifting consumer desires and sensitivities.[18] In this essay, I argue for a combined approach that sets both sides—production and consumption—in relation to each other. Presuming contemporary consumer culture to be broadly encompassing and inescapable, thoroughly permeating everyday practices, I also presume that it frames and shapes processes of production and consumption. Successfully marketed religious products are the result neither of a genuine contribution ex nihilo on the side of religious suppliers nor of passive social actors uniformly consuming these products.[19] Producer and consumer inhabit a social and material world that enables and simultaneously restricts, a world that structures and simultaneously is structured by knowledge regimes and practices. A case study of Joel Osteen as a religious brand and his "message of hope"—the product on offer—will show how both production and consumption are tied to broader cultural patterns and discourses that structure the social world and the ways that actors on both supply and demand sides engage that world.

## I  *Religious Branding*

Are Joel Osteen and his obviously popular brand of Christianity just the latest product, rehashed, advertised, and marketed in the contemporary marketplace of religion, or is there something genuinely innovative here? According to media studies expert Mara Einstein and James Twitchell, a professor of advertising, although the use of marketing in the propagation of religious goods is not new, the extent and the sophistication of the initiatives employed in recent decades are. These scholars argue that a strategy called "religious branding" is crucial to these newer marketing campaigns.[20] Branding is a commercial process of storytelling that gives consumers something to think and feel about a commodity that goes beyond its physical attributes and that attaches those associations to a brand name. A brand transforms a commodity into an expressive, memorable, named product. Branding as a marketing strategy aims to achieve emotional attachment, which marketers seek to utilize whenever there is an overflow of interchangeable goods. Applying a story to a product or service creates a means of differentiation that distinguishes it from competing products or services. Market-oriented practices like branding include the identification of target audiences and the quest to appeal to consumer needs in changing and repackaging a product.[21] Moreover, branding as strategy is about the creation of meaning and a sense of community.[22] Marketing expert Lee Cow reminds us that "brands aren't just a way of remembering what you want to buy any more: They've become part of the fabric of our society. Brands are part of our system of ordering things—they even create context about who we are and how we live."[23] Branded commodities and services thus contain meaning for people's lives and become part of the process of identity-creation, influencing the tastes of people who have learned to purchase "culture" as a means of self-improvement, relaxation, or recreation.[24] Brands do more than simply market and sell a product or service; they create a sense of affiliation and community and therefore can be conceptualized as a form of cultural production and as providers of contexts for interaction.[25]

Branding as a competitive device is not restricted to "fast-moving consumer goods"; it has also entered the public sphere of "slow-moving cultural institutions" such as museums, colleges, hospitals, and religious institutions.[26] In the contemporary religious marketplace, Christian denominations are no longer as clearly identified as brands as they might have been previously. The label "United Methodist," for example, may not convey a clear enough picture of what this denomination is all about to attract prospective attendees.[27] Denominational ties increasingly fail to function as identity markers, and a trend of de-emphasizing denominational affiliations is visible among seeker-sensitive churches and megachurches.[28] Contemporary churchgoers seem to lack "brand loyalty"[29] to established denominations; this means that they tend to be more loyal to a particular local community institution than to a more abstract and remote religious bureaucracy. Fast-growing churches, which are usually seeker-oriented and increasingly nondenominational, offer prospective attendees a sense of belonging, emphasizing the search for individual meaning and purpose but situating that pursuit in the context of a distinct community.[30] As marketing experts argue, both denominational and nondenominational churches need to promote themselves as brands to create differentiation and attachment in a crowded market and attract return customers.[31]

## *II   Joel Osteen as a "Faith Brand"*

Seeing branding strategies at work in promoting and establishing Joel Osteen as "the smiling preacher" and "one of the most recognizable faces of U.S. Christianity," Einstein describes and analyzes Osteen as a "faith brand" and his Lakewood Church as a "brand extension." She defines faith brands as "spiritual products that have been given popular meaning and awareness through marketing," such as religious books, programs, classes, practices, services, a pastor, or combinations of these products.[32] Like other marketed products, faith brands have a brand name and a recognizable logo sometimes accompanied by a tag line. In the present case, the brand name is made up of the pastor's name, "Joel Osteen"; a stylized rendering of the name functions as a logo. The accompanying slogan— "Discover the champion in you!"—is accentuated with a recognizable musical theme and opens Osteen's televised services and every service recorded and distributed on DVD. According to Einstein, a tag line or slogan makes the brand distinguishable and identifiable. A "humanizing icon,"[33] a smiling Joel Osteen on book and DVD covers and in diverse advertising campaigns enhances the recognition value of the brand. Faith brands, like other branded commodities, are supported by a brand "mythology."

Here that "brand mythology" begins with Joel's father, John Osteen (1921–1999). The elder Osteen, a Southern Baptist minister, preached love, salvation, prosperity, and the gifts of the spirit. This brought him into conflict with the denomination and resulted in John Osteen leaving the Southern Baptist Convention to found a nondenominational church—the then-ninety-member Lakewood—in a converted feed store in Houston. Another important part of the brand mythology is Joel's mother, Dodie Osteen, who miraculously recovered after being diagnosed with terminal liver cancer in 1981.[34] That part of the brand mythology is literally cast in bronze, in the form of a statue of John and Dodie Osteen in the entrance area of Lakewood Church. In the 1980s, Joel Osteen dropped out of Oral Roberts University and convinced his father to create a television ministry, which helped grow the church tremendously. Joel had shown no intention of stepping into his father's line of work but was instead known as some-one who preferred working behind the scenes. In early 1999, however, John fell seriously ill and asked Joel to preach the Sunday service in his place. At first, Joel refused, but something changed his mind: "Daddy's words kept flitting through my mind, and with no other provocation, I began to have an overwhelming desire to preach."[35] Joel decided to take up the task, although he had never preached before. To fight his insecu-rity, he literally wore a pair of his father's shoes when he stepped onto the stage for the first time. His first Sunday service was reported to be a tre-mendous success. Shortly afterward, John Osteen died, and Joel Osteen became the new leader of Lakewood Church. Since then, he has grown the church from 6,000 to 45,000 weekly worship attendees.[36]

The brand mythology tells a story of growth, success, prosperity, and happiness. It is a story of overcoming all kinds of obstacles by faith and trust in a miracle-working God. It is also a classic "American success story," with one generation founding a "mom-and-pop" business and bequeathing it to their child, who continues to grow the business and to prosper. This brand myth authenticates the brand message, which for the "Joel Osteen" faith brand is an overwhelmingly positive message of suc-cess, prosperity, and happiness. Message and product are thus a single unit. As Einstein argues, the image of "the smiling preacher" must match the form and content of Osteen's services in order to sustain the brand. To make Osteen's religious products appealing, their form and content are adapted to contemporary consumer tastes, as can be seen in entertaining and uplifting services and the omission of terms such as *sin* and *salvation*. Thus, faith brands are repackaged and adjusted to consumer needs just like any other branded commodity and ultimately pursue the growth of market share.

In Osteen's case, as Einstein explains, the combination of highly sophisticated production values and a positive message on improving your life makes his televangelist program entertaining as well as effective. Einstein asks whether the reason for Osteen's success lies in his ability to be a good preacher but answers that it is more likely that the audience finds the product—that is, the message, the pastor, and the branding strategy—appealing.[37] As insightful as her heuristic approach in analyzing contemporary religion in the terms of marketing and branding may be, one central question remains: *Why* is it that the audience finds the product appealing?[38] This question calls for a more complex approach, as the branding explanation focuses mainly on the supply side and how a product is marketed and fails to address the demand side or to account for the ways in which consumer tastes and needs are shaped. Taking these considerations as a point of departure, I argue that it is not just the process of branding that guarantees a steadily growing consumer base. Above all, it is Osteen's firm rootedness in dominant discourse regimes on religion, spirituality, and the nature of the human self that makes his message so persuasive and enables him to be one of the most successful "pastorpreneurs" in the contemporary American marketplace. To engage this line of argument, I analyze the narrative and rhetorical devices at work in Osteen's "message of hope"—his product—and contextualize my findings in the broader discourses of self-help, therapy, and the modern regime of the self.

## III  Joel Osteen's "Message of Hope"

A detailed analysis of different material resources, including Osteen's recorded Sunday messages, his books, and notes from the worship services I attended during my fieldwork, will help us take a closer look at how this "message of hope" is constructed and the rhetorical and narrative devices it employs. We should note that Osteen does not call his preaching in worship services at Lakewood Church a sermon but, rather, a "message."[39] His messages from the Sunday worship services are recorded and broadcast on TV. Additionally, each Sunday message can be purchased on CD after the service. What viewers and listeners experience is the final portion of the service, which accounts for approximately 30 percent of the whole service. A typical Sunday service at Lakewood Church lasts about one hour and forty minutes and is composed of two main parts. The first part is an hour of contemporary praise and worship music interspersed with short inspirational messages, periods of praying, and tithing. The second part, thirty to forty minutes long, is reserved for Osteen's message and the altar call. The extended praise and worship part engages the participants at Lakewood Church physically as well as emotionally and prepares them for the message, whereas the viewers in front of their TV only hear and see the spoken word performance of Joel Osteen. Therefore, the two different audiences might have different reasons for their repeated consumption of the particular products at offer.

A regular Sunday service is structured as follows: After a short video welcoming the audience, the Lakewood Church music ministry band takes the stage to perform the first praise and worship song. Joel Osteen and his wife, Victoria, then walk out on the stage and welcome the audience. He asks, "How many of you are ready to worship the Lord?" In response people in the audience cheer, applaud, and raise their hands. Before leaving the stage, the couple offers a short prayer to God and invites everyone to celebrate God's goodness with praise and worship. People in the audience are standing, raising or clapping their hands, singing, and moving to the beat. Most of the songs are well-known contemporary Christian praise and worship songs, with lyrics projected on large video screens.[40] After a couple of more vigorous praise songs, the lights in the auditorium are dimmed, and the golden globe—the only dominant symbol displayed on stage—disappears into the ground, revealing another large screen at the far end of the stage.[41] The lyrics of the next three worship songs usually center on Jesus the savior, his Crucifixion, and God's willingness to sacrifice His own flesh and blood to wash humankind clean of sin. The songs here are modeled on popular rock and pop ballads. The large screen at the center of the stage shows pictures of Jesus and crosses; these change with every song. After the final song, Osteen comes up on stage and offers a prayer. He stands with his eyes closed and arms stretched out while thanking God for everything good He has done and for everything He still has in store for everyone. Meanwhile, the lights on stage and in the auditorium slowly brighten. At the end of the prayer, the ceiling lights are a soft blue, and we can see the golden globe back in place, rotating slowly. Osteen adds a short message of hope and encouragement and invites people in special need of a personal prayer to pray with prayer partners in front of the stage.[42] During prayer time, the band and singers perform a slow ballad, while worship attendants in the ranks pray alone, watch, reflect, or even check e-mails on their smartphones. A more upbeat song follows this prayer time, inviting people to stand up again, to praise and worship the Lord. Then Victoria takes the stage, speaks a prayer, gives a short inspirational message, and invites people to give for the work of God. Another vigorous song closes this hour of praise and worship before, finally, Joel Osteen comes on stage to give his extended message.

The television broadcast begins at this point in the service. Osteen greets his extended viewing audience and begins with a joke before inviting the audience to stand and recite the following words with their Bibles in hand:

> This is my Bible. I am what it says I am. I can do what it says I can do. Today, I will be taught the Word of God. I boldly confess, my mind is alert, my heart is receptive. I will never be the same. I am about to receive the incorruptible, indestructible, ever-living seed of the Word of God. I will never be the same. Never, never, never. I will never be the same. In Jesus's name. Amen.

Before launching into his message, he asks his audience members to open their Bibles. Many people in the auditorium are sitting with open Bibles, open notebooks, or prayer journals and pen in hand, ready to take notes or highlight biblical passages. Osteen develops the topic of the day by telling different short stories. After each story, he comes back to the main message of the day he wants to convey. By connecting every story to the main message, he develops a cohesive narration. That narration often only loosely refers to the chosen part of scripture for the day. What the stories typically have in common is that they relate to everyday life and to the experiences of those in the audience. Some stories are sentimental; others have a funny twist and make the audience laugh and applaud. All are intended to be testimonials of God's grace and inspirations for the audience. People in the audience comment with loud exclamations of "Amen!" "Thank you, Father!" or "Praise the Lord!" Osteen's narrative abilities are enhanced by smooth, slow gestures and interspersed encouragements. The message ends with Osteen asking the audience, "Did you receive it today?" and the altar call for people to accept Jesus as their savior. People scattered throughout the audience stand up as a sign that they want to (re) dedicate their lives to Jesus Christ. They are greeted with a large round of applause. With closed eyes and in unison with the audience Osteen at last declares: "Lord Jesus, I repent of my sins, come into my heart, wash me clean, I make you my Lord and Savior. Amen." He offers another prayer of thanks and speaks a blessing, the TV broadcast ends, and the service concludes with a song.

Osteen's messages follow a basic structure, whether a recorded spoken message or a chapter from his books, which are repackaged versions of his sermons. They combine encouragements with different small stories, creating uncountable variations of the main theme. His basic message is the promise that there is hope for everyone and a solution to every problem. Every struggle one faces can be overcome with the right perspective and the right action and by remaining faithful to God's promise of restoration, happiness, and prosperity. Consider an example drawn from the CD/DVD resource *Overflow—Discover the God of More than Enough*. The title of that particular Sunday message is "Going from Believing to Expecting." As usual, Osteen starts by naming and elaborating on the topic of the day, supporting his explanations with short Bible quotations. He describes the topic of the message as "making preparations for the good things God has in store for everyone" and explains that this usually implies a period of waiting for those good things to happen. He goes on to state that there is a "right way of waiting" and a "wrong way of waiting." He elaborates on the right way of waiting with a quote from James 5:7: "Be patient, as you wait. See how the farmer waits expectantly." He thereby lays out the main frame for his explanations. That main theme is that one "has to wait with expectancy," meaning that one is "not supposed to sit around discouraged, negative and thinking that one's situation is never going to change." Waiting expectantly, Osteen explains, means that one is "hopeful and positive." Waiting therefore should not be passive; it should be active. That means that one should "be on the lookout, talk like it is going to happen, act like it is going to happen, and make preparations for those good things to happen." Each of the anecdotes that follows this introduction is an example of how "making preparations," "going from believing to expecting," and "putting action behind one's faith" helped make the dreams of the people in those stories come true.

Here we can see how Osteen integrates the stories into his main narrative:

It may be just something small, a dream to lose weight. I know this young lady. She was so tired of being overweight. But I'm telling you, she had dieted, she had tried, she had fought it. Nothing seemed to work. Finally, she just gave up and accepted where she was in spite of the fact that she knew that wasn't God's best. And this is so easy to do in any area of life, to kind of just sit back and settle for mediocrity. But one day this young lady got fed up. She put her foot down and started to put actions behind her prayers. She went up to the mall and on purpose she bought a new outfit that was two sizes too small for her. She knew she couldn't wear it. What was she doing? Making preparations to lose the weight. She went from believing to expecting. She told how she put that outfit in her closet right by her mirror so she could see it every day. You'd say, "Joel, that would depress me!" No! This inspired her! Every time she saw it, she would say, "Father, thank you that I will lose that weight. Thank you that every gland, every organ, every cell in my body functions normally. Thank you that I have discipline and self-control." Day after day, she kept watering her seed. I saw her about a month ago. You know what she was wearing? Her new outfit. She said, "Joel, I not only lost 30 pounds but I feel better today than I've ever felt before." I gave her a high five and said "You go, girl!" [Applause.] God rewards people like that. Keep the vision in front of you! Stay determined! . . . Stretch your faith! Put some action behind what you're believing for![43]

Here, Osteen recounts the story of an overweight woman dreaming about losing weight and thereby touches upon "an abiding, daily preoccupation of millions of American people."[44] Osteen tells his audience how the young woman gave up after failing several times to lose weight. At this point in the story, Osteen leaves the frame of that particular narrative and reminds his audience that defeat and mediocrity are too easily accepted in any area of life, not just in repeatedly unsuccessful attempts to lose weight. His appeal not to "settle for mediocrity" is a recurring and strongly emphasized point in his messages and publications. He then returns to the storyline and reveals the narrative's core point. Despite her previous failures, the young woman starts a final attempt to lose weight by putting "actions behind her prayers," by going "from believing to expecting." Acting like her dream was already coming true—buying a dress too small for her and "speaking change into existence"[45] through her prayers—she loses weight and makes her dream into reality. This part of the narrative articulates the idea that even a hopeless situation can be successfully transformed with the right attitude and right action. That combination is, as Osteen states, what will get God's attention, causing Him to work in the life of the believer: "God rewards people like that." Osteen concludes this short tale of success by directly addressing his audience in the imperative: "Keep the vision in front of you! Stay determined! . . . Stretch your faith! Put some action behind what you're believing for!" The last sentence relates back to Osteen's topic of the day and thereby connects the different examples and stories recounted during the whole sermon into a cohesive narrative. That narrative is structured to convey one message to his audience, namely, that it is possible to achieve anything if one decides to talk, to act, and to live as though "good things are going to happen." The message's central theme is that agency ultimately lies within the individual. All people have the power to make their dreams come true by putting action behind their faith and prayers. The right attitude supported by the right action will enable individuals to transform themselves from a currently undesirable to a more desirable state.

What is particularly interesting is that here we can see Osteen using the same rhetorical and narrative devices that are used in self-help literature and workshops from the broader field of alternative spiritualities, popular therapeutic discourse, and the Human Potential Movement.[46] For example, psychologist Helen Lee has analyzed eight books from the mind-body-spirit genre, which comprises ideas from alternative religious traditions, contemporary spirituality, self-help, and psychology,[47] and identifies ideas of transformation and liberation as central themes in those books. The narrative construction of transformation and liberation is based on specific assumptions about human nature and responsibility. Those narratives place the individual at the center "as the one who is in control of, and responsible for, improving his/her own life,"[48] and they offer psychological liberation as a means of personal transformation. The person, and, more specifically, the mind, is the focus of change in those narratives. We can see these ideas of liberation and transformation at work in Osteen's book *Every Day a Friday: How to Be Happier 7 Days a Week*, which works in a similar way. Looking at this book will help us understand how the mind is constructed as the venue where personal transformation and liberation are implemented.

Osteen starts his narration with the story of John, an old blind man who decides to move into a seniors' home. When the young aide shows him through the corridors of the home, she describes his new room in great detail. It is, she tells him, a nice, sunny, comfortable room. The old man interrupts her description and states that he loves the room, prompting the bewildered aide to reply that he has not even seen it yet. John's answer contains the lesson that Osteen wants to impart:

> John said, "No, you don't have to show it to me. Whether I like my room or not doesn't depend on how the furniture is arranged. It depends on how my *mind* is arranged. Happiness is something you decide ahead of time." As wise old John understood, happiness is a choice. When you wake up in the morning you can choose what kind of day you want to have. You can choose to be in a good mood, or you can choose to be in a bad mood. . . . My purpose in writing this book is to help you arrange your mind so that you choose happiness each and every day. Whatever challenges you may face, whatever circumstances are weighing you down, you can choose your response. How you live your life is totally up to you. It's not dependent on your circumstances. It's dependent on your choices.[49]

The passage conveys the idea that life can improve, that difficulties can be overcome, and that a better life full of happiness will result if one chooses to arrange one's mind in the right way. The focus of change is not external circumstances that may lie beyond the individual's reach and influence but, rather, the individual's mind. The mind is construed as both the problem and the solution. Negativity and discouragement are consequences of a wrong mindset, a wrong perspective on things. Liberation from negativity and unhappiness is thus a question of consciously reworking one's mind in the right way.

Discourses on personal responsibility are, according to Lee, intimately related to the construction of liberation from pessimism, discouragement, and unhappiness.[50] The individual is portrayed as solely responsible for bringing about personal and internal change as a means to a better life. Another rhetorical device that further emphasizes the notion of personal responsibility in these narratives is the recurrent use of personal and possessive pronouns. For example, the pronouns *you* and *your* are dominant in the quotation above. Phrases such as "you can choose," "your choices," and "you arrange your mind" imply personal accountability and thereby construct an individualistic concept of responsibility.

At the same time, as Lee explains, the use of the pronoun *you* functions inclusively to draw the reader or listener in by personalizing the message. Similarly, the collective pronoun *we* directly addresses readers and listeners while uniting them with the author or speaker as well as with the other readers and listeners, as the following quotation shows:[51] "That's the excitement God has placed inside every one of us. We should never forget how to celebrate each day. But so often as we get older, we let the challenges of life push us down and sadden our spirits. We have to realize every day is a gift from God. Once this day is gone, we can never retrieve it. If we make the mistake of being negative, discouraged, grumpy, or sour, we've wasted the day."[52] Although the author tells his readers that the reason for discouragement and unhappiness lies in subjugating oneself to the wrong perspective, the use of the collective pronoun *we* marks him as his audience's equal in that respect, not their superior. He, too, is someone who, like them, needs this personal transformation: "Listen here, self. Cheer up. Put on a new attitude. We're not staying down. We're not staying defeated. We're putting our hope in the Lord."[53] The prolific use of the collective pronoun *we* further assists in establishing the idea of personal responsibility.

Moreover, the extended use of exercises, visualizations, affirmations, prayers, and questions causes the reader or listener to pause, think, answer, and become involved. Lee calls this "practicising reality."[54] The listener or reader actively engages in a practice that works to enable a personal transformation, a practice that visualizes the ultimate aim, the transformed self. Others have called such practices "speaking change into existence."[55] We encountered one example in Osteen's story of the overweight woman who acted as though she had already lost weight and thereby encouraged herself to actually lose the weight. Osteen recounted the daily prayer that empowered her to fulfill her dream: "Father, thank you that I will lose that weight. Thank you that every gland, every organ, every cell in my body functions normally. Thank you that I have discipline and self-control." Osteen's books provide similar passages and prayers, which can be employed by the reader in everyday life, assisting in bringing about the self-transformation: "When you wake up in the morning and that negative thought comes to your mind saying, *It's a lousy day*, don't just agree and say, 'Yeah. It's a lousy day, I feel terrible.' Instead turn it around and talk to yourself. Make a declaration of faith out loud: 'This will be a great day. I will get well. God will restore health to me.' "[56]

Journal versions of most of Osteen's books are available for purchase. These journals are intended to further support readers in applying the insights from the book to their everyday lives. The journal is another request to become active; it demands that readers engage with the text and actively enact its advice in their lives. Alongside inspirational daily readings, the journal offers step-by-step instructions and space to write down personal thoughts and encourages the reader to keep a written report of progress in the project of self-transformation.[57]

What distinguishes Joel Osteen's books and Sunday messages from those books Helen Lee has analyzed is the reference to the power of a supernatural God. Although Osteen is a Christian, his audience of readers and viewers includes Christians and non-Christians alike.[58] Despite the reference to a powerful God, the individual is solely responsible; the individual has to make the choice to change his or her life. Only then will God work in supernatural ways to help make those dreams come true.

Osteen's approach to self-fulfillment is comparable to similar products on the market that combine self-help, positive thinking, and the pursuit of happiness and prosperity with spirituality.[59] They all place happiness and contentment solely within the agency of an individual and thereby dovetail with a neoliberal discourse that naturalizes the idea of individual autonomy while simultaneously concealing the supra-individual forces of the social and material world. The language employed in those self-help books and similar programs—whether Christian-inspired, like the material analyzed above, or from the field of alternative spiritualities or secular providers—is shaped by the therapeutic culture prevalent in contemporary societies. The therapeutic discourse strongly influences notions of self and personhood in contemporary America.[60]

## IV    *Religion and Therapeutic Culture*

In the 1980s, social theorist Pierre Bourdieu observed that the boundaries of the religious field were increasingly blurred:

> Today there is an imperceptible transition from clerics of the old school . . . to members of sects, to psychoanalysts, to psychologists, to doctors . . . to sexologists, to teachers of diverse forms of bodily expressions and Eastern martial arts, to life counselors, to social workers. They all take part in a new field of struggle over

the symbolic manipulation of the conduct of private life and the orientation of one's vision of the world, and they all develop in their practice competing and antagonistic definitions of health, of healing, of the treatment of bodies and of souls.[61]

Although Bourdieu might have had contemporary France in mind, his observations apply to other Western countries as well. Joel Osteen is one of those experts in the "new field of struggle over the symbolic manipulation of the conduct of private life and the orientation of" the worldview where religious and therapeutic discourses overlap and coalesce. This will become clear by setting the material presented thus far into the broader context of the modern discourse on the self.

As sociologist Nikolas Rose argues, in current postmodern societies there seems to be one core value that is beyond reproach: the self and the concepts that are assembled around it, such as autonomy, identity, individuality, liberty, choice, and fulfillment. The conception of "our selves" as autonomous, individual, and free is the basis on which we come to understand our endeavors, desires, lifestyle choices, and relationships. The way we consume and choose our commodities, how we display our tastes and our distinctiveness, the way we shape and fashion our bodies—all of these everyday practices are borne out by the idea that they express our authenticity, our "true self." Thus, Rose concludes that "this ethic of the free, autonomous self seems to trace out something quite fundamental in the ways in which modern men and women have come to understand, experience, and evaluate themselves, their actions, and their lives."[62] He terms that set of values clustered around the idea of an autonomous self the "regime of the self"[63] that characterizes postmodern societies. Following Foucault's genealogical approach, Rose unearths the history of that particular regime of the self. Specifically, he argues that the idea of the autonomous self is not ontological but was "invented" in collaboration with the development of psychology in the late nineteenth century.[64]

Sociologist Eva Illouz follows a similar line of argument and describes the therapeutic discourse as one of the dominant narrative structures in twentieth-century America. The therapeutic discourse developed enormous cultural resonance "because the language of psychotherapy left the realm of experts and moved to the realm of popular culture, where it interlocked and combined with various other key categories of American culture, such as the pursuit of happiness, self-reliance, and the perfectibility

of the self."[65] Neither Rose nor Illouz considers psychology or the therapeutic discourse to be confined to academic discourse or psychotherapy
in the narrow sense of the term. Instead, therapeutic discourse has thoroughly permeated all of contemporary life and has generated and popu-
larized a language and a conception of self and personhood in therapeutic
terms.[66] Central to this understanding of the self are the ideals of autonomy, self-reliance, and personal responsibility, all of which imply agency.
The discourse describes the autonomous self as the center of personal
agency, which can act upon itself, others, and the world.

This concern with our selves and the conduct of our selves was termed
by Michel Foucault as "technologies of the self," "which permit individuals
to effect by their own means or with the help of others a certain number
of operations on their own bodies and souls, thoughts, conduct, and way
of being, so as to transform themselves in order to attain a certain state of
happiness, purity, wisdom, perfection or immortality."[67] In the modern
discourse of the self, ideals of autonomy and self-responsibility are tied to
notions of self-development, self-realization, and self-fulfillment. By con-
ventionalizing self-realization as the core of modern selfhood, "most lives
become 'un-self-realized,'"[68] denoting an undesirable state responsible for
different forms of failures or weaknesses. Success and happiness thereby
become intrinsically implicated with the fulfillment of the self.[69] It is the
cultural matrix of an encompassing consumer culture that facilitates the
commodification of the therapeutic narrative that naturalizes the need for
self-development and self-fulfillment. Wade Clark Roof has described that
process as the "commodification of the self in modern society."[70]

Producer and consumer, the pastorpreneur and his audience, inhabit
the same social and material world, a world that structures and simultaneously is structured by hegemonic knowledge regimes and practices
of contemporary Western liberal societies, such as consumer capitalism,
the regime of the self, and therapeutic culture. Joel Osteen's "message of
hope" is shaped by and an answer to the prevalent therapeutic ethos in
today's consumer societies. The "smiling preacher's" brand offers hope
and encouragement in the face of hardship, misery, or unhappiness,
which current discourse regimes place solely within the responsibility of
the individual, thereby obfuscating larger societal and material structures
of inequality. Osteen's message in its different formats thus resonates
with the self-understandings of his diverse audiences and offers a way
to comply with the ubiquitous imperative of self-fulfillment. As we have
seen, Osteen encourages his audiences to become active, to be expectant,

and to be positive that with the help of God they will be "overcomers, and not be overcome," that they will be "victors, and not victims," in the face of life's challenges. In their strivings toward self-development, Osteen's readers, viewers, and worship attendees are assured divine support if they first believe right and act right—in other words, if they become the agents of their change and self-transformation. This case study of Joel Osteen and his products has shown that production and consumption are tied to broader cultural patterns, discourses, and practice regimes that frame and shape the social world and the ways that actors on both supply and demand sides engage this world.

## V   *Conclusion*

Joel Osteen—best-selling author, famous televangelist, and pastor of what is currently the largest megachurch in the United States—is one of the most successful "pastorpreneurs" in the American religious marketplace. He is at once a savvy businessman and a cultural broker; he combines business and marketing strategies with a message that resonates with the self-understanding of modern consumers shaped by contemporary discourses and practices of the self. This analysis of the rhetorical and narrative devices employed in Osteen's books, recordings, and sermons has shown how his "message of hope" is shaped and sustained by the same discourses and practices. Postmodern consumer culture and the regime of the self frame and mold both processes of production and consumption of cultural products.

The modern discourse of the self naturalizes the idea of an autonomous self. It inculcates and nourishes the need for self-development and self-fulfillment supported by the therapeutic ethos of contemporary consumer societies. Sociologist and marketing expert Jennifer Rindfleish has argued that due to the specific cultural conditions of postmodern consumer societies, there is a need to "consume the self."[71] As different scholars from religious studies such as Jeremy Carrette, Richard King, and Paul Heelas have shown, assumptions about the modern self and personhood function as interfaces to the contemporary discourse on religion and spirituality in a market where the naturalized need for self-development and self-transformation becomes commodified.[72] The culturally produced and commodified need for self-fulfillment tends to homogenize consumers and products and simultaneously offers options for differentiation.[73] Technologies of the self—whether provided by secular counselors, New

Age spiritualities, Buddhist experts, or Christian suppliers such as Joel Osteen—are diversified answers to the naturalized and marketed need for self-development.

## *Notes*

I gratefully acknowledge the support of the Deutsche Forschungsgemeinschaft (German Research Foundation), which funded the research that resulted in this chapter.

1. Jaweed Kaleem, "Televangelist's Motivational Message Comes to AmericanAirlines Arena," *Miami Herald*, November 28, 2010, A1.

2. Mara Einstein, *Brands of Faith: Marketing Religion in a Commercial Age* (London: Routledge, 2008), 124, 135.

3. Joel Osteen, *Every Day a Friday: How to Be Happier 7 Days a Week* (New York: FaithWords, 2011).

4. Osteen's other books are *Your Best Life Now: 7 Steps to Living at Your Full Potential* (New York: FaithWords, 2004), *Become a Better You: 7 Keys to Improving Your Life Every Day* (New York: Free Press, 2007), and *It's Your Time: Activate Your Faith, Achieve Your Dreams, and Increase in God's Favor* (New York: Free Press, 2009). All of them made it onto the *New York Times* "Advice, How-To and Miscellaneous" bestseller list, with *Your Best Life Now* reaching #1. The books are accompanied by a "Daily Readings from . . ." version in printed and audio book format and an additional journal containing inspirational messages, step-by-step instructions, and a place for writing down personal notes and reflections.

5. Grammy Award–winning singer Israel Houghton serves alongside Cindy Cruse-Ratcliff and the gospel duo "Anointed" as worship leader in the Lakewood Church music ministry and might be considered an attraction himself.

6. William Martin, "Prime Minister," in *Southern Crossroads: Perspectives on Religion and Culture*, ed. Walter H. Conser Jr. and Rodger M. Payne (Lexington: University Press of Kentucky, 2008), 80–83. One of Osteen's harshest critics is theologian Michael Scott Horton from Westminster Seminary California. See, for example, Michael Horton's *Christless Christianity: The Alternative Gospel of the American Church* (Grand Rapids: Baker Publishing Group, 2008); and his statement on "Joel Osteen Answers His Critics," *60 Minutes*, CBS News, October 14, 2007.

7. See, for example, William Martin, "Prime Minister," *Texas Monthly*, August 2005, 106–113, 167–175.

8. As described by Byron Pitts on "Joel Osteen Answers His Critics."

9. Martin, "Prime Minister," in *Southern Crossroads*, 65; Ruth Marshall, *Political Spiritualities: The Pentecostal Revolution in Nigeria* (Chicago: University of

Chicago Press, 2009), 280. While conducting fieldwork in Singapore in 2013 and 2014, I found an assortment of books written by Osteen in all big "secular" bookstores as well as in all Christian bookstores; the latter usually also had Chinese translations of his titles on offer.

10. François Gauthier, Tuomas Martikainen, and Linda Woodhead, "Introduction: Religion in Consumer Society," *Social Compass* 58, no. 3 (2011): 291.

11. John Jackson, *Pastorpreneur: Pastors and Entrepreneurs Answer the Call* (Friendswood, Tex.: Baxter Press, 2003), 2.

12. Shayne Lee and Phillip Luke Sinitiere, *Holy Mavericks: Evangelical Innovators and the Spiritual Marketplace* (New York: New York University Press, 2009), 2; Roger Finke and Laurence R. Iannaccone, "Supply-Side Explanations for Religious Change," *Annals of the American Academy of Political and Social Science* 527 (1993): 30–36.

13. Laurence R. Moore, *Selling God: American Religion in the Marketplace of Culture* (Oxford: Oxford University Press, 1994), 45–52; Jon Butler, Grant Wacker, and Randall Balmer, *Religion in American Life: A Short History* (Oxford: Oxford University Press, 2003), 129; Lee and Sinitiere, *Holy Mavericks*, 15. A common critique leveled against evangelical preachers at the turn of the nineteenth century referred to the mechanical, rote, and theatrical elements of revival preaching. See Kathryn E. Lofton, "The Preacher Paradigm: Promotional Biographies and the Modern-Made Evangelist," *Religion and American Culture: A Journal of Interpretation* 16, no. 1 (2006): 104–106.

14. Robert D. Putnam and David E. Campbell, *American Grace: How Religion Divides and Unites Us* (New York: Simon and Schuster, 2010), 163–164.

15. Moore, *Selling God*, 243.

16. Ibid., 9, 43, 55.

17. Ibid., 209–218.

18. Finke and Iannaccone, "Supply-Side Explanations for Religious Change," 27; Stephen Ellingson, *The Megachurch and the Mainline: Remaking Religious Tradition in the Twenty-First Century* (Chicago: University of Chicago Press, 2007), 11.

19. Stewart M. Hoover, "Audiences," in *Key Words in Religion, Media and Culture*, ed. David Morgan (New York: Routledge, 2008), 34–39.

20. James B. Twitchell, *Branded Nation: The Marketing of Megachurch, College Inc., and Museumworld* (New York: Simon and Schuster, 2004), 47; Mara Einstein, "Evolution of Religious Branding," *Social Compass* 53, no. 3 (2011): 331–338.

21. Twitchell, *Branded Nation*, 1–46; Einstein, *Brands of Faith*, 67–94; Einstein, "Evolution of Religious Branding," 332.

22. Melissa Aronczyk and Devon Powers, "Introduction: Blowing Up the Brand," in *Blowing Up the Brand: Critical Perspectives on Promotional Culture*, ed. Melissa Aronczyk and Devon Powers (New York: Peter Lang, 2010), 10.

23. Lee Cow, "Lee Cow—TBWA Worldwide," in *The Future of Brands: Twenty-Five Visions*, ed. Rita Clifton and Esther Maughan (New York: New York University Press, 2000), 71.

24. Moore, *Selling God*, 5.

25. Aronczyk and Powers, "Introduction," 7.

26. Twitchell, *Branded Nation*, 9.

27. Mary Jones, "Branding Methodism: Media Campaign Seeks New Ways to Draw, Keep Younger Members," *e-Review Florida United Methodist News Service*, March 13, 2009, accessed February 4, 2014, http://www.flumc.info/global_connect_archives-0309.shtml; Einstein, "Evolution of Religious Branding," 334.

28. Kimon Howland Sargeant, *Seeker Churches: Promoting Traditional Religion in a Nontraditional Way* (New Brunswick, N.J.: Rutgers University Press, 2000), 59–61; Scott Thumma and Warren Bird, "A New Decade of Megachurches: 2011 Profile of Large Attendance Churches in the United States," Leadership Network, accessed February 4, 2014, http://www.hartfordinstitute.org/mega-church/New-Decade-of-Megachurches-2011Profile.pdf, 6.

29. Einstein, "Evolution of Religious Branding," 334.

30. Sargeant, *Seeker Churches*, 156; William H. Swatos, "Beyond Denominationalism? Community and Culture in American Religion," *Journal for the Scientific Study of Religion* 20, no. 3 (1981): 226.

31. Einstein, "Evolution of Religious Branding," 334–337.

32. Einstein, *Brands of Faith*, 92.

33. Ibid., 122.

34. Richard Young, *The Rise of Lakewood Church and Joel Osteen* (New Kensington, Pa.: Whitaker House, 2007), 49, 55, 77–83.

35. Osteen, *Your Best Life Now*, 215.

36. Martin, "Prime Minister," in *Southern Crossroads*, 66–70.

37. Einstein, *Brands of Faith*, 121.

38. Einstein's book contains a lot of interesting and innovative ideas and, most importantly, reminds us that religion is a commodity product and as such is packaged and sold like any other product. Her book is a reminder that religion is not something "holy" or "sacred" in itself and therefore untouched by the supposed "triviality" or capitalist materiality of consumerism. At the same time, it is important to make two critical notes here. First, Einstein tends toward an essentialist and ahistorical notion of religion. Consider, for example, her questions in the section "From Enlightenment to Enterprise" in the preface of the book: "How did a once esoteric, Jewish tradition become a religious commodity? How did Kabbalah get to be a pop cultural phenomenon instead of a serious religious practice? How did it turn into a product for enterprise and entertainment instead of enlightenment?" (ibid., x). I would respond by asking whether pop culture phenomena and serious religious practices must

be mutually exclusive. Must enlightenment and entertainment likewise be mutually exclusive? These questions urge us to reflect upon our own underlying assumptions about religion as something serious and profound or the aspiration toward enlightenment. Furthermore, Einstein argues that marketing changes the product to suit the market: e.g., due to the process of marketing and branding, religion will become something different. Religion has changed from "what people need to what people want" (192). Her view that religion is fundamentally changed in the process is already expressed in her introduction: "It is safe to say that marketing religion likely has been a contributing factor in transforming religion into 'religion lite' and religion probably is watered down and that may not be a good thing" (14). Such notions of religion tend to be value-laden, but religious studies scholars must be careful not to assign different moral values to different styles and forms of religious practice. My second critical remark refers to the explanatory scope of the branding approach. Her argument basically works along the lines of analogies: today's televangelists, Oprah, Kabbalah, and other religious products are branded and marketed in the same way as an Apple or a Nike product. But the analogy works the other way around, too: Branding as a marketing process is about storytelling and the creation of meaning and imaginaries; marketing shares those very characteristics with religion. Einstein employs a good deal of marketing language and concepts in her description of contemporary religious organizations, their products, and their practices. Yet most of her elaborations remain at the surface, more descriptive than explanatory. Most of her explanations are based on assumptions about consumers without ever really looking at what consumers actually do and thereby just assuming that they react in the presumed way. I think that one could have used the heuristic category "brand" even more creatively and toward a more pointed end, by focusing on the relationship between consumers and religious brands as about more than the consumption of a certain product or service; consumption, after all, also enables the formation of social relations, sensual experiences, certain lifestyles, and a sense of belonging to a community. See Aronczyk and Powers, "Introduction," 7.

39. This preference for certain terminology is not limited to Lakewood Church but is also observable in other contemporary megachurches. See Twitchell, *Branded Nation*, 94.

40. Songs I heard regularly during my fieldwork at Lakewood Church services included Darrell Evans's "Trading My Sorrows," from his album *Freedom* (1998), lyrics and music by Darrell Evans, an American evangelical Christian musician and songwriter of contemporary Christian worship music; "Majesty (Here I Am)" from the album *World Service* (2003), lyrics and music by Martin Smith and Stuart Garrard from the British Christian rock band Delirious?; and "Our God" from the album *And if Our God Is for Us . . .* (2010), lyrics and music by Chris Tomlin, Matt Redman, Jesse Reeves, and Jonas Myrin. Chris

Tomlin is another American Christian contemporary musician and song-writer. For a study of contemporary worship music, see Robert Woods and Brian Walrath, eds., *The Message in the Music: Studying Contemporary Praise and Worship* (Nashville: Abingdon Press, 2007).

41. The central part of the stage design at Lakewood Church is a three-dimensional, slowly rotating golden globe in front of a sky-blue wall, which simultaneously provides the background for Osteen's stage presence in the TV broadcast. The pulpit—Osteen calls it a podium—is decorated with a stylized dove, the logo of Lakewood Church. The apparent lack of Christian symbolism at Lakewood Church is a recurring point in writings and comments about that church. See, for example, John Leland, "A Church that Packs Them In, 16,000 at a Time," *New York Times*, July 18, 2005, A1; Einstein, *Brands of Faith*, 128. However, the physical absence of Christian symbols is suspended by temporarily changing video projections of corresponding images such as crosses, stained-glass orna-ments, and Jesus statues during the praise and worship part of the service.

42. Joel Osteen and members of his family act as prayer partners, too. Therefore, the prayer time offers the rare opportunity to have a personal moment with Joel Osteen, with him praying for one's personal problems.

43. Transcript of "Going from Believing to Expecting," from *Joel Osteen: Overflow—Discover the God of More than Enough*, CD/DVD (2009), time stamp 00:25:24–00:27:11.

44. Peter N. Stearns, *Fat History: Bodies and Beauty in the Modern West* (New York: New York University Press, 2002), 4. The popular ideal of cultivat-ing thin, lean, and healthy bodies is central to both secular and evangelical dis-courses on diet, body size, and health in contemporary American culture, which constitutes the body as a means to self-transformation and self-cultivation and equates the slender body with beauty, health, success, and self-mastery. See R. Marie Griffith, *Born Again Bodies: Flesh and Spirit in American Christianity* (Berkeley: University of California Press, 2004); and Katharina Vester, "Regime Change: Gender, Class, and the Invention of Dieting in Post-Bellum America," *Journal of Social History* 44, no. 1 (2010): 39–70.

45. Lee and Sinitiere, *Holy Mavericks*, 31.

46. Good examples are est (= Erhard Seminars Training) and Landmark Forum workshops (Landmark Education Corporation), which are influenced by ideas formulated by Carl Rogers and Abraham Maslow. See Eva Illouz, *Saving the Modern Soul: Therapy, Emotions, and the Culture of Self-Help* (Berkeley: University of California Press, 2008), 186–196.

47. The label "mind-body-spirit" is an umbrella term that encompasses a variety of books from different fields such as complementary health, psychology, busi-ness, ecology, and philosophy and different religious traditions that empha-size self-development. See Elizabeth Puttick, "The Rise of Mind-Body-Spirit Publishing: Reflecting or Creating Spiritual Trends?" *Journal of Alternative*

*Spiritualities and New Age Studies* 1 (2005): 130–131; and Helen Lee, "'Truths that Set Us Free?' The Use of Rhetoric in Mind-Body-Spirit Books," *Journal of Contemporary Religion* 22, no. 1 (2007): 91.

48. Lee, "Truths that Set Us Free?" 94.

49. Osteen, *Every Day a Friday*, 3–4; emphasis in original.

50. Lee, "Truths that Set Us Free?" 96–97.

51. Ibid., 98.

52. Osteen, *Every Day a Friday*, 6.

53. Ibid., 14.

54. *Practicising* is an amalgamation of the terms *practice* and *exercise*. The neologism implies the notion of doing something and shows an orientation toward action. See Lee, "Truths that Set Us Free?" 96.

55. Lee and Sinitiere, *Holy Mavericks*, 31.

56. Osteen, *Every Day a Friday*, 13–14; emphasis in original.

57. On reading and journaling as tools of renewal, transformation, and self-actualization in the context of spiritual practices, see Kathryn E. Lofton, "Practicing Oprah; or, The Prescriptive Compulsion of a Spiritual Capitalism," *Journal of Popular Culture* 39, no. 4 (2006): 607–614.

58. Take, for example, the following statement on Amazon.com of a reader and reviewer of Joel Osteen's *Every Day a Friday* as well as a viewer of the TV broadcast: "I am not a 'Christian'—but I like Joel Osteen. His TV talks are gently inspiring and uplifting. In our world with all its troubles that are either real or imagined—he shines a light that enables one to move forward. He has the gift of encouragement, that is not something to be denigrated in any way" (rk, "Read It if You Want to Live Life Better," Amazon.com, September 15, 2011, accessed February 4, 2014, http://www.amazon.com/review/R1SLZ6X07N7IZU/ref=cm_cr_pr_perm?ie=UTF8&ASIN=0892969911&linkCode=&nodeID=&tag=).

59. The products and practices from Oprah Winfrey's empire function in a similar way, as they aim at individual spiritual transformation through material means. See Lofton, "Practicing Oprah."

60. Illouz, *Saving the Modern Soul*; Vincent J. Miller, *Consuming Religion: Christian Faith and Practice in a Consumer Culture* (New York: Continuum, 2009), 85–88; E. Brooks Holifield, *A History of Pastoral Care in America: From Salvation to Self-Realization* (Nashville: Abingdon Press, 1983), 259–324; Katja Rakow, "Therapeutic Culture and Religion in America," *Religion Compass* 7, no. 11 (2013): 485–497.

61. Unfortunately, Bourdieu's short paper "La dissolution de religieux" (a lecture from 1982) has not been included in the English translation of *Choses dites*. Hence this is my translation of the quote from the German version: Pierre Bourdieu, *Rede und Antwort*, trans. Bernd Schwibs (Frankfurt am Main: Suhrkamp, 1992), 233.

62. Nikolas Rose, *Inventing Our Selves: Psychology, Power, and Personhood* (Cambridge: Cambridge University Press, 1996), 1.

63. Ibid., 2.

64. Ibid., 17.

65. Illouz, *Saving the Modern Soul*, 155.

66. Rose, *Inventing Our Selves*, 10–11; Illouz, *Saving the Modern Soul*, 5–8.

67. Michel Foucault, *Technologies of the Self: A Seminar with Michel Foucault*, ed. Luther H. Martin, Huck Gutman, and Patrick H. Hutton (Amherst: University of Massachusetts Press, 1988), 18.

68. Illouz, *Saving the Modern Soul*, 161.

69. Jennifer Rindfleish, "Consuming the Self: New Age Spirituality as 'Social Product' in Consumer Society," *Consumption, Markets and Culture* 8, no. 4 (2005): 345.

70. Wade Clark Roof, *Spiritual Marketplace: Baby Boomers and the Remaking of American Religion* (Princeton: Princeton University Press, 2001), 35. A similar process is described in Rindfleish, "Consuming the Self," 345.

71. Rindfleish, "Consuming the Self," 358.

72. Jeremy Carrette and Richard King, *Selling Spirituality: The Silent Takeover of Religion* (London: Routledge, 2005); Paul Heelas, *Spiritualities of Life: New Age Romanticism and Consumptive Capitalism* (Malden: Blackwell, 2008). See also Heidi Marie Rimke, "Governing Citizens through Self-Help Literature," *Cultural Studies* 14, no. 1 (2000): 61–78; Rindfleish, "Consuming the Self"; and Lee, "Truths that Set Us Free?"

73. Jean Baudrillard, *The Consumer Society: Myths and Structures* (London: Sage, 1998), 89.

## 10

# *Unsilent Partners*

### SPORTS STADIUMS AND THEIR APPROPRIATION AND USE OF SACRED SPACE

*Anthony Santoro*

ON FEBRUARY 5, 2012, the New England Patriots and New York Giants met in Indianapolis in Super Bowl XLVI. The host stadium and the attendant spectacle hit all of the buttons that the Super Bowl as a two-week festival loves to hit: football fervor served up with a helping of patriotism and anything that can be called "all-American." Visually, there was little to break the theme: two teams whose colors are different shades of red, white, and blue; the blue NFC "N" logo contrasted with the red AFC "A"; the military presence in the stadium and within the confines of the broadcast; the invocative power of the call to "honor America" by standing for the national anthem; and the "unisonance"[1] of the "selfless" community singing its national anthem—all of the standard elements of civil religious ceremony were on display.

In several crucial senses, the spectacle unfolding before hundreds of millions of viewers worldwide was the embodiment and enactment of American civil religion (ACR) par excellence.[2] In the days before the game, coaches, media personalities, and the athletes themselves made any number of comments dealing with the themes of self-sacrifice in pursuit of a goal or a vision; of finding the proper role for the individual within the corporate body of the team and the organization; of the simple values of hard work, dedication, devotion, and sacrifice in pursuit of a dream; and of the openness and levelness of the playing field. The sheer scope of the spectacle notwithstanding, this was little different from any other NFL game day. The same affirmation of core American cultural myths and values, the same expression and embodiment of ACR, the same sense of coalescing discrete bodies into one larger body in pursuit of a higher goal—all are on display throughout the season.

In this essay, I want to shift our focus to the venues, integral components and "unsilent partners" in the spectacles. Stadiums are not simply host venues for the games, nor do they simply enhance and narrativize the spectacle on the field via various media and sensory devices. Instead, I argue that these stadiums are sensational forms, communicative devices designed to evoke certain affects by providing a space within which the American civil religious mythos is embodied and enacted and within which spectators participate in contesting and affirming that mythos.[3] They are both "flagship tourist attractions" and "key component[s] of the cultural landscape."[4] These spaces are half-constructed and half-ascribed.[5] They address beholders with sets of signs and symbols offering a narrative best understood as the product of the cultural and historical contexts that determine how the space is read, and they involve beholders in affirming, consenting to, or contesting the narratives on offer as the beholders accept those narratives for themselves.

My argument proceeds in four sections. First, I engage criticisms of civil religion as an explanatory vehicle and argue that it remains a useful analytic vehicle in this context. Second, I describe these stadiums as stars, locating them within the sporting and cultural marketplaces as such. Third, I take readers on a tour of these spaces and show how the popular perception of these stadiums combines with the willful marketing of nostalgia and the tenets of ACR to create spaces that need to be taken seriously and read as any sacred space would be. Finally, I show how these stadiums generate and market nostalgia to unite the dispersed fan nation and drive the franchise brand. This marketed nostalgia incorporates and acknowledges racial and class conflicts in society, while the stadiums provide a space for fans to react to these problems. This provision of space, however, simultaneously contains and minimizes these responses while adapting them both to the enhancement of the brand and to the furtherance of the civil religious narrative.[6]

# *I   Civil Religion and Professional Football in the United States*

Before proceeding to analyze the way these stadiums communicate civil religious values and ideas, a few words about my approach to ACR are in order. A number of scholars have raised trenchant objections to

ACR, questioning its usefulness given its tendency to promote a homogeneous nationalism and reinforce stereotypes while distorting our ability to see the complexity around us. Ira Chernus, for example, objects to ACR's chauvinism and its glorification of and in military might, as well as its deleterious effect on "a thoughtful open-minded public life—and study of public life—that truly values diversity."[7] As Arthur Remillard has shown, however, the fault may lie less with the idea and more with its application; that is, civil religion can be used profitably if we reject consensus-based, homogeneous definitions and use ACR as a vehicle by which to examine the various definitions of "the good society." This essay follows Remillard's lead in looking at these stadiums as spaces within which these various definitions are posited, contested, and accepted as expressions of *the* "American way of life."[8]

Consider the following declaration by current NFL commissioner Roger Goodell: "There is so much about [football] that captures the spirit of our country. When you combine the physical challenges, collective goals, and multiple sacrifices that are required to play football, you are talking about the same values that are at the core of our national spirit. America [like football] is about the freedom to compete and be successful on a level playing field. . . . You can look at football and see the heart of America."[9] Had Goodell said this in a relative vacuum, it could perhaps be written off as hyperbole directed at driving a product, but in fact, football has always been interpreted in this way. As folklorist Danille Lindquist notes, football "performs national identity (including tropes of competitive opportunity, mechanized teamwork, and homeland defense) in terms of shared experiences . . . [and] endors[es] efficient skill, physical strength, inventive achievement, and coordinated effort."[10] Football is the quintessentially industrial game, combining Taylorian concepts of how to manage not only labor but the act of laboring with rigid hierarchies with notions of sacrifice, dedication, hard work, and the tension between the need to subsume individual desires or needs into the collective and glorifying individual achievement in its own right. In this sense, football is the quintessentially Taylorist game, referring to the principles of scientific management developed by Frederick Winslow Taylor, who sought to maximize worker efficiency by studying and quantifying labor according to tasks performed, optimizing the amount of work performed in each action, selecting for the individuals best suited to particular physical tasks, and bringing management and labor into collaborative effort to achieve maximal efficiency via teaching and enacting these optimized motions.[11] Football has historically combined a strict division between management and labor with an "intense legality" that codifies conceptions of proper behavior.[12] Football also embraces, and indeed glories in, the idea of redemptive violence and territorial conquest; while Robert Bellah worried that his idea of ACR could be construed as endorsing the idea of "manifest destiny," Sal Paolantonio, a prominent sports journalist, entitled a chapter in his book *How Football Explains America* "How Football Explains Manifest Destiny."[13]

Football is a combination of sport, business, physical combat—to the point that the game is frequently metaphorized as war—and patriotic nationalism.[14] It is also a moralizing game, offering a definitive model of what it means to be an American. The spaces within which this game is played communicate this and incorporate elements of this idealized picture into their construction, which we can see when we read the stadiums in light of the way they communicate the "American dream."[15] If the stadiums are more than simply venues where the games are played and the fans spectate, if they are "unsilent partners" communicating these values, then we should be able to read them functionally and see embodied in them and in their use of space the values at the "heart of America," "the freedom to compete and be successful on a level playing field," as Goodell put it. We would also expect to see, as Lindquist argues, these values rooted in the locality but used within a national context.[16] In both cases, we would be right, as we will see when we look at these buildings via the stadium tours offered by nearly all NFL franchises.[17] Before taking a tour, however, we should begin by looking at where these star stadiums fit into the broader sports marketplace.

## II   *Stars*

Stars drive the sports market by serving as the face of the franchise and thereby of the brand; by, in some cases, transcending that franchise and becoming a brand unto themselves; and by serving as "the humanized content of sports that fans can relate to and, through this relationship, express a wide number of emotions."[18] Stars are one of two *essential connectors* in sport: by driving how sport becomes rooted in a particular community and its identity, they connect the fans to the franchise, the franchise to the community and the wider sport-consuming market, and so on.[19] The second essential connector is *place*, the facility within which the games are played. Most NFL stadiums are quite young: twenty-two of the league's thirty-two teams play in stadiums less than twenty years old. This means that two-thirds of the league's franchises play in stadiums built during what is variously called the "Highlight Generation" or the "postmodern" era of stadium design, when stadiums were built to be stars in their own right.[20]

Speaking of these stadiums as attractions, though, is less an observation than an advancement of two specific claims about their design and function. First, these attractions are clearly defined discrete units "that are accessible and motivate large numbers of people to travel some distance from their home, usually in their leisure time, to visit them for a short, limited period."[21] Second, these stadiums are man-made structures designed both to attract visitors for these short, limited periods and to cater to their needs during that period.[22] This is surely the case on game day, when many sporting pilgrimages are made, but it is also true at other times as well. The stadium tours offered by most NFL franchises are such discrete times designed to cater to highly and lowly identified fans alike and to capitalize on the stadium as an attraction and pilgrimage site.[23] More specifically, the tours are among the tools that franchises use to enhance feelings of community among fans, and thereby feelings of association with the team, by providing an experience that caters to the respective fan nation.

There are two essential components of this experience, apart from the game itself. The first is the generation of affect via media and sensational technologies that link fans into a single corporate body, providing sensory cues and guiding the community through its experience.[24] The second is the conspicuous, deliberate offering of nostalgia and heritage in these stadiums. We will look at these two ideas in more detail below, but here we can take Detroit's Ford Field as an example. Ford Field was built on the site of the flagship Hudson's department store, at one time the tallest and, according to Hudson's, the second-largest (square footage) department store in the country. Ford Field is located in the former Paradise Valley, a prominent, thriving Jazz Age African American neighborhood. The stadium's pedestrian concourses are named for prominent local streets. The bricks paving the Adams St. concourse date from the 1920s and were recovered from the demolished Hudson's, while the concession stands along Adams St. are named for famous Detroit landmarks. The brick interior facade behind Adams St. gives the impression that the stadium grew up alongside the old Hudson's warehouse, which is exactly the impression intended. These selective uses of historical names and materials and visual cues are meant both to link Ford Field to Detroit's past and to make it appear to be a part of the organic development of that history.[25]

## III   *Touring These Sacred Spaces*

In spring 2011, I took stadium tours at four NFL facilities: Ford Field in Detroit, Paul Brown Stadium in Cincinnati, Cleveland Browns Stadium in Cleveland, and Heinz Field in Pittsburgh.[26] The basic outline of these tours is representative of NFL stadium tours anywhere. The group meets at a designated location, where a guide joins you and introduces the facility while leading you through it. My tours all included stops in the press box; the luxury suites; historical or otherwise important places along the public concourses; the facilities that the public can rent for proms, weddings, or other events; the locker rooms (visitor, home, or both); and the playing field itself. Each tour focuses on showcasing the elements that make that facility unique among its peers or how it is rooted in its particular community. In Pittsburgh, we were walked through the Great Hall, with its giant replica Vince Lombardi Trophies housing the Steelers' Super Bowl trophies, its Fan Zone, and its Walk of Fame honoring past Steeler greats.

Tour patrons can take photographs of virtually everything they see, but, in accordance with NFL and Department of Homeland Security policies, videotaping is forbidden. We were shown replay booths and the coaches' boxes, though those doors remained locked, as did the stadium's official time clock. While these tours provide access to areas closed off to fans on game day, we were denied access to what each franchise and the league deemed most important, most central, to the stadium's function on game day, as well as to what we could damage. In Cleveland and Pittsburgh, we were prevented from stepping onto the natural grass field surface, though Detroit and Cincinnati allow fans onto their artificial surfaces. In Cincinnati, we were shown the visitor's locker room rather than the Bengals' facilities—privileged space, reserved exclusively for the team and not open to the public. Likewise, NFL rules prohibit all but the official personnel responsible for replay and timekeeping functions from entering those respective rooms; to make either place more widely accessible would be to undermine the sanctity of two of the most important features of the game-day spectacle: accurate recording and utilization of organized time and the ability to obtain the truth of the on-field action when necessary (or permitted).

These tours have also inspired commercials that draw on the stadiums' cultural resonances to enhance the appeal of their products. Kemps, a dairy producer headquartered in St. Paul, Minnesota, and with production facilities in Wisconsin, drew on Lambeau Field's cachet in a 2011 commercial featuring one of its dairy cows taking a tour of the Green Bay Packers' home field.[27] After welcoming the guests to "the home of the world champion Green Bay Packers," the guide takes them around the facility. After we see the cow gazing down onto the field from the press level, we are shown the group walking through the tunnel onto the field while the guide tells them that "every Packer great has walked out this tunnel"; the time and space that ordinarily separate tour patrons from Packers players past and present are here erased as customers walk through the same tunnel onto the same field as the athletes. On the field, the cow drops its head to munch on the grass, presumably conferring the mystical benefits of that grass—that field, with its history and tradition— to the cow, to her milk, and to Kemps's Packers Touchdown Sundae ice cream, the product featured in the spot. As the group is guided back off the field, the cow looks over its shoulder, surveying the unbroken green expanse while the words "Sacred Pasture" appear on screen. Only now that the field has been declared sacred is the ice cream mentioned.

We should observe several noteworthy elements of this commercial. First, these tours are sufficiently well known to form the basis for advertisement in the context of transferring the credibility and value of one brand—a football franchise—to another—dairy products. Second, the stadium is enough of a star both to carry the narrative of the advertisement and to serve as the nexus of exchange, the place where this value is exchanged. Third, while football is touted as the "industrial" game and baseball is the game that hearkens back to the pastoral ideal, football expresses its own pastoral ideal at the culmination of the quest. Finally, the idea that this football field is "sacred" is both emphasized and taken for granted. We can infer from the fact that the word *sacred* appears at all that there is an expected agreement with that description of the place, while the placement of the text within the commercial and its apposition to the product being advertised suggest that the idea is meant not as simple hyperbole but as an idea to be taken at face value. By invoking the idea of the sacred in this way, commercial forces lend credence to the idea that these spaces ought to be taken seriously as sacred spaces.

Sporting events and venues are frequently discussed in loosely or analogically religious language. A number of scholars and commentators have assessed sport in these terms along a continuum ranging from declaring that sport links with religion and shares some of its features and functions to declaring that sport *"is religious."*[28] Stadiums, meanwhile, are frequently discussed in terms traditionally denoting sacred spaces: stadiums are our "cathedrals," "hallowed" spaces and grounds, "modern day shrines," "sanctuar[ies] for the spirit," and our "monasteries."[29] Within these cathedrals, people have experiences that they can only explain with recourse to religious language; as Eric Bain-Selbo notes, a majority of the respondents in his survey of college football fans "used at least one religious . . . metaphor to explain the game-day experience."[30]

One important question that arises when we encounter such language is whether these comparisons are meant literally or figuratively, that is, whether they are meant literally or are simply linguistic signifiers denoting importance. A full engagement with this problem is beyond the scope of this essay,[31] but I want to argue that it is not necessary to resolve this problem to analyze these spaces in terms of their civil religious content.[32] Sufficient grounds exist for taking them seriously as sacred spaces that we can profitably examine them as such, as the following examples demonstrate.

In his study of Alabama Crimson Tide fans, Warren St. John repeatedly calls attention to the "religious" or "near-religious" nature of the fans' devotion, the "sacred" action of the game, and the "sacred shrine[s]" associated with Alabama football.[33] Being there, however, is only part of the story; getting to the stadium is a major component of the game-day experience. In a comment left on the *Oakland Tribune*'s *Inside the Oakland Raiders* blog, BigTed07 mentioned that he was "making the pilgrimage down to the bay this afternoon," in time to attend the Kansas City–Oakland game that weekend.[34] This representative comment deserves a closer look. These kinds of comments show us that place, movement, and motivation are all elements of this travel.[35] That BigTed07 does not live in the San Francisco Bay area we can ascertain from his making the trip "down." That his motivation for the trip is to attend the game is also clear, while the context dictates that we read "the bay" as a metonym for the O.co Coliseum, where the Raiders play their home games.

Most interestingly, and furthering the parallel, is the definite article in place of a pronoun—*the* pilgrimage rather than *my* pilgrimage, for example. This implies that BigTed07 knows that other fans and other commenters will make the same association between traveling to the game and a pilgrimage. This expectation informs the "Raider Mecca" event, an annual congregation of Raider fans from all around the world for a week-end that includes a tour of the team's facility, meet-and-greets with legends, and a tailgate party.[36] We can see similar motivation in fan practices revolving around life-cycle events. Fans request to be buried with game tickets in their pocket or to have their ashes scattered at specific stadiums; this latter practice is reportedly relatively widespread.[37] Fans can be buried in team-themed caskets, so long as the respective league has granted the appropriate licensing, while some companies offer sports-themed wedding decorations and planning materials.[38] You can also rent out a portion of an NFL stadium for a wedding, prom, or other significant event.[39]

Nor is it only the fans who ascribe special status to these places. The playing surfaces as viewed on the tours differ from those same surfaces on game day because they are conspicuously incomplete: they have not been branded with the team's name, colors, logos, and whatever other designs adorn the field for the games. In Cleveland and Pittsburgh, the field is painted before each game, and the paint is taken down afterward. The same is true in Detroit, according to our guide, even though the artificial surface could certainly be permanently branded. Even in Cincinnati, where the end zone markings are fixed onto the surface, the NFL logo is applied before and taken down after each game. In each case, this pairing of dedicative and de-dedicative actions defines the space both spatially and temporally. This singularization, this marking of this space (and time) as special relative to other things in its class, works in at least two ways. First, this dedication of space and time differentiates this space and time from the franchise's peer—and rival—franchises. Second, stadiums are multipurpose sites, in that they host a variety of mass-mediated, mass-public spectacles, such as rock concerts, political rallies, and religious services.[40] These acts transform a multipurpose space into a specific space by rededicating it to the spectacle of the game.[41]

These examples of how important sports are to some fans returns us to BigTed07's maybe not-so-casual use of the word *pilgrimage*. Recent reassessments of pilgrimage have sought to come to terms—figuratively and literally—with modern, secular forms of pilgrimage. We can draw on this growing body of literature to focus more fully on sporting venues. On the one hand, we need to recognize that these tours promote the stadiums both as places to be consumed and, in the pairing of nostalgia with the American dream, as heritage attractions.[42] On the other hand, we need to recognize that their status as pilgrimage sites derives not just from their association with the game but from their association with the civil religious and nationalistic ideals that the sport purports to embody and from which football derives some of its cultural power and attractiveness.[43] Journeys to these sites, which Gammon calls "a modern form of pilgrimage," are journeys not to places of worship but to sites that inspire particular reverence within certain historical, mythical, or cultural traditions or understandings.[44] We can see these various elements at work by returning to the stadium tours and looking at how they trade in expressions of the American dream.

## IV   *Nostalgia, Resistance, and Adaptation*

The Heinz Field tour begins and ends in the "Great Hall,"[45] a massive expanse of public concourse dedicated to celebrating the Steelers, their history, and their fans. This primacy and ultimacy of location underscores its importance, but we should note right away that this is the "Coca-Cola Great Hall," a triply branded space. Hanging between the words *Great* and *Hall* on the sign above the concourse is a modified Steelers logo. Complementing the familiar red, yellow, and blue hypocycloids of the U.S. Steel logo that forms the basis for the Steelers insignia is a fourth icon, a red Coca-Cola icon. The Great Hall is thus marked as belonging not only to the Steelers but also to trademarked logos representing both the production—U.S. Steel—and consumption—Coca-Cola—elements of the consumerist continuum.

Just inside the Great Hall is the Steeler Nation display, which honors the fans and their imagined community.[46] Fan nations are "comprised mostly of fans who are not citizens of cities" and whose identity rests on a shared "imagined cohesiveness" created via the use of myths, symbols, rituals, and narrative.[47] Stadium tours help enhance these fan nations, which we can describe as "communities of feeling,"[48] both by giving them a special, "capital" location and by providing physical access to nostalgia. The fans then consume this nostalgia, and with it the brand, via the "storying of the past" as embodied in the stadium and communicated via the tour.[49] This, in turn, enlists the fans consuming this nostalgia in enhancing the touristic appeal of the site by taking the tour and taking away mementos of the experience.[50]

On offer on this tour, however, is not simply nostalgia—a discrete set of positive memories or associations from the past that seem preferable in comparison with the perceived present—but *heritage*, which Ramshaw and Gammon define as an attempt to "remember, enliven, teach—and even create—personal and collective legacies for contemporary audiences. Its purpose is often to celebrate the achievements, courage, and strength of those who have come before."[51] This combination of positive associations and the celebration of achievement is on full display in the Great Hall. The six oversized Lombardi trophies dominate the space, while a wall mural depicting past Steeler greats includes a portrait of Byron "Whizzer" White, a former Steeler who later served as an associate justice on the U.S. Supreme Court. The Walk of Fame is a semienclosed space bounded on the left by lockers relocated from Three Rivers Stadium, the Steelers' former home, and a gigantic pair of black-and-white photographs depicting the Immaculate Reception, the play that sealed the Steelers' victory over the Oakland Raiders in the 1972 AFC Divisional playoffs and inaugurated the 1970s Steelers dynasty.

This sequence and juxtaposition of images is instructive. The apposition of the mural including Justice White and the oversized championship trophies point to two measures of success. The lockers rescued from the demolished Three Rivers include items worn by Steeler legends. Even though they are safely enshrined behind glass panels, these jerseys, cleats, pads, and other items relocate "ghosts" from the previous facility into the new one, physically rooting tradition, nostalgia, and heritage in the new building, where, in Novak's words, "tradition instantly begins."[52]

The gigantic depiction of the Immaculate Reception, meanwhile, enlists the patron in creating the imagined community and the "storying" that the stadium embodies. What are we to make, for example, of the fact that the paired photographs are in black and white? One can find full-color footage of that play via YouTube,[53] and certainly pivotal moments from a game played in 1972 were captured on color film. The black and white is a stylistic touch that imparts a sense of temporal distance that increases the "historic" feel both of the event depicted and of the space that it oversees and dominates. At the same time, this combination of objects and pictures both highlights and erases the divide between individual and collective memory. One may or may not remember the Immaculate Reception, but the Steeler Nation does, and because the imagined community remembers it, the individual fan receives and recreates the memory of that event.

This goes to several of the elements of these spaces as sacred. The depiction of the Immaculate Reception and the lockers opposite are simultaneously authentic and symbolic. Likewise, the walk from the locker room through the tunnel and onto the field is at once authentic and symbolic. It is authentic in the sense that tour patrons physically traverse that space, or, more appropriately, traverse those spaces, and it is authentic in the sense that every Steeler player makes that same walk. Given the material inclusion of vital elements from Three Rivers in Heinz, this walk is also both an authentic and a symbolic reproduction of the walk made by Steeler greats in the previous stadium. The walk is symbolic, however, because the field is unmarked, incomplete, and undifferentiated, and we may walk only out *to* the field, not *onto* it.

The tour also helps focus our gaze on the ways in which the very construction of the stadiums reveals that they are self-consciously designed as "sweeping" spaces—that is, they have been designed in awareness of the fact that various publics will lay claim to the spaces in furtherance of their beliefs or in promotion of their values.[54] These stadiums, and football generally, are part of a long tradition of sports moralism, to the point that, beyond the ascription of sacred qualities to these spaces by individual fans, it is the civil religious content that they embody that marks these stadiums as sacred spaces. Moreover, given that both "space" and "sacred" are social constructions, and given that audiences both receive and actively participate in the creation of nostalgia,[55] these tours are simultaneously well beyond the various times and timelines encapsulated in the architectural design, material objects, and visual displays, such as the Fan Zone at Heinz Field. The "simultaneity of place"[56] extends to how these stadiums incorporate and depict understandings of class and race in society.

The Fan Zone features two large crowd shots. In each of these, we see Steelers fans decked out in black and gold, waving their Terrible Towels, and wearing black-and-gold hard hats with the Steelers logo, reflecting the city's blue-collar, industrial history. One shot is taken from the top of the end zone seats looking out—the worst seats in the house, which nevertheless clearly boast a decent view of the field. The other is run through from lower right to upper left by a visible yellow seam, the yellow plastic seats that dominate the stadium's color scheme. With framed displays of fan artwork and craftsmanship and photos of fans sporting Steeler gear all over the world—and aboard the International Space Station—the message conveyed here has an "everyman" effect. There is a fundamental projected equality, a linking of all fans into one equal, and equally valued, body. The same effect is accomplished in Cleveland architecturally; the steel I-beams that obstructed views within parts of the old Municipal Stadium were incorporated into the southeast and southwest gates of the new Cleveland Browns Stadium. Past obstructions—makers and markers of inequality of access—were reformed into makers and markers of equality of access: gates, through which any ticket-holding member of the public may pass.

A different set of barriers is symbolically removed in the new Cleveland Browns stadium as well. Among the names memorialized in Cleveland's Ring of Honor are Bill Willis and Marion Motley, both of whom have been enshrined in the Pro Football Hall of Fame and who together with Kenny Washington and Woody Strode broke pro football's color barrier in 1946, the year before Jackie Robinson more famously did the same in baseball. A separate portion of the ring is dedicated to Willis and Motley as "Pioneers of the Game." This static memorialization and this phrasing are problematic for at least two reasons. First, in laying claim to Willis and Motley as "Pioneers *of the Game*," these players' achievement is appropriated within the teleological narrative of the game and is thus merely representative of, but decoupled from, the larger civil rights struggles and movements of the twentieth century. Second, while the intent of this memorial is to recognize the American dream as lived out by two pioneers who had the courage and strength to stand up to an unjust system and begin changing it, the communicative effect is to retroactively—and misleadingly—declare the NFL postracial as of 1946.

There is a similar moment on the Heinz Field tour. One stop looks over the Ohio River at the Duquesne Incline, one of the Mount Washington funiculars that took laborers, largely immigrants, to and from the steel foundries. Nothing was said about the complex history of labor in Pittsburgh or in the United States or about the violence and deaths that were part of the labor movements of the nineteenth and twentieth centuries. Rather than mentioning these historical struggles, the tour used the funicular to link Pittsburgh with its past, thereby symbolically Americanizing those immigrants who worked in the foundries, highlighting the distance between home and work that is a core part of the American dream, and thus a core part of the ACR, and linking the local with the national in the "storying" of the place.[57]

In a sense, this is nostalgia done "right." As Andreea Ritivoi has noted, nostalgia, improperly managed, can be alienating where it seeks to be inclusive.[58] While there is an element of this in these examples, they remain effective tools in differentiating and branding the franchise. They link the present with the past; they provide spaces within which cultural and societal problems can be metaphorically addressed and which celebrate the resolution of those problems. At the same time, the celebration of those resolutions links the franchise and the fan nation within the local and national historical narratives and histories, expanding the reach of this simplistic, touristic history within the collective memory.[59] These kinds of spaces also dispense effectively with the uneasiness that could be caused by a perceived "secular numinous." This postmillennialist idea holds that while we can see where we fail to live up to our highest values, we can yet achieve them with the right combination of dedication, hard work, and sacrifice.[60] Lindquist argues that "the football celebratory complex articulates, enacts, and invites conversation about . . . political and economic worldviews," while Laderman notes that football "encompasses and resolves—however temporarily and precariously—a variety of social realities that are less clear, more chaotic, in the world outside the field of play, such as . . . [instances] where winners and losers do not always represent a just, moral order."[61] Football—both spectacle and stadium—enacts and works through social problems, resolves them, and moves on, reaffirming the American dream within the civil religious tradition.

Just as these stadiums root the local within the national and the failures of the past within the success of the present, they provide space within which these narratives and triumphs can be challenged. Spectator sports are polysemic phenomena, incorporating festival, ritual, and play; this characteristic of sport combines with the ambivalence discussed above to confound any attempt to discuss sport in terms of a simple subordination/protest binary.[62] Nevertheless, subordination and protest are elements both of the game and of the fan experience within the stadium, and this engagement with space is part of the ongoing engagement with complex social issues that are part of the teleological civil religious narratives put forward by both game and space. We will briefly look at fan behavior to see how stadiums both permit and circumscribe symbolic challenges to the social status quo, all to the benefit of further defining the franchise brand.

The respective fan nations have helped differentiate a number of NFL brands. The Oakland Raiders, for example, have the elaborately costumed Raider Nation in the Black Hole; the Green Bay Packers have the Cheeseheads; the Cleveland Browns have the Dawg Pound; and the Pittsburgh Steelers have the Steeler Nation, waving the "sacred" flag of that nation, the Terrible Towel.[63] Despite the impact that these fan nations have on how a brand is recognized, these are all examples of *minimal transformations*—changes to the sports product that "are minor in scale and do not disrupt the core of the product."[64] None of these fan flourishes materially change the core product—the team that plays the game—but each franchise benefits from the differentiation from peers, the heightened sense of fan "nationalism" that is generated via these minimal transformations, and the merchandising opportunities to which these fan actions contribute.

The fan nations also engage directly with the idea of the "secular numinous" in defining their community. As one unnamed Raider fan noted, "You look at this group of people behind me, and I don't know any of them. I don't know what they do for a living. Are they criminals? Maybe! You know, according to the media, some of them are. Are some of them the assistant district attorney of Alameda County? Yes, yes they are. They are professional, they come from all walks of life. . . . [O]n Sunday? That's my sister, my brother, and everybody is together."[65] Here again we see family metaphors employed in the imagining of community. More than that, we can see the democratic, egalitarian ethos of the American dream. But if the quote were rendered in full, we would also see the self-perceived limits of that community. In the portion that I replaced with an ellipsis, the fan says: "And from Monday through Saturday, I don't care. But on Sunday. . . ." So while this fan says that "nobody sees black, nobody sees white, nobody sees Mexican, nobody sees Asian. We all see Silver and Black," this realization of that portion of the American dream is bounded, temporally, spatially, and metaphorically.[66] It is, then, the ambivalent realization of the dream and the simultaneous expression of the problem.

On Sundays, the fan nations occupy specific, significant pieces of real estate. The Black Hole and the Dawg Pound are exemplary in this respect. The Black Hole consists of four sections of seats ringing the south end zone in Oakland, while the Dawg Pound consists of a roughly equivalent space around the north end zone in Cleveland. Both are noted for their flamboyant fans and are prized pieces of real estate within each fan nation. Arguably the two NFL properties most defined by the fans who occupy them, the Black Hole and the Dawg Pound show both the extent to which the fans can challenge the distance between the real and the ideal in terms of the secular numinous and the limits that can be imposed on their space to embody these challenges. The elaborate costuming helps both to cement the affiliation with the team and to erase racial and class distinctions to a certain extent.

These spaces are also subject to control from without, by stadium personnel, by other fans, and by instruments of state power. Local and state police maintain a presence between the stands and the field, establishing a boundary between fan and field that is less conceptual than it is based on state power. Moreover, both the Black Hole and Dawg Pound are bounded on three sides—along each sideline and above—by other seating sections. Though confined to one end of the stadium, these two sections are the choicest of these locations because they abut the field; those in the front row are close enough to catch players leaping into the stands as they celebrate touchdowns. Despite being close enough to touch the players sometimes, both the Black Hole and the Dawg Pound are far from either sideline and thus out of proximate reach of both home and visitor teams. In part, this is simply a result of a phenomenon developing in one space and being perpetuated there. It is also a consequence of planning: when the NFL awarded an expansion franchise to Cleveland, to replace the original Browns (now the Baltimore Ravens), the team made sure to incorporate plans for a restored Dawg Pound in the new Cleveland Browns Stadium. The fans had in this instance dictated stadium design and status within that new building, while the franchise effectively transferred a "ghost" from its past and used that to reroot the brand while enhancing its reach. Even so, these spaces are minimal transformations that enhance the brand without altering the core of the product.

Black Hole fans are also acutely aware that they are perceived in terms of class differences. As Black Hole Rob, acknowledged founder of the Black Hole, claims in the *Raider Nation* documentary, the disdain shown the denizens of the Black Hole has nothing to do with their antics but, rather, the fact that they are perceived as "lower class"; this perception of them as lower class, Rob says, makes them a target for ridicule.[67] While Rob's real concerns over class and perception may not be the full story, class is clearly marked in NFL stadiums. Recall the description of the photos in the Heinz Field Fan Zone and the yellow chairs that unite them. The "everyman" quality of that photograph is undercut by the belt of gray seats that ring the stadium on the suite level. These are the luxury seats, twenty-one inches instead of the standard nineteen (measurements that are the norm league-wide); they are also by far the most expensive seats in the house. Luxury suites themselves can cost well over $100,000 per year; a ten-year lease is standard. These seats offer the best views of the field, and in most NFL stadiums, luxury suites abut the press booth, further signifying their value. The fans in the photograph in Pittsburgh thus are not "anyone, anywhere" in the stadium; they are instead "anyone, *except*." The class markers in Detroit are more explicit: luxury-level seats are taken from the Ford Explorer and the Lincoln Navigator, two Ford vehicles whose 2010 suggested base retail prices were around $29,000 and

$58,000, respectively.[68] Compare this with the median 2010 American household income of slightly less than $50,000/year,[69] and it becomes clear that while fans may form a community that differs structurally from the broader society, and while they may champion an egalitarian ethos that corresponds with the values espoused by the ACR, and while they may engage in acts of deliberate resistance against what they recognize as an unjust status quo in pursuit of the distant teleological ideal, they do so within spaces and spectacular practices that both permit and confine that resistance.

## V  *Conclusion*

Peter King, a prominent sportswriter, claims that "football tells universal truths in our society."[70] One of the ways it does so, according to Gary Laderman, is to provide temporary clarity and resolution to complex social realities, as noted above. Yet this clarity, which extends to the way these spaces incorporate and diminish complex historical and social problems, distorts and minimizes these realities. This is not surprising; these spaces are not designed to engage in serious historical or social analysis. The fact that their engagement with complex historical and social problems necessarily presents both a teleological progress narrative in the American civil religious tradition and clear evidence that these problems persist in these spaces is remarkable only for how clear the markers on both sides are. More remarkable is the capacity of these stadiums to communicate these moralistic ideas and to merge the game and its embrace of the ACR with opportunities to contest the social and societal status quo and adapt it to suit the needs and visions of the spectators. In the stands and on the tours, these stadiums provide the space for individual visitors to create their own narrative of place and derive their own meaningful content from that place even within the context of an overarching normativizing, homogenizing metanarrative—to enact, in other words, a different civil religion. The stadiums are both flagship tourist attractions and spaces that embody and promote civil religious ideals and values. We should thus take them seriously both as "civil sacred spaces" and as avenues of deeper exploration into the interactions among sacred values; the demands and capacities of the market, especially its capacity to both facilitate and contain challenges to the status quo; and those challenges themselves in the messy workings of the democratic process in the public sphere.[71]

## *Notes*

I gratefully acknowledge the support of the Deutsche Forschungsgemeinschaft (German Research Foundation), which funded the research that resulted in this chapter.

1. Benedict Anderson, *Imagined Communities: Reflections on the Origin and Spread of Nationalism*, 2nd ed. (New York: Verso, 2006), 149.
2. On football and/as civil religion, see Craig A. Forney, *The Holy Trinity of American Sports: Civil Religion in Football, Baseball, and Basketball* (Macon: Mercer University Press, 2007); Barry Hankins, "Prayer, Football, and Civil Religion in Texas," *Liberty Magazine*, November/December 2000, http://www.libertymagazine.org/article/prayer-football-and-civil-religion-in-texas; and Joseph L. Price, "From Sabbath Proscriptions to Super Sunday Celebrations: Sports and Religion in America," in *From Season to Season: Sports as American Religion*, ed. Joseph L. Price (Macon: Mercer University Press, 2001), 15–38. Except where otherwise indicated, all websites cited in this essay were accessed February 1, 2012.
3. Birgit Meyer, "Religious Sensations: Why Media, Aesthetics, and Power Matter in the Study of Contemporary Religion," in *Religion: Beyond a Concept*, ed. Hent de Vries (New York: Fordham University Press, 2008), 704–723.
4. Daniel H. Olsen, "Management Issues for Religious Heritage Attractions," in *Tourism, Religion and Spiritual Journeys*, ed. Dallen J. Timothy and Daniel H. Olsen (New York: Routledge, 2006), 114.
5. Meyer, "Religious Sensations." My operative definition of *space* tracks closely with Bremer's definition of place: socially constructed, predicated on relationships, constantly changing, contested, and temporal as well as geographic. Thomas S. Bremer, "Sacred Spaces and Tourist Places," in Timothy and Olsen, *Tourism*, 26–29. For an overview of academic definitions of *space* and *place*, and the difference between these two ideas, see generally Kim Knott, *The Location of Religion: A Spatial Analysis* (London: Equinox, 2005), 11–58. In this essay, I use *space*, *place*, and *site* interchangeably.
6. In my functional analysis of stadiums as sacred places, and in my attempt to use a functional analysis to address commonly acknowledged deficits in such analyses, I am responding primarily to Jay Coakley, *Sport in Society: Issues and Controversies*, 6th ed. (St. Louis: Times Mirror/Mosby, 1998), 34–35; D. Stanley Eitzen, "Classism in Sport: The Powerless Bear the Burden," *Journal of Social Issues* 20 (February 2006): 95–105; and Daniel L. Wann, Merrill J. Melnick, Gordon W. Russell, and Dale G. Pease, *Sport Fans: The Psychology and Social Impact of Spectators* (New York: Routledge, 2001), 200ff.
7. Ira Chernus, "Civil Religion," in *The Blackwell Companion to Religion in America*, ed. Philip Goff (Malden: Wiley-Blackwell, 2010), 68.

8. Arthur Remillard, *Southern Civil Religions: Imagining the Good Society in the Post-Reconstruction Era* (Athens: University of Georgia Press, 2011). I am aligning Remillard with Will Herberg's definition of civil religion, rather than Robert Bellah's classic definition or its subsequent modifications. See Will Herberg, "America's Civil Religion: What It Is and Whence It Comes," in *American Civil Religion*, ed. Russell E. Richey and Donald G. Jones (New York: Harper and Row, 1974), 77; Robert Bellah, "Civil Religion in America," *Daedalus: Journal of the American Academy of the Arts and Sciences* 96, no. 1 (Winter 1967): 1–21; Robert Bellah, *The Broken Covenant: American Civil Religion in a Time of Trial*, 2nd ed. (Chicago: University of Chicago Press, 1992); Robert Bellah, *Beyond Belief: Essays on Religion in a Post-traditionalist World* (Berkeley: University of California Press, 1991). Eric Bain-Selbo makes a similar move in "From Lost Cause to Third-and-Long: College Football and the Civil Religion of the South," *Journal of Southern Religion* 11 (2009), accessed February 13, 2014, http://jsr.fsu.edu/Volume11/Selbo.htm. Chernus and Remillard continue to argue for their respective positions in a number of important recent writings. See, for example, Ira Chernus, "Confronting the Mythical Beast," *Immanent Frame*, March 19, 2010, http://blogs.ssrc.org/tif/2010/03/19/confronting-the-mythical-beast/; and Arthur Remillard, "Civil Religious Revivals and Awakenings," *Religion in American History*, June 12, 2012, http://usreligion.blogspot.de/2012/06/civil-religious-revivals-and-awakenings.html. See also Heike Bungert and Jana Weiß, "Die Debatte um 'Zivilreligion' in transnationaler Perspektive," *Zeithistorische Forschungen/Studies in Contemporary History* 7 (2010): 454–459. Of particular note is Chernus's observation that Remillard's plural position still takes for granted a "we" at the core of the debate, which, Chernus says, returns us to the core problem with ACR, which is that "whenever 'we' are imagined and supposedly common values are articulated, the process is hardly shared equally by all the inhabitants of the land" (Ira Chernus, "We Need to Stop Using the Phrase 'American Civil Religion,'" *History News Network*, June 18, 2012, http://hnn.us/article/146831). Though this particular issue lies beyond the scope of this essay, I point it out to underscore the fact that, as this essay shows, the stadiums and people described herein likewise take the normative function for granted. That said, this essay is also mindful of Remillard's observation that our task in using civil religion as a category of analysis is to "purge [it] of its normative assumptions." This, of course, need not include ignoring the normative assumptions of the various civil religious discourses as deployed in the broader public discourse. Arthur Remillard, "Can Civil Religion Be Saved?" *Religion in American History*, September 9, 2012, http://usreligion.blogspot.de/2012/09/can-civil-religion-be-saved.html.

9. Quoted in Sal Paolantonio, *How Football Explains America* (Chicago: Triumph Books, 2008), 186.

10. Danille Christensen Lindquist, "'Locating' the Nation: Football Game Day and American Dreams in Central Ohio," *Journal of American Folklore* 119 (Fall 2006): 445–446.

11. Frederick Winslow Taylor, *The Principles of Scientific Management* (New York: W. W. Norton, 1967).

12. David Riesman and Reuel Denney, "Football in America: A Study in Culture Diffusion," in *Individualism Reconsidered and Other Essays*, ed. David Riesman (Glencoe, Ill.: Free Press, 1954), 248.

13. Bellah, "Civil Religion," 10; Paolantonio, *How Football Explains America*, 1–13. On this history and description of American football, see Forney, *Holy Trinity*; Thomas P. Hughes, *American Genesis: A History of the American Genius for Invention* (New York: Penguin, 1989); David F. Noble, *America by Design: Science, Technology, and the Rise of Corporate Capitalism* (New York: Oxford University Press, 1977); Michael Novak, *The Joy of Sports: End Zones, Bases, Baskets, Balls, and the Consecration of the American Spirit* (New York: Basic Books, 1976); Michael Oriard, *Brand NFL: Making and Selling America's Favorite Sport* (Chapel Hill: University of North Carolina Press, 2007); Michael Oriard, *Reading Football: How the Popular Press Created an American Spectacle* (Chapel Hill: University of North Carolina Press, 1993); Karsten Senkbeil, *Ideology in American Sports: A Corpus-Assisted Discourse Study* (Heidelberg: Winter, 2011); Peter Williams, *The Sports Immortals: Deifying the American Athlete* (Bowling Green, Ohio: Bowling Green State University Popular Press, 1994).

14. See, for example, Maurizio Viroli, *For Love of Country: An Essay on Patriotism and Nationalism* (Oxford: Oxford University Press, 1995).

15. It is important to note that other sports have been promoted as typifying "America," "American values," and the "American dream" just as professional football has. While these other sports are beyond the scope of this essay, a comparison can be profitably made between the civil religious ascriptions and functions of other sports, particularly baseball, boxing, and stock car racing. On baseball, see especially Christopher H. Evans, "Baseball as Civil Religion: The Genesis of an American Creation Story," in *The Faith of 50 Million: Baseball, Religion, and American Culture*, ed. Christopher H. Evans and William R. Herzog (Louisville: Westminster John Knox, 2002), 13–33; Forney, *Holy Trinity*; Joseph L. Price, *Rounding the Bases: Baseball and Religion in America* (Macon: Mercer University Press, 2006), esp. 111–175. On stock car racing, see Joshua I. Newman and Michael D. Giardina, "Neoliberalism's Last Lap? NASCAR Nation and the Cultural Politics of Sport," *American Behavioral Scientist* 53, no. 10 (May 2010): 1511–1529; and Daniel S. Pierce and Harvey H. Jackson III, "NASCAR vs. Football: Which Sport Is More Important to the South?" *Southern Cultures* 18, no. 4 (Winter 2012): 26–42. On other sports, see the respective essays in Steven A. Riess, ed., *A Companion to American Sport History* (Oxford: Blackwell, 2014).

Along these lines, sport has long been a vehicle for acculturation and adaptation, both to and of national norms, particularly for religious and ethnic minorities. The literature on this is likewise extensive. In addition to works cited elsewhere in this essay, see, for example, Lawrence Baldassaro and Richard Johnson, eds., *The American Game: Baseball and Ethnicity* (Carbondale: Southern Illinois University Press, 2002); Jeffrey S. Gurock, *Judaism's Encounter with American Sports* (Bloomington: Indiana University Press, 2007); Richard Kimball, *Sports in Zion: Mormon Recreation, 1890–1940* (Urbana: University of Illinois Press, 2003); Jack Kugelmass, ed., *Jews, Sports, and the Rites of Citizenship* (Urbana: University of Illinois Press, 2007); Peter Levine, *Ellis Island to Ebbets Field: Sport and the American Jewish Experience* (New York: Oxford University Press, 1992); and Steven A. Riess, ed., *Sports and the American Jew* (Syracuse, N.Y.: Syracuse University Press, 1992).

A different perspective on civil religion, one that sees civil religion as centered on war and the nation, would likewise hew toward football as the exemplary civil religious sport in America. This would enable expanding the conversation to include recent work on questions of the militarization of both game and nation. On civil religion and war, see Raymond Haberski Jr., *God and War: American Civil Religion since 1945* (New Brunswick, N.J.: Rutgers University Press, 2012). On the links between the militarization of the nation and of sport, see Michael Atkinson and Kevin Young, "Shadowed by the Corpse of War: Sport Spectacles and the Spirit of Terrorism," *International Review for the Sociology of Sport* 47, no. 3 (May 2012): 286–306; Pete Fussey and Joan Coaffee, "Balancing Local and Global Security Leitmotifs: Counter-terrorism and the Spectacle of Sporting Mega-events," *International Review for the Sociology of Sport* 47, no. 3 (May 2012): 268–285; Richard Giulianotti and Francisco Klauser, "Sport Mega-events and 'Terrorism': A Critical Analysis," *International Review for the Sociology of Sport* 47, no. 3 (May 2012): 307–323; Tricia Jenkins, "The Militarization of American Professional Sports: How the Sports–War Intertext Influences Athletic Ritual and Sport Media," *Journal of Sport and Social Issues* 237, no. 3 (July 2013): 245–260; and Gavin Weedon, " 'I. Will. Protect This House': Under Armour, Corporate Nationalism, and Post-9/11 Cultural Politics," *Sociology of Sport Journal* 29, no. 3 (September 2012): 265–282.

It will also be important to bring the civil religious functions of sport in the United States into greater conversation with civil religious elements of sport globally. The literature on this subfield is increasingly diverse and illuminating, and useful comparisons can be drawn by comparing more "classically" civil religious discourses with postcolonialist nationalisms. This is not to conflate the two but, rather, to suggest that broader comparative study of the functions of sport within civil religious and nationalist discourses and practices would be worthwhile. It is impossible to

summarize the body of literature that addresses portions of this broad ques-
tion here, but see Mahfoud Amara, *Sport, Politics, and Society in the Arab World* (New York: Palgrave Macmillan, 2011); Joseph L. Arbena and David G. LaFrance, eds., *Sport in Latin America and the Caribbean* (Wilmington, Del.: Scholarly Resources, Inc., 2002); Snejanka Bauer, *Helden–Heilige–Himmelstürmer: Fußball und Religion* (Tübingen, Germany: Legat-Verlag, 2006); David R. Black and John Nauright, *Rugby and the South African Nation* (New York: Manchester University Press, 1998); Claire Brewster and Keith Brewster, *Representing the Nation: Sport and Spectacle in Post-revolutionary Mexico* (New York: Routledge, 2010); John Cash and Joy Damousi, *Footy Passions* (Sydney: University of New South Wales Press, 2009); Patricia Cormack and James Cosgrave, *Desiring Canada: CBC Contests, Hockey Violence, and Other Stately Pleasures* (Toronto: University of Toronto Press, 2013); Tamas Doczi, "Gold Fever(?): Sport and National Identity—The Hungarian Case," *International Review for the Sociology of Sport* 47, no. 2 (March 2012): 165–182; Jon Fox, "Consuming the Nation: Holidays, Sports, and the Production of Collective Belonging," *Ethnic and Racial Studies* 29, no. 2 (August 2006): 217–236; Annika Hvithamar, Margit Warburg, and Brian Arly Jacobsen, *Holy Nations and Global Identity: Civil Religion, Nationalism, and Globalisation* (Leiden: Brill, 2009); Heather Levi, *The World of Lucha Libre: Secrets, Revelations, and Mexican National Identity* (Durham, N.C.: Duke University Press, 2008); Joseph Maguire and Masayoshi Nakayama, eds., *Japan, Sport and Society: Tradition and Change in a Globalizing World* (London: Routledge, 2006); Andrew D. Morris, *Colonial Project, National Game: A History of Baseball in Taiwan* (Berkeley: University of California Press, 2011); Arthur Remillard, "Playing on Sacred Ground: Uncovering the Religious Dimensions of Athletic Venues around the World," in *The Changing World Religion Map*, ed. Stanley D. Brunn (Berlin: Springer, forth-coming); Tom Sinclair-Faulkner, "Some Puckish Reflections on Hockey in Canada," in *Religion and Culture in Canada/Religion et Culture au Canada*, ed. Peter Slater (Waterloo, Canada: Wilfrid Laurier University Press, 1977); Tracy J. Trothen, "Hockey: A Divine Sport?—Canada's National Sport in Relation to Embodiment, Community and Hope," *Studies in Religion/Sciences Religieuses* 35, no. 2 (June 2006): 291–305; and Kath Woodward, David Goldblatt, and James Wyllie, "British Fair Play: Sport across Diasporas at the BBC World Service," in *Britishness, Identity and Citizenship: The View from Abroad*, ed. Catherine McGlynn, Andrew Myock, and James W. McCauley (Oxford: Peter Lang, 2011), 171–190.

16. Lindquist, "'Locating' the Nation," 446.
17. Seifried and Meyer's study of nostalgia at NFL and MLB facilities notes that stadium tours are offered at twenty-seven of the thirty-one NFL stadi-ums. Chad Seifried and Katherine Meyer, "Nostalgia-Related Aspects of

Professional Sport Facilities: A Facility Audit of Major League Baseball and National Football League Strategies to Evoke the Past," *International Journal of Sport Management Recreation and Tourism* 5 (2010): 63.

18. Irving Rein, Philip Kotler, and Ben Shields, *The Elusive Fan: Reinventing Sports in a Crowded Marketplace* (New York: McGraw-Hill, 2006), 57.

19. Ibid., 56; italics in original.

20. Ibid., 42–50; George Ritzer and Todd Stillman, "The Postmodern Ballpark as a Leisure Setting: Enchantment and Simulated De-McDonaldization," *Leisure Studies* 23 (2001): 97–113.

21. John Swarbrooke, *The Development and Management of Visitor Attractions*, 2nd ed. (Oxford: Butterworth-Heinmann, 2002), 4–5.

22. Ibid., passim; Sean Gammon, "Secular Pilgrimage and Sport Tourism," in *Sport Tourism: Interrelationships, Impacts and Issues*, ed. Brent W. Ritchie and Daryl Adair (Bristol, England: Channel View Publications, 2004), 30–45.

23. On the classification of fans into highly and lowly identified categories, see Wann et al., *Sport Fans*, 2–7. See also Richard Giulianotti, "Supporters, Followers, Fans, and Flaneurs: A Taxonomy of Spectator Identities in Football," *Journal of Sport and Social Issues* 26 (February 2002): 25–46. Garry Crawford critiques these "static" categorizations, which, he argues, do not accurately reflect the behaviors and self-identifications of fans. Crawford also emphasizes the role of commerce in imagining and sustaining fan communities at all levels of engagement. See Garry Crawford, ed., *Consuming Sport: Fans, Sport and Culture* (London: Routledge, 2004), 30–38, 77–88. I use the two terms here to underscore Crawford's broader point while noting that the nostalgia, community, and history on sale at these spaces are by no means limited to highly involved fans. See generally David L. Andrews, *Sport–Commerce–Culture: Essays on Sport in Late Capitalist America* (New York: Peter Lang, 2006); and Seifried and Meyer, "Nostalgia-Related Aspects."

24. Crawford, *Consuming Sport*; Meyer, "Religious Sensations"; Seifried and Meyer, "Nostalgia-Related Aspects."

25. This description of Ford Field is from my notes of the stadium tour taken April 29, 2011. See also Andrew L. McFarlane, "Remembering Detroit's Paradise Valley," *Absolute Michigan*, March 6, 2007, http://www.absolutemichigan.com/dig/michigan/remembering-detroits-paradise-valley/.

26. Guided tours: Ford Field, Detroit, Michigan, April 29, 2011; Paul Brown Stadium, Cincinnati, Ohio, May 23, 2011; Cleveland Browns Stadium, Cleveland, Ohio, May 25, 2011; Heinz Field, Pittsburgh, Pennsylvania, May 27, 2011. Cleveland Browns Stadium was renamed FirstEnergy Stadium in January 2013. See Mark Naymik, "Browns Owner Jimmy Haslam Has Spell over Football Fans and Politicians Alike," *Cleveland.com*, March 8, 2013, http://www.cleveland.com/naymik/index.ssf/2013/03/browns_owner_jimmy_haslam_has.html, accessed September 7, 2014.

27. Kemps Cows, "Kemps TV Spot: 'Sacred Pastures' Lambeau Field Tour," YouTube, November 3, 2011, http://www.youtube.com/watch?v=UPVdUGYj2_g.

28. Charles S. Prebish, "'Heavenly Father, Divine Goalie': Sport and Religion," in *Sport and Religion*, ed. Shirl J. Hoffman (Champaign: Human Kinetics Books, 1992), 48; italics in original. See also Forney, *Holy Trinity*, 60–64; Gary Laderman, *Sacred Matters: Celebrity Worship, Sexual Ecstasies, the Living Dead, and Other Signs of Religious Life in the United States* (New York: New Press, 2009), 43–62; Novak, *Joy of Sports*, 18–34; Charles S. Prebish, "The Sports Arena: Some Basic Definitions," in Hoffman, *Sport and Religion*, 19–43; Price, "From Sabbath Proscriptions to Super Sunday." Many authors have provided detailed lists of the points on which they see sports and religion overlapping. In addition to those cited above, see, for example, Eric Bain-Selbo, *Game Day and God: Football, Faith, and Politics in the American South* (Macon: Mercer University Press, 2009), 70ff.; Jim Miller and Kelly Mayhew, *Better to Reign in Hell: Inside the Raiders Fan Empire* (New York: New Press, 2005), 20–21; Joseph L. Price, "An American Apotheosis: Sports as Popular Religion," in *Religion and Popular Culture in America*, ed. Bruce David Forbes and Jeffrey H. Mahan, rev. ed. (Berkeley: University of California Press, 2005), 197–201; Wann et al., *Sport Fans*, 181, 198–200.

29. Roberta Newman, "The American Church of Baseball and the National Baseball Hall of Fame," *NINE: A Journal of Baseball History and Culture* 10 (Fall 2001): 50; Joshua Fleer, "The Church of Baseball and the U.S. Presidency," *NINE: A Journal of Baseball History and Culture* 16 (Fall 2007): 56; Gammon, "Secular Pilgrimage," 30; Price, "From Sabbath Proscriptions to Super Sunday," 28; and Novak, *Joy of Sports*, 126, respectively. See also the discussion above in note 16 on the various civil religious narratives embodied in different sports.

30. Bain-Selbo, *Game Day and God*, 70.

31. In addition to the sources already cited, see, for example, John Bale, *Sport Geography*, 2nd ed. (New York: Routledge, 2003); and Robert J. Higgs and Michael C. Braswell, *An Unholy Alliance: The Sacred and Modern Sports* (Macon: Mercer University Press, 2004).

32. Gary Laderman gets us close to a resolution with his acknowledgment that this "awkwardly employed religious vocabulary . . . [is] . . . for many the best way to communicate" what these places and experiences mean to them (*Sacred Matters*, 50). Two excellent surveys of the literature on sport and religion have recently been published. See Annie Blazer, "Religion and Sports in America," *Religion Compass* 6, no. 5 (May 2012): 287–297; and Richard Kimball, "Sport and American Religion," in Riess, *Companion to American Sport History*, 601–614.

33. Warren St. John, *Rammer Jammer Yellow Hammer: A Road Trip into the Heart of Fan Mania* (New York: Three Rivers Press, 2004), 124, 185, 126, 206.

34. Jerry McDonald, "Looks Like Rayner Will Be Kicking," *Inside the Oakland Raiders*, October 22, 2011, 10:18 a.m., comment #17, 10:28 a.m., http://www.ibabuzz.com/oaklandraiders/2011/10/22/looks-like-rayner-will-be-kicking/#comment-682765. Comments from most of the articles in the blog's archive were deleted when it was upgraded, but this post and comment can still be seen via the Wayback Machine, http://web.archive.org/web/20111024153124/http://www.ibabuzz.com/oaklandraiders/2011/10/22/looks-like-rayner-will-be-kicking, accessed September 7, 2014.

35. See Simon Coleman, "Pilgrimage," in *The Blackwell Companion to the Study of Religion*, ed. Robert A. Segal (Malden: Wiley-Blackwell, 2006), 385–396.

36. Rebecca Corman, "Fans Travel to Raider Mecca," Raiders.com, September 18, 2010, http://www.raiders.com/news/article-1/Fans-Travel-to-Raider-Mecca/c6a85247-4132-4298-a077-dde10ac871f4; Raider Mecca, http://www.raider-mecca.com/.

37. For examples of sport fans being buried with game tickets in their pockets or stipulating that they want their ashes scattered at sporting venues, see Eric Christensen, *Win It for . . . : What a World Championship Means to Generations of Red Sox Fans* (Champaign: Sports Publishing, LLC, 2005), 36, 77, 185. On the scale of such practices, see Mary Foster, "Fans Long to Have Their Ashes Scattered on Sporting Sites," *Seattle Times*, May 9, 2008, http://seattletimes.nwsource.com/html/sports/2004402982_apathleticashes.html.

38. Kevin Cowherd, "Sporty Caskets Offer Fandom for an Eternity," *Baltimore Sun*, December 22, 2008, http://articles.baltimoresun.com/2008-12-22/news/0812210184_1_caskets-eternal-image-swoosh-logos. Sports Themed Weddings, http://www.sportsthemedweddings.com/.

39. The Heinz Field "Book an Event" website features a picture of a bride and groom gazing into the afternoon sun from the field surface: http://www.steelers.com/tickets-and-stadium/book-an-event.html.

40. Price, "From Sabbath Proscriptions to Super Sunday," 26–27, provides a short list of religious and life-cycle events held in stadiums. More recently, Joel Osteen's "Night of Hope" events have been held in stadiums following the success of the event held in Yankee Stadium in September 2009. See Angurah Kumar, "Joel Osteen Takes 'Night of Hope' to Chicago Ballpark," *Christian Post*, August 6, 2011, http://www.christianpost.com/news/joel-osteen-takes-night-of-hope-to-chicago-ballpark-53484/; and Katja Rakow's essay in this volume.

41. Ann Taves, *Religious Experience Reconsidered: A Building-Block Approach to the Study of Religion and Other Special Things* (Princeton: Princeton University Press, 2009).

42. Dallen J. Timothy and Stephen W. Boyd, *Heritage Tourism* (Harlow, England: Prentice Hall, 2003).

43. E. Alan Morinis, "Introduction: The Territory of the Anthropology of Pilgrimage," in *Sacred Journey: The Anthropology of Pilgrimage*, ed. E. A. Morinis (Westport, Conn.: Greenwood Press, 1992), 1–28; Wilbur Zelinsky, "Nationalistic Pilgrimages in the United States," in *Pilgrimage in the United States*, ed. Gisbert Rinschede and Surinder M. Bhardwaj (Berlin: Dietrich Reimer Verlag, 1990), 253–267.

44. Gammon, "Secular Pilgrimage," 30. See also Justine Digance, "Religious and Secular Pilgrimage: Journeys Redolent with Meaning," in Timothy and Olsen, *Tourism*, 36–48.

45. Heinz Field is one of a minority of NFL stadiums with an on-site hall of fame—the "Walk of Fame"—making both stadium and tour exemplary in this respect. See Seifried and Meyer, "Nostalgia-Related Aspects," 63.

46. Anderson, *Imagined Communities*.

47. William M. Foster and Craig G. Hyatt, "Inventing Team Tradition: A Conceptual Model for the Strategic Development of Fan Nations," *European Sport Management Quarterly* 8 (September 2008): 266, 269. See also Miller and Mayhew, *Better to Reign*.

48. David Morgan, "The Look of Sympathy: Religion, Visual Culture, and the Social Life of Feeling," *Material Religion* 5 (July 2009): 133.

49. Seifried and Meyer, "Nostalgia-Related Aspects," 58.

50. Crawford, *Consuming Sport*, 77–82, 87–88; Greg Ramshaw and Sean Gammon, "More than Just Nostalgia? Exploring the Heritage/Sport Tourism Nexus," *Journal of Sport and Tourism* 10 (2005): 229–241; Rein, Kotler, and Shields, *Elusive Fan*.

51. Ramshaw and Gammon, "More than Just Nostalgia?" 230.

52. Novak, *Joy of Sports*, 123.

53. "Immaculate Reception—Original Broadcast," https://www.youtube.com/watch?v=GMuUBZ_DAeM. Other videos of this play have been taken down due to the NFL lodging copyright claims.

54. Erika Doss, "Disputation over Sacred Space in Contemporary America," *Material Religion* 7 (July 2011): 269–271. See also David Chidester and Edward T. Linenthal, "Introduction," in *American Sacred Space*, ed. David Chidester and Edward T. Linenthal (Bloomington: Indiana University Press, 1995), 1–42.

55. Fred Davis, *Yearning for Yesterday: A Sociology of Nostalgia* (New York: Free Press, 1979). See also Stuart Hall, "Encoding and Decoding," in *Culture, Media, Language: Working Papers in Cultural Studies, 1972–1979*, ed. Stuart Hall, Dorothy Hobson, Andrew Lowe, and Paul Willie (New York: Routledge, 1996), 117–127.

56. Bremer, "Sacred Spaces."

57. See Chad Millman and Shawn Coyne, *The Ones Who Hit the Hardest: The Steelers, the Cowboys, the '70s, and the Fight for America's Soul* (New York: Gotham Books, 2010).

58. Andreea Deciu Ritivoi, *Yesterday's Self: Nostalgia and the Immigrant Identity* (Lanham, Md.: Rowman and Littlefield, 2001).

59. Marita Sturken, *Tourists of History: Memory, Kitsch, and Consumerism from Oklahoma City to Ground Zero* (Durham, N.C.: Duke University Press, 2007).

60. Forney, *Holy Trinity*; Miller and Mayhew, *Better to Reign*; Newman, "American Church of Baseball"; Novak, *Joy of Sports*.

61. Lindquist, "'Locating' the Nation," 445; Laderman, *Sacred Matters*, 54–55.

62. Lindquist, "'Locating' the Nation," 448.

63. Robert Dvorchak, "The 'Terrible Towel' that Changes Lives," *Pittsburgh Post-Gazette*, August 30, 2009, http://www.post-gazette.com/pg/09242/ 994215-66.stm; Greg Garber, "'Terrible' Influence Yields Good Results," ESPN. com, January 29, 2009, http://sports.espn.go.com/nfl/playoffs2008/columns/ story?columnist=garber_greg&page=hotread20/garber.

64. Rein, Kotler, and Shields, *Elusive Fan*, 140.

65. Peter Hathaway, *Raider Nation*, dir. Leonard Spoto (Oakland: Rise Above Entertainment, 2003), 18:48ff.

66. Ibid., 22:40ff.

67. Ibid., 28:50ff. Miller and Mayhew make similar claims in their study of the Raider Nation: *Better to Reign*, 37–44, 181–208.

68. See http://www.ford.com/suvs/explorer/pricing/; http://www.lincoln.com/ suvs/navigator/.

69. Carmen DeNavas-Walt, Bernadette D. Proctor, and Jessica C. Smith, *Income, Poverty, and Health Insurance Coverage in the United States: 2010*, U.S. Department of Commerce, Economics and Statistics Administration, U.S. Census Bureau, September 2011, http://www.census.gov/prod/2011pubs/ p60-239.pdf.

70. Quoted in Paolantonio, *How Football Explains America*, 186.

71. An example of such an analysis is Kevin J. Delaney and Rick Eckstein, *Public Dollars, Private Stadiums: The Battle over Building Sports Stadiums* (New Brunswick, N.J.: Rutgers University Press, 2003).

# PART FIVE

# *Critical Reflection and Prospects*

## *II*

# *Considering the Neoliberal in American Religion*

### *Kathryn Lofton*

NEOLIBERAL IS A term impossible to avoid when facing a twenty-first-century volume devoted to intersections of religion and marketplace. It is impossible to avoid because *neoliberal* is a summary of the historical and historiographic moment recorded in this edited collection. This book represents a very recent detente between the history of religion and economic analysis. The sources for this relational reprieve between religion and economics are multiple, but perhaps none is more significant for both history and historiography than the revolutions of 1989. The fall of communism does not figure strongly in this collection as a literal series of political events, but it is a powerful specter, insofar as the revolutions that overthrew the communist states in various Central and Eastern European countries indicated, simultaneously, a failure of a certain critical ideology and a triumph of market logic. Those decrying the end of communist rule mourned the loss of its potential as a critique of the social effects of modern economic life. Those celebrating its demise did so on behalf of a confidence in the social order brought about by capitalist rule. One term for this era of the inescapable logic of markets is *neoliberal*.

In the wake of the revolutions of 1989, political pundits, historical observers, and moral commentators agreed that capitalism would inevitably determine every ideological conflict and frame every choice within everyday life. What is religion within a world of such market determinism? This collection offers a picture of religion in such an economic frame while proffering a series of methodological options for the study of religion in such a market climate. In some essays, we have read examinations of the religious valences in ostensibly consumer-driven sites, as is the case in Anthony Santoro's analysis of the Heinz Field tour in Pittsburgh and Sarah Pike's examination of youth festivals such as Bonnaroo and Coachella. In others, we have learned about the market contexts of ostensibly religious artifacts, as in Daniel Silliman's evaluation of the publishing culture that situated the emergence of the *Left Behind* series and the advertising strategies that Katja Rakow observes as critical to evangelist Joel Osteen's meteoric success. No matter the object, one central insight of this volume is that religious life and economic life are inextricable in the United States, with one producing the other in a recursive round. Indeed, to me, it is notable how religion and economics are not merely inextricable from one another but also now seem so rarely to conflict with one another. Although it is clear that religious thinkers work to reconcile certain market emphases with their preferred practices, and that certain religious critics may indict other religious actors for being overly acceding to the marketplace, the stunning consistency in this diverse array of analytical testimony is the combination of religious aspirations and economic practices.

It seems, in this sense, that this is a good time for scholarship to consider how religion and economics have blended. The marketplace is indeed robust with the sale of spirituality. Let me pause to offer a specific example of what I mean by way of continuing to pursue the neoliberalism of American religions. Here I mean "the neoliberalism of American religions" in two senses: first, as a sociological description, that is, religious practice in the United States is usefully described as neoliberal; second, as a theme for historiography, that is, scholars of religion increasingly pursue themes reflective of their neoliberal era. How might we describe this era? To begin, in the twenty-first-century marketplace of consumer goods it is almost impossible to buy something without also buying into a promised reclamation of your spirit. This phenomenology of commodity includes but is not limited to associations drawn between taking an Alaskan cruise and reviving family love, between buying a car and reclaiming lost masculinity, and between wearing a certain lipstick and revealing your true beauty. Each of these instances indicates the broader pattern in which twenty-first-century producers and advertisers collaborate to sell goods not only as aspirational but as targeted personally to the you that you already are. You already have family love; you already are quite a man; you already possess real beauty. You just need a quickening agent for its reminder. The purpose of any good is to unearth something understood to be natural, be it love, manliness, or beauty, through the application of something manufactured. The product is a material way of accessing something ineffable.

In my book on the multimedia productions of Oprah Winfrey, I described this era as propounding a form of "spiritual capitalism," in which sellers succeed through marketing their goods as spiritually consequential and in which buyers purchase in order to achieve a right spirit. Oprah recommends her relentless practices of consumption to her massive reading and viewing audience not just to improve their looks (since you already are beautiful) or their status in society (since you already are worthy) but to change the experience of living for her viewers. Once they have found the right array of products to coordinate with their truth, they will literally wear their sanctification. To illustrate this, let us focus briefly on one object among the many advertised in the world of Oprah Winfrey in order to focus the terms of this consumer era into a specific spiritual proposition. Introduced in a 2007 issue of *O, the Oprah Magazine*, "The O Bracelet" was designed specifically for *O* magazine, a piece of jewelry presented as "handbeaded by women in Rwanda and Zambia." The descriptive copy in her magazine continues: "Let's just assume (A) you know that women in Africa face a pileup of hardships—serial rape, AIDS, illiteracy, hunger, poverty, genocide. (B) You care and would like to help, although *how on earth* is the daunting question. (C) If we changed the subject to jewelry—hey, catch that sudden glint of spirit, the lift of pleasure? Without doubt, tiny bits of shimmer and color release slaphappy chemicals in the brain. (Science will prove it; you watch.)"[1] The practice of purchase advocated by Winfrey here achieves a climactic global effect. Uncomfortable observers, be at peace (the narrative proceeds): we aren't girls who just want to have fun. We are girls using jewelry to "get" our spirit. If you answer yes to (A), (B), and (C), the article suggests that this bracelet is the right prescription against such political angst, political indecision, and love of goods.

Purchasing is a form of spiritual politics for Oprah's imagined audience. Carefully conscientious economic practice rims the advertising annotation: "One hundred percent of the profits on these bracelets go to the women, who are employed full-time for the duration of the project." We learn that the designer of the O bracelet was Mary Fisher, "the well-heeled suburban mother from a prominent family who stunned the country in 1992 by announcing at the Republican Convention that she was HIV-positive." Mary's story proceeds predictably apace, matching the beats of transformational biography popularized on *The Oprah Winfrey Show*. We learn that Mary's ex-husband, who infected her, had died, but Mary "hit life running," spending a lot of time in Africa working with AIDS victims who are "blown away to meet a white woman with the disease, much less one sitting on the ground next to them, talking frankly and trading crafts skills." Readers are told that Rwandans call Mary *Mirarukundo*, which means "full of love." Mary connected with Willa Shalit, head of Fair Winds Trading, an organization "that develops markets for the arts of the world's poorest." Willa's Path to Peace project in Rwanda (where, we are told, "she's called *Uwacu*, meaning 'ours'") provided trading and a connection to the eventual buyers. The bracelets would be sold exclusively at Macy's department store. "To complete the circle," the article concludes, "there's you: We hope that wearing an O magazine bracelet will make you feel good—and that you'll feel even better knowing how it's improved the life of the woman who made it for you. Call it an ethical luxury. A conscientious indulgence. If nothing else, it's a really good buy."[2]

This is an example of how spiritual life and political life are connected in contemporary culture through consumer transactions. As an artifact of this moment, the O bracelet translates the global pulse of this consumer culture, as the bracelet simultaneously sells a transnational brand (that "O") through the coordination of multiple agencies and individuals (in addition to Mary and Willa, several nongovernmental organizations joined the O project, including Women for Women International and the Centre for Infectious Disease Research in Zambia). But this is not just about institutional synergy, since we are told through their retitling that the women at the helm are truly, authentically present on the ground and embraced by natives. Mary is "full of love," and Willa is "ours," labels recounted to O magazine readers so as to underscore the perceived decency of these occupying Westerners. These women, with their stories of struggle and success, with their friendly colonial encounters and empowered entrepreneurship, are the centerpiece of Oprah's particular spiritual economy. Every fissure is sealed with squatting talk about crafts; every confusion is alleviated by purchase. The moral is ensured as the advertisement-as-article concludes: "If nothing else, it's a really good buy." The making of the *good* buy (how it is done and for whom) is central to any description of contemporary spiritual life and the economic principles upon which it depends.[3]

The immediate reply of critics to this episode could be made on neoliberal grounds. *Neoliberalism* is a term that has been used to describe the hegemonic relationship between the United States and the rest of the world.[4] Neoliberalism in this sense is a continuation of colonialism, but with a twist: if colonialism was primarily an extractive economy in which raw materials were drawn from one geography into another, neoliberalism is an expanding occupational economy in which entire manufacturing systems and consumer markets are erected for the benefit of foreign corporations. The paradigmatic neoliberal statement is that by Paul Bremer, head of the Coalition Provisional Authority in Iraq, who promulgated four orders for Iraqi economic reformation in 2003, which included "the full privatization of public enterprises, full ownership rights by foreign firms of Iraqi U.S. businesses, full repatriation of foreign profits . . . the opening of Iraq's banks to foreign control, national treatment for foreign companies and . . . the elimination of nearly all trade barriers." Bremer thus concocted what David Harvey has described as a "full-fledged neoliberal state apparatus whose fundamental mission was and is to facilitate conditions for profitable capital accumulation for all comers."[5] As agents for the manufacture and distribution of the O bracelet, the Fair Winds Trading and Path to Peace projects seem to be cheerful versions of the same apparatus, as they facilitate trade for (what is understood to be) the benefit of the Rwandans, who get earnest work and new purpose, as well as for the foreign investors and Macy's shoppers, who get to profit from "really good" buys.

This perhaps moves too quickly to a condemnatory appraisal of these Oprah women and their beaded bracelets. We miss the glee of the enterprise and its beaming advertised tone; we miss the earnest intention to make the world a better place while also healing a dark past; we miss the hope to create new communities of friends through international economic communities; and we miss the positive value of globalized markets. Writing about spiritual tourism in Australia, Elizabeth Povinelli notes, "The market itself relies upon a complex set of textual mediations generating both an object for and a limit to capital forms of commodification."[6] We see in the O bracelet promotion a complex set of mediations, with hugs to the suffering Mary in all of us, winks to potential investors, political recommendations for the plaintive, and economic savvy to spare. The materials of the Oprah empire—like those of so many twenty-first-century celebrities, consumer-packaged goods, and international brands—are not trying to hide their multiple desires: for money, for authenticity, for friendly relations, for peace, for product, for beauty. The O bracelet advertisement exposes these many feelings in and through an object that needs this text to mediate its potentially explosive spiritual and economic power. The moral of the story is simple: through the right practices within a free market, we can have it all. We can have money and peace, good beauty and right spirit.

In this essay, I want to think about *neoliberal* as a diagnosis for such a commodity and its era. This edited collection is one specifically attending to the conjunction of religion and the marketplace. In it, we learn about the consumer strategies of the Billy Graham Evangelistic Association, which oversaw saturated revival-campaign advertising and coordinated neighborhood prayer meetings, as well as the spirituality-infused marketing practices of middle-class book marketers, a phenomenon not unfamiliar to those who have studied Oprah. We learn about eighteenth-century networks of financially minded evangelicals and about late twentieth-century evangelist James Dobson's endorsement of Ronald Reagan's supply-side policies. We learn, in other words, about a *coordinated* conjunction, wherein the identifiably religious do not hesitate to connect their mission with that of financial remuneration for the spiritual practice of their best lives. Such an accord between religious and market experience invites a further exploration of the neoliberal era that produced this set of essays and of the possibly neoliberal suppositions that encouraged its economic realities. Is all religion neoliberal? And what does this mean?

In a 2014 interview, anthropologist James Ferguson warns against any narrow definition of neoliberalism: "It is important to recognize that this thing we call neoliberalism is an intellectually complex field, and that there is not a single politics that we can neatly and unproblematically attach to the style of reasoning that we identify as neoliberal."[7] Ferguson signals an understandable wariness with the category, since it is hard to find a political theory or anthropological study from the last ten years that does not take up neoliberalism as a presumptive designation or critique. In these studies, neoliberalism is alternatively described as a doctrine and a description, a friend and an enemy, a position and a polemic against a position.[8] More specifically, neoliberalism might be seen as an ideology, a mode of governance, and a set of affects regarding market culture. One could even see these in sequential procession: As an ideology neoliberalism appeared as Reaganomics and Thatcherism; as a mode of governance it can be discerned in Bill Clinton's espousal of market globalism and Tony Blair's Third Way; and as a set of affects neoliberalism may be found in the increasing role of corporate power, nongovernmental organizations (NGOs), and private government contractors in the management of political reality and everyday life, as signaled in the on-air "militainment" promotions of the Second Gulf War and the on-the-ground market restructuring of Iraq in its wake. In this progression, "we drifted from *having* a market economy to *being* a market society," writes Michael J. Sandel.[9] *Neoliberalism* is the summary term for that drift toward a society determined by markets.

In *Ill Fares the Land,* historian Tony Judt argues that this society is one shaped by a generation of Austrian thinkers—business theorist Peter Drucker; economists Friedrich A. von Hayek, Ludwig von Mises, and Joseph Schumpeter; and philosopher Karl Popper—who witnessed liberalism's collapse in the face of fascism and concluded that the best way to defend liberalism was to keep government out of economic life.[10] Neoliberalism describes the resultant emphasis on market systems, which political theorist Wendy Brown has narrowed to four elements: "(1) the devaluation of political autonomy, (2) the transformation of political problems into individual problems with market solutions, (3) the production of the consumer-citizen as available to a heavy degree of governance and authority, and (4) the legitimation of statism."[11] In their writings, Judt and Brown mount serious critiques of such a market-oriented political landscape. Yet, for advocates of the relevant policies, neoliberalism is not a craven plot for elite profit as much as it is a democratization of resources and of informational access. If during the nineteenth century leading colonial powers informed by liberal writings sought to civilize the world, in the twenty-first century elite nations informed by neoliberal writings labor to expand their economies through the development of untapped markets and an emphasis on consumption as political practice. "We can, therefore, examine the history of neoliberalism either as a utopian project providing a theoretical template for the reorganization of international capitalism or as a political scheme aimed at reestablishing the conditions for capital accumulation and the restoration of class power," writes David Harvey, summarizing the divide.[12]

For students of religion, three aspects of the varied definitional terrain for *neoliberalism* invite particular interest. First, to define something as neoliberal is to contrast it immediately with something else; most obviously, to call something neoliberal is to invoke the difference between some condition of the market now and the conditions of liberal yore. Varied contrasts could then emerge. For example, one could return to the archive of product advertisements from, say, the 1940s and 1950s, which tended to emphasize how certain products could, if purchased, contribute to your occupation of a certain location, whereas advertisements since the 1990s are more likely to emphasize a product's role in your quest for personal wellness. Thinking analogically within religion, one could think about the difference between the heyday of denominational religious life within congregations in the early to mid–twentieth century and contrast that sectarian religious participation and congregational structure with the parachurch organizations of the later twentieth century. In her reflections on the relationship between liberalism and neoliberalism, Catherine Chaput underlines this differential sense of social emplacement between liberalism and neoliberalism through a description of space. "Unlike liberalism's clearly assigned spaces for public life and private life or work time and leisure time, neoliberal spaces bear few obvious markers," she writes: "The neoliberal landscape consists of blurred boundaries that fold into one another: information flows almost instantaneously, commodities and people transgress national boundaries, time accelerates, space collapses, and distinctions between such classic demarcations as agent and subject or politics and economics erode."[13] If liberalism clarifies your role as a social actor (defined by social identities such as class or denomination), neoliberalism ostensibly maps a borderless world in which the star player is not a social unit or a governing body but is instead your particular self, growing and prospering as an independent agent through fluid multimedia networks of communication, access, and exchange. Think here of the congregants Katja Rakow describes in Joel Osteen's church, using their smartphones to check personal e-mail during the designed prayer time in the service. The congregants do what they need to do, no matter the liturgy or the leadership. And *neoliberal* describes the sense that this is new—that once upon a time, checking e-mail during services would have been socially inconceivable. Descriptions of the neoliberal moment emphasize this contrast, that there was a preceding time and social experience, one that is understood as more static in comparison with our contemporary permeability and mobility.

Second, to define something as neoliberal is to focus attention upon economic life as determinative to human experience and, particularly, an emphasis on free markets as constructing moral economies. In his examination of neoliberalism, David Harvey summarizes this

imperative: "Neoliberalism is a theory of political economic practices pro-
posing that human well-being can best be advanced by the maximization
of entrepreneurial freedoms within an institutional framework characterized by private property rights, individual liberty, unencumbered markets, and free trade." Harvey continues, "The role of the state is to create
and preserve an institutional framework appropriate to such practices."[14]
For a scholar of American religion, such a description of neoliberalism
is especially alluring. Reflect on Harvey's definition of neoliberalism as
a theory that emphasizes the positive power of entrepreneurship and
unencumbered markets. How is this description of economic freedom
different from the circulating ideal of religious freedom propagated in
the United States? I draw this connection with full acknowledgment of
its limits—that is, the limits placed on religious freedom by the prefer-
ences goaded by American jurisprudence and by majoritarian social control.[15] What I want to underline, however, is the ideal at play: within the
promissory discourse of neoliberalism, market freedom is the only route
to true self-expression. The state's job is to provide as permeable a frame
as possible so as to encourage its fruition and limit any severe detriment.
Throughout the history of the United States, a similar idealism surrounds
religious freedom, insofar as its proponents suggest that a total disestablishment (an unencumbered market) will encourage radical religious
creativity (entrepreneurial innovation). To be sure, certain religious ideas
will be more rewarded in such a market-driven environment than others.
In his post-9/11 analysis *Holy Terrors*, Bruce Lincoln argued that American
Protestantism, lacking a central bureaucracy, has historically identified
entrepreneurial success and affluence as themselves measures of spiritual success.[16] Although asceticism exists in the United States, the vast
majority of religious lives—Protestant and otherwise—concur with this
account of the relationship between financial success and spiritual superiority, and religious movements in favor of prosperity have been more
likely to flourish than those that have emphasized sacrifice. As Hilde
Løvdal Stephens explains in this volume, Protestants may mandate sexual
abstinence and financial discipline—and, indeed, may suggest that these
regulations are interconnected—but these displays of self-denial only represent the excess of a believer's specifically gendered power, phenomenal
spiritual strength, and possible material holdings. We abstain only insofar as we occupy seats of abundance.

Third, to define something as neoliberal is to try to summarize
the way that apparatuses of late-modern corporate existence focus

individuals on a particular concept of the self that vehemently denies the effective hegemony of those matrices. To continue the analogy with religious freedom, to define something as free by the terms of neoliberalism is to summarize the way it focuses individuals on their individuality without highlighting the sense that—again, in religious terms—this individuality may derive from a larger normalizing system of belief and identity. In the case of religion in the United States, the connection would be between such corporate matrices and the persistent effects of Protestantism, which, as Tracy Fessenden has effectively argued, determine American religious experience and identity.[17] The specific theological concepts of democracy and divinity within Protestantism allow for its adhering participants to imagine that they are fiercely antinomian and antiauthoritarian, so that they do not imagine they are within a structure of obedience but, rather, think they act within a structure of liberation, independence, and revelation. There is no conflict between the self and any system, since any success indicates the capacity of the self to master any system.

Such a self cannot be out of control or in trouble due to structural factors; indeed, the only explanation for why the self may be struggling is related to psychological or biological reasons (hence the increase in pharmacology in the era described as neoliberal). No structures intercede in your possibility; only *your* actions, or your biology, keep you from your best life (to borrow from an Oprah idiom). This is why the neoliberal self is one exhausted (perpetually "stressed out") from trying to seem in control of a world that demands unending calculation and decision. As Ilana Gershon has written:

A neoliberal perspective presumes that every social analyst on the ground should ideally use market rationality to interpret their social relationships and social strategies. This concept of agency requires a reflexive stance in which people are subjects for themselves—a collection of processes to be managed. There is always already a presumed distance to oneself as an actor. One is never "in the moment"; rather, one is always faced with one's self as a project that must be consciously steered through various possible alliances and obstacles. This is a self that is produced through an engagement with a market, that is, neoliberal markets require participants to be reflexive managers of their abilities and alliances.[18]

Accounts of religious identity in America reflect this sense of participatory option and management, as sociologists have observed believers combining disparate sectarian practices ("various possible alliances") into individualized regimes and historians have described spirited charismatic leadership (the best "reflexive managers") derived from newly imagined ecclesiastical bodies. To be sure, there are also adherents guided by more orthodox concepts of adherence within the United States, but the primary metric of religious freedom seems to be determined by participants who understand themselves as managers of their religious lives rather than managed by religious authority.

William Arnal has written convincingly about this dynamic, arguing that such an idea of individualism is not as oppositional to authority as it may seem. Instead, he suggests that individuals in such a self-managing role are quite dependent upon authority, however imperceptibly perceived. "The state as conceived by modernity serves the purpose of creating a framework in which the individuals who are imagined to constitute the state are best poised to pursue and create *their own* meanings," Arnal writes, "to be free from the aggression of others so that they may seek and realize whatever it is that they may regard to be their own particular selfish self-interest." As a result, Arnal proceeds, " 'religion' comes to form a special *political* category in modernity—one that creates a peripheral space for, and serves to account for and *especially* to domesticate, whatever forms of persistent social and collective action happen to retain a positive or Utopian orientation."[19] Religion becomes, in Arnal's rendering, a particular space in late modernity because it concocts a reprieve from the optional chaos. Late capitalism produces violent disruptions of nation, community, and family, such as the downsizing of industries, the privatization of public services, and the commodification of every form of social life, thus "parsing human beings into free-floating labor units, commodities, clients, stakeholders, strangers, their subjectivity distilled into ever more objectified ensembles of interests, entitlements, appetites, desires, purchasing 'power.' "[20] Against these disruptions, certain spaces—be they fundamentalist sects or fantasy theme parks, Hasidic shuls or LAN parties—"would seem to offer a stable realm: a return to community, a resurgence of civil society, sanctity for the individual."[21] Yet such specific enclosed social experience functions within a broader frame where the subjective choice of the individual is lionized as the determining interactive principle.

Interactive to what? What or who determines the options for that con-
sumer/citizen/believer? The easiest answer—the one invoked most often
within analyses of neoliberalism—is that of the corporation. A corporation is a group of people authorized to act as a single entity and recognized
as such in law. Corporations enjoy most of the rights and responsibilities
that an individual possesses; that is, a corporation has the right to enter
into contracts, loan and borrow money, sue and be sued, hire employees,
own assets, and pay taxes. Yet a corporation is separate and distinct from
its owners (hence the difference between a corporation and a collective).
In the late twentieth century, historians suggested that corporations had
gained increasing sway over public interests, with a resultant decrease
of popular power. Yet, as Monica Prasad has demonstrated, the story of
the 1981 individual income tax cuts—the largest part of the tax-cut bill
and the central element of domestic economic policy over the next three
decades—is a story of political response to public opinion, and not political reply to corporate pressure. "That it was public opinion that played the
key role in bringing the tax cuts onto the agenda suggests that we do not
need to fear secret plots by business having led to the current era of market dominance," she writes. It may be nice to maintain a "business-power
narrative" that casts oligarchs as our puppeteers, but it is not accurate to
the social history of the economics associated with neoliberalism.[22] Prasad
argues that it was popular opinion that encouraged Reaganomics as much
as it was corporate intervention into political life, suggesting that despite
the protests against supply-side policies by leftist critics, a celebration of
the market is as much a populist position as it has been a business boon.[23]

But let us not move too far into a celebration of the impact that popular
opinion can have on electoral life. The genius of the late-modern corporation is the way that it can claim to speak for the people, thus rendering its private ambitions as seemingly good for everyone. For example,
in 2012, IBM released a new advertising campaign promoting a set of
"augmented-reality" applications for mobile devices.[24] Founded in the
1880s, International Business Machines, or IBM, is now a multinational
technology and consulting firm headquartered in Armonk, New York. It
manufactures computer hardware and software, but its profits are increasingly derived from the development of informational infrastructure,
such as hosting and consulting bent upon organizing the billions of data
that individuals produce in a given day. Its 2012 advertising campaign
explains this transition from manufacturing objects to organizing knowledge, arguing that we have all the technology we need; what is needed,

now, is new applications of what we know. "The technology is here," the copy explains: "People are ready. The time is now." Ready for what? This is explained in a series of posters:

> *Power grids reduce energy bills for you.*
> *Intelligence turns information into insights.*
> *Roads reduce their own congestion.*
> *Data helps prevent crimes before they happen.*
> *Medical histories alert doctors before patients get sick.*
> *Store shelves know exactly what customers want.*[25]

Beneath each of these boldfaced slogans is the repeated line, "Smarter x for a smarter planet." Under "Power grids reduce energy bills for you," the tag line reiterates: "Smarter energy for a smarter planet." Under "Store shelves know exactly what customers want," the copy underlines, "Smarter retail systems for a smarter planet." Smarter energy, smarter business, smarter traffic, smarter public safety, smarter histories, smarter retail systems: all make for a smarter planet. The closing summation: *Let's build a smarter planet* (http://www.ibm.com/smarterplanet/us/en/index.html).

Observe how IBM invokes unifying infrastructures (such as power grids, roads, medical records) to specify individual frustration (high bills, congested traffic, illness). The store shelves will know what you want, the medical histories will alert doctors, the roads will limit their jams—all you have to do is accede to the totality of their knowledge about you. The job of the consumer is merely to trust in that capability, to believe that the data set is smarter than the consumer, the bill payer, the driver, or the patient. There are a lot of data in this data-driven world, and those who want to live on the smartest planet will accede their power. This is our neoliberal freedom: the freedom to decide what matrix will determine your cognizance. The corporation has done all the thinking *on your behalf.*

For Arnal, this acquiescence by individuals to the power of companies should be familiar terrain for the scholar of religion. He suggests that capitalism succeeds because it provides this kind of corporate safe haven in the form of sanctified locations such as Disney World where individuals can locate themselves as both specific and statistical. These IBM advertisements do something similar, albeit without the same rituals of social experience as Disney. IBM has reduced your diversity to a predictable type and can resolve your trouble (be it high bills or strange illness) through an effective algorithm. If you are worried, worry not: a better system than you can conceive is on the case. IBM has a product that resolves your worries, just as the O bracelet has solved your anxieties. The commodity has done all your work for you, leaving you alone to just be you.

Such a description of the corporation invites connections to religion, especially one with a high ecclesiology. Indeed, Wendy Brown identifies religious thinking as essential to neoliberal operations, although she locates the function of religion within the populace more than she does its overarching structures. According to Brown, certain religions soften the self to receive such a resolved consumer landscape. She writes: "A religiously interpellated populace, and an increasingly blurred line between religious and political culture, and between theological and political discourse, facilitates the reception of the de-democratizing forces of neoconservativism and neoliberalism."[26] An overt example of this blurred line would be the *Left Behind* series, addressed by Daniel Silliman in this volume, which offers a multivolume apocalyptic pulp plot laced with confidence about the rectifying wisdom of free-market capitalism.[27] Anthropologist Daromir Rudnyckyj suggests that religious commodities like the *Left Behind* books are components of a broader pattern in economic life. In the heyday of liberalism, the market was understood to be immoral; in the epoch of neoliberalism, the economy is understood not just as an operational good but actually as an entity capable of the highest spiritual accomplishment, hence the increased diagnoses of the *spiritual economy* or the *spiritual marketplace*.[28] Neoliberalism might therefore be understood as a form of religious occupation of the economy: a way of seeing the self in the world as a technologically capable, fiercely independent, thoughtfully calculating entity, gaining for one's individual good and (if universalized as a principle for all people) for the creation of that smarter planet.

Religion on such a planet functions in reply to the religious; the religious is more likely to emerge from certain kinds of religions rather than others. "In a sense . . . the logic of what is now called neoliberalism penetrates deep into a certain history of evangelical faith," writes Andrew Strombeck.[29] The interdenominational evangelicalism espoused by Dwight Moody (and continued by others well into the twentieth century) propagated a large number of missionary agencies bent upon assisting the world regardless of borders.[30] Scholars of neoliberalism emphasize that the number of NGOs has increased dramatically since the fall of communism and through the emergent global economy of the late twentieth century. However, NGOs have a history prior to that of the U.N. charter, as evangelical laborers flooded foreign mission fields under the auspices of highly bureaucratized organizations, and reform movements, including those for abolition, suffrage, and disarmament, were guided by similarly transnational operations.[31]

Contemporary humanitarianism continues to be guided by NGO labor. Even when a particular international economic development program, such as Mercy Corps or Water.org, is not overtly religious, anthropologist Jill Detemple invites scholars to consider these agencies as religiously significant. "Due to their colonial heritages, implementation strategies, sites of action, on-the-ground realities, and epistemological structures, development programs often utilize, incorporate, or share the infrastructure, language, delivery systems, rituals, and spaces of religious life and institutions," she writes: "Even the most secular of economic development projects, and certainly their faith-based counterparts, are often perceived as 'religious,' or as having an effect on religious identity and practice, by people who receive development assistance."[32] With her work, Detemple demonstrates how much of contemporary internationalism possesses an ongoing missionary bent, one that makes sense of the arrival of new economies by casting them in familiar ritual and churchly forms.

This returns us to where we began, namely, the figure of Oprah Winfrey in her promotion of international aid provided through the sale of the commodity fetishes forged through international sisterhood. Increasingly, philanthropic labor of all stripes circulates via an advocating celebrity, who conveys the difficult details of actual humanitarian instance through a smoothed and soothingly resolved iconic ease. "As a rock star, I have two instincts," said Bono, the lead singer for U2: "I want to have fun, and I want to change the world. I have a chance to do both."[33] This is what transports the celebrity from the entertainment section of the newspaper to its front page, as our celebrities increasingly work within politics, politicians increasingly need to think like celebrities, and both practice their millennial ambitions for world-saving with a superhero confidence and a missionary zeal that coordinates well with the new geopolitics of neoliberal power. Celebrities offer their aura as a delimited public where all confusions regarding political or economic difference are smoothed into a consolidated iconic space. Oprah is, of course, perhaps the most famous of these celebrity do-gooders, though there are few causes without a celebrity (and very few celebrities without a cause).

For instance, in February 2011, actor George Clooney appeared on the cover of *Newsweek*. Clooney was not promoting a film or television show. Instead, he was promoting an international problem and himself as a missionary seeking to resolve it on our behalf. While the cover announced, "Mr. Clooney, the President Is on Line 1," the article head-lined with more declarative ascription, calling Clooney "A 21st Century Statesman." "In January, Clooney was back in South Sudan," we learn, "directing his star power toward helping its people peacefully achieve independence from the northern government of Khartoum after two decades of civil war." No mention of religion is made in the article—no spiritual awakening seems to have brought Clooney here. Instead, the article infers that Clooney possesses a basic decency inherited from his journalist father. Indeed, it was the influence of his hard-nosed patri-arch that led Clooney to cowrite and direct *Good Night, and Good Luck* (2005), a film depiction of Edward R. Murrow's famed face-off with U.S. senator Eugene McCarthy. *Newsweek* presents Clooney as a form of responsible rationalism of a pre-infotainment age. He is the celebrity who wields his celebrity to the good beyond celebrity. The article con-cludes: "In this new environment—fueled by social networking—fame is a potent commodity that can have more influence on public debate than many elected officials and even some nation-states."[34] Every prob-lem has a celebrity to solve it—and to entertain you as they do. The pur-chase of the O bracelet helps African women *and* your fashionable life (there's that bracelet, on my wrist); watching a George Clooney movie helps African countries *and* your fantasy life (there's that handsome devil, charming me again).

As the political necessity of celebrity and the celebrity circulation in politics continue to expand, it is useful to recall that such projects do not merely have their origin in ideologies of secular reason. The power of celebrity to expand and contract, to fit the image of the given moment, and to belong in the crevice of every crisis is not because that image is denuded of meaningful religious authority. It is precisely because they possess such spectral power that they may direct attention to their causes. In a strictly liberal age, Clooney would have needed to be elected, or helm a major social movement, in order to become a political cover boy. In a neoliberal age, he just needed to articulate his specific charismatic caring after accumulating enough iconic interest. While it may be tempting to imagine Clooney's predecessor as the similarly dashing screen idols Cary Grant and Errol Flynn, this edited volume invites us to think about evan-gelist Billy Graham as a preamble to his particularly suave incursion into politics. Celebrities—be they preachers or actors—never make us think deeply about any Gordian dilemma. Rather, they give us a sharply moral punch line while charming us with the cut of their suits and the calming pitch of their voices. For better and for worse, these charismatic figures define an enormous swath of the moral debates of our time.

In the early twentieth century Émile Durkheim argued that religion defined social life. "For we know today that a religion does not necessarily imply symbols and rites, properly speaking, or temples and priests," Durkheim explains: "The whole exterior apparatus is only the superficial part. Essentially it is nothing other than a body of collective beliefs and practices endowed with a certain authority."[35] We live in a time with fewer mandated rituals or closely tended temples. We live, instead, in a society determined in and through its authoritarian heroes, as well as its anti-authoritarian networks of dissent. As Manfred Steger and Ravi Roy have written, the neoliberal modes of public administration "redefined citizens as 'customers' or 'clients' and encouraged administrators to cultivate an 'entrepreneurial spirit.'"[36] All ideologies propose that they will result in a better world for you. Neoliberalism says, in its simplest form, that the better world comes through free markets. In this age, the agent of the better world is conceived always as *consumer*.

It is a good moment, then, for an edited volume to consider the multiple interrelationships between religion and the marketplace. And the contributors to this volume have proved that neoliberal logic can be found throughout the empire of American religions. A word of warning, then, is perhaps in order, as we proceed from this good work: namely, that those who observe, annotate, and classify religions in the modern period can easily slip into an acceptance of the logic and valuations of markets. The apparent inevitability of capitalism is that a better world comes through free markets. In our own lives, we often perceive ourselves most essentially as consumers, which can mask the pervasive hermeneutic effects of neoliberalism. In the analytic work of this volume, religion and economic practices rarely disagree with one another. This should prod us to think about the truths illuminated and obscured by such a symphonic commiseration of economy and ideology. Is all of American religion now neoliberal? Or is it merely the case that our scholarship has become so determined? As we continue to follow the inspiring work of this volume, we would do well to continue to ask what spiritual and economic conflicts inform the lives of our chosen religious subjects, as well as what economic and spiritual challenges tug upon us, the scribes of their markets, the historians of their religions.

## *Notes*

1. "The O Bracelet," *O, the Oprah Magazine*, May 2007, 152.
2. Ibid.
3. This analysis is taken from Kathryn Lofton, *Oprah: The Gospel of an Icon* (Berkeley: University of California Press, 2011), 199–201.
4. Gary Prevost and Carlos Oliva Campos, eds., *Neoliberalism and Neopanamericanism: The View from Latin America* (New York: Palgrave Macmillan, 2002). *Neoliberalism*, translated as *neoliberalismo*, is a word used by Central and South American economists to describe the pro-market model for Latin American economic development.
5. David Harvey, "Neoliberalism as Creative Destruction," *Annals of the American Academy of Political and Social Science* 610 (March 2007): 25.
6. Elizabeth Povinelli, "Consuming Geist: Popontology and the Spirit of Capital in Indigenous Australia," *Public Culture* 12, no. 2 (2000): 501.
7. "Humanity Interview with James Ferguson, Pt. 2," *Humanity*, June 10, 2014, http://www.humanityjournal.net/blog/humanity-interview-with-ja mes-ferguson-pt-2-rethinking-neoliberalism/.
8. This description of neoliberalism derives from my reading of the follow-ing texts: Robert Brenner, "The Boom and the Bubble," *New Left Review* 6 (November–December 2000), accessed on August 12, 2013, http://www.newleftreview.org/?view=2286; Gérard Duménil and Dominique Lévy, *Capital Resurgent: Roots of the Neoliberal Revolution* (Cambridge: Harvard University Press, 2004); Gérard Duménil and Dominique Lévy, *The Crisis of Neoliberalism* (Cambridge: Harvard University Press, 2011); Stephen Gil, "Globalization, Market Civilization, and Disciplinary Neoliberalism," *Millennium* 24, no. 3 (December 1995): 399–423; Jerry Harris, *The Dialectics of Globalization: Economic and Political Conflict in a Transnational World* (Cambridge: Cambridge Scholars Publishing, 2008); David Harvey, *A Brief History of Neoliberalism* (New York: Oxford University Press, 2005); William Robinson, *A Theory of Global Capitalism: Production, Class, and State in a Transnational World* (Baltimore: Johns Hopkins University Press, 2004).
9. Michael J. Sandel, *What Money Can't Buy: The Moral Limits of Markets* (New York: Farrar, Straus, Giroux, 2012), 10.
10. Tony Judt, *Ill Fares the Land* (New York: Penguin, 2010), chap. 3, 81–136.
11. Wendy Brown, "American Nightmare: Neoliberalism, Neoconservatism, and De-democratization," *Political Theory* 34, no. 6 (December 2006): 703.
12. Harvey, "Neoliberalism as Creative Destruction," 28–29.
13. Catherine Chaput, "Rhetorical Circulation in Late Capitalism: Neoliberalism and the Overdetermination of Affective Energy," *Philosophy and Rhetoric* 43, no. 1 (2010): 2.
14. Harvey, "Neoliberalism as Creative Destruction," 27.

15. David Sehat, *The Myth of American Religious Freedom* (New York: Oxford University Press, 2011).

16. Bruce Lincoln, *Holy Terrors: Thinking about Religion after September 11* (Chicago: University of Chicago Press, 2002), 48.

17. Tracy Fessenden, *Culture and Redemption: Religion, the Secular, and American Literature* (Princeton: Princeton University Press, 2007).

18. Ilana Gershon, "Neoliberal Agency," *Current Anthropology* 52, no. 4 (August 2011): 539. Wendy Brown extends this description of the neoliberal agent, writing that "this aspect of neoliberalism also entails a host of policies that figure and produce citizens as individual entrepreneurs and consumers whose moral autonomy is measured by their capacity for 'self-care'—their ability to provide for their own needs and service their own ambitions, whether as welfare recipients, medical patients, consumers of pharmaceuticals, university students, or workers in ephemeral occupations" ("American Nightmare," 694).

19. William Arnal, "The Segregation of Social Desire: 'Religion' and Disney World," *Journal of the American Academy of Religion* 69, no. 1 (2001): 4–5.

20. Jean Comaroff and John L. Comaroff, "Millennial Capitalism: First Thoughts on a Second Coming," *Public Culture* 12, no. 2 (2000): 333.

21. Andrew Strombeck, "Invest in Jesus: Neoliberalism and the *Left Behind* Novels," *Cultural Critique* 64 (Fall 2006): 184.

22. Monica Prasad, "The Popular Origins of Neoliberalism in the Reagan Tax Cut of 1981," *Journal of Policy History* 24, no. 3 (2012): 375.

23. For a classic (and tendentiously liberal) account of this dynamic, see Thomas Frank, *What's the Matter with Kansas? How Conservatives Won the Heart of America* (New York: Holt, 2005).

24. "Augmented Reality Makes Shopping More Personal," IBM Research, accessed August 12, 2013, http://www.research.ibm.com/articles/augmented-reality.shtml.

25. Sean Patterson, "IBM's New Augmented Reality App Will Track Your Grocery Shopping," WebProNews, July 2, 2012, accessed August 12, 2013, http://www.webpronews.com/ibms-new-augmented-reality-app-will-tr ack-your-grocery-shopping-2012-07.

26. Brown, "American Nightmare," 706.

27. Strombeck, "Invest in Jesus," 161. See Daniel Silliman's essay in this volume for a wonderful treatment of the market conditions for the appearance of *Left Behind* within the broader publishing industry.

28. Through his anthropological research in Indonesia, Rudnyckyj has described spiritual economies as spaces where religious ethics and business management knowledge converge. Daromir Rudnyckyj, "Spiritual Economies: Islam and Neoliberalism in Contemporary Indonesia," *Cultural Anthropology* 24, no. 1 (February 2009): 104–141.

29. Strombeck, "Invest in Jesus," 183.

30. Bruce J. Evensen, *God's Man for the Gilded Age: D.L. Moody and the Rise of Modern Mass Evangelism* (New York: Oxford University Press, 2003); Michael D. Hamilton, "The Interdenominational Evangelicalism of D. L. Moody and the Problem of Fundamentalism," unpublished paper.

31. Charter of the United Nations, accessed August 13, 2013, http://www.un.org/en/documents/charter/. See also Victoria Bernal and Inderpal Grewal, eds., *Theorizing NGOs: Feminist Struggles, States and Neoliberalism* (Durham: Duke University Press, 2014); Dana L. Roberts, *Christian Mission: How Christianity Became a World Religion* (Malden, MA: Wiley-Blackwell, 2009).

32. Jill Detemple, "Imagining Development: Religious Studies in the Context of International Economic Development," *Journal of the American Academy of Religion* 81, no. 1 (2013): 108.

33. Edna Gunderson, "Bono: You Too Can Make Y2K Better for 3rd World," *USA Today*, October 7, 1999. On Bono as the soundtrack to neoliberalism, see Chad Seales, "Burned over Bono: U2's Rock 'n' Roll Messiah and His Religious Politic," *Journal of Religion and Popular Culture* 14:1 (Fall 2006): 1–27.

34. John Avlon, "A 21st Century Statesman," *Newsweek*, February 21, 2011, accessed August 12, 2013, http://www.newsweek.com/2011/02/20/a-21st-century-statesman.html.

35. Emile Durkheim, "Individualism and the Intellectuals," in *Emile Durkheim on Morality and Society*, ed. Robert N. Bellah (Chicago: University of Chicago Press, 1973), 50–51.

36. Manfred B. Steger and Ravi K. Roy, *Neoliberalism: A Very Short Introduction* (Oxford: Oxford University Press, 2010), 13.

# Index